HOSTILE TAKEOVER

HOSTILE TAKEOVER

HOW BIG MONEY & CORRUPTION CONQUERED OUR GOVERNMENT —AND HOW WE TAKE IT BACK

DAVID SIROTA

 CROWN PUBLISHERS NEW YORK

Published in the United States by Crown Publishers, an imprint of the
Crown Publishing Group, a division of Random House, Inc., New York.
www.crownpublishing.com

Crown is a trademark and the Crown colophon is a registered
trademark of Random House, Inc.

Library of Congress Cataloging-in-Publication Data

Sirota, David, 1975–
Hostile takeover : how big money and corruption conquered our
government—and how we take it back / David Sirota.—1st ed.
Includes index.
1. Corporations—Political aspects—United States.
2. Business and politics—United States.   I. Title.
HD2785.S434   2006
322'.30973—dc22   2005025230

ISBN-10: 0-307-23734-6
ISBN-13: 978-0-307-23734-7

Printed in the United States of America

10 9 8 7 6 5 4 3 2 1

First Edition

For Emily,

the most blatant of blatancies.

I HOPE WE SHALL CRUSH IN ITS BIRTH THE ARISTOCRACY OF OUR MONIED CORPORATIONS WHICH DARE ALREADY TO CHALLENGE OUR GOVERNMENT TO A TRIAL OF STRENGTH, AND BID DEFIANCE TO THE LAWS OF OUR COUNTRY.

—THOMAS JEFFERSON, 1816

Contents

HOSTILE TAKEOVER

INTRODUCTION

★

AT ABOUT 4:30 A.M. I finally had the epiphany. On my way back from a friend's wedding and struggling to finish this book on deadline, I was trapped in Minneapolis International Airport, relegated to sleeping on the floor by the airline I was flying home on. My wife, wedged onto a filthy plastic bench, groaned as she turned over and forced a weak smile at me.

We had been that day's corporate roadkill—just another casualty in Big Business's unbridled quest for profits. In this case, we were speed bumps on an airport floor, barely big enough for one of those beeping golf carts to even slow down, much less stop. I was tired from the trip, and frustrated that I couldn't think of a way to start this book, until suddenly it hit me: what my wife and I were going through at that moment was the perfect introduction to the hostile takeover.

Our story was one of a million—not one in a million, but one of a million that happen every day in all different ways. On our connecting flight back to our home in Montana, the airline sat a planeload of us out on the tarmac for two and a half hours. Then, just before we were supposed to take off at midnight, the pilot told us the radar had broken and the flight would be canceled.

I was grateful we hadn't found out about the malfunction while we were in the air, but, then, I had no idea what abuse was coming. When we got off the plane, the pilot reiterated to an airline representative that the flight was canceled because their plane was busted. But the airline representative proceeded to mark it down as a weather cancellation—a straight-up, unadulterated lie right to all of our faces, and a lie with a motive: weather-related cancellations meant the company did not have to pay for a hotel room for us or rebook us on another airline. It was a cash-saver for them, and a big middle finger to us.

All of us passengers protested, but the airline employees let us know the decision was made by the higher-ups, and they were powerless to do anything about it. A soldier coming home from Afghanistan had been flying for sixty hours straight—he got the best treatment: they said they could fly him to a destination 250 miles away from where he had originally paid to go, but that they wouldn't pay for a rental car for him to make the last leg.

The rest of us, including the elderly and families with infants, were told that we could be rebooked on the next open flight home—which would leave four days from then. Pull up a food-stained bench, they said, and get comfortable: the multimillion-dollar airline that screwed you is not paying the $43 it would cost to put you up at a Motel 6. No matter anyway—by the time they decided to tell us they would be lying to us to avoid the cost, there were no rooms available. That's right. After forking over hundreds of hard-earned dollars to a big corporation (in this case, an airline), we had been treated like idiots, then brazenly lied to, then thrown to the floor like a piece of trash—and thanks to our government's lack of consumer protection laws prohibiting this sort of flagrant abuse, there was nothing any of us could do about it.

"Just shut up, you whiner," you are probably thinking. "We've all been through an ordeal like this, so just suck it up and shut up."

You are right. We have all been through episodes like this, whether with the airlines, or with an abusive employer, or with some other corporation trying to scam us for an extra couple of bucks. It's why when *Planes, Trains and Automobiles* comes on television at Thanksgiving, we always laugh so hard—because we've all been there before and felt that helpless.

You are also right that most of us do just suck it up and take it. We know we shouldn't, but we do. Even those of us who wait on hold for three hours through Kenny G lullabies just to vent our frustration to the helpless "customer service" representative ultimately sit there and take it. Why? Because there's really no other choice.

And that's exactly the problem—at the very same time corporate abuse has been allowed to become such a regular part of daily life, average citizens have been stripped of the rights and the tools to protect themselves. Our government—which used to be in the business of protecting us, now sits by and allows us to be abused, or worse—actually helps the abusers. Put another way, government's business has become protecting business, not people.

Being forced to sleep in airports is the least of it.

Some fat cat is taking a cut of your paycheck? "Suck it up," says the boss, and "Sorry," says your government, which long ago stopped seriously enforcing wage violations. Your pension gets stolen? "Tough," says your employer, and "Too bad," says your government, which provides you little, if any, protections. Credit card company using the financial hardships of a death in the family to go after your life savings? "Deal with it," says the collection agency, and "Talk to the hand," says your government, which long ago legalized the most disgusting forms of usury.

I'm not naïve. I know that corporations exist for one reason and one reason only: the relentless, single-minded pursuit of profit, no matter who gets shafted. That is their stated purpose in a capitalist society, and that's fine. But in our country, corporations aren't supposed to be allowed to pursue this purpose in a vacuum, unchecked, unregulated, unopposed. There is supposed to be a counterweight, a government separate from Big Business whose job is to prevent the corporate profit motive from destroying society. That government once passed laws protecting the environment, so the profit motive wouldn't end up eliminating breathable air. That government once protected workers, so the profit motive wouldn't result in Americans toiling in sweatshops. And that government once demanded better wages, so the profit motive wouldn't result in a race to the bottom for poverty-level paychecks.

But that government, as we all know, is long gone.

Just as the mom-and-pop store in your town was bought out by the big corporate conglomerate, so has our government been the victim of a hostile takeover. Over the last thirty years, Corporate America has applied its most effective business tactics to the task of purchasing the one commodity that's not supposed to be for sale: American democracy. From the model of the door-to-door salesman, we get the slick business lobbyist. From the ad campaigns that push this or that brand of soap, we get the well-oiled PR machine that pushes this or that piece of corporate-written legislation. And from the art of buying out competitors, we get a river of money to buy off politicians.

This last tool, money, is clearly the most important of them all. Big Business now buys off politicians in the most brazen ways. Whereas in eras past, bribery happened behind closed doors, now it has become such a part of the political culture, it happens right out in the open. Whether funding politicians' vacations to luxurious locations, or lending them corporate jets for their campaigns, Corporate America makes lawmakers feel as if they are living in *Lifestyles of the Rich and Famous* — as long as those lawmakers pay back their sponsors with legislative favors.

Added to this is a political system that requires candidates to raise huge amounts of money to run for office, whether at the local, state, or national level. When congressional candidates start their campaign, they are told by their political parties that the most important priority is getting on the phone and calling big donors and corporate political action committees to ask for huge contributions—contributions that will pay for expensive television advertising. By election night, typical candidates have spent most of the race not meeting voters, not giving speeches, not touring their districts, not researching issues—they have spent most of their time on the phone or at fundraising parties shaking down donors for cash.

The net effect of this is a *Clockwork Orange*-style system of brainwashing, where the supremacy of corporate cash is drummed into politicians' heads from day one of their candidacies. By the time they assume public office to represent regular people, these politicians have learned that the key to their political survival is to ignore those regular people in favor of corporations and the very wealthy, because that's where the campaign cash is. And the campaign cash is only where the hostile takeover begins. Politicians, once in office, benefit from the junkets and gifts that come their way. Lucrative jobs seem to appear out of nowhere for their friends and relatives. And if lawmakers play their cards right, they can spend the rest of their careers spinning in a revolving doorway—one that allows them to move back and forth between important regulatory posts in the government and the private sector they're supposed to be regulating.

For their part, corporations and the wealthy are happy to give, because they get it all back once the politician they funded gets into office.*

---

*There are many references throughout this book about industries, companies, and wealthy individuals giving money to politicians or political parties. To clarify: Federal election law technically bars corporations from using the company treasury to make political donations to candidates, and there are limits on how much a candidate can take from any one individual. However, companies and wealthy individuals are able to easily get around this prohibition. Companies, for instance, can establish a Political Action Committee (PAC), funded by company employees (usually executives), and then the company PAC can make contributions to candidates. Additionally, companies can give to politicians through their individual employees—many of whom "bundle" many contributions together. Wealthy individuals can also bundle contributions (that's what President Bush's Rangers/Pioneers do). This says nothing about the fact that corporations and the wealthy can give unlimited amounts to 527 organizations which now dominate political campaigns through television ads and other key expenditures. Therefore, for brevity's sake, when this book refers to industries/companies/ wealthy individuals giving large sums of money to politicians or parties, it is (unless otherwise stipulated) referring to the aggregate amount that the companies'/industries'/individuals' PACs and employees have donated to that politician/party or how much those wealthy individuals have bundled in contributions.

For instance, look at just one report from one local paper to see this corruption-as-investment-strategy at work. In 2005, the *Toledo Blade* reported that "the Ohio business leaders and lobbyists who steered at least $4.1 million to President Bush's re-election campaign last year collected more than $1.2 billion in taxpayer dollars for their companies and clients," including "millions from unbid contracts."[1] The paper also reported that in Texas, "the federal government has awarded more than $3 billion in contracts to the President's elite 2004 fundraisers, their businesses, and lobbying clients."

Remember, that's just two states out of fifty.

In state government, it's the same story: buying off policy has become a commonplace, out-in-the-open practice—as if legislation is just another trinket for sale in a flea market. Just look at Utah for an example. In 2005, the *Salt Lake Tribune* reported that Republican lawmakers in the statehouse there set up a "speed dating" event with corporate lobbyists. The event would "let lobbyists 'date' [lawmakers] for a few precious minutes—as long as they donate to their political action committee." When questioned about the event's obvious overtones of overt bribery, "organizers said the idea is simply a fun, new way to raise campaign cash." The lobbyists undoubtedly got their money's worth when Utah's next legislative session opened for business.

For a more individual-centered example of how big donors get their money's worth, take the tale of California Rep. Randy "Duke" Cunningham (R). He took tens of thousands of dollars in campaign contributions from a defense contractor,[2] while living on a yacht provided by the company.[3] Things went a step further when Cunningham got the company to buy his house for far higher than its market value, meaning a huge windfall for Cunningham.[4] At the very same time, the committee that oversees Pentagon spending—on which Cunningham served—was directing millions of dollars' worth of contracts to the same company.[5] Think that's a coincidence? Because if you do, then I have some real estate to sell you.

Lawmakers and the media feigned outrage at Cunningham when his exploits were exposed. But really the only thing different about his case was that he got caught. The sad truth is that Cunningham's behavior is as disgusting as it is commonplace in our country's bought-and-paid-for political system. In fact, all you had to do was look in Cunningham's hometown paper weeks after he pleaded guilty to bribery charges to know that the corruption he got nailed for is the rule in politics today, not the exception. "From powerful positions on the House Appropriations Committee, California Rep. Jerry Lewis has greenlighted hundreds of millions of dollars in federal projects for clients of one of his closest friends, lobbyist and former state Congressman Bill Lowery," the *San Diego Union Tribune* reported in a December 2005 story barely noticed because it was so mundane. "Meanwhile, Lowery, the partners at his firm, and their clients have donated 37 percent of the $1.3 million that Lewis' political action committee received in the past six years."

It is legislation for sale—and thanks to lax laws, little oversight and almost no enforcement, it is totally legal and happening all the time. And while that's clearly bad for the American public, it has meant a royal lifestyle for politicians, who are now living the good life auctioning off public policy. What does "the good life" mean exactly? Just look at one 2005 Associated Press story about House Majority Leader Tom DeLay (R-TX):

> As Tom DeLay became a king of campaign fundraising, he lived like one, too. He visited cliff-top Caribbean resorts, golf courses designed by PGA champions, and four-star restaurants—all courtesy of donors who bankrolled his political money empire. Over the past six years, the former House majority leader and his associates have visited places of luxury most Americans have never seen, often getting there aboard corporate jets arranged by lobbyists and other special interests. [He took] at least 48 visits to golf clubs and resorts with lush fairways; 100 flights aboard company planes; 200 stays at hotels, many world-class; and 500 meals at restaurants, some averaging nearly $200 for a dinner for two. . . .

Remember, this was not a story about a Saudi sheik or some king. This was a story about the second-highest ranking member of the U.S. Congress selling off legislative favors in exchange for corporate cash that he then used to finance his life of luxury. And that kind of thing is happening all the time, with all sorts of politicians, all throughout the political system. As DeLay himself once said, "I am the federal government." Yup, that about says it all. Corruption is government, and government is corruption—they have become one and the same.

But then, that's not what you hear from politicians themselves—they engage in this kind of corruption, selling out their constituents, all the while parroting Corporate America's spin, and telling us they are really defending our interests. Just look at DeLay himself—while Corporate America was flying him all over the world to resorts and he was paying companies back with legislative favors, he was publicly portraying himself as Mr. Clean. Here is what he said in a speech on the floor of the U.S. House in 1995:

The time has come that the American people know exactly what their Representatives are doing here in Washington. Are they feeding at the public trough, taking lobbyist-paid vacations, getting wined and dined by special interest groups? Or are they working hard to represent their constituents? The people, the American people, have a right to know.

Remember, politicians like DeLay say this kind of thing all the time. They want us to believe they are "working hard to represent their constituents" even when they themselves are the ones "feeding at the public trough, taking lobbyist-paid vacations, and getting wined-and-dined by special interests." But he is right about one thing: we do have a right to know. The problem is that politicians like him are conspiring with Big Money interests to make sure we *don't* know.

If you dare to read this book, you will see the sad truth: despite all the hot air about America's political system representing the will of the "people," it really represents the will of Big Money. Because not a single day goes by in Congress where an industry isn't using huge amounts of money to buy favors from politicians—favors like tax breaks, regulatory loopholes, and all sorts of other goodies that screw over average citizens while padding Big Business's bottom line.

But as this book also shows, the buying of legislative favors is really only one small part of the corruption that is afflicting America's political system. The far more important and pervasive problem than money buying politicians' votes is money buying politicians' rhetoric—rhetoric that artificially limits the entire political debate exclusively to the dishonest terms Big Money interests want.

In speeches, town meetings, community events, television advertising, and all the other channels of modern political communication, corrupt lawmakers parrot Big Business's lies, myths, and half-truths—all designed to make us believe policies that sell us out are actually in our best interest. The result, much to the pleasure of Big Money interests, is a deliberately distorted and dishonest political debate wholly divorced from the day-to-day economic realities facing ordinary Americans.

Why is this form of corruption more troubling than simple vote buying on this or that specific issue? Because when the whole political debate is owned by moneyed interests, individual votes to sell out ordinary Americans don't have to be bought—they come naturally and almost invisibly on every single issue. Think about it—if you artificially set the boundaries of what politicians talk about and define the political debate on dishonest terms favorable to you, you ensure that the outcome of *every* public policy debate is one or another version of exactly what you want. That's what Big Business has done—used corruption to perform a hostile take-over not only of America's day-to-day partisan battles, but of America's political discourse as a whole.

Most people, of course, sense this takeover, sense the corruption, and sense they are being lied to on a regular basis, even if they can't put their finger on exactly what it all results in. And yet everywhere we turn, we hear these laughably disingenuous promises that government is working for us. The dichotomy between the rhetoric and the facts creates a hazy unreality to it all—as if we are in the movie *The Matrix*, and know something's wrong, but haven't yet woken up.

Corporate profits have risen, but so have poverty levels. Our politicians tell us they really care, tell us tax cuts and "free" trade are the only policies that can alleviate the problem. And yet, strangely, the only people who get tax cuts are the super-wealthy and the only people who benefit from "free" trade are the executives at the large corporations who funded both parties' presidential candidates in the last election. CEO compensation is skyrocketing while workers' paychecks get cut, yet few members of Congress say a thing about the inequity. Energy industry profits rise, more people can't pay their heating bills, our government promises to do something—and yet, Congress's energy policy discussions are limited to a debate about which form of new taxpayer handouts should be given to which oil companies. HMO executives make millions while almost one in five Americans has no health care at all. Polls show Americans want a universal health care program—and yet any discussion of that very concept is labeled "out of the mainstream" or "unrealistic" by elites in Washington, D.C.

But just like in *The Matrix,* you have a choice: you can swallow the blue pill and continue living in Big Business's fantasy where you are told that all these contradictions and abuses are just "facts of life." Or you can take the red pill by reading this book, and start exploring what's really going on.

Undoubtedly, Big Business has used its media conglomerates and the money-driven political process to keep us addicted to the blue pill. We get feel-good industry ads, and politicians claiming Congress's latest multibillion-dollar giveaway to an already-wealthy corporation is going to fix society's problems. We get pundits preaching the virtues of America's economy, and Fox News pumping in right-wing PR to soothe the masses. Worst of all, we get a flood of Orwellian messages from the Establishment that deny the existence of our very own beliefs. Almost every time you tune in to politics on television, some know-it-all is claiming the solutions that polls show the public widely supports are actually considered "out of the mainstream."

It is, in short, as though we are being force-fed an alternative reality, like we are merely watching a depressing, poorly made drama, instead of starring in it.

On almost every major issue affecting your wallet, you are told a different version of the same basic story. There is a deified "free market" that we all must bow down to and never question, under punishment of getting tarred and feathered as a pinko commie bastard by whatever Attila the Hun radio host happens to be on the air. This free market, we are told, means we must have fewer regulations that protect citizens' rights, less taxation of the rich, and no mandates on business to fulfill any social responsibilities other than increasing corporations' bottom line. At the same time, this "free market" is to be ignored when it might actually benefit ordinary citizens.

Thus, in one breath, politicians tell us price controls for medicine are bad, but restrictive patent laws that keep drug prices high are good; regulations against energy price gouging are bad, but government handouts to energy companies are good; protecting American jobs is bad, but government help in outsourcing our jobs is good. In short, they tell us government is Big Business's personal sidearm, instead of the middle-class's flak jacket against corporate abuse.

Sure, there is the occasional instance where government seems to act on our behalf. But upon further inspection, we usually find out all that happened was Congress forked over a massive taxpayer handout to an already-profitable industry as a payoff to get that industry to deal with a mess that could have been solved with just a bit of commonsense government intervention.

For instance, instead of regulating drug and health insurance prices like every other industrialized country, our government hands out corporate welfare checks to the pharmaceutical and HMO companies as a bribe to get them to improve their medical benefits (which, invariably, they don't). Instead of forcing companies to pay their workers better through minimum wage mandates, we get proposals to give companies even more tax breaks if they agree to consider pay increases. Instead of laws that prohibit oil companies from gouging Americans with higher and higher gas prices, we get billions of dollars' worth of new tax breaks to the petroleum industry. In other words, problems for average Americans become opportunities for lawmakers to shower Corporate America with taxpayer cash, instead of an impetus to reform a broken system.

But if polls are any indication, more people are becoming aware that something is very, very wrong—and they are looking for the red pill. A 2000 Harris poll found three-quarters of Americans believe big corporations and moneyed interests have too much power in Washington.[6] As *BusinessWeek* reported, the survey also found that more than four in five believe "business has gained too much power over too many aspects of American life."[7] A 2002 *Washington Post* poll found that 88 percent of Americans distrust corporate executives, and more than half believe their government is "not tough enough" in fighting corporate abuse.[8] A 2004 CBS poll found well over half of Americans believe the White House cares more about protecting the interests of the wealthy than about average people.[9] And a 2005 Associated Press poll found 88 percent of Americans believe corruption is a serious problem and 67 percent said a moderate number to a lot of public officials are involved in that corruption.

Corporate America and its political cronies have tried to whitewash this reality by co-opting the word *centrist,* and using it to describe an extreme agenda. You've heard it before. Whenever politicians write a bill selling out ordinary citizens, they are labeled "centrists"—as if they represent the mainstream of American political opinion. Likewise, whenever anyone opposes selling out, they are labeled an "extremist." Yet on issue after issue after issue, polls show that ordinary Americans overwhelmingly support far more populist policies than their government permits.[10] Furthermore, the public is not fooled by this attempt to redefine the political center; polls show most Americans are acutely aware that the people who are supposed to represent them in Washington do not represent their views.[11]

The public, in short, isn't as stupid as the Washington political establishment or the media make us out to be—and we are starting to demand answers about why our government is selling us out.

Who Is This Book For?

This book is for you, a member of that all-too-ignored majority outlined in those polls.

This book is for you, the young person who would be interested in the political process except that you know in your heart that almost everything you read or hear about politics is just another greasy, burning lie designed to manipulate you.

This book is for you, the middle-aged middle-class working person who has heard so many empty promises from politicians that you've decided to give up paying attention to politics, yet you now feel frustrated that in giving up on the political system, you are giving up on your country and letting those bastards who cheated you out of your pension win.

This book is for you, the reader whom the media and political Establishment ignore and forget about, as if your day-to-day concerns about making ends meet are far less important than the newest Paris Hilton sex video or the latest exposé about Michael Jackson's genitals. Your concerns about your dwindling paycheck, your ballooning health care bills, or your job insecurity are considered unimportant by the political system until about two weeks before a presidential election, when suddenly every desperate-for-camera-time CNN reporter and every political pollster looking to make a fast buck wants to know which of the two clowns you are going to vote for.

This book is for you, the Republican, the Democrat, the independent, the Libertarian, the Green, and whomever else, because the hostile takeover of our government doesn't affect just people of one party or another, and isn't the fault of just one party or another.

This book is for you, the teacher, the student, the construction worker, the fireman, the retiree, and all the rest of us "regular" or "ordinary" people, regardless of party affiliation.*

Let's be honest: most books about politics aren't written to explore the real-life day-to-day economic challenges facing the "regular people" demographic. There's a reason for that. Very few political operatives, politicians, or pundits actually *want* to explore those challenges, because exploring them would ultimately force them to admit that the political system they venerate is totally corrupt.

Think about some of the idiotically simple questions that are almost never asked in the normal course of this country's political debate:

– How come we hear so much about how well-off America is, yet our country has the highest number of uninsured citizens in the industrialized world?

– How come Congress refuses to raise the minimum wage, even though it is reaching a fifty-year low and provides less income than is necessary to rise above the poverty line?

---

*This book often refers to "regular" or "ordinary" or "average" Americans—it is a term meant to represent "the rest of us" who aren't part of the political or corporate establishment. It in no way is meant insultingly or to denigrate "average" people—it means the real Americans who make this country great, as opposed to the elitists who are trying to drive our country into the ground.

― How come America is the richest nation on earth, yet poverty in our country is rising?

Why aren't these questions asked? Because you can't answer any of them honestly without exploring how Big Business has bought off enough politicians to make sure our government helps the perpetrators of these travesties.

But ignoring these questions doesn't make them go away. Even though TV rarely gives voice to the economic obstacles we face, and even though politicians lie to our faces about trying to help, we know every time we pay a new fee on a bill, or get a smaller paycheck, or get pushed around by a company wanting more money, that those obstacles are very real, and few, if any, in government are really looking out for us.

It would be one thing if we knew exactly why we are getting screwed, and exactly how we are getting lied to, so that we could fight back. But most people, understandably, don't. You see that extra charge on your utility bill, you don't understand why it's there, but you either have to pay it or wait on the phone for an hour to try (most often unsuccessfully) to fight it. You may have a vague sense that some politician had a hand in passing or gutting a law that allowed this to happen, but you can't be sure.

That's where this book comes in. *Hostile Takeover* is more than just the story of how our government was bought. It is a guidebook to help you see exactly how corrupt politicians' lies, myths, and half-truths justify government policies that allow Corporate America to rip us off. It is your decoder ring to an intricate sequence of dishonesty that is making your life and the lives of millions of Americans worse. And it is a window into the one fact that the corporate lobbyists and their tools in the government don't want you to know: that the problems undermining America on a daily basis can be fixed if our government starts representing the interests of ordinary people.

This book is, in other words, your very own red pill, engineered to let you see how the entire political system is built on lies—lies specifically designed to justify making your economic situation worse.

Who Is This Book Not For?

I'll admit that it's a bit unconventional to use this introduction to say who this book is *not* for—narrowing the reading audience, even a little bit, probably gives my editor and publisher heartburn. Then again, it is critically important for you, the reader, to know at the beginning what you can and cannot expect in the pages that follow. And knowing who this book *isn't* written for will give you a sense of exactly what you are getting yourself into.

If you are a bought-off politician who has helped run our political system into the ground, you can stop reading right here—this book is not for you, because you already know all too well just how dishonest you are. Nothing in here is news to you.

This book is not for people like former Senators Don Nickles (R-OK)[12] and John Breaux (D-LA), both of whom, immediately after leaving their public offices, sold their knowledge of government to the highest bidder and became big-time corporate lobbyists. Again, people like that specialize in making government an accomplice to the worst corporate desires to bleed the middle class dry—they have nothing to learn from this book.

This book is not for mindless partisans who, at the mere mention of any political issue, start vomiting up the day's prefabricated talking points from dolts like Rush Limbaugh or Bill O'Reilly. This book takes a brutally honest look at the major economic issues that face citizens in their daily lives—and that means its analysis crosses party lines, and isn't ready-made for the next set of Democratic or Republican Party press releases.

This book is not for people like Tom Friedman, the *New York Times* columnist who, from the comfortable confines of his cushy six-figure job, regularly insults ordinary workers by telling us the keys to America's success are for us to work longer hours at lower wages and sit quietly as our government sells off our jobs to the last Third World "hot spot" he just vacationed in. Friedman is not alone—he is merely the most high-profile example of how many political reporters and pundits are so comfortably removed from the realities of ordinary Americans' economic lives that they have no problem regurgitating Big Business's latest lie as if it were fact. This book does the opposite: instead of reinforcing dishonest corporate/government propaganda, this book challenges it.

This book is not for people like Senator Rick Santorum (R), who call themselves "moral," then say we must cut programs for the poor because "making people struggle . . . is not necessarily the worst thing,"[13] and then support massive tax breaks for America's superwealthy. People like that are such wild-eyed, deranged lunatics, no amount of sanity in this book or any other is going to get through to them.

This book is not for prominent figures who claim to be Democrats but who have spent the better part of two decades using money from the likes of Enron, Philip Morris, Chevron, and the rest of Corporate America to push the Democratic Party to stop representing ordinary people and to start acting as just another vehicle for Big Business's PR. It is also not for that slew of gutless Democratic politicians whose only convictions seem to be their own self-promotion and successful reelections, rather than actually standing up for America's middle class. These people have long ago made a decision to undermine their party and support the hostile takeover that this book indicts.

Finally, this book is not for those who see politics only as another kind of infotainment or reality TV show, instead of the arena where millions of people's lives are affected by huge decisions. Many have said that Washington is Hollywood for ugly people—it's usually said with a laugh, but there's nothing funny about it. The top officials in government and media who treat public policy as a televised sport to be played only by the rich and powerful are the reason why Americans feel so divorced from their political process.

To be sure, there are many hardworking, sincere, and courageous people working in our nation's capital. Some of them are featured in this book. But they are far outnumbered and outgunned by the bought-off, the dishonest, and the cynical who see our government as their exclusive, gated country club from which they can play games while the rest of us are locked out.

Just a quick read of the most prominent political publications verifies how dominant this elitist world view is in Washington. Consider ABC News's *The Note*—a daily inside-the-Beltway publication from one of America's biggest media outlets. The newsletter's entire premise is to reinforce the arrogant, conceited, and self-important attitude among Washington insiders that has helped transform public policymaking into just another bidding war between moneyed interests. The writers of *The Note* regularly let readers know that they believe the only people who matter in politics are "the Gang of 500"—a cute name for a group of 500 Washington insiders who they claim "set the political agenda for the country."[14] That is the bipartisan consensus within Washington's media/political establishment today: forget about regular people; forget about state and local political initiatives; forget about grassroots organizing; forget about democracy—a handful of corrupt suits in Washington get to decide everyone's fate, period.

The arrogant aristocracy in Washington does everything it can to brush away anyone who has the nerve to challenge the powers that be, or oppose the government's carnal relationship with Corporate America. It is why we rarely, if ever, hear a congressional debate where lawmakers openly discuss how much money a given industry has spent to pass a piece of legislation. It is why any effort to oppose the hostile takeover is labeled "fringe" or "crazy" by the Washington establishment. And it is why this book is not written to get applause from those currently pulling the levers of power—because their applause comes only when the truth about economic reality is suppressed.

Why Should You Read This Book?

There are certain tools any person who faces a challenge needs. Rocky Balboa couldn't have won the heavyweight championship of the world without his trainer Mickey and a pair of boxing gloves; Superman couldn't save the world without his superpowers and his Fortress of Solitude; and Luke Skywalker couldn't defeat Darth Vader without a decent lightsaber and the Force.

If we are ever to make our government start working for us, the ordinary people who constitute the real America, the first thing we will need is information about exactly what's wrong, exactly how we are being deceived, exactly how our government has been the victim of a hostile takeover, and exactly how to start fixing things. Without that information, we can't know where to focus our energies, we can't know where the biggest problems are, and we can't know how to fight back. We would be waging a battle without a battle plan.

This book is designed to be a key part of that battle plan—one that systematically reviews in plain English how we're getting screwed, debunks the lies that are used to justify the screwing, and shows the very simple things our government could be doing to improve the lives of millions of citizens. It is designed to arm you with knowledge you can use to help reclaim our government.

Mind you, the "battle" is not one distinct event—it is millions of different interactions on front lines you may never have known were front lines in the first place. It is you talking to your colleagues at work. It is arguing politics with the guy next to you on the bus. It is discussing with your children how the government *actually* works, meaning making sure they get a dose of reality along with their sugarcoated civics curriculum. It is writing letters to the editor, organizing meetings with groups of citizens and your state legislator, and knocking on doors during elections. It is all of these things and more, and this book will help you be as informed as possible, and therefore all the more effective a foot soldier in taking our country back.

How Do You Use This Book?

This book certainly can be read cover to cover, and as the author, I don't want to encourage readers not to read the whole thing.

That said, however, this book is constructed first and foremost to serve as a user-friendly handbook to help people decode America's corrupt political system. That means you don't have to read every chapter. You don't even have to read every section of a given chapter. Ideally, you will have this book nearby when, say, you watch the evening news, or when you go to a town meeting held by your local elected official. When an issue comes up that affects your wallet, simply flip to the relevant section in the book, and there you will hopefully find a section on one of the main assertions you are hearing about. And suddenly at your fingertips you will have the proof you need to know that what that self-important media pundit or that smiling politician is telling you is simply not true.

For this reason, each chapter is designed in the same way. First comes an explanation of how Big Business has bought politicians' complicity in screwing you over in a certain aspect of your economic life. They've raised our taxes and lowered our wages. They've reduced the quality of our health care and increased the prices for our medicines. They've eliminated any semblance of job security and created obstacles to fighting for our economic rights in court. They've jacked up our energy bills and tamped down our ability to get bankruptcy protections when we can't pay those bills. They've made it easier for companies to steal our retirement nest egg and harder for us to join unions that protect that nest egg. And the list goes on.

But it isn't enough just to identify what has happened—we need to explore *how* all this has come to be. Big Business's hostile takeover of our government took place right in front of us over a course of years, but we barely noticed it happening. How is that possible? How could such a brutal conquest occur so silently?

Because they had what *Star Trek*'s Captain Kirk would call a "cloaking device"—a gadget that allows a threatening adversary to become invisible. Their particular cloaking device is a spin machine fueled by dishonest story lines, all designed to make us still believe our government is looking out for us when in fact it is doing exactly the opposite. Almost every policy that harms your economic situation is dressed up by politicians and corporate lobbyists as a policy that is supposed to help you.

Thus, following the explanation of how we're getting squeezed in a given area, each chapter is broken into sections that analyze the major lies, myths, and half-truths used to publicly rationalize the corrupt policies that make your economic situation worse and make the profit-at-all-social-cost agenda a reality.

To be sure, the chapters could end right there. Many a book has been written that is all doom and gloom. But the truth is, there are at least some honest souls in politics who have courageously fought the hostile takeover, and who have proposed concrete ways to start making government work for ordinary people. Big Business wants us to believe that the only way to solve society's economic challenges is for the government to hand over more power and more taxpayer money to Corporate America. Anything else, we are told, is unpatriotic or unrealistic. But nothing could be further from the truth.

That's why each chapter concludes with a set of concrete proposals that, if implemented right now, would start improving most Americans' quality of life without selling our country out. It is not enough to only detest the liars and debunk the scoundrels—we must also create the alternatives and construct a new reality.

IN the movie *The Matrix*, there is a scene where the main character is forced to choose which pill to swallow. But before he decides, his mentor, Morpheus, takes him aside and explains what is really going on. The intricate system of lies "is everywhere," Morpheus says. "It's all around us, here even in this room. You can see it out your window, or on your television. You feel it when you go to work, or go to church or pay your taxes."

The same can be said for the hostile takeover. You can see it everywhere—in the media, at your job, when you fill out your IRS forms. As Morpheus says, "It is the world that has been pulled over your eyes to blind you from the truth"—the world where citizens' ignorance is corporate bliss. The more we are distracted from the painful realities foisted on us by corporations and their agents who have infiltrated our government, the more we can be bled for all we're worth.

Therefore you have a decision to make: close this book now and go back to believing your corporate-owned government works for you, or believing there's nothing you can do to fight back. You take the blue pill and live in the fantasy world so carefully prepared for you by the establishment.

Or as they say in *The Matrix*, "You take the red pill . . . and I show you how deep the rabbit hole goes."

That means a whole different look at the way our political system works, a look that exposes all the ugly, smelly, rancid ways the most greedy people on earth have hungrily feasted on our country for their own pleasure—a look you may not be used to seeing in a world dominated by corporate media and a corrupt political system that has every financial incentive to hide these truths from us.

Just remember, like Morpheus, "All I am offering is the truth—nothing more."

The choice is yours.

CHAPTER 1

TAXES

★

IN THE spring of 2003,[1] American soldiers began massing on Kuwait's border with Iraq, preparing for what some experts feared could be a horrendous Iraqi counterattack[2] should President Bush order an invasion. It was a tense time in a nation both on the verge of war and strapped for resources to defend itself against terrorism thanks to massive budget deficits.

Every day, it seemed, there was a reminder of how serious the situation was. Color-coded alerts warned that another 9/11 could occur at any moment, as police and fire departments reported severe budget shortfalls; more than a year after the World Trade Center attacks, air marshals were still protecting only a fraction of the 35,000 daily flights in the United States;[3] in an urgent plea to the White House, federal officials warned that budget shortfalls were leaving the nation's nuclear material dangerously unprotected from al Qaeda;[4] and possibly worst of all, many soldiers awaiting the command to invade Iraq did not have adequate body armor to protect them.[5]

So when House Majority Leader Tom DeLay (R-TX) gave a major speech on March 12—just weeks before the invasion—the average onlooker might have expected a demand for national sacrifice, a patriotic call to make sure the country was protected and our troops were safe. Instead, we got a glimpse of just how far our political leaders will go to reward the wealthy.

"Nothing is more important in the face of a war than cutting taxes,"
DeLay proudly declared.[6] Nothing? Not securing our country, not preventing another 9/11, not protecting American troops heading into battle? No, to DeLay, the impending violence was just another excuse to
reward the rich donors who fund political campaigns.

You might think this comment was the strange babbling of an un-
hinged lunatic and was greeted with outrage or at least dismissive scorn.
You would be half right: the source of the comment was, in fact, a babbling fool—Tom DeLay is the same slime who, according to his hometown paper, justified dodging the draft during Vietnam by claiming he
really wanted to join up but was unable to find a spot because too many
poor minorities were enlisting.[7]

But in today's Washington, the absurd notion that cutting taxes is the
noblest and most important mission of the government—even in a time of
war—is so commonplace that few reporters thought DeLay's comments
newsworthy enough to write about. Big Money's hostile takeover of our political system has made DeLay's logic the rule, rather than the exception.

Look, no one likes paying taxes, and everyone wants them lowered.
But at the end of the day, we have to pay for things we need—things like
roads, bridges, schools, police, firefighters, national security, and the military. The ever-present question, then, is not whether taxes need to be
paid, but how they should be paid and by whom.

By the beginning of the twentieth century, America seemed to have
reached a consensus answer. As *Christian Science Monitor* columnist
David Francis noted in 2003, the United States opted to "rely on a simple
rationale: the well-to-do pay a larger share of their income in federal taxes
than the rest of Americans, because the rich can afford it." In return, "the
government protects their wealth and property."[8] Thus, the birth of a progressive income tax structure. It seemed simple enough—the Rockefellers
and the Mellons would pay a higher tax rate than their servants because
they could afford to. In return, the wealthy were the disproportionate
beneficiaries of a safe, secure, well-run national infrastructure.

The income tax on corporate profits was also established at the beginning of the century—a simple way to make sure business does its fair
share. Then, in 1916, the estate tax was created.[9] This one-time levy on
inherited wealth above a certain (very high) level falls almost exclusively
on the rich, raises money for social programs, and is supposed to prevent
the kind of hereditary aristocracy that had mutated into corrupt governing royalty in so many other parts of the world.

The system was, in short, government intervention at its best—

demanding that everyone throw in what they can. Lower tax rates at the bottom—which minimize the barrier to the middle class—were financed by higher rates for those at the very top who had already made it.

And then, slowly but surely, arguments opposing this perfectly functional system began to take hold. At first they were promoted only by a small coterie of tax-cutting zealots who possess a cultish devotion to the idea that allowing the superwealthy to accumulate more wealth is the highest economic good. But soon this crusade to change our tax code found converts in the highest levels of government. And the result has been a tax structure flipped on its head.

Using everything from subtle loopholes to brazen tax cuts targeted at the wealthy, moneyed interests have used huge campaign contributions and lobbying resources to transform a once-progressive system into one with one single goal: making the rich richer. During the Reagan era, the top 10 percent of the population saw its effective tax rates plummet, while almost every other segment of the population saw an increase.[10] During the George W. Bush era, things got much worse. In Bush's first term, he gave the top 1 percent of the population (those who make an average of $1 million a year) more than a half-trillion dollars' worth of tax cuts.[11] Meanwhile, the bottom 60 percent of the population—who make below about $42,000 a year—got about half of that.[12]

This kind of greed has been replicated at the state level. In 2005, for instance, Texas Republican legislators pushed a bill that would raise taxes by more than $1 billion a year on people earning less than $100,000 a year, in order to finance a half-billion-dollar tax cut for people earning more than $100,000 a year.[13] As the *Houston Chronicle* reported, the largest political donors to that cause were "the businesses [and individuals] that receive the biggest tax breaks."[14]

The elimination of corporate taxes has also been remarkable. Corporations have used the courts to win many of the same rights to free speech and legal protection as individual citizens. Yet they are allowed to simultaneously shirk the responsibilities of citizenship—especially that of paying taxes. Big Business argues that corporate taxes must be eliminated in the United States to keep American companies competitive with companies based in Third World tax havens, as if we should blindly engage in a race to the bottom for status as the world's biggest and best corporate banana republic.

In truth, the whole argument is designed to increase Big Business's bottom line at the expense of individual U.S. taxpayers, who are forced to shoulder an ever increasing and disproportionate cost of America's economic infrastructure (roads, bridges, security, defense, energy, patent enforcement, etc.)—much of which serves Corporate America. Between 1996 and 2000, ten large companies raked in $50 billion in corporate tax breaks. These run the gamut from tax breaks for stock options, to abusive offshore tax shelters, to specialized tax breaks for certain idiosyncratic activities granted by bought-off politicians.[15]

Hundreds of millions of dollars in taxes are dodged by other companies through smaller loopholes. By 2004, Big Business did not even try to hide the mockery it was making of the tax code. A bill that year designed to fix a small export tax problem was seized on by Congress as a prime opportunity to pass scores of narrow special-interest tax breaks for politicians' corporate donors: $92 million for NASCAR track owners, $189 million for Oldsmobile dealers, and $64 million for those who sell horses.[16] There was even a $25 million break for the dog and horse track gambling industry.[17] Meanwhile, American companies and individuals are being allowed to buy mailboxes in offshore tax havens, claim they are thus no longer "American" companies even though their operators are here, and then avoid paying up to $70 billion they owe in taxes.[18]

Politicians fuel this bonanza because they have a stake in it. Major donors to both political parties tend to be very wealthy individuals or very wealthy corporations. These are the same people and interests who stand to gain the most out of a tax policy rigged to reward the wealthy. Thus, a politician knows that if you give the rich or a corporation a new tax break, some of that cash will likely make it back into that politician's own campaign coffers. Just ask George W. Bush: his tax policies gave a total of $1.6 million in new tax cuts to his six top money men, and they returned the favor by raising him more than $1.4 million.[19]

On some issues, lawmakers actually have an even more personal interest in soaking the rich: their own bank account. Take the recent proposal to repeal the estate tax. Because the current law exempted the first $1 million of assets, repealing it would almost exclusively reward the richest 2 percent of America with billions of dollars—and would give almost nothing to everyone else. But repealing it also would give a huge chunk of change to about one in five elected officials in Washington, as roughly a hundred members of Congress are multimillionaires. The president and vice president, who aggressively support the proposal, would save their families roughly $6 million and $10 million, respectively.[20]

And then, of course, there are the lobbyists who game the process. According to the Center for Responsive Politics, there are 4,000 registered lobbyists in the nation's capital[21] who list taxes as one of their specialties. In terms of sheer manpower, this army could rival many "coalition" countries' forces in Iraq. These sharks are armed with the best propaganda and the fattest checkbooks to intimidate and cajole lawmakers into doing their bidding. In Washington's corporate feeding frenzy, lobbyists now jokingly equate their manhood with how big a loophole they are able to weave into tax bills. "Any lobbyist worth his salt has something in this [tax] bill," one lobbyist told the *Washington Post,* as Congress was passing a $136 billion corporate tax cut. The shakedown, he bragged, had "risen to a new level of sleaze."[22]

It is this sleaze, however, that is packaged in populist rhetoric and myth—all designed to force average Americans to pay an ever-increasing tax burden to sustain the lifestyles of the rich.

MYTH: Tax cuts mean lower taxes for average Americans.

During the 2000 election campaign, George W. Bush knew that in order to sell his tax cuts, he would have to convince working-class Americans they would be getting most of the benefits. "By far the vast majority of [my tax cut] goes to people at the bottom end of the economic ladder,"[23] he said during the second presidential debate.

This turned out to be a straight-up lie. According to the nonpartisan Citizens for Tax Justice, when Bush's tax cuts are fully implemented in 2010, the top 15 percent of income earners will have received roughly two-thirds of the tax cuts, with the top 1 percent of Americans receiving almost $600 billion in tax cuts. The bottom 60 percent of Americans will receive less than 18 percent of the total benefits.[24]

President Bush, we later found out, knew all his talk of tax cuts helping the average Joe was malarkey. According to journalist Ron Suskind, White House aides started pushing a new round of tax cuts for the wealthy in 2002. "Haven't we already given money to rich people?" Bush asked, acknowledging that he knew exactly whom his policies were benefiting.[25]

"Not enough" was the apparent answer. He soon introduced a bill eliminating all taxes on dividend income (aka money made from stock and bond holdings), an even bolder giveaway to his Big Money donors than before. The White House repeatedly claimed "92 million taxpayers would receive, on average, a tax cut of $1,083" under the legislation. The key word was *average*. In reality, 80 percent of taxpayers will receive less than $1,083, with most Americans getting an average tax cut of just $226. The reason the average was so high was because those who make $1 million or more will get more than $90,000 each.[26] It was the equivalent of putting Bill Gates and his $2 billion next to a broke homeless person and claiming the average net worth between the two is $1 billion. It is true— but it is also misleading.

It would have been just bad if ordinary people simply did not receive tax cuts they were promised. But the story gets worse: many Americans not only were cut out of the payday, they actually got a tax increase. In 2004, the *Christian Science Monitor* analyzed the net effect of Bush's tax policies and found "millions of American individuals and businesses face tax hikes" that "will shrink or even possibly wipe out the savings" that the White House had promised would come from its tax cuts."[27] A few months later, the *Washington Post* reported that in Bush's first four years, the top 1 percent of income earners—those making an average of more than $1 million a year—saw their share of their federal tax burden drop substantially, while the middle tier of income earners was forced to shoulder more.[28]

This reverse Robin Hood phenomenon was fueled by two things. First, the "tax-cutting" Bush administration quietly raised federal fees to suck billions out of ordinary citizens' pockets.[29] In Washington-speak, *fee* is another word for tax. These are all those charges you have to pay when you enter a national park, or when you apply for your veterans' medical benefits, or when you get on an airplane. And here's the kicker: because fees are the same for everyone regardless of income, they hit people with less money the hardest.

Second, Bush's policies forced states to raise taxes on the middle class by almost $22 billion since he was elected.[30] Here's what happened: the huge deficits Bush's federal tax cuts created became a justification for the White House to cut federal grants to states under the guise of "necessary belt-tightening." These cuts came at the very same time the White House passed a slew of laws that forced states to spend more money—without giving them the money to spend. According to *Stateline*, the publication that tracks state politics, these "unfunded mandates" cost states more than $50 billion from 2004 to 2005 and over the coming decade will cost states another $300 billion.[31] That money doesn't just magically appear. It comes from state and local tax increases,[32] and not only in "blue" states headed by "liberal" Democratic governors. In recent years, Republican governors in "red" states like Arkansas, Idaho, Ohio, and Texas have raised taxes and fees on their citizens to deal with budget shortfalls.[33]

HACK: Grover Norquist, Washington, conservative power broker

LIKENS TAXING THE RICH TO THE HOLOCAUST

As President of Americans for Tax Reform, Grover Norquist runs one of Corporate America's most powerful front groups in Washington. From an ideological perch to the right of Genghis Khan, Norquist uses corporate cash to bankroll hateful and dishonest propaganda that justifies more and more tax cuts for the wealthy. For instance, in an October 2003 radio interview, he equated the rationale of the estate tax to "the morality of the Holocaust." Three months later, when a Jewish newspaper asked him why he supported tax cuts for fat cats, Norquist attacked the questioner, saying, "The Nazis were for high marginal tax rates."

At the same time, local property taxes—which fund priorities like education and police—rose by more than 10 percent.[34] Those increases were making up for Bush's cuts to law-enforcement programs[35] and refusal to adequately fund his own No Child Left Behind education bill— moves the White House said were necessary because of deficits, deficits that Bush's tax cuts created.

So while it may seem counterintuitive, these so-called tax-cutting eras have left most Americans feeling more pinched by taxes than ever. This is why, for example, by early January 2004, a *New York Times*/CBS poll found fewer than one in five Americans said their tax burden was easing.[36] Four months later, as tax day approached, an Associated Press poll found roughly half of all Americans said their tax burden had actually increased after three years of much-ballyhooed federal tax cuts. That was four times the number who said their taxes decreased. "Every time you turn around, there's a new gasoline tax, more property taxes, a library tax," said one poll respondent, proving that no matter how much happy tax-cut talk is in the air, ordinary citizens know they are getting the shaft.[37]

MYTH: We should feel sorry for the persecuted billionaire.

On April 15, 2004, some of Colorado's wealthiest residents gathered at the ritzy Denver Country Club to feast on a lavish meal and to collectively mourn the plight of having to pay taxes. The evening was called the "Hard Times Tax Relief Party" and featured the local elite singing songs bemoaning the IRS.[38] The scene, far from humorous, was a pristine example of how our country has lost its moral compass when it comes to economic issues. Far from believing we are all in this together, the most extreme elements of America's rich and powerful are waging a merciless campaign to convince the public that America's wealthy are grossly overtaxed, and forced to pay more than their fair share. And they give huge amounts of money to politicians, political parties, and lobbying organizations who help them spread their dishonest story line.

This "persecuted-billionaire" myth is as fictional as a common fairy tale. On average, ordinary Americans are hit far harder by taxes than the wealthy. As *New York Times* tax writer David Cay Johnston notes, "people making $60,000 paid a larger share of their 2001 income in federal income, Social Security and Medicare taxes than a family making $25 million."[39] This stark reality is no accident. It is the product of enrich-the-already-rich economic policies justified by the myth of the persecuted billionaire, and by disproven "trickle-down" economic theories that dishonestly claim tax cuts for the rich will result in benefits for everyone else. They never do.

The truth is, if the wealthy were ever really persecuted (which they weren't), President Reagan, the first major "trickle-down" president, did everything he could to ease their pain. He reduced the rate of taxation on the tax code's very top income bracket.[40] He also cut the tax rate on capital gains[41] (i.e., gains from stock, bond, real estate, and other sales)—a tax cut that primarily benefits the wealthy, because they tend to own the most investments. Reagan's giveaways to the wealthy were followed by President George W. Bush's similar gifts that yet again showered the wealthy with billions in new tax breaks.

Far from having a glut of "persecuted billionaires," America now has a problem of a persecuted middle class, thanks to these tax policies. As Johnston notes, the regressive tax system today "literally takes money from those making $30,000 to $500,000 per year and funnels it in subtle ways to the super rich—the top $1/100$th of 1 percent of Americans."[42]

Still, that hasn't stopped the lies. People like South Carolina's Jim DeMint (now a U.S. senator) insist that "today, a near majority of voters pay little or no income taxes while they receive an increasing number of benefits from the government."[43] He is joined by right-wing outfits like the *Wall Street Journal* editorial page, which, in its piece headlined "The Non-Taxpaying Class," claimed "fewer and fewer people are responsible for paying more and more of all taxes."[44]

These propagandists are particularly crafty in their arguments—they narrowly focus on *income* tax, which remains modestly progressive. But if you account for all taxes—including regressive payroll, state, and local levies—government data proves the rich pay almost exactly the same overall tax rate as the rest of us. In fact, as *Slate* magazine's Tim Noah points out, "the tax bite is probably *higher* for many poor people, percentage-wise, than it is for the rich," especially considering the growing use of complex tax avoidance schemes by the wealthy.[45]

Nonetheless, the myth of the persecuted billionaire lives on in the highest reaches of government. In late 2002, Deputy Assistant Treasury Secretary J.T. Young penned a breathless op-ed in the right-wing *Washington Times* claiming that we are "seeing the end-result of class warfare: A shrinking group is shouldering virtually as large a tax burden as [has] ever been supported by the nation."[46]

Young's rhetoric was part of a bigger strategy of dishonesty, as the *Washington Post* reported two weeks later that the White House was secretly "refining arguments for why it may be necessary to shift more of the tax load onto lower-income workers." No matter that hard numbers showed the rich were already living large off the taxes of everyone else. White House officials simply changed the numbers, modifying the way the raw data was calculated "to make the poor appear to be paying less in taxes and the rich to be paying more."[47]

And thus the myth of the persecuted billionaire lives on. . . .

MYTH: A flat tax is a fair idea that would be good for the middle class.

Why all the effort to make the rich appear persecuted? So that the tax-cut zealots have one key public justification for their ultimate dream:

replacing the graduated income tax with one flat tax rate or a national sales tax.

The dishonest justification for this comes from extremists like Steve Forbes and House Speaker Dennis Hastert (R-IL),[48] who claim that making everyone's tax rate the same would be more fair and even lower taxes for most Americans. They say it would also be simpler: Instead of the long tax forms you have to fill out every year, they say all you'd have to do is fill out a simple postcard.

The problem is that when you filled out the postcard, you'd probably have to pay much more in taxes than you do now. As simple arithmetic shows, flattening the progressive tax system would be a huge tax cut for the wealthy, and a huge tax increase for everyone else.

If you don't believe that, just look at what Ronald Reagan's own Treasury Department said in 1982: "Any [flat tax plan] would involve a significant redistribution of tax liability" away from the wealthy and onto average taxpayers.[49] Remember, this is from the Reagan administration—a crowd that did everything it could to tilt the tax code toward the wealthy (in fact, they were probably trying to brag about the flat tax in noting that it would squeeze the middle class).

In the 1990s the flat tax proposal was once again resurrected. But as tax expert Robert McIntyre reported to Congress, the government's own analysis "shows that the typical family would pay close to $2,000 a year in additional taxes" under the proposal, while "very rich people would get tax cuts averaging more than $50,000 each."[50]

If all of this is true, how can politicians today keep advocating for a flat tax with a straight face? Because it is a highly deceptive proposal—at a cursory glance, a flat tax seems like a commonsense, simple, and brutally fair concept, even though it is none of those things.

First, there is nothing commonsense about a flat tax, because most flat tax propositions propose hitting only earned income like wages while eliminating taxes on unearned income like capital gains, interest, and stock dividends. These proposals, therefore, punish those who work for a living (the majority of Americans), while rewarding those who can afford to live off the work of others (the superwealthy, those who inherit money, etc.). That is insane.

Second, there is no reason that having a single tax rate is much simpler than having a graduated tax rate. The fact is, America's tax code is complex not because of its progressive income tax rate, but because of all the special-interest tax loopholes bought-off politicians have created over the years. In truth, a graduated tax can be applied with just about the same amount of paperwork as a flat tax. And if the aim is to simplify paperwork for most Americans, there are many easier and more fair ways to do it. You could, for argument's sake, classify all revenues—whether wages or capital gains or interest—as income, and tax it all the same, instead of what we do today, which is create often lower tax rates for capital gains and higher tax rates for wages.

Finally, there's nothing fair about taxing the subsistence income poor and middle-income people need to survive at the same rate that we tax the excess income of the wealthy. In truth, the flat tax is the baldest, most audacious scheme of all for finally and completely undoing a progressive tax system that has served this country well for decades.

LIE: Average Americans are bankrupted by the estate tax.

There is no issue debated in Washington that evokes more deliberate dishonesty than the estate tax. Politicians and interest groups literally lie through their teeth about it, pretending their push for repeal is all about the common man.

"Repeal of the 'death tax' means the next generation of young farmers and ranchers may inherit what is rightly theirs, instead of having to consider selling off a part of the family operation just to satisfy a tax penalty from the federal government,"[51] said Representative Larry Combest (R-TX) during one debate over repealing the estate tax.

Indiana's Democratic senator Evan Bayh has made the same case, claiming, "Instead of allowing families to pass their businesses to the next generation of entrepreneurs, the death tax forces these families to liquidate their assets."[52]

The American Farm Bureau, a front group for giant corporate agribusiness,[53] does what it always does and pretends to represent small farmers. The organization says, "The loss of these family businesses to pay the death tax hurts the families of deceased producers, the rural communities that depend on farming and the general health of American agriculture."[54]

Topping them all, antitax advocate Grover Norquist argues that taxing very wealthy estates is similar to "the morality of the Holocaust."[55]

Here are the facts: 98 percent of Americans pay no estate tax at all. Of the 2 percent of Americans who do, the vast majority of the tax is paid by the extremely wealthy. As the IRS has reported, half of all the revenues paid in estate taxes are paid by the one-tenth of 1 percent of the population whose estates are worth more than $5 million.[56] In other words, it is a tax almost exclusively on those appearing on MTV's *Cribs* or on the cover of *Cigar Aficionado*.

Politicians claim the estate tax is crushing poor farmers, but they know that's not true. According to IRS data, almost no working farmers ever pay the estate tax.[57] That is worth repeating and putting in all capital letters because it flies in the face of everything we hear from politicians who claim their anti-estate-tax positions are motivated by concern for rural America: ACCORDING TO IRS DATA, ALMOST NO WORKING FARMERS EVER PAY THE ESTATE TAX.

One prominent Iowa economist actually searched for families who had lost their farms to estate taxes but failed to find a single one. When the *New York Times* wanted to write a real-life feature about a farmer who lost his farm because of the estate tax, it went to the American Farm Bureau. The newspaper expected the organization to match its fiery rhetoric against the estate tax with hundreds of examples. The Farm Bureau was unable to produce even one.[58]

But facts no longer seem to matter: the lies about the "death tax" hurting average Americans have been so often repeated by politicians at the behest of their wealthy campaign donors that the tax was repealed in 2001,[59] handing over almost $60 billion a year to America's richest families by 2009. Though many ordinary Americans have been led to think this repeal will help them, in truth most of them will get nothing.[60] The repeal of the estate tax was a victory for the superrich champions of hereditary wealth.

Thankfully, the repeal is slated to expire after 2010, and with record deficits making headlines, even the most extreme politicians are hesitant to publicly back a permanent repeal. But that doesn't mean they aren't looking for backdoor ways to attack the tax, meaning a whole new fight is brewing. As the *Washington Post* reported in 2005, "The very rich and the merely rich are fighting over the fate of the estate tax," and "so far, the very rich are winning." The "merely rich want to exempt from taxation inheritances of up to $10 million"—exempting all but the most incredibly wealthy citizens. But that's not acceptable to the incredibly wealthy. These very rich people, "whose estates are worth tens of millions or even billions of dollars," say "a $10 million exemption isn't nearly enough for them." They want a plan like the one Arizona senator John Kyl (R) has pushed, which preserves an estate tax but lowers it to an almost negligible rate. His plan would cost a quarter-trillion dollars by 2015,[61] 57 percent of which would go to the three-hundredths of 1 percent of Americans who have estates worth more than $20 million. In other words, Kyl's bill would be a massive tax cut, the majority of which would go to the wealthiest 900 estates in the entire nation.[62]

Not surprisingly, lost in this argument between fat cats is the fact that a permanent repeal of the estate tax would deprive the government of tens of billions of dollars it needs to provide services to ordinary Americans. As one tax expert said, "Wealthy people will get tax cuts they don't need at the expense of important public services like food stamps and health care." That, in a nutshell, is what the push for an estate tax repeal is really all about.[63]

FAIRY TALE: Companies are forced to pay higher taxes in the United States than in most other industrialized countries.

Groups like the Cato Institute and Americans for Tax Reform, which are funded by some of America's wealthiest corporations, have for years pushed to eliminate all corporate taxes. They claim "the federal government takes 35 percent" of corporate income[64] for taxes, and that such a rate is the fourth-highest in the industrialized world, meaning U.S. companies are oppressed and the economy is harmed.[65]

Yes, it is true, the official corporate tax rate in America is 35 percent. It is also true, however, that because of lax enforcement, loopholes, and evasion, most corporations never come close to paying that rate. As the Government Accountability Office (GAO) reported in 2004, 94 percent of major corporations pay less than 5 percent of their income in taxes.[66] Because of this, corporate tax payments in the United States are at their second lowest level in sixty years.[67] In all, the actual corporate tax rate (as opposed to the official one) is lower in America than in every other industrialized country other than Iceland.[68] Put another way, unless your company studies subarctic volcanic islands in the middle of the Atlantic Ocean or can't survive without the music of Björk, there is no better place in the industrialized world than this country to base a corporation intent on evading taxes.

It all started back in the 1970s with the campaign to open up more and more corporate tax loopholes—a death-by-a-thousand-cuts strategy. Under the guise of creating a more "business-friendly" climate, lawmakers of both parties made an art out of riddling the tax code with special-interest provisions that rewarded their corporate campaign donors. The result today is that for every dollar the federal government receives from corporate and individual income taxes, it gives away at least 75 cents in the form of deductions, exemptions, exclusions, credits, preferences, and deferrals.[69]

Drug companies, for instance, are perennially among the most profitable businesses on the planet. They are also among the biggest givers of political campaign contributions, which means they continue to receive hundreds of millions of dollars a year in various tax write-offs from the U.S. government.[70] Likewise, American firms such as Accenture and Ingersoll-Rand—which receive huge taxpayer-funded government contracts—are allowed to purchase a mailbox in the Caribbean to avoid paying their fair share of U.S. taxes.[71] These are not petty amounts that corrupt politicians are permitting to be ripped off, mind you. This is theft on a scale barely even referenced in Hollywood bank robber movies for fear the audience wouldn't believe it—only it's legal and entirely commonplace. As just one example, in a mundane story about Ireland, the *Wall Street Journal* flippantly noted in 2005 that "a law firm's office on a quiet downtown street here houses an obscure subsidiary of Microsoft Corp. that helps the computer giant shave at least $500 million from its annual tax bill."

These subsidies and loopholes—and an unwillingness by government regulators to go after tax cheats—have made a mockery of the corporate tax rate. Under lax oversight by the Clinton administration, forty-one of the wealthiest companies in America reported $25.8 billion in total pre-tax profits between 1996 and 1998, yet paid no income taxes. Then, on tax day, they received $3.2 billion in tax rebates.[72] From 2001 to 2003 it got even worse: eighty-two companies that made $102 billion paid no taxes and received $12.6 billion in tax rebate checks.[73] Imagine what a scam that is by putting it in individual terms: it is like pulling in $1 million a year, evading your taxes, and then being rewarded with a fat check from Uncle Sam on April 15.

External auditors, who are hired by companies to make them comply with tax laws, are supposed to prevent this kind of behavior. Instead, they are aiding and abetting it. Between 1998 and 2003, government regulators found sixty-one Fortune 500 companies avoided a total of $3.4 billion in taxes through tax shelter schemes the companies' own auditors helped them create.[74]

In reality, America is operating like a Third World tax haven. As a *St. Petersburg Times* editorial put it, "April 15 is just another day [companies] don't have to worry about paying taxes [because] corporations have been allowed, even encouraged, to dodge their tax responsibility."[75]

HACK: Tom DeLay, House majority leader

DRAFT DODGER SAYS TAX CUTS MORE IMPORTANT THAN TROOPS IN COMBAT

House Majority Leader Tom DeLay (R-TX) says he supports protecting U.S. troops fighting in combat. Yet when lawmakers in March 2003 tried to prevent the passage of new tax cuts for the wealthy in order to save resources for the imminent Iraq War, DeLay ignored the pleas for prudence and pushed through the new tax cuts—even as troops were being sent into combat with inadequate body armor. "Nothing is more important in the face of war than cutting taxes," he said just days before officially crushing the tax cut opponents on the House floor. It was a statement that could only come from a man who, after dodging the Vietnam War draft, actually told the *Houston Press* that he had wanted to fight but was prevented from joining the military because too many poor minorities had enlisted and taken his spot.

Far from being overtaxed, American corporations are lavishly rewarded by a tax system they've helped design for maximum exploitation.

MISPERCEPTION: The IRS does a good job preventing cheating.

Every spring as tax season rolls around, thousands of Americans inevitably fear they are going to be audited by the IRS. It's not that most people are tax cheats. It's that most Americans feel like Alan Arkin in the movie *Glengarry Glen Ross*. Before being interrogated, the innocent Arkin says apprehensively, "When I talk to the police, I get nervous." But as Al Pacino reminds him, "Yeah, you know who doesn't? Thieves."

Pacino's line, while snappy, was only partly right. He should have added "and big corporations." That's because the policeman that makes sure Corporate America pays its taxes is as powerless as the unarmed rent-a-cop at your local mall.

Over the last few years, the IRS has been deliberately neutered by Congress and the White House, even as corporate scandals have ravaged the economy. Tax enforcement has fallen dramatically. The IRS now has about half the law-enforcement resources it had in 1988. The audit rate for the 11,000 largest companies fell by half over the past decade.[76] In 2003, only 0.73 percent of business tax returns were audited, down from 0.88 percent the year before.[77] And Congress continues to prohibit the IRS from going after companies that acquire a post office box in places like the Cayman Islands and then refuse to pay American taxes. The result is fewer penalties, fewer prosecutions, and a huge incentive for companies to continue evading.

And evade they do. A 2004 GAO report found that more than 27,000 Pentagon contractors owe the federal government $3 billion in unpaid taxes.[78] A follow-up study the next year found an additional 33,000 contractors for civilian agencies owe $3 billion more.[79] The government could cut off these cheats by terminating their federal contracts. Or at the very least, officials could follow a 1997 law that requires federal agencies to withhold 15 percent from payments to individuals or businesses with unpaid tax bills.[80] Yet that hasn't happened, likely because many of those tax evaders are big donors to politicians of both parties.[81] Meanwhile, companies that abuse offshore tax havens continue to receive almost $1 billion in U.S. government contracts each year, despite the fact that they are brazenly stealing money from American taxpayers.[82] In all, corporate delinquency, refusal to pay, and tax evasion rob America of up to $40 billion a year—more than the annual budget of the Department of Homeland Security.[83]

Regulators' lax attitude extends to their posture toward wealthy individuals, too. As David Cay Johnston notes, Congress was told in 2004 that more than three-quarters "of known tax cheats in investment partnerships are not even asked to pay because there are not enough tax collectors to go after them." In the late '90s, for example, the Justice Department prosecuted just 49 out of 1,600 cases of suspected tax fraud a Cayman Islands banker had handed over to the agency in a confession.[84]

For its part, the White House has never seriously addressed the problem of offshore tax havens. President Bush gave a clue as to why in 2004 when he dismissed efforts to raise taxes on the wealthy by saying that "real rich people figure out how to dodge taxes anyway."[85] It was the equivalent of a police chief saying we shouldn't fight crime because "criminals will figure out how to commit crime anyway." And it was wink-and-nod approval for wealthy people to continue cheating with impunity.

But even the Bush administration knows it needs money to run the government. So the White House began to squeeze more tax revenues from the people who can't afford to buy political power in today's corrupt system: low-income Americans. Today, Johnston notes, "those who make less than $16,000 a year are eight times more likely to be audited than millionaire investors in partnerships."[86]

And the audits are particularly aggressive. For instance, even if there is no reason to suspect someone is committing tax fraud, applicants for low-income tax credits can now be preemptively audited, with IRS agents demanding that the applicants provide pay stubs, rent receipts, and school transcripts in order to qualify.[87] As the *New York Times* noted in 2005, the preemptive audits ask the working poor "to provide the most exhaustive proof of [tax credit] eligibility ever demanded of any class of taxpayers."

This persecution has only increased over time. In 2003—the very year President Bush proposed eliminating all taxes on stock dividends— the IRS requested a 69 percent increase in funds to catch those who cheat on the Earned Income Tax Credit (a credit for the working poor), yet requested only a 3 percent increase in tax enforcement in all other areas.[88] After Hurricane Katrina in 2005, instead of eliminating billions in future tax breaks for the wealthy in order to pay for reconstruction, Republicans pushed a plan to once again increase audits of EITC recipients (many of whom had been victims of the hurricane).[89] These proposals play right into the age-old stereotype that lazy poor people—and not wealthy tax cheats—are supposedly the cause of America's problems. But just look at the numbers to see how dishonest that assertion is: Experts estimate that a total of about $300 billion in taxes goes unpaid every year, and that EITC fraud constitutes just 3 percent of that.[90]

You can bet much of the rest of that $300 billion gap comes from corporations and the wealthy using loopholes to avoid paying their fair share. And our government seems to encourage stealing. In 2002, for instance, Connecticut congresswoman Rosa DeLauro (D) authored legislation to prevent government contracts from going to companies that abuse U.S. laws and evade their tax obligations by incorporating in offshore tax havens. The rationale was simple: Taxpayer money should not go to subsidize companies that actively avoid their patriotic responsibility to pay taxes, especially at a time of war and of record budget deficits. The measure initially won approval, but was then eliminated by Republican lawmakers behind closed doors.[91]

She brought it up again in 2005, and this time 28 Democrats joined Republicans in defeating it.[92] Illinois congressman Rahm Emanuel (D), formerly an investment banker, provided the best example of how comfortable politicians are misleading the public about taxes. Claiming to be a defender of ordinary Americans, he had penned a 2003 op-ed in the *Wall Street Journal* saying he wanted to mount "an aggressive attack on the tax code" and its most unfair provisions, and that "should start with corporate expatriates." He claimed he was appalled that "some corporations are actually rewarded with federal contracts while they move their corporate headquarters to Bermuda."[93]

"I know of no middle-class family that sets up a shelter in Bermuda to pay for college education for the kids," Emanuel told the *Christian Science Monitor* in 2005, just four months before the DeLauro legislation came up.[94]

But in Washington, talk is cheap—votes are where the big money action is. And so when it came time to actually crack down on these tax cheats, Emanuel voted with Corporate America, and against DeLauro's legislation, helping defeat it once and for all.

FICTION: Spending—not tax cuts—is the reason we're in the red.

One of politicians' most repeated legends is the one about how government spending—not tax cuts—is the reason we now have record budget deficits. It started with Ronald Reagan's attempt to blame trillion-dollar deficits on lazy "welfare queens" supposedly driving around in Cadillacs and living off government handouts. And it continues today (though in more tacit terms). "Unless Congress controls its spending," says President Bush, "we'll face a decade of deficits."[95] He doesn't mean defense or homeland security spending, mind you. He means spending on things like health care for the poor, welfare, low-income housing, and inner-city schools.

It's a tall tale meant to subtly stir up all sorts of racial and class stereotypes, blaming poor people (read minorities, immigrants, and any group of "others") for bankrupting America. And it is being taken to the extreme. As one "scholar" at the corporate-funded Heritage Foundation wrote, the problem is not that tax cuts have depleted government revenues, "The real problem is government spending, and rising deficits are merely a symptom of that problem."[96]

But consider just one example to illustrate how shamefully dishonest this argument is: In 2004 the *Detroit News* found that the cost of Bush tax cuts for "the richest 10 percent this year alone will total $148 billion." The paper noted this is "twice as much as the government will spend on job training, $6.2 billion; college Pell grants, $12 billion; public housing, $6.3 billion; low-income rental subsidies, $19 billion; child care, $4.8 billion; insurance for low-income children, $5.2 billion; low-income energy assistance, $1.8 billion; meals for shut-ins, $180 million; and welfare, $16.9 billion."[97]

In other words, blaming the budget deficit on spending and not tax cuts is like eating a steady diet of deep-dish pepperoni pizza for a month, and then blaming the diet soda you drank for making you gain weight.

But that is exactly what is being argued. Bush's demand for Congress to "control its spending," for instance, came one year after he forced Congress to pass almost $2 trillion worth of tax cuts, most of which will go to the wealthiest Americans. According to a 2003 Congressional Budget Office report, those tax cuts were so large, they were the number-one reason America went from a projected $5.6 trillion surplus to a projected $4 trillion deficit in just four years.[98] More than war costs, 9/11 reconstruction, and new homeland security improvements, tax cuts are the main reason we went into the red.

But apparently this reality has not satiated those who would do anything to fork over more cash to the rich. The Bush administration is now pushing a series of new tax cuts that is expected to increase the federal debt by another $2 trillion.[99]

Then again, increasing those deficits may be just the point. As antitax activist Grover Norquist has said, one of the primary goals of tax-cut proponents "is reducing the size and scope of government by draining its lifeblood."[100] What better way to do that than create massive deficits? These zealots and their bought-and-paid-for politicians really do believe it is better to take Americans' hard-earned tax money and give it to a handful of rich people than it is to provide basic health care to families, education to our children, and food assistance to the poor.

That may sound like too harsh a characterization, but just look at the comments of one top Republican defending huge cuts to welfare. Senator Rick Santorum, the third-ranking Republican in the Senate, said at a public hearing that the cuts were justified because "making people struggle a little bit is not necessarily the worst thing."[101] These words came from his lips only months after he voted to give wealthy investors a massive tax break on their stock profits. As one pundit put it, Santorum and his ilk really do "believe in the class struggle, as long as it's only the poor who struggle."[102]

Santorum's comments are not uncommon—they are echoed by right-wing think tanks like the Heritage Foundation, which says the problem in society is not cuts to basic government services but not cutting basic government services enough. "Government spending undermines the nation's social fabric," wrote one of the foundation's operatives. "When the federal government increases outlays for social programs, it causes social damage."[103]

This logic asks us to forget about the social damage that comes when you kick the sick, the old, and the middle-class in the gut. Over the last few years, tax-cut-induced deficits have been the overarching justification for "belt-tightening" proposals to kick 90,000 low-income students off college grants,[104] 438,000 families off winter heating assistance,[105] and 300,000 low-income parents off child care assistance.[106] They have been used to rationalize proposals to halve housing aid for the disabled[107] and eliminate medical grants to people who have no health care insurance.[108] And they have been used to justify efforts to cut off 300,000 low-income families from food stamps at the very same time the White House pushed a provision to give 300,000 millionaires a brand-new $19,000 annual tax cut.[109]

Even soldiers wounded on the battlefield are not immune from being sacrificed on the altar of tax cuts. Just look at what happened in the lead-up to the Iraq war. In late 2002, as the president began formulating plans to send our soldiers into Iraq, the Bush administration ordered veterans' hospitals to stop publicizing health care benefits that veterans were entitled to.[110] The reason? Budget deficits meant VA hospitals needed to lower costs, and the fewer veterans who knew about their health benefits, the less money would have to be spent.

Yet on January 7, 2003, Bush said the government was so flush with cash that America could afford his $364 billion plan[111] to eliminate all taxes on stock dividends—a proposal that gave the average American $226 and the average millionaire more than $90,000 a year.[112]

But then, ten days later, the Bush administration said the government was so strapped for money it had to cut off health care benefits for 164,000 veterans.[113] Deficits, though, weren't enough to stop Bush from signing the dividend tax cut into law in September 2003. But deficits were enough to prevent adequate funding of health care services for soldiers wounded in battle. As United Press International discovered a month after Bush signed his dividend tax cut, "hundreds of sick and wounded U.S. soldiers including many who served in the Iraq war are languishing in hot cement barracks here while they wait—sometimes for months—to see doctors."[114]

In 2004, it was the same. In January, the president proposed spending

$2 trillion[115] on new income tax cuts,[116] primarily for the wealthy. That very same month, the White House refused a request by its own Veterans Affairs Secretary for $1.2 billion in emergency funding for veterans' health care.[117]

In February, it got worse. *Slate* magazine reported that the White House was skimping on funds to provide adequate armor for the thousands of troops being sent into combat in Iraq. In the very same budgets that proposed new tax cuts,[118] the White House earmarked zero dollars for various armor production programs.[119] The consequences were severe. As *Newsweek* reported in April of that year, a study by one defense consultant circulating throughout the Army noted that up to "one in four of those killed in combat in Iraq might be alive if they had had stronger armor around them" and "thousands more who were unprotected have suffered grievous wounds, such as the loss of limbs."[120]*

In 2005, this tax and deficit bait-and-switch reached a new low. On January 25, the *Wall Street Journal* reported that a top Bush administration official publicly blamed veterans' health care spending—not tax cuts—for jeopardizing national security resources. "The amounts [spent on veterans] have gotten to the point where they are hurtful. They are taking away from the nation's ability to defend itself," said David Chu, the Pentagon's undersecretary for personnel and readiness.[121] Yes, as hard to believe as it may be, it is true—the Pentagon was blaming veterans' need for health care, and not budget-busting tax cuts, for hurting America's defenses. The nauseating statement was clearly designed to prepare the public for more budget cuts. Two days later, reporters uncovered evidence that the Bush administration was forcing wounded soldiers to pay for their own hospital meals.[122] The next month, the White House released a budget that proposed raising health care premiums on veterans, citing (you guessed it) deficits.[123]

But still, it wasn't enough for the tax cut zealots. A few weeks later, right-wing pundit Tony Blankley authored a column with a headline claiming that the "Bush budget cuts are insufficiently draconian."[124]

Of course, that's easy for someone like Blankley to say. Famous on the Washington cocktail circuit for his grotesque corpulence,

---

*These statistics may have actually underestimated the consequences, as the *New York Times* reported in early 2006 that "a secret Pentagon study found that as many as 80 percent of the marines who have been killed in Iraq from wounds to the upper body could have survived if they had had extra body armor" that the administration refused to provide at the very same time it was spending billions on new tax cuts.

x-British-aristocrat accent, and flashy power suits, Blankley and his well-heeled friends are the ones who get to enjoy the protection of our brave soldiers while never having to sacrifice anything themselves. If you are a fat cat, it is easy to sip white wine by the pool, bloviate about the need to cut government programs, and pocket your big tax cut. That is, as long as you've never been maimed in a mortar attack on your inadequately armored Humvee, denied proper medical attention, and then told by a smiling politician that it is because of deficits.

HALF-TRUTH: Spending cuts are more than offset by the extra money most people get from tax cuts.

Whenever someone decries draconian spending cuts, inevitably there is a mouthpiece for the rich ready to claim that those spending cuts will be offset by tax cuts. We're told these tax cuts will put enough money in people's pockets to help them more than overcome the reductions in government services.

In one sense, the argument is true. In 2005, those in the top 1 percent of the population—who make an average of $1 million a year[125]—received almost $60,000 each from President Bush's tax cuts.[126] These folks will surely be able to cope with cuts to low-income housing, poverty assistance, and Medicaid. They are so rich, they don't need any of those programs. But those in the bottom 40 percent of the population received only between $100 and $400 in tax cuts that year[127]—hardly enough to cover a cut in even one of these services.

In September 2004, the *Detroit News* tried to find out whether recent tax cuts were, on the whole, helping or hurting America's middle class. Interviewing scores of people across the United States and examining thousands of pages of federal and state financial records, the newspaper reported that "the loss of services cost many poor Americans more money than they saved from the tax cuts," with working families now "increasingly likely to be placed on waiting lists for help, receive reduced services, or be denied service entirely."[128]

Remember, this tax and deficit policy came at a time when the need for government services was greatest. As the Associated Press reported in October 2004, "one in every five U.S. jobs [is] pay[ing] less than a poverty-level wage for a family of four," leaving 39 million Americans with "barely enough money to cover basic needs."[129]

HERO: David Obey, Wisconsin congressman

TRYING TO REDUCE TAX CUTS FOR THE WEALTHY
TO PAY FOR PRESSING NATIONAL PRIORITIES

Dave Obey has been in Congress since 1969, and in that time, he has learned how to use the legislative process to draw a sharp contrast. Case in point was his series of amendments in 2003 that showed exactly how our government is willing to put tax cuts for the wealthy ahead of everything else. Obey's proposals were simple: they would have slightly reduced scheduled tax cuts for the roughly 200,000 Americans who make more that $1 million a year in order to pay for a select few pressing priorities. His first amendment, for instance, would have reduced millionaires' 2003 tax cuts from $88,326 to $83,546 in order to restore most of the $1.5 billion cut to military family housing that the White House was proposing. Another amendment would have reduced the tax cut by the same amount, in order to pay for $1 billion in additional port and border security programs. Other amendments proposed to plug holes in health care and education funding. Though all of Obey's proposals were voted down, he managed to force a normally secretive Congress to declare out in the open that it is more interested in the welfare of millionaires than the welfare of everyone else.

MYTH: "Tax and spend" is a recipe for economic disaster.

In the spring of 2004, President Bush began formally kicking off his reelection bid by holding a series of public events to preview his major campaign themes. Nothing was very surprising about his agenda—it was the standard fare America had become used to from Republican incumbents. First, there was the salute to cultural conservatives with his

-profile introduction of a constitutional amendment banning gay
riage. Then there was the chest-thumping on national security and the
war on terror (sans any mention of the still-at-large Osama bin Laden).
And then, finally, there was the most familiar theme of all: economics.

Bush proudly promoted the trillions in tax cuts he had passed as supposedly helping the economy, and then went on the attack. "The tired, old
policies of tax and spend," Bush said, referring to Democrats, "are a
recipe for economic disaster."[130]

The inference in Bush's statement is one America has been hearing
for years: that an agenda of tax cuts and spending cuts is not tired, is
somehow "new," and, most important, is a path to economic success.

But look no further than the Hurricane Katrina catastrophe—and
the billions it caused in economic damage—to see how that simple, seemingly impenetrable axiom in American politics suddenly crumbled almost
as quickly as the infrastructure that was supposed to be protecting America's Gulf Coast. As the disaster showed, "tax and spend" is not the recipe
for economic disaster; tax cuts and spending cuts are.

In 2001, Republicans passed a $1.3 trillion tax cut[131] at the same time
they pushed massive cuts to America's flood and hurricane protection programs.[132] In 2003, President Bush pushed a $125 billion plan to eliminate
taxes on stock dividends[133] while cutting funds that his own Army Corps of
Engineers said were needed to maintain flood-control infrastructure in
southeast Louisiana.[134] The next year, the White House pushed a $1 tril-
lion plan to make the president's previous tax cuts permanent[135]—the
same year the New Orleans *Times-Picayune* reported that "for the first
time in 37 years, federal budget cuts have all but stopped major work on
the New Orleans area's east bank hurricane levees."[136] Just before the
storm in 2005, the White House and Republicans pushed to repeal the estate tax on the wealthiest 2 percent of Americans, while proposing a budget that would provide almost $300 million less than the Army Corps of
Engineers said was needed to complete critical infrastructure improvements in and around New Orleans.[137] This, in the face of a report by the
American Society of Civil Engineers that warned 3,500 dams were at risk
of failing unless the government spend $10 billion to fix them.[138]

Remember, these tax and budget decisions—made in the name of
fighting against "tax and spend" policies—happened while experts such
as Bush's own Army Corps chief warned that leaving these infrastructure
priorities unaddressed could lead to a disaster[139] (Bush's Army Corps
chief, Mike Parker, was immediately fired by the White House when he
said exactly this).[140] They also came as the insurance industry warned
that, unless infrastructure was improved, a major storm could cause be-

tween $27 billion and $150 billion in damage to the Gulf Coast.[141] In other words, it was the "tax cut and spending cut" agenda that left America vulnerable to so much economic damage after Hurricane Katrina—and it was a "tax and spend" agenda that might have protected us with better infrastructure investments in the first place.

Incredibly, though, this simple truth didn't seem to break through even after the storm. In his first nationally televised interview after Katrina—with Americans still drowning and starving—the president made sure to reiterate that he would not consider repealing the $336 billion in new tax cuts that he was set to give the richest 1 percent of Americans over the next five years.[142] Congressional leaders soon promised not to spend more money, but instead promised—you guessed it—more new tax cuts.[143]

But then, Hurricane Katrina is only the latest real-world consequence of the war against "tax and spend" and the promotion of tax cuts and spending cuts.

In 2002, our government faced serious revenue shortfalls right when we needed a big investment in homeland security. An ABC News national poll taken three months after the September 11 terrorist attacks found a majority of Americans supported canceling the Bush tax cuts.[144] But Congress refused, and instead opted to plunge our country into record deficits, while underfunding critical programs to beef up America's security and emergency response capabilities. Today, experts say America still has not invested adequate resources to protect itself from a terrorist attack.

In 2004, it was America's jobs crisis. With unemployment up and wages down, a *Money* magazine poll showed three-quarters of Americans would rather the government invest in job creation programs than the Bush tax cuts.[145] In response, the White House proposed big cuts to job training programs[146] while proposing to make the Bush tax cuts permanent.

As the aforementioned polls show, the public strongly supports a "tax and spend" agenda, because the public understands the obvious: The government plays a key role in spending money that is needed to protect and grow our economy. Tax cuts for the wealthy don't protect American cities from floods that cause billions in economic damage—infrastructure spending by the Army Corps of Engineers does. Tax cuts for the wealthy don't stop terrorist attacks that cost billions in economic damage—spending by the Department of Homeland Security does. Tax cuts for the wealthy have never given a single worker new skills—job training spending by the Department of Labor does.

In short, tax cuts for the wealthy do nothing more than give away money to people who don't need it but who give lots of money to politicians. Government spending, on the other hand, is critical to supporting and protecting America's economy for the long haul. Sure, there are examples of government spending excess (such as, say, billions in no-bid contracts to companies like Halliburton), just as there are examples of excess in every other operation involving large sums of money. But those only highlight a need for better oversight by regulators—they do not negate the simple fact that government has a responsibility to invest taxpayer money in our country's economic future, not just give it away to politicians' Big Money donors. Without such an investment in our future, we leave our country vulnerable to all sorts of problems that we could have avoided.

Solutions

The mistake we make when it comes to reforming America's tax code is to keep falling for "trickle-down" rhetoric that masks tax policies devised to simply reward the wealthy. The most effective reforms are those that make the system more fair, not more unfair, and those that provide enough revenue for critical priorities, like health care, education, job training, antipoverty initiatives, and adequate armor for our soldiers.

Roll back the Bush tax cuts immediately. In 2004, Meals on Wheels faced a $180 million shortfall, which meant 139,000 eligible, hungry seniors would be unserved by the program.[147] Preventing that shortfall would have required a little more than one-tenth of 1 percent of what the government spent on President Bush's dividend/stock tax cut package that year.[148] This is just one small example of how desperately we need to repeal the recent Bush tax cuts. Then again, if this relatively small example isn't your fancy, how about a big one: The Bush tax cuts cost three times as much as it would cost to fix Social Security's deficit[149]—the same Social Security deficit the president claims will bankrupt the entire system (more later on how that Social Security claim is, unto itself, dishonest). Repeal even some of the tax cuts and Social Security can be shored up, with plenty of money to spare.

Stop letting companies rip off American taxpayers by using offshore tax havens. The federal government needs to tighten laws that allow companies that have most of their operations in America to shirk their taxes by simply renting a mailbox in a tax haven country. The practice is the equivalent of living and working in Wichita, Kansas, but then on April 15 donning a flowered shirt, grabbing a piña colada, blowing up an inflatable pool in your backyard, and saying, "Hey mon!" in hopes you can trick the IRS into thinking you live in Jamaica and are therefore not subject to U.S. tax law. It would not fly for the average Joe, and it should not fly for Big Business. Instead of cutting taxes on offshore profits by $40 billion, as Congress did in 2004,[150] regulators need to hunt corporate tax evaders down and collect the cash that America is owed. This is no small problem—a report by nonpartisan congressional investigators found in 2005 that the federal government could increase tax revenues by $311 billion over the next ten years if it fixed the problem.[151]

Stop doing business with tax cheats and start punishing them. It seems no matter how much a company lies, cheats, and steals its way out of paying taxes, the federal government is there ready to hand that company a new government contract. While everyone else has to pay taxes or face consequences, companies are using abusive tax shelters to steal up to $8 billion a year—and many are still being rewarded with tax-payer largesse.[152] Instead, contracts should be made contingent on companies' paying what they owe, and contracts shouldn't be given to any company that hides its profits in Caribbean tax havens. You watch— within a year of this policy's passing, hundreds of companies that owe back taxes would pay up, for fear they would lose their government graft.

Force CEOs to certify corporate tax returns. Legally, corporations have fought for years to have the same legal rights as citizens. But that means they should also have the same responsibilities. Thus, if citizens can be held liable for falsifying their tax returns, so should corporations and their executives. In 2005, lawmakers attached a version of this proposal to a highway funding bill, and soon after, Corporate America started freaking out. A spokeswoman for a CEO lobbying group actually argued, "This is like asking a member of Congress to be personally liable for understanding everything in the budget resolution they just voted for."[153] Umm . . . what the hell is wrong with that? Nothing. And there's also nothing wrong with making a CEO stand by his/her company when it comes time to pay taxes. Too bad the proposal was ultimately killed behind closed doors[154]—but it is a good idea and should be law.

Give the IRS back its teeth and start making it do its real job. In 2003, the IRS told Congress that budget cuts would mean 75,000 audits would not be completed.[155] In 2004, IRS commissioner Charles

Rossotti said because of budget cuts, "the IRS doesn't have anywhere near the capacity to even deal with the most obvious cheaters." But he also said that if Congress started reversing the 20 percent reduction in IRS enforcement resources that was enacted during the 1990s, America could recover up to $300 billion in missing tax revenue.[156] But that money won't be recovered just with more resources—it will be recovered by the IRS focusing on the wealthy and large corporations, instead of overauditing the working poor, as happens now. To get the big money we're owed, the IRS has to go after big money.

When cutting taxes, give everyone the same tax cut . . . literally. To be sure, there is a time and a place for tax cuts in American politics when we have surpluses. But instead of telling folks we're going to cut taxes for everyone, and then giving most tax cuts to the wealthy, we can make those tax cuts more fair. For instance, the government can issue equal tax cuts to every man, woman, and child in America. And by equal, that means the same exact dollar figure. A middle-class couple would receive the same tax cut as Bill and Melinda Gates. For the Gates family a tax cut of $600 or $1,000 might be nothing, but for the other couple, it would be much-needed help. The Bush administration was actually forced to accept a version of this proposal in 2001 when a coalition in Congress pushed it.[157] The result was that taxpayers were given $300 rebate checks. And though these rebates were far outweighed by larger tax cuts for the wealthy, they were a step in the right direction, because they moved toward treating every American equally.

Fix the regressive payroll tax. In 2001, President Bush appointed an "independent" bipartisan commission to study Social Security, but specifically banned the panel from exploring proposals to address inequities in the payroll tax (i.e., Social Security and FICA taxes all workers pay regardless of income).[158] It was the most explicit example of how the wealthy are frightened of a debate about the issue. You see, right now, all income earners, whether they make $25,000 a year or $10 million a year, pay Social Security and Medicare taxes on the very first dollar they earn. This 12.4 percent payroll tax, however, applies only to wages below about $90,000,[159] meaning the $25,000-a-year earner pays a higher effective payroll tax rate than the millionaire. To fix the problem, the government could exempt a portion of an employee's salary from the payroll tax, as the conservative Business Roundtable proposed in 2002. Exempting the first $10,000 of wages from payroll taxes would cut $765 off the average worker's tax bill.[160] To make up for the lost tax revenue, we could simply raise the cap on what income is subject to payroll taxes.

Start taxing wealth instead of just work. A few weeks after President Bush took the oath of office for his second term, the *New York Times* analyzed the net effects of his tax policy. "Bush's cuts have brought the United States tax code closer to a system under which income from savings and investments aren't taxed at all and revenues would be raised exclusively from taxes on labor," the paper wrote,[161] noting that taxes on wages are now two and a half times greater than taxes on investment income.[162] In real-world terms, that means a janitor's hourly pay or a teacher's salary is often taxed at a higher rate than a CEO's stock earnings or a fat cat's inheritance. As billionaire Warren Buffett admitted, recent tax cuts on stock income mean "[my secretary's] overall federal tax rate would be 10 times what my rate would be."[163] The way to fix this is for Congress to scrap the current tax system and adopt something like the one the Center for American Progress has proposed—one that creates one simplified, progressive income tax that treats all money equally.[164] There would be no difference between capital gains earnings on stock trades and money earned sweeping floors—it would all be classified as income, subject to the new income tax. And there would be an elimination of all tax loopholes and deductions, except for the few that help the middle class, such as the home mortgage deduction and the child tax credit. The result would be a system that taxes exorbitant wealth, rather than disproportionately taxing an honest day's work.

Limit the home mortgage deduction. Speaking of the home mortgage deduction, it is time to limit this tax break once and for all. Currently, taxpayers get to write off the interest they are paying on their home mortgages, up to a $1 million mortgage. Here's the thing—anyone who wants to spend $1 million on a house has every right to do that. But should taxpayers really be subsidizing all $1 million of that home? The answer is no—taxpayers should be helping citizens reach the American dream of owning a home, but taxpayers shouldn't be subsidizing the wealthy in their million-dollar mansion purchases. That's why a cap of $500,000 for this tax break makes sense. Such a limit would save $17 billion, and also preserve the tax break for the home buyers who most need that extra boost. Alternatively, the tax could be targeted by letting folks deduct all of their interest on the first $300,000 of their mortgage, write off a slightly smaller amount on the next $200,000, and continue

HERO: Bob Riley, Alabama governor

TAKES ON HIS OWN PARTY IN FIGHT TO MAKE TAXES MORE FAIR

As a protégé of Newt Gingrich's in Congress, Alabama's Bob Riley (R) had been an ardent tax cutter. But when he took office as governor in 2003, Riley decided enough was enough. He followed his religious belief in fairness, and courageously tried to reform his state's unfair tax system—a system whereby the lowest-earning one-fifth of the population pay a 10 percent tax rate while the richest 1 percent pay just 3.7 percent. Riley's move highlighted the problem of tax unfairness that is plaguing states all over America: in 2002, the lowest-earning 20 percent of Americans faced an average state and local tax rate that was twice the rate being paid by the richest 1 percent of the population. Riley's solution was simple: Raise taxes on the top third of Alabama income earners, and on corporations that were paying almost nothing, while lowering taxes on the working class. In all, Riley's plan would have meant either no change or lower taxes for two-thirds of Alabamans—all while raising the necessary money to plug his state's massive budget deficit and increase funding for education. And though his plan was defeated in a statewide referendum at the hands of a corporate-funded campaign, Riley's efforts were a critical step in the fight to make taxes more fair.

diminishing on up to a certain cutoff point.[165] The bottom line remains the same—we should start limiting tax breaks for those who don't really need them.

Bring back the estate tax. Restoring and reforming the estate tax, as opposed to eliminating it, is a must. There is no reason to scrap the estate tax and forfeit billions to the superrich over the next two decades, especially at a time when poverty and budget deficits continue to rise. Instead, a reformed estate tax could be enacted that would fall only on estates valued at more than $5 million (as opposed to $1 million, where it stood before it was eliminated). That reform is strongly supported by the public: a 2002 poll showed more than two-thirds of Americans want the estate tax reformed instead of fully repealed.[166] In most states, raising the estate tax to this level would mean it would hit fewer than fifty of the biggest estates each year. It would preserve the tax as a levy exclusively on moguls and dynasties—not on regular families.

IMMEDIATELY after Hurricane Katrina, almost every political leader in America said they would do "whatever it takes" to help rebuild the Gulf Coast. Images of bodies floating through streets and destitute citizens swimming for their lives seemed to momentarily shock even the most dishonest politician's conscience.

Within days, however, these politicians were back doing what they do best: ignoring serious crises and focusing on protecting their wealthy campaign contributors. In his first nationally televised interview after Katrina—with people still starving, struggling, and drowning in the streets of New Orleans—the president made sure to reiterate that he would not consider repealing billions in new tax cuts scheduled for the rich.

The specifics of what followed provided Americans a clear view of how skewed politicians' priorities really are. Lawmakers simultaneously proposed making Bush's tax cuts for the wealthy permanent[168] while floating a plan to gut programs that serve military families. The *Navy Times* reported that congressional Republicans were asking troops to "accept reduced health care benefits for their families" and closures of elementary and secondary schools that serve children of soldiers.[169] Days later, CBS News reported that even as the White House refused to back off plans for more tax cuts, the administration was pleading poverty and "blocking a bipartisan $9 billion health care package for hundreds of thousands of evacuees" from the hurricane.[170]

Even the emergency relief legislation that was approved by Congress for hurricane victims was laced with tax cuts for the rich. The Associated Press reported that when Congress passed a package of tax breaks for victims, many provisions "would do more for wealthier taxpayers."[171] For instance, the *Washington Post* reported that "national gambling companies would be granted access to millions of dollars in tax breaks" under President Bush's proposal. When asked why hugely wealthy casinos should get special tax breaks, Mississippi governor Haley Barbour (R) claimed,

"They should be treated like any other business [because] that's the way we do it in Mississippi." It was a flat-out lie: As the *Post* noted, "The gambling industry largely has been excluded by statute from economic development incentives"—but now our government was using a human tragedy to shower the industry with new tax breaks.[172]

By the Christmas season in Washington, it was as if Katrina had never happened. All the rhetoric from politicians about their supposed heartfelt concern for the needy was gone—and so was the pretense that government exists to do anything but shower the wealthy in cash.

Weeks before the holiday, the *New York Times* reported that Congress passed a budget cutting food stamps and raising premiums on Medicaid recipients. Yes, that's right—cutting food stamps for people so poor they can't afford food, and raising health care premiums on people who are so poor they are forced to go on Medicaid. And where the money went was even more disgusting.

In the same budget, Congress enacted $56 billion in new tax cuts for the wealthy. How wealthy? According to the *Times,* experts calculated that more than half of the tax cuts "would flow to the top 1 percent of filers, people with average annual incomes of $1.1 million. Put another way: half the entire tax cut would go to about 1.4 million households."

All of this prompts critical questions:

When will the madness end?

If tax cuts for the wealthy can now routinely come before all of America's pressing priorities, what will they not come before?

If America's Gulf Coast suddenly submerged under water can't shock the insulated political establishment into reevaluating its tax-cuts-at-all-cost orthodoxy, what can?

And, perhaps most disturbing, if today's politicians are so corrupt and heartless as to use a human tragedy like Hurricane Katrina to justify more tax cuts for their big campaign contributors, what disaster *won't* they use to justify more tax cuts in the future?

Think about it—are we headed for a day in America's future where a leading politician will say an earthquake or a tsunami means we need more tax cuts for the wealthy? Or how about a terrorist detonating a nuclear weapon in an American city—will congressional leaders tell us in the shadow of a mushroom cloud that giving Bill Gates and the Walton family another tax cut will protect us?

Seriously, folks—what is next?

CHAPTER 2

WAGES

★

THE U.S. HOUSE's Financial Services committee is corporate-owned soil, one of the first conquered territories in Big Business's hostile take-over of our government. To most onlookers, its proceedings probably seem like a good cure for insomnia. And that is by design—the more bor-ing things look on the surface, the more Big Money interests can enact policies that squeeze average citizens.

But amid the committee's drone one summer day in 2001, those pay-ing attention were treated to a very public glimpse of exactly how our government has been engineered to work against us on even the most basic economic issues.

Federal Reserve Chairman Alan Greenspan was giving the committee his regular report on the economy. He was perhaps the single most pow-erful economic policymaker in America (if not the world), and his words had for years been treated like they were the Almighty's echoing down from Mt. Sinai. What a Fed chairman says during speeches usually goes when it comes to federal law—and few people have the nerve to chal-lenge that kind of power.

So things suddenly ground to a standstill when Representative Bernard Sanders (I-VT) confronted Greenspan about his position on the minimum wage—the law that says all American workers must be paid at least $5.15 an hour.

"Are you for abolishing the minimum wage?" Sanders asked.

The scene was right out of TV's *Happy Days:* the jukebox had cut out, the dancing suddenly stopped, and all went quiet—someone had challenged the Fonz to a fight. Greenspan paused, probably preparing to hide his out-of-the-mainstream ideology with his usual monotonous response that deliberately puts people to sleep. But that day, he got flustered.

"Yes," Greenspan told a surprised panel. Then, insulting millions of Americans toiling at or near the minimum wage, he added, "The minimum wage does no good."[1]

Greenspan is the same person who once said a measure of a person is whether one succeeds "without leaving a trail of casualties in your wake."[2] Yet, in one swift statement, he gave a huge boost to Corporate America's efforts to keep workers' pay as low as possible—efforts that are leaving casualties scattered throughout America.

Today, the minimum wage is nearing a fifty-year low,[3] when adjusted for inflation. A full-time minimum-wage worker makes about $10,700 a year—more than $5,000 below the official poverty line for a family of three.[4] If Greenspan had his way, these workers would be permitted to be paid even less.

The wage squeeze doesn't just affect minimum-wage workers—it affects everyone. Researchers at the University of California found in 2004 that jobs in the bottom third of the pay scale were growing almost twice as fast as those in the middle.[5] These are the Wal-Mart jobs that have been steadily replacing well-paying manufacturing jobs.[6]

The wage squeeze is happening as other economic forces bear down on the average citizen. As the *Washington Post* reported in 2004, those lucky enough to make a decent wage will have to "stretch further than ever as they pay more for health care or risk doing without insurance, and assume much or all of the burden for their retirement."[7] (More on these topics in later chapters.)

Those with a solid education or technical skills used to brush off these troubling trends, believing they were immune. Yet even in traditionally high-paying industries, workers are starting to feel the pinch. For instance, in 2003, the Institute of Electrical and Electronics Engineers found computer professionals saw a 1.5 percent decrease in their salaries—the first drop since the group began surveying their members in 1972.[8] In 2004, a national survey found these workers lost roughly another 1 percent of their salaries.[9] And by 2005, a real crisis had started solidifying. The Economic Policy Institute reported on government data that showed "real hourly wages have gone up by 1% in total" since 2001—a rate that isn't even keeping pace with inflation.[10] A month later, the *Financial Times* released a new report finding that "real wages in the U.S. are falling at their fastest rate in 14 years."[11]

It would be one thing if workers' paychecks were being cut because corporate profits were declining. But that's not the case. Since the economy picked up in 2002, corporate profits have risen almost 91 percent, while wages have stagnated.[12] As the *Boston Globe* reported, in the last quarter of 2003 "corporate profits as a share of the entire economy reached their highest level in more than 50 years," while "the share of the pie going to wages and salaries hit a 50-year low."[13]

The wage squeeze also might be understandable if American workers were becoming less productive. But as the *Christian Science Monitor* reported in 2005, "wage growth has been lackluster despite strong gains in worker productivity." In ages past, "as employees are able to produce more in each hour of work, the result is greater cash flow that can be divvied up between workers and owners." But now, with our bought-and-paid for government eliminating or ignoring worker safeguards, "most of the gains in the economy have gone into profits rather than wages," said one top economist.[14]

While workers suffer through this situation, corporate executives are hitting the jackpot. CEOs now make, on average, more than $9 million a year.[15] That's almost 300 times what their average workers make.[16] And they are using scandalous schemes to pump up their salaries even more. For instance, the *Wall Street Journal* reported in 2005 that "amid soaring CEO compensation, a number of companies are paying extra sums to cover executives' personal tax bills." These are not small sums—they can run into the millions, on top of the millions executives are already paid. In all, the *Journal* found more than half of the 100 largest corporations pad executives' salaries with such packages. And, not surprisingly, "details of the little-known payments . . . are often buried in impenetrable footnotes or obscure filings"—a deliberate move by executives to hide the rip-off schemes from their own shareholders and the public at large. Meanwhile, government regulators who are supposed to stop this kind of nefarious behavior look the other way.

But shouldn't CEOs be paid well when their companies do well? Sure, except many of the wealthiest CEOs are giving themselves huge bonuses at the very same time they are demanding wage concessions from employees, and running their companies into the ground. As one of Wall Street's most respected news services reported in 2005, "companies that sweeten executive compensation with unusually large bonuses or options plans tend to have deeper and more frequent credit downgrades and higher bond-default rates than those that don't offer such plum packages."[17]

To understand what that means in real numbers, check out what *USA Today* reported in late 2005:

> At 60 of the worst-performing companies in America, which lost $769 billion in market value over the past five years, the aggregate pay for the top five executives of those 60 companies over the same period was $12 billion. In other words, since January of 2000, some 300 executives who were responsible for more than three-quarters of a trillion dollars in shareholder value vanishing were rewarded by their shareholders with salary, bonuses, and stock options worth $12 billion. That averages out to $40 million for each of those companies' top five executives over the five-year period, or $8 million per executive per year.

It's the Ken Lay phenomenon: executives are frantically pocketing as much they can get while the rest of us—shareholders and workers—are trapped on the sinking ship.

With CEOs having such a huge amount of cash at their disposal—and with workers having so little—executives are able to buy lawmakers' support for policies that keep wages down. In 2004, business interests that had a stake in preventing a minimum-wage increase gave members of key House and Senate committees more than $7 million in campaign contributions.[18] This kind of massive influence buying is the norm. Not surprisingly, Congress hasn't considered a minimum-wage bill in years.

CEOs make no bones about what they are doing. After the 2004 election, the *Wall Street Journal* reported that Domino's Pizza CEO David Brandon is "counting on the president to counter any potential moves to increase the minimum wage."[19] Brandon, a longtime Republican donor, has many weapons at his disposal. Since 1997, Domino's has given the Republican Party more than $100,000.[20]

Then there was Betsy DeVos, of the billionaire family that controls the retailing giant Amway. As chairwoman of the Michigan Republican Party in 2004, she issued a press release claiming "most of the economic problems in Michigan are a result of high wages."[21] It was quite a thing to say to Michigan workers who were still making, on average, less than $39,000 a year,[22] even as energy and health care costs were spiking. And it was particularly poorly timed, considering the *Detroit News* had reported one month before that "Michigan ranks dead last among the states and the District of Columbia in personal income growth since 2000."[23] Yet far from distancing himself from this rhetoric, President Bush embraced DeVos afterward. Why? Maybe it had to do with the fact that she was one of his elite fundraisers in 2004. "I want to thank my friend, Betsy DeVos, for her leadership and her community spirit," Bush said at a speech in Michigan a few months after DeVos's insulting comments.[24]

DeVos was just one of eighty-five Bush Pioneers and Rangers (i.e., those who raise more than $100,000 for Bush) who head industries that have a direct stake in keeping wages as low as possible. These include CEOs from construction firms, agribusiness, manufacturing, and nursing home companies.[25] They include people like Dirk Van Dongen, president of an industry trade group that helped sponsor millions of dollars' worth of ads defending politicians who voted against the modest minimum-wage increase in 1996.[26]

Big Business's relentless efforts, of course, aren't limited to the White House or Congress. In 2004, the Chamber of Commerce spent $300,000 on a series of parties for California governor Arnold Schwarzenegger (R) at the Republican National Convention in New York.[27] Days after he returned home to Sacramento, he vetoed legislation that would have raised California's minimum wage.[28] That same year, the Florida Retail Federation fought a campaign against a statewide minimum-wage ballot initiative. The organization's CEO actually told reporters that "there would never be a good time to raise the minimum wage" and said "the minimum wage is an artificial number that means nothing."[29] Governor Jeb Bush (R) aligned himself with the group—no doubt a payback to Corporate America for its strong support of his reelection two years before. Luckily, voters ignored the lies and passed the initiative.

Big Business even has its tentacles in local politics. After a number of cities began enacting their own minimum-wage laws, bought-off state legislators started introducing bills to invalidate these local statutes in their midst.[30] Not surprisingly, these "Minimum Wage Repeal Acts"[31] were originally drafted by the American Legislative Exchange Council—a right-wing think tank funded by major corporations who have a financial interest in eliminating the minimum wage.[32]

These efforts to keep wages down aren't just supported by Republicans. As usual, some of these efforts were actually aided by corporate entities within the Democratic Party. For example, in 1999, when Montgomery County, Maryland, was considering raising its minimum wage, the industry-funded Democratic Leadership Council (DLC) issued a policy paper saying the move would result in "an unnecessary boost in pay" for some workers. "The problem with living wage ordinances, and minimum wage

increases generally," wrote the DLC, "is that they are not narrowly focused on the poor." In other words, this big-business-funded group was
publicly arguing that because the bill would increase the paychecks of lots
of workers, it was a bad idea. The DLC then endorsed an alternative plan
that would have eliminated the mandated pay increase and replaced it
with a government subsidy to companies that raised wages. That's not
necessarily a bad policy in a vacuum. But as a substitute for a minimum
wage, it is really just a giveaway to corporations, as it forces taxpayers to
foot the bill for a minimum-pay increase that should have been required
at no cost to taxpayers at all.[33]

If you are breathing a sigh of relief because you think the battle over
workers' pay is limited only to the minimum wage, don't get comfortable.
There are many other public policies Big Business is using to bring down
everyone's paycheck. In 2003, for example, President Bush proposed
eliminating overtime pay protections for up to 8 million workers.[34] These
are the basic laws that force companies to pay workers a higher wage
when they are asked to work longer hours. When Democrats joined with
Senator Arlen Specter (R-PA) to stop the move, White House allies in
Congress threatened to slash roughly $5 billion out of health care and ed-
ucation programs for the middle class. Their message: Let us put the
squeeze on workers or we'll put the hurt down on their families. For corporate hacks who supposedly hate "class warfare," it was a spectacularly
successful attempt to pit the middle class against itself. And it worked.
Specter backed down and the overtime cuts went through.[35]

But cutting off 8 million people apparently wasn't enough. Within
months, the Associated Press reported that Bush's Labor Department was
"giving employers tips on how to avoid paying overtime"[36] to the roughly
1.3 million low-income workers who were still eligible under the new
rules. Suggestions from the government included cutting workers' hourly
wages and adding the overtime to equal the original salary.

When Hurricane Katrina hit the Gulf Coast in 2005, the White House
decided to use the catastrophe as just another way to lower wages. In the
days after the storm, President Bush said the disaster justified him signing
an executive order revoking a seventy-four-year-old law that required federal contractors to pay their workers at least the region's prevailing wage
on construction projects.[37] The move allowed companies given federal
contracts for reconstruction to both pocket taxpayer cash and squeeze
down workers' wages. And because of whom the Bush administration
awarded those contracts to, the executive order ended up being exposed as
a deliberate gift to the GOP's corporate campaign donors.

For instance, the executive order helped Bechtel and Fluor,[38] both top

HACK: Sonny Perdue, Georgia governor

USES STATE LAW TO INVALIDATE CITY LAWS RAISING WAGES

In January 2005, the Atlanta City Council voted to give contract preferences to companies that pay their workers a "living wage" (aka a wage that allows people to rise out of poverty). Soon, though, corporate lobbyists and Georgia governor Sonny Perdue (R) went to work. Within months, they had crafted a bill in the state legislature that prohibited cities from enacting living-wage laws. Though Perdue's Republican Party often says it wants to give local communities "local control" over their own affairs, when it comes to paying workers well, that doesn't apply. Perdue signed the legislation in May, invalidating Atlanta's living-wage laws.

donors to the Republican Party which, immediately after the storm, had been granted no-bid contracts for reconstruction by the Bush administration.[39] It was also a boondoggle for President Bush's former campaign manager, Joe Allbaugh, who had set up a lobbying firm to help corporations profit off catastrophes (for instance, the front page of Allbaugh's Web site says his company was "created specifically with the aim of assisting clients to evaluate and take advantage of business opportunities in the Middle East following the conclusion of the U.S.-led war in Iraq[40]"). Ignoring all regard for human suffering, Allbaugh was, according to the *Washington Post*, "helping coordinate the private-sector response to the storm"[41]—a euphemistic code for Allbaugh's efforts to use the disaster to score as many federal contracts for his corporate clients as possible. He was wildly successful, corraling two huge federal contracts for his clients Shaw Group and Halliburton subsidiary Kellogg, Brown & Root.[42] And thanks to Bush's wage-destroying executive order, these companies would be able to pay workers a pittance while cashing in.

These examples of government helping Corporate America drive down workers' paychecks are the most overt. But there is a far less visible and equally nefarious campaign to drive down wages being channeled through America's trade policy. Under the guise of creating better-paying jobs at home, Corporate America has lobbied vigorously for legislation that eliminates U.S. tariffs on goods coming from low-wage countries. That sounds pretty positive at first glance. But then, the tariffs were created to construct a financial barrier against companies who try to reap a financial reward for eliminating U.S. jobs and exploiting desperate, low-wage workers in developing countries. It makes less business sense for a company to pick up and relocate to China in order to exploit $1-a-day labor if the goods made with that kind of slave labor face a tariff. Not only do such tariffs create an incentive for oppressive countries to clean up their act and treat their workers better, they also make sure Americans don't have to directly compete for jobs with slave labor.

Unfortunately, those commonsense policies conflict with the wishes of corporate executives who want to troll the world for the poorest people and cheapest labor to exploit. So in 1993, business interests hired at least thirty-three former U.S. government officials and spent at least $25 million on a lobbying campaign to pass the North American Free Trade Agreement (NAFTA)—a pact that included no wage protections at all.[43] They were joined by President Bill Clinton, who, despite data showing the contrary, promised that the deal would benefit America, "since," he said, it "will [bring] higher-paying jobs."[44] Clinton put the full weight of the White House behind the effort, having his staff convene regular meetings with top corporate lobbyists to plot strategy and strong arm lawmakers into selling out their constituents. They did.

That campaign was topped only by the effort in 2000 to enact a "free" trade deal with Communist China. Stung by wage losses in the seven years after NAFTA's passage, roughly four in five Americans in 2000 opposed a pact that didn't include wage/human rights standards[45]—standards that would prevent American workers from having to compete with workers who make $1 a day. But using $113 million worth of campaign contributions, lobbying, and advertising,[46] Big Business joined the Clinton administration in convincing Congress to pass such a pact.

And yet, there's more coming: The Bush administration and Big Business recently passed a corporate-written trade deal with Central America—again, with almost no wage, environmental, or labor standards. Politicians claim this so-called free trade policy is designed to raise living standards both in America and in the developing world, but it does exactly the opposite: it rewards countries that have the most oppressive regimes—regimes that persecute workers and keep wages down. And it begs the simple question: where does it all end? When Americans' wages rose, during the early and mid-twentieth century, "free" trade deals like

NAFTA, the China pact, and CAFTA forced us to choose either lower wages or the elimination of our jobs (more on that in the next chapter). As Latin Americans' wages rise, their jobs are now getting shipped off to China. If Chinese wages eventually rise because workers there start demanding a better life, where's next? Will we suddenly see a "free" trade agreement with North Korea—a country whose dictator has quite literally enslaved his population? Forget about "low-wage" labor—Big Business would have "no-wage" labor. Are our politicians going to suddenly start telling us that's a good thing that America's trade policy should encourage and reward?

If you think this is hyperbole, remember: Corporate America has admitted this downward spiral is precisely its goal. As GE CEO Jack Welch has said, Big Business's objective is "ideally [to] have every plant you own on a barge." Exactly, with U.S. government trade policy encouraging that barge to move away from whatever country's workers demand better wages.*

Welch, a Bush campaign donor whose company gave more than $2.4 million to the Republican Party since 2000,[47] was one of the corporate executives who attended Bush's first economic summit as President-elect in 2000.[48] You can bet Welch's desire to squeeze down wages carried a lot more weight at that meeting—and with our government in general—than the concerns of regular workers.

But then that's to be expected from a political system run by corporations. The lower the wages, the less overhead for business, the bigger the salaries for executives, the more campaign contributions for politicians, and the more lies that are created to justify policies that persecute America's working families.

LIE: "Free" trade is free.

Before delving into trade policy and its monumental role in driving down wages in America, you must first understand that "free" trade is not free. True—politicians of all stripes certainly say "free" trade is free. "It is in the best interest of the consumers of America to have true 'free'

---

*Welch might actually get his wish: in 2005, the *Los Angeles Times* reported that one American technology company released a proposal to house 600 software engineers "on a cruise ship moored three miles off the California coast, thus undercutting U.S. wage rates and circumventing local labor rules."

trade," said George H. W. Bush's White House chief of staff John Sununu in 1989.[49] "[Clinton's] concept of free trade is true free trade," Clinton Treasury Secretary Robert Rubin bragged to a conference of stockbrokers in 1993.[50] "Let's start talking now about genuinely having a true 'free' trade zone," said House Speaker Newt Gingrich two years later.[51]

But this "true free trade" line is a lie (and why this book puts quotations around "free" when referring to "free" trade). The truth is, "free" trade is anything but free. It is, instead, just a nice-sounding, poll-tested phrase to make it seem as if corporate-written, highly restrictive trade deals bring us closer to a utopia of less regulation and a borderless world. How could you possibly oppose "free" trade? Are you a backward, crazy Luddite who hates freedom? Those are exactly the misguided questions Big Business wants us to ask of those who oppose its trade agenda.

But at a 2000 conference on trade issues, an uncomfortable scene exposed the dishonesty behind the "true free trade" farce. Holding aloft a 900-page copy of one of America's recent pacts, a questioner asked why such a long list of restrictions was necessary for supposedly "free" trade? If "free" trade pacts are really truly free, couldn't they be written on just a few sheets of paper that say no tariffs, no regulation, no nothing?[52]

The answer can be found in the quiet admissions of trade officials long after they've left public office. Former Reagan official Bruce Bartlett—one of the original "free" trade zealots—recently acknowledged that he's never been interested in real "free" trade. "We don't have anything remotely like true 'free' trade," Bartlett said.[53] Same thing for Mickey Kantor, the lead proponent of "free" trade for President Clinton—a man who, soon after passing these "free" trade deals, became a corporate lawyer helping companies exploit them.[54] "I don't believe in free trade," he said, defying his entire career as one of Big Business's highest profile "free" trade advocates. "There is no such thing. We want rules-based trading systems, not free trade."[55]

At least the honest truth came out, even if it was years too late, and came with absolutely no remorse. That is what we have: "rules-based trade"—but rules that only benefit Corporate America. Trade deals today are "free" of wage protections for ordinary citizens but filled with restrictions that protect corporate interests. That is why those trade pacts are hundreds of pages long: they are teeming with very specific limitations to protect Corporate America's bottom line, but barely a single enforceable word about protecting average people.

Look no further than Robert Rubin for proof of this reality. In 2005, CNN reported that in the name of "free" trade, the former treasury secretary was urging "Congress to set aside environmental and labor concerns in supporting free-trade agreements."[56] Rubin apparently considers efforts to save American jobs, preserve decent wages, and prevent environmental degradation an affront to his devotion to "free" trade, or in another parlance that many use, negative "protectionism." But protectionism for Corporate America . . . well, that's okay by Rubin. After all, in 1996, it was Rubin who was crafting a trade deal with China that included almost no provisions to preserve American wages, but made sure to include restrictive intellectual-property protections desired by wealthy software and pharmaceutical executives. Intellectual property "is a matter of enormously serious concern," Rubin said at one press conference to reassure his Big Business friends. "It's a matter we take with the utmost seriousness, and we intend to pursue it with great seriousness."[57] Worker rights? Pollution standards? Anything to prevent companies from using the threat of heading to low-wage China to force down U.S. wages? Silence.

The proof of this "true free trade" lie, of course, is not limited to one person or one political party. In 2001, for instance, President Bush began pushing the so-called Free Trade Area of the Americas. In the name of "free" trade, he stressed that the pact would remove all tariffs and widen NAFTA to cover the entire South American continent. "We've embraced a collective responsibility to break down the barriers of poverty [and] disease," he said. "Open trade is an essential foundation for that prosperity and that possibility."[58]

Yet six months later, the *Washington Post* reported that the Bush administration was employing previously negotiated restrictions in supposedly "free" trade treaties "to keep Brazil and other developing countries from securing broad rights to override patents and lower the prices of drugs for treating AIDS and other illnesses" plaguing their populations.[59] It was overt protectionism for Bush's drug industry campaign donors.

This hypocrisy doesn't even stop when it endangers the health and safety of our own people. In 2005, for instance, critics called for restrictions on importing vegetables and meat from our trading partners in the wake of a mad cow scare. The Bush administration responded by claiming that, in the name of "free" trade, we must continue allowing unrestricted importation.[60] It didn't matter that mad cow disease had been found in Canada. It didn't matter that Mexican vegetables,[61] possibly grown in polluted water,[62] had recently caused a hepatitis outbreak in Pennsylvania. It didn't even occur to politicians to ask whether NAFTA's lax environmental standards—weakened in the name of "free" trade— might have set the conditions for permitting those vegetables to be tainted and then imported in the first place. The only thing that mattered was preserving "free" trade for the international agribusiness industry, which has flooded the political process with more than $360 million in campaign contributions since 1990.

Yet "free" trade was nowhere to be found just months before as these same shills in our government wrote provisions into a 2004 Australian trade pact that specifically prevented American seniors from importing lower-priced FDA-approved medicines. In other words, politicians' "free" trade rhetoric justified allowing companies to freely import things that make Americans sick, but it prevented Americans from freely importing things that will cure them. As Montana governor Brian Schweitzer (D) asked in 2005, "Why allow bad beef to enter the U.S. from Canada and not allow safe medicine?"[63] The answer is simple: Because agribusiness gave Bush more than $7 million in his career[64] to pose as a "free" trader when "free" trade supports Big Business's interests, and the drug industry gave him another $1.5 million to be the corporate protectionist he really is.[65]

Now, as this destructive and hypocritical policy is wreaking havoc, Corporate America and its political allies are using even more bareknuckled tactics to get their way. During the lead-up to the Central American Free Trade Agenda (CAFTA) in 2004, for instance, Guatemala passed a law speeding cheaper generic medicines to market there,[66] fearing CAFTA's restrictive patent provisions. Similarly, Costa Rica's legislature threatened to reject the treaty outright because of similar concerns. In response to both, the Bush administration's trade negotiators threatened economic consequences for Guatemala,[67] while the *Wall Street Journal* reported that two U.S. congressmen, Jim Moran (D-VA) and Dan Burton (R-IN), traveled to Costa Rica to warn "that Congress would eventually cut off existing trade preferences if Costa Rica's legislature didn't approve the CAFTA."[68] Both countries relented, and CAFTA passed with provisions limiting cheaper generic medicines and strengthening procorporate economic restrictions.

What becomes clear from all of this is simple: Corporate America tries to paint trade debates as occurring between "free" trade policies on one side and "protectionist" trade restrictions on the other. But these debates really are between two versions of restricted trade—one with restrictions that exclusively benefit Big Business and one with restrictions that actually benefit ordinary people. That is a debate Big Business and the corrupt politicians don't want to have out in the open, because all of their arguments quickly fall apart. As economist Mark Weisbrot has pointed out, tariffs—the taxes on imported goods designed to prevent an economic race to the bottom—"rarely increase the price of a good by more than 20 or 25 percent." That's no small amount, to be sure. But all the other restrictive tenets in our current "free" trade pacts can mean a far higher cost. For instance, according to Weisbrot, patent-protected prices "can be ten or twenty times the competitive price" for goods (think things like overpriced prescription drugs). He correctly notes that these corporate-written restrictions are really what our current "free" trade policy is all about: expanding this "lucrative form of protectionism across international borders."[69]

In interviews after the passage of NAFTA, then–House minority leader Dick Gephardt (D) explained how this destructive and hypocritical trade policy has been allowed to persist for so long, even as it has decreased American wages and ballooned our trade deficit. "Intellectual property, capital, what I call the finance issues are very important to ["free" traders]," he said. "But labor and workers and environmentalists are just not at the table. They've never been part of trade discussions."[70] As long as that's the case, we will have a policy that frees corporations to eliminate jobs and drive down U.S. wages—all while restricting citizens' economic rights.

LIE: "Free" trade creates better-paying American jobs.

In October 2004, Treasury Secretary John Snow visited Ohio to campaign for President Bush's reelection. A month earlier, the *Cincinnati Enquirer* reported that despite "free" trade deals like the China pact in 2000 that were supposed to help workers, studies showed that Ohio's real median wage had fallen three straight years from 2001 on.[71] But instead of acknowledging the disastrous effects of "free" trade—or even avoiding the issue—Snow went on the offensive for Corporate America.

"Free trade," he said defiantly, "helps to create more higher-paying jobs for American workers."[72]

In politics, we've come to accept half-truths, myths, and garden-variety dishonesty. But then there are the pathological lies, statements so utterly dishonest that only people who have a sick, maniacal disregard for the truth utter them publicly. This was one of them.

The facts are very stark: trade deals that allow companies to freely search the world for the cheapest labor have driven down Americans' wages. In 2001, economists estimated that three-quarters of American workers had lost about 12 percent of their current wages because of these trade deals.[73] For a worker earning $25,000 a year, that's more than

$3,000, thanks to trade deals that corporate America and politicians of both parties promised would mean better wages. In the period from World War II to 1972, when our government was not aggressively using trade policy to sell out American workers, wages grew by 85 percent. By contrast, in the next three decades of "free" trade dominance, real wages grew only 7 percent, even as corporate profits skyrocketed.[74]

The reason is simple: a government policy that forces Americans to compete for jobs with workers in other countries who have no minimum-wage or union rights forces Americans to either accept pay cuts or see their jobs shipped overseas. As the *New York Times* reported six years after NAFTA's passage, "Wage increases are being held down, especially in manufacturing, by a persistent fear among workers about losing their jobs despite the strong economy."[75] That fear is exploited by CEOs who use the leverage "free" trade policies granted them to make overt threats. As Delphi's CEO Robert "Steve" Miller told *Fortune* magazine in 2005, "There's nothing to be gained [by unions who strike over lost wages] other than to accelerate and expand the number of plants that have to be closed" here at home.[76]

Thanks to "free" trade and corporate executives who exploit it, workers today are forced to accept wages that don't keep up with inflation even when workers are increasing their own output.

As economist Mark Weisbrot noted, over the last three decades wages have barely increased, even though worker productivity has grown by 82 percent. "Normally we would expect wages and salaries to grow with productivity," Weisbrot wrote. "[But] these trade agreements have helped keep wages from growing here by increasing competition with workers making 60 cents an hour and by making it easier for employers to threaten to move when workers demand their share of rising productivity."[77]

If you don't care about Americans' wages and instead support "free" trade because you buy the politicians' line that it helps impoverished workers in the developing world, even that myth has been debunked. Just look at what's happened to the factories on the Mexican border. During the first seven years of NAFTA, 700,000 jobs were created in these *maquiladoras*, often paying workers up to $4 a day.[78] But since 2000, more than 40 percent of those jobs have been eliminated.[79] Have they moved back to the United States? Far from it. They headed for China to take advantage of $1-a-day labor now opened to exploitation by the new China "free" trade deal. As one prominent Mexican economist told the *New York Times* in 2003, "Ten years after, there is no conclusive evidence that real wages have increased because of Nafta."[80] The race to the bottom is on.

HACK: Mickey Kantor, President Clinton's U.S. trade representative

CRAFTS WAGE-DESTROYING TRADE DEAL, THEN SAYS THE EFFECTS DON'T MATTER

As President Bill Clinton's chief trade negotiator, Mickey Kantor crafted the North American Free Trade Agreement. That was the agreement that forced American workers to compete with Mexican workers who make poverty-level wages, thus creating downward pressure on wages in America. That was exactly the point of the corporate-written deal, and it was no surprise that Kantor later cashed in as a corporate lawyer. But perhaps worse, he publicly insulted workers whose wages have been devastated by the deal, saying that politicians shouldn't really care about the effects of unfair trade deals. "The NAFTA vote had about a two-week half-life," he told author John R. MacArthur, adding that "trade has very little political impact in the country."

Polls today show Americans are no longer believing the fraudulent argument that "free" trade means better paychecks for anyone. A 1999 poll done on the five-year anniversary of NAFTA found only 24 percent of Americans said they wanted to "continue the NAFTA agreement," while 58 percent expressed dissatisfaction with the pact.[81] In January 2004, a nationwide poll conducted by the University of Maryland found that "the majority of the American public is critical of U.S. government trade policy."[82]

Yet that doesn't seem to matter on the Washington cocktail party circuit, where corporate lobbyists, politicians, and the elite media alike look upon the interests of working Americans with disdain. As Big Business's traditional home, the Republican Party almost uniformly supports "free" trade. Worse, an increasing portion of the Democratic Party—the party that purports to represent the working class—is also clinging to the corporate line. President Clinton's chief trade-negotiator-turned-corporate-lawyer Mickey Kantor is Exhibit A. Years after NAFTA's effects on wages were well documented, he said that in terms of significance, "the NAFTA vote had about a two-week half-life." He then added that "even today trade has very little political impact in the country."[83] What an easy thing to say from the plush confines of a ritzy law firm whose clients' bottom line was undoubtedly fattened by Kantor's "free" trade advocacy.

And then there was, once again, former Clinton treasury secretary Robert Rubin. As mentioned previously, CNN reported in 2005 that he told Congress to set aside wage/labor concerns in supporting "free" trade agreements.[84] Now head of Citigroup,[85] Rubin has an interest in making sure capital can flow anywhere it wants. Even so, his brazen willingness to shill for corporate profits at the expense of workers' wages is shocking. In a 2005 speech, he actually argued against including serious wage protections in trade deals because he said such provisions "do not relate to the economic realities of the countries involved." Try telling that to the American family whose wages were decimated by Rubin-negotiated "free" trade deals during the 1990s.

Congressional Democrats have unfortunately listened to this corporate PR. Every few weeks, it seems a cadre of self-described "New" Democrats lands a story in a Capitol Hill publication explicitly reassuring corporate lobbyists that they fully support a trade policy that sells out America. As just one example, look at *Roll Call* newspaper in September 2005—a few months after many Democrats mustered the courage to vote against the Central American Free Trade Agreement (CAFTA). Instead of being proud that Democrats for once stood up for workers on trade, "New" Democrats were focused on making sure their corporate campaign donors were happy. *Roll Call*'s headline blared, "New Democrats Try to Assuage K Street" (a reference to the Washington, D.C., street where business lobbyists' offices are). "We want to be sure the business community knows that we are at the ready to work with them" in passing "free" trade deals, said California representative Ellen Tauscher (D)—a surefire signal that the "party of the working class" would not soon be abandoning its effort to sell out that working class in the future.[86]

But it is more than just "free" trade rhetoric that comes from Democrats—it is also action. Just look at what Democrats did in 2005 when a slot opened up on the House Ways and Means Committee—the panel that oversees all trade legislation. Instead of filling the position with a lawmaker who had tried to defend American workers against unfair trade, the party filled it with Illinois Representative Rahm Emanuel (D), who, as a White House aide during the 1990s, was responsible for forcing NAFTA through Congress. It was the same Rahm Emanuel who penned a

May 2000 op-ed piece in the conservative *Wall Street Journal* pressuring Democrats to capitulate and pass the China "free" trade pact—a move perfectly timed to help secure the critical votes that ultimately passed the deal.[87] It was the same Rahm Emanuel who pocketed more than $16 million in just two and a half years as an investment banker almost immediately after leaving the White House in what the *Chicago Tribune* described as "a tale of money and power, of leverage and connections, of a stunningly successful conversion of moxie and a network of political contacts into cold, hard cash." Yet now, instead of keeping Emanuel away from the trade policies he has been so instrumental in deforming over the years, Democrats promoted him to the Ways and Means Committee, where he can once again make his corporate donors' wage-destroying "free" trade agenda legislative reality.

LIE: Low wages are offset by low prices.

Talk to most politicians or economists in Washington, D.C., about "free" trade, and invariably the "low price" argument will be unveiled. You've heard a version of it before: Sure, they might admit, workers' wages are stagnating—but cheap goods produced by slave labor in places like China has meant incredibly low prices for American consumers. The implication is that the low prices more than compensate for the decline in workers' paychecks.

The argument sounds powerful. After all, wage levels are only important compared to what those wages can purchase. If, as we are led to believe, prices are declining faster than wages are declining, then workers may actually be making relative gains, because they will be able to afford more goods and services.

But here's the problem—that's not happening. As Jared Bernstein of the Economic Policy Institute reported in 2005, government data shows that "wages after adjusting for inflation are actually lower today than they were when the so-called economic 'recovery' began a few years ago." This has happened despite workers increasing their overall output. Put another way, workers are producing more per hour, but being paid less in real, inflation-adjusted dollars.

But beyond all the statistics and economic terms, we can see just how dishonest this "low-prices-trump-low-wages" argument is in a 2003 report that looked at a single parent of two children employed full-time at a Wal-Mart in Salina, Kansas—the middle of middle America. The report was done by local Salina writer Stan Cox and its premise was straight-forward: Wal-Mart is one of the main economic forces driving down wages in America—but it is also famous for supposedly super-low prices. So the question was, could that poorly-paid Wal-Mart worker afford her family's absolute minimal needs only if she shopped at low-priced Wal-Mart? If prices were dropping faster than wages, as we're led to believe, then of all places, Wal-Mart would certainly reflect that. But, alas, the results showed exactly the opposite: even when the Wal-Mart worker shopped only at Wal-Mart, she did not make enough income to survive.

None of this, of course, seems to matter to corrupt politicians. A front page *Washington Post* story in April 2005 sounded the alarm bell, but also noted that most lawmakers were playing the distraction game, using episodes like the Terry Schiavo controversy to divert attention from the basic truth: "free" trade's lower prices do not offset "free" trade's negative impact on workers' wages. "Inflation and interest rates are rising, stock values have plunged, a tank of gas induces sticker shock, and for nearly a year, wages have failed to keep up with the cost of living," the paper reported. In all, inflation-adjusted earnings had not risen in four years. Yet, as the *Post* pointed out, there remains a severe "disconnect between pocketbook concerns of ordinary Americans and the preoccupations of their politicians" who simply don't want to talk about the issue.

LIE: Politicians of all stripes actually support increasing the minimum wage.

No policy is more hated by Big Business and its political allies than the minimum wage. And yet no policy gets so much public pooh-poohing than the minimum wage. Even as cutthroat lobbying against it occurs behind closed doors, politicians tell the cameras they really do support an increase. No elected official who ever has to face voters wants to be openly against it, because polls consistently show wide public support for a raise.

That's why in early 2001 President Bush's new labor secretary, Elaine Chao, promised that "the president's position on the minimum wage is that it should be increased."[88] White House spokesman Ari Fleischer later insisted to the national media that "the president has indicated an openness to increasing the minimum wage."[89]

In Washington-speak, however, "should be" and "openness to" are code for "willingness to feign support for." It was true—Bush did say in the 2000 campaign he would sign a minimum-wage increase. But only one that would allow states to opt out and refuse to comply. Put another way, he would support a minimum wage increase as long as it was unenforceable.

Dick Cheney was asked about this contradiction. If Bush really did support a minimum-wage increase, why did he only support one that allows states to sabotage it? "Why not?" Cheney asked innocently in an effort to play off the ploy. "I don't see any reason why we shouldn't have that kind of flexibility."[90]

No reason? Not one? How about the simple hypocrisy of it all? A bill that purports to increase the nation's minimum wage but allows states to veto that minimum wage increase isn't worth the paper it's written on. Cheney might have called that "flexibility," but it was nothing more than a cynical and dishonest ruse—one that clearly made Big Business happy.

For the next three years, Bush didn't lift a finger to make his sham plan or any other minimum-wage bill a reality. He preferred to let workers' paychecks stagnate—a position that no doubt thrilled his big corporate donors who were being allowed to simultaneously rake in record profits while shafting workers. But when it came time to face voters again in 2004, Bush cynically put a note on his campaign's website claiming he would "continue to work with Congress to study the various minimum wage proposals."[91]

The dishonesty of Bush's position was not lost during the 2004 presidential campaign. Bush had gone from publicly supporting a fake increase during the 2000 campaign, to only expressing "openness" to an increase once elected, to only being willing to "study" proposals as a candidate for reelection. And by July 2004, when he was asked about the minimum wage, he knew he needed to explain his position, so he claimed in a public forum that Kentucky senator "Mitch McConnell is working on [a minimum wage] idea on the Senate floor, and I'm going to continue working with Mitch."[92] Sounded like a pretty concrete effort, right? After all, it was supposedly "on the Senate floor"—the place where bills get voted on.

Months later, though, there was still nothing happening on the minimum wage, and Bush was again asked about the issue, this time during the presidential debates. Stumbling for an answer, he claimed McConnell "had a minimum-wage plan that I supported that would have increased the minimum wage."[93]

Again, sounded as though Bush had been working hard, right? Too bad the lazy reporters covering the presidential campaign refused to let the voting public know what *The Hill* newspaper sadly reported only after the election: While McConnell once told a reporter of his desire to craft a loophole-riddled minimum-wage bill that would give Republicans cover on the issue, "McConnell never formally introduced his bill." In other words, there was no plan and certainly not one "on the Senate floor." The president had been misleading the country for months about one of the most important economic issues in America.[94]

After the election, of course, no one—not the White House, Mitch McConnell, or any other corporate shill in Congress—was talking about the minimum wage. Bush's bob-and-weave avoidance strategy seemed to have worked. That is, until 2005, when Massachusetts senator Ted Kennedy (D) forced a Senate vote on a proposal to raise the minimum wage to $7.25 an hour—not quite a radical idea, considering it still would provide a worker with a salary near the poverty line.

Panicking that the raise was so modest it might pass, Corporate America dispatched one of its most reliable allies, Pennsylvania senator Rick Santorum (R), to defuse the situation. "I have not had any ideological problem with the minimum wage," Santorum said upon introducing his own alternative to Kennedy's. He billed it as a minimum-wage increase—a shock to other senators, since it was Santorum who had voted seventeen times against raising the minimum wage in the past.[95]

That disbelief, however, quickly subsided when the bill's fine print was exposed. It was true, Santorum's bill would have raised the minimum wage by $1.10 for almost 2 million workers. But because of a tiny provision exempting businesses with revenues up to $1 million, it would have eliminated *all* minimum-wage protections for almost 7 million workers, opening the door to massive pay cuts, and the effective legalization of sweatshops. The bill also would have nullified various state minimum-wage laws, eliminated overtime pay protections for millions of workers, and exempted businesses from being fined for violating workplace safety, health, and pension laws—all in the name of "promot[ing] job creation" and "family time," as the legislation's text claimed.[96]

Kennedy's bill was defeated and, thankfully, so was Santorum's. But while the defeat of Kennedy's bill was a loss for workers, the mere existence of Santorum's bill was a big win for Big Business because it had done what it was supposed to for its proponents: namely, provide just the right cover for corporate-owned politicians. The lawmakers who had voted for Santorum's sham and then against Kennedy's real legislation headed home to dishonestly tell their constituents they really had tried to pass a minimum-wage increase and that they really do support a minimum-wage increase in the future—even though nothing is further from the truth. For his efforts, Santorum got a nice wet kiss from Corporate America: Wal-Mart, one of the country's largest low-wage employers and strongest opponents of raising wages, lent him its corporate jet a few weeks later so he could travel to a slew of big-dollar fundraisers and let the fat cats know he's their guy when it comes to keeping wages down.[97]

LIE: Raising the minimum wage kills jobs and hurts low-income workers.

One of the most effective arguments used to defeat minimum-wage increases comes disguised as compassion.

"Decades of research on the increases in the minimum wage have shown that when you raise the minimum wage, you tend to hurt the very people you're trying to help," said Craig Garthwaite of the Employment Policies Institute, when Kennedy's minimum-wage increase was being debated.[98] Because raising the minimum wage forces businesses to spend more on each employee, he argued, the policy supposedly kills jobs and therefore hurts the working poor.

Before even analyzing this fraudulent argument, understand that the Employment Policies Institute is a right-wing outfit created in the early 1990s and given the same acronym as the Economic Policy Institute (the similar name was likely a deliberate effort to confuse the media). The latter is a much older and better-respected research organization that represents the interests of working-class citizens. In 1992, the *Los Angeles Times* discovered that the sham Employment Policies Institute was really a front group "financed mostly by low-wage companies such as hotels and restaurants"[99] that have a big stake in keeping wages as low as possible.

Not surprisingly, then, the Employment Policies Institute's argument that minimum-wage increases hurt the economy and job growth is totally dishonest. In a comprehensive 2004 study, the nonpartisan Fiscal Policy Institute reported that since 1997, states that had boosted their minimum wage above the federal minimum actually created jobs faster than those that did not.[100] In higher-minimum-wage states, employment grew by 50 percent more than it did in states still at the pathetic federal level. Even in tough economic times, the minimum wage doesn't hurt jobs: Berkeley economist David Card found that even the minimum-wage increases during the 1990–91 recession "were not associated with any measurable employment losses."[101] As Republican senator Arlen Specter (PA) once admitted, "history clearly demonstrates that raising the minimum wage has no adverse impact on jobs."[102]

But that doesn't stop the most corrupt politicians like Utah senator Orrin Hatch (R) from lying about the minimum wage, even though raising the minimum wage would immediately provide a raise to more than 7 percent of his state's workforce.[103] Hatch said in 2005 that "raising the minimum wage closes the doors of many small businesses."[104] He made this inaccurate claim knowing full well the hard data shows that states that raised their wages saw small businesses grow at almost double the rate of states that didn't.[105]

Hatch is supported in his efforts by the corporate-funded Heritage Foundation, which claims that raising the minimum wage even a little bit would "result in the loss of hundreds of thousands of jobs" in the small-business sector. Yet nine out of ten small businesses surveyed in a 1998 study reported that the recent minimum-wage increases had no effect on their employment or hiring decisions.[106]

The truth is that raising the minimum wage is the best, most economically benign way to boost the pay of those who need it most. In Oregon, for instance, the state raised its minimum wage in 1998, and the average earnings of newly employed welfare recipients climbed by 9 percent, while the percentage of welfare recipients who found a job actually rose.[107] Similarly, in the four years after the last federal minimum-wage increase, Senator Specter noted that "the economy experienced its strongest growth in over three decades."[108]

The economics of the minimum wage make perfect sense: As opposed to providing tax cuts to the wealthy for them to simply save, raising the minimum wage gives a boost to people who are more likely to immediately spend the money on necessities, giving the economy a big job-creating shot in the arm.

LIE: The minimum wage should be abolished, because the government is not in the business of picking economic winners and losers.

You can't really blame New Hampshire senator John E. Sununu (R) for being out of touch with average Americans. The son of Republican operative/über-lobbyist John H. Sununu,[109] he grew up right around the

HERO: Jim Sinegal, CEO of Costco

SHOWS THAT PAYING WORKERS GOOD WAGES IS GOOD BUSINESS

The most often heard argument against policies that force companies to raise worker wages is that they are "antibusiness." But Costco CEO Jim Sinegal's track record is proof that it simply isn't true. As the *New York Times* reported in 2005, Costco's average pay "is $17 an hour, 42 percent higher than its fiercest rival, Sam's Club," while its "health plan makes those at many other retailers look Scroogish." Has that hurt business? No. "Costco's profit rose 22 percent in 2004, to $882 million, on sales of $47.1 billion," the *Times* reported. "In the United States, its stores average $121 million in sales annually, far more than the $70 million for Sam's Clubs." Sinegal says paying workers well "is not altruistic—this is good business," because it reduces worker turnover, raises productivity, and keeps customers loyal because they know the low prices aren't coming at workers' expense.

moist underbelly where Corporate America and politicians do their dirtiest work.

So it was no great shock that when the Senate debated raising the minimum wage in 2005, Sununu was appalled, claiming such a move "suggests that as Federal legislators it is our job to reward work." (Remember, that's a particularly disgusting proposition to someone like Sununu, who, growing up so close to power, never really needed laws that rewarded work.)

Taking it a step further, Sununu then claimed the government is not in the business of choosing economic winners and losers. "[It] is not the role of the Federal Government" to decide "whose work is worth more than someone else's and what kind of rewards" people should get, Sununu said. Proponents of the minimum wage were "try[ing] to control the levers of the economy," he said, and then claimed that is only done in places like Cuba and North Korea.[110]

This is one of the most oft-used lies in preventing the government from protecting the middle class. When regular people need the government to step in and defend them from abusive companies, we are told that's an unpatriotic, Communist idea and not the government's role. But when corporations ask for the same thing, they get that and more.

So, for instance, it is a Communist idea to have government intervene to raise wages of Wal-Mart's low-paid workers, thousands of whom make so little they are on Medicaid. But it is perfectly acceptable for the government to continue intervening in the economy to give Wal-Mart $1 billion in annual subsidies that help the giant company destroy local businesses.[111] Sununu rails that minimum-wage proponents "try to control the levers of the economy," but it was Sununu who pulled an economic lever in 2001 when he voted to give the airline industry $15 billion in taxpayer handouts[112] that were used to maintain airline executives' salaries in the face of decreasing profits. It was bought-and-paid-for politicians in Congress who voted in 2005 to reject a minimum-wage increase because they said they wanted the government out of the economy. But it was those same lawmakers three years before[113] who voted to continue giving General Motors the tens of million of dollars in taxpayer handouts it had received from the government's Export-Import bank since 2001 — a subsidy that helped the company ship almost 40,000 American jobs overseas in that same time period.[114]

In short, it's hands-off when it comes to helping average Americans, but it's hands-in-the-cookie-jar when it comes to serving Corporate America.

MYTH: We don't need to increase wages because low-wage workers aren't poor—they're just lazy.

In 2004, Heritage Foundation fellow Paul Kersey testified to the U.S. House of Representatives that "increasing the minimum wage will do little to improve conditions for the working poor ... because relatively few of the recipients of such an increase are living in poverty."[115]

Technically, he may or may not be correct because the official poverty line is roughly $16,000 for a family of three, and it is possible many minimum wage workers live in families barely over this line (though that also doesn't mean they aren't destitute).[116] But more important than a debate over official lines is how his rhetoric is emblematic of the broader effort by Corporate America and right-wing politicians to essentially deny the plight of low-wage workers. To support his argument, for instance, Kersey pointed out that nearly three-quarters of low-wage workers "have a family income that is at least 50 percent higher than the poverty line." Sounds great, until you realize all that means is that these families make $24,000—not exactly the high life.

This pseudoscience may seem tame on its own—but consider that it is regularly translated into some of the most inflammatory demagoguery on talk radio. As just one example, Rush Limbaugh, who rakes in roughly $30 million a year,[117] claimed similar Heritage Foundation data shows "that the poor in this country are not really all that poor."[118]

But consider some statistics:

– In almost every county in America, a person needs to earn three times the minimum wage to realistically afford a two-bedroom rental apartment. In fact, there are only four counties in the entire country where a household working forty hours a week, fifty-two weeks a year at a minimum-wage job can even afford a one-bedroom apartment at prevailing rates.[119]

– According to a comprehensive 2001 study by the Economic Policy Institute, nearly one in three families with an income double the poverty line or lower reported facing hardships like missing meals, being evicted from housing, having utilities disconnected, doubling up on housing, or not having access to needed medical care. Again, these are folks who make up to double the poverty line—far more than the minimum wage.[120]

– In that same study, researchers found nearly one in three working families in America does not earn enough income to afford basic necessities like food, housing, health care, and child care. Many of these families work full time and earn almost twice the official poverty rate, yet still remain destitute.[121]

– A 2004 U.S. Conference of Mayors study found that 34 percent of adults requesting emergency food assistance were already employed. Officials in half the cities surveyed identified low-paying jobs as a primary cause of hunger.[122]

No matter. Corporate shills can come up with ways to deflect even the most disturbing facts. Heritage's Kersey claimed that increasing wages won't help the poor because of "the low amount of hours that parents in poor families actually tend to work." The real problem, he seems to be saying, isn't that Corporate America shafts workers with terrible wages—it's that poor people are lazy. His prescription? Don't raise the minimum wage—make poor families work more because that "nearly doubles the average income of these families." Amazing! If we just get people to work more at the same low pay, their problems will be solved!

What Kersey and the Heritage Foundation's corporate benefactors who benefit from low wages don't want you to know is that many workers work part time only because there are fewer and fewer full-time jobs available. More companies are converting a larger share of their workforce to part-time or temporary labor so they can avoid paying for health care and retirement benefits. Today, there are 5 times the number of temporary workers in America than there were just two decades ago.[123]

But for argument's sake, let's just say the working poor could find more work. How many more hours would a typical family have to put in to achieve a minimally acceptable standard of living? "A couple with two children would have to work a combined 3.3 full-time minimum wage jobs to make ends meet," writes expert Holly Sklar in her seminal book on the minimum wage. "That's 132 hours a week. It just doesn't add up."[124] And even if these families could deal with this kind of indentured servitude, what are they supposed to do with their kids? President Bush's 2004 budget cut off 200,000 families from child care assistance, and his subsequent budget aims to cut off another 300,000 by 2009.[125] Following the Heritage Foundation's advice would make the movie *Home Alone* look more like a frightening prophecy than a lighthearted comedy.

MYTH: Higher wages mean much higher prices.

A good way to scare Americans into opposing better pay for themselves is to claim that higher wages will mean astronomically higher prices for essential goods. The Heritage Foundation claimed in 2001 that "economic research indicates that those who pay the most" for a minimum-wage increase are "consumers through higher prices."[126] That research probably comes out of places like the Employment Policies Institute—the group whose "mission is to oppose increases in the minimum wage so restaurants can continue to pay their workers as little as possible,"[127] according to the nonpartisan Center for Media and Democracy. In 2001, the Employment Policies Institute issued a report claiming "3 in 4 of the poorest workers lose from shouldering the costs of higher prices" that supposedly result from a higher minimum wage.[128]

As usual, that malarkey is parroted by bought-off politicians. "A minimum-wage increase is paid for by higher prices that hurt poor families the most," said Wyoming senator Mike Enzi (R) in 2004,[129] as he opposed a minimum-wage bill that would have meant an immediate raise for almost 9 percent of his state's workforce.[130] In other words, raise the minimum wage and the average family won't be able to put food on the table.

Sounds pretty scary. Thank the Lord it's not true. The U.S. Department of Agriculture issued a comprehensive report in 2000 analyzing what would happen if the minimum wage was increased by 50 cents an hour. The agency found that such a move would raise food prices "by less than one-quarter of a percentage point."[131] That's like going to the grocery, spending $100 on food for your family, and having to pay less than a quarter more on the whole bill. For minimum-wage earners working below the poverty line, the extra $1,000 per year from such a raise is sure to cover that.

The proof is in the pudding. As economist Ross Eisenbrey said, in 1996 and 1997 "we raised the minimum wage by 90 cents for about 9 million workers and inflation remained so low the effect was almost undetectable."[132]

How can you raise wages and not see huge spikes in prices? Look no further than the right-wing, corporate-funded Cato Institute for answers. In opposing the minimum wage, Cato accidentally admitted in a report that many companies are simply "unable to pass on their increased costs to consumers." Because of competition, "businesses cannot always arbitrarily increase the prices of their products" when wages rise. Thus, they may be forced to simply pay their workers better, which is exactly the point of minimum-wage laws.[133]

MYTH: We don't need policies that increase wages because wages are already growing.

One of the ways the Bush administration has deflected attention from its corporate-backed opposition to policies that raise wages is by pretending wages are already increasing. In four separate speeches in 2004, for instance, Vice President Dick Cheney told Americans that their "real incomes and wages are growing."[134] To be sure, Cheney's own bank account was growing—he was, after all, still collecting a fat paycheck from Halliburton,[135] even though he was vice president of the United States and not officially working for the company anymore. And a month before his declaration about wages, he filed his tax return flaunting a one-year $88,000 personal windfall from the Bush tax cuts.[136]

But the same certainly couldn't be said for everyone else.

Between 2001 and the time Cheney gave his speech claiming that "real incomes and wages are growing," hard economic data showed that American workers' wages decreased by 0.6 percent. If that's "growing," we'd be in real trouble when wages were "shrinking."[137]

When the economy finally started to add jobs after the recession of 2001 and 2002, President Bush reassured us in 2004 that "many of the new jobs are being created in industries that pay above-average wages."[138] Again, a dishonest claim with almost no factual basis. A study that same year showed definitively that the industries adding jobs in today's economy pay 21 percent less than industries that are slashing jobs.[139] Worse, many of these are low-paying temp jobs that have little or no benefits. According to Bush's own Labor Department statistics, 97 percent of the jobs added in the months before Bush's declaration were part-time positions.[140]

MYTH: Wage protection laws prevent necessary wage cuts when things are bad, and aren't necessary when things are good.

In 2003, the then-CEO of American Airlines told his blue-collar workers that they needed to accept a massive pay cut to keep the company afloat. "We realize that what we're asking is far from trivial," said CEO Donald Carty. "But we've always been honest with our employees, and that's not going to stop now."[141] He later told workers, "I just hope all of you realize we're in this mess together."[142]

Fearing for their jobs, the workers accepted the blow and took the pay cut. They bought the argument that decreasing profits at the airline was forcing lower wages—the same argument corporations use against government-mandated wage increases. When the company is in trouble, the logic goes, all employees' pay is in jeopardy. And any government policy that gets in the way of that supposed economic axiom will stunt the economy.

But look no further than Donald Carty for proof that this "we're all in this mess together" mantra is not always true. At the very same time Carty used the poverty argument to extort wage concessions from workers, he quietly drew up plans to have the company give him a $1.6 million bonus and donate $41 million to a special pension fund for forty-five top executives.[143] Details of the perks were discovered in the company's annual financial report, whose publication was delayed until after workers agreed to cut their own pay.[144] Apparently, there was plenty of cash available for executive perks, but not for workers' wages.

The same story goes for the converse. We'd like to believe that we don't need wage protections, because we'd like to believe that when good times come for Corporate America, good times come for workers. Not so. Since the economy picked up in 2002, corporate profits have risen almost 91 percent but wages have stagnated. The share of Big Business revenues that go to workers is now at the lowest level since World War II.[145]

The leftover cash during good times—some of which used to go to workers—is now being funneled to the same corporate executives who lobby against raising the minimum wage and who slash workers' paychecks. In 2004, CEOs at America's biggest companies made an average of $9.6 million, while workers at those same companies made an average of $33,176. Put another way, CEOs now make more in one workday than their average workers make in a year.[146] That's the widest pay gap in recent history.[147]

Look at the Comcast Corporation to see what this means in real-world terms. In 2004, the telecommunications company made $970 million in profits.[148] It also convinced Pennsylvania governor Ed Rendell (D) to give the company $30 million in taxpayer handouts for the construction of a new corporate headquarters.[149] There was so much cash lying around, Comcast's top six executives paid themselves $86 million in 2004 (including $2.1 million for David L. Cohen, who had previously been Rendell's chief of staff).[150] Yet when it came time to reward workers, the company still insisted on paying its top technicians almost 20 percent less than competitors, while thwarting unionization efforts.[151]

Or check out Caterpillar. In the first quarter of 2004, the construction equipment manufacturer reported a 200 percent increase in profits. Three days after the earnings announcement, Caterpillar sent its 8,000 workers a contract that rejected their raise requests, and instead asked them to shoulder higher health care costs and accept significantly lower pay for new hires.[152] Caterpillar then dragged out contract negotiations and tried to squeeze more concessions from workers.[153] By the end of the year, the company had reported a record $2 billion in profits,[154] paid CEO Jim Owens $15.2 million in total compensation[155]—and forced workers to accept the wage cuts.

Remember, it wasn't always like this. There was a time when we really

HERO: Bertha Lewis, ACORN Leader

COMMUNITY ORGANIZER HARNESSES GRASSROOTS POWER TO RAISE WAGES

As head of New York's Association of Community
Organizations for Reform Now (ACORN), Bertha Lewis
has built a serious grassroots movement that is fighting
for better wages. In 2002, Lewis and ACORN were
instrumental in passing New York City's living-wage law.
In 2004, ACORN scored another victory, this time helping
pressure New York's Republican State Senate to override
Governor George Pataki's (R) veto of a minimum-wage
hike—no small task. ACORN has started the national
Living Wage Campaign at www.livingwagecampaign.org,
developing grassroots resources all over America with the
specific goal of raising citizens' wages. Lewis and ACORN
prove that the hard work of community organizing and
creating local political pressure can ultimately result in
wins for workers.

were "in this together"—or at least more together than we are now. Sure, CEOs made more money than average workers, but not *that* much more. In 1970, for instance CEOs made about 38 times what workers made. Now they make an average of about 280 times what workers make.[156] And an exploding wage gap isn't just one of those indelible facts of business life in an industrialized economy. As just one example, Knight Ridder noted that "studies have shown salaries for executives in Japan"—a country with a solid economy—"are about five times those of their average employee."[157]

Think about it this way: If the minimum wage had grown at the same rate as CEO pay between 1990 and 2000, it would now be more than $25 an hour—five times the current rate of $5.15. If the average American's wage had grown at the same rate, most people would be making $120,000 a year.[158]

But that's not about to happen. Lawmakers are more than happy to take campaign contributions from CEOs and then vote against wage laws that would force those CEOs to give the average American a raise.

Solutions

The wage gap in this country is not just an insult to people at the bottom of the wage scale. It's a threat to our economy and social cohesion. The solutions are not aimed at punishing the rich but at making sure the floor does not drop out from beneath the rest of us.

Raise the minimum wage to a living wage. The richest country on earth should not have a minimum wage that is below the poverty line. Period. As the Economic Policy Institute reports, raising the minimum wage would not only help the 7 million workers toiling at the lowest level, but also create upward wage pressure for 8.2 million additional workers who earn near the minimum wage.[159] The argument that this raises prices or hurts low-income workers is a lie. So is the argument that it hurts business profitability. Just look at Costco: The company pays its workers more than triple the minimum wage, and 65 percent more than what Wal-Mart pays its workers, while providing better health care and retirement benefits than its competitors.[160] The result? In 2004, the company made almost $1 billion in profits,[161] beating Wall Street's expectations. How do they do it? A study by *BusinessWeek* found that by paying its employees more, the company gets lower turnover and higher productivity.[162] The minimum wage can be raised to the kind of wage that Costco pays its workers—a living wage that permits workers to afford the bare necessities. Already, one hundred municipalities[163] have passed living-wage ordinances. The *Christian Science Monitor* noted that though skeptical of living-wage laws, researchers concluded that slight job losses caused by the law in a few cities "are more than compensated by the decrease in family poverty."[164]

Use other tools to raise wages. "Increasing the minimum wage would represent a substantial unfunded mandate," wrote one Heritage Foundation scholar in 1998, concisely summarizing one of Corporate America's arguments. If we are to believe that business simply opposes economic mandates and has no problem with higher wages, then it would have no problem with other, less intrusive policies. For instance, some state lawmakers have proposed slapping a modest, 1 percent tax on companies' profits above $20 million if they aren't paying their workers a living wage.[165] That money would then be used to pay the increased Medicaid and welfare costs these workers incur from having such low wages. Or local governments can tell companies they aren't going to get government contracts or tax breaks unless they pay their workers better.[166] Under both scenarios, Big Business would be free to continue its abusive practices. Only under these circumstances, Big Business would face consequences for its socially irresponsible behavior.

Use tax policy to tie executives' pay to workers' pay. What's good for the goose should be good for the gander, meaning when CEOs rake in the cash, so should workers. One way to promote this concept is to reform America's corporate tax code. Instead of one corporate tax rate riddled with loopholes (as discussed in the tax chapter), we can establish a sliding rate based on the gap between a company's best-paid and worst-paid employee. The lower the gap, the lower the corporate tax rate, and vice versa. The policy would effectively be a tax incentive for companies to pay their workers better. It would also be a way to generate government revenue in order to pay for the safety-net services low-paid workers inevitably need—and it would be a way to get that revenue specifically from the companies paying the low wages instead of from everyone. To imagine what this could do, take a look at Wal-Mart. In 2001, the *Arkansas Democrat Gazette* reported that the company's CEO was paid $15.6 million.[167] That same year, Wal-Mart's salesclerks made an average salary of about $13,800—about $800 less than the federal poverty line for a family of three,[168] and more than 700 times less than the CEO. If a well-crafted sliding corporate tax had been in effect, it might have been more financially attractive for Wal-Mart to pay its CEO "only" $5 million a year, while giving more than 13,000 of Wal-Mart's employees an $800 raise—thus lifting 13,000 people over the poverty line.

Repeal trade pacts that don't have wage protections. According to a 2004 national poll, more than three in four Americans believe the U.S. government has paid too little attention to workers in trade deals.[169] It's time to renegotiate the trade deals that have driven workers' wages into the ground. That doesn't necessarily mean we need all our trade partners to agree to enforce U.S.-level minimum wages in their own countries. But it does mean they need to enforce *some* minimum wage that improves the lives of their own people and doesn't force Americans to compete with slave labor. That minimum-wage level can be lower than in the United States but should at the very least provide enough to achieve a basic standard of living. If our trade partners refuse, they need to face sliding tariffs that move up when their minimum wage level goes down, and move down when their wage level goes up. Opponents of this idea will scream "protectionism"—but it's far from that. It's a commonsense way to prevent Americans from having to compete on unfair terms. It is also a way to turn the economic race to the bottom into a race to the top by providing financial incentives for countries to increase wages.

WHEN THE Bush administration was criticized in 2003 for helping companies cut overtime pay for workers, its choice of a front man on the issue was illustrative of just how cozy our government is with Big Business, and how comfortable our officials are lying to ordinary Americans about their paychecks.

"We're not saying anybody should do any of this," said Labor Department spokesman Ed Frank, promising that government wasn't helping companies slash wages.[170] He might have been believable, except for the fact that before taking his government job, Frank was the top spokesman for the National Federation of Independent Business (NFIB)—the major business group that pushed for the overtime rollback in the first place.

An outrageous conflict of interest? Sure. Unfortunately, though, that's become the rule in Washington these days. Big Business and government are one and the same when it comes to keeping workers' wages down. Lower paychecks for ordinary employees means more money for higher CEO salaries, more campaign contributions for corrupt politicians who regurgitate corporate PR, and more industry shills like Ed Frank filling top government positions. Certainly, there is a veneer of independence. "We're not here to represent business," Frank told the *Denver Post* upon moving over from NFIB to his government job. "We're here to represent workers, and that is at the core of every decision we make."

That pseudopopulist rhetoric is designed to sound reassuring, but all it does is more crisply illustrate the dishonesty. We need look no further than White House political guru Karl Rove to see as much.

"NFIB and the Bush administration do walk hand in hand," Rove said in a brief moment of candor, essentially discrediting Frank's claim that government officials put workers' interest first.[171] They don't—they're walking hand in hand with the business interests that buy their elections, and buy public policies that keep ordinary Americans as destitute as possible.

CHAPTER 3

JOBS

HAN SOLO didn't crack jokes about Luke Skywalker when Darth Vader cut his arm off. Lois Lane didn't heckle Superman when kryptonite hurt him. Captain Kirk didn't make fun of Mr. Spock when he was dying from radiation poisoning after saving the *Enterprise*. But during the last recession, our own government laughed at American workers as they lost their jobs.

Specifically, the White House issued an official report in early 2004 officially endorsing Corporate America's efforts to ship U.S. jobs overseas. When releasing the document, the president's chief economic adviser, Greg Mankiw, claimed that outsourcing was "a plus for the economy." Eliminating jobs in America and sending them overseas, Mankiw explained, is "the latest manifestation of the gains from trade."[1]

At that point, more than 2 million Americans had lost their job since President Bush had taken office,[2] and almost one in ten Americans could not find a full-time job.[3] Yet the White House was calling their plight a "gain." The U.S. government had, in effect, given these workers the big middle finger.

This brazen insult to workers was quickly followed up with an equally brazen lie. Sensing that ordinary Americans might not like being flipped off, the White House put Labor Secretary Elaine Chao in front of the cameras to claim President Bush "doesn't sign this report" that Mankiw was hawking. Funny, it must have been that other "George W. Bush" whose oversized signature was proudly displayed on page four of the report.[4]

But that's the bait and switch for you. While our government helps companies reduce our wages, as the previous chapter showed, politicians also deceive us by helping publicly justify Big Business eliminating our jobs altogether.

From the 2001 recession to early 2005, the economy added a net total of just 415,000 jobs. That represents the worst record since the government began collecting jobs data at the end of the Great Depression. If the economy had grown at the average rate that it has in the past, we would have added 7.1 million new private-sector jobs.[5]

The jobs crisis is reaching into all sectors of the economy. The *New York Times* reported that America lost more than 2 million manufacturing jobs between 2001 and 2004.[6] That's more than 1,300 jobs lost every single day, all as the government continues to push corporate "free" trade deals and cuts to job-training programs. In the high-tech industry, it's the same. Between 2001 and 2004, almost one in five U.S. technology jobs were eliminated.[7] That's more than 400,000 jobs. Don't try to pawn that off on 9/11 and the subsequent economic downturn—more than half of those lost jobs were eliminated after 2001's post-9/11 recession officially ended,[8] and experts believe this job loss will go on well into the future. For instance, University of California researchers estimated in 2004 that up to 14 million American jobs are at risk to outsourcing,[9] while Gartner Research predicted that 30 percent of high-tech jobs could be shipped overseas by 2015.[10]

The blame for this goes to both parties, who have allowed Corporate America's hostile takeover of our government to threaten one of the most fundamental foundations of any economy—the ability of workers to find work.

When he ran for president in 1992, Bill Clinton made a face-to-face promise to Americans that he wouldn't sell out their jobs. Using his classic I'm-biting-my-bottom-lip-to-show-you-I-really-care presentation, Clinton told a town hall meeting that he would sign trade deals "only— only—if [trading partner countries] lifted their wage rates and their labor standards and they cleaned up their environment so we could both go up together, instead of being dragged down."[11] That was encouraging rhetoric for workers—he was promising them they would not have to worry about trade deals that rewarded companies for relocating U.S. jobs in countries where lax wage/environmental laws encourage exploitation. He also promised that "I wouldn't have done what [the first President] Bush did and give all those trade preferences to China when they're locking their people up"—again, a promise to American workers that they would not have to worry about trade deals that let Corporate America exploit poor human rights conditions and ship U.S. jobs to countries that provide no labor protections at all.[12]

Once Clinton assumed office, however, those promises were promptly ignored in favor of a trade agenda that satisfied the new president's Big Money donors. In his very first year in office, Clinton organized a coalition of business lobbyists to help him crush opposition and pass the North American Free Trade Agreement (NAFTA).[13] A few years later, he used the same tactics to ram the China "free" trade deal through Congress. Both pacts included almost none of the strong labor, environmental, or human rights standards Clinton promised would be necessary to get his signature. As the millionaire CEO of American Express proudly said after NAFTA passed, "[Clinton] stood up against his two prime constituents, labor and environment, to drive it home over their dead bodies."[14] For Corporate America, running roughshod over workers and ecological protection is something to be proud of. And thanks in part to Clinton's obscene, corporate-driven flip-flop on trade, American workers now must compete with slave labor in the developing world, and companies have a financial incentive to continue shipping millions of U.S. jobs overseas.

At the very least, though, Clinton did try to maintain some semblance of a safety net for the workers he had sold out, increasing education funding and assistance to those who had seen their jobs eliminated because of "free" trade.[15] But that's where the Republicans came in. They not only push Big Business's trade agenda and openly encourage companies to outsource jobs, they also do everything in their power to eliminate public assistance and job training to unemployed workers. Some are brutally honest about their goals. For instance, the right-wing Cato Institute's official handbook given out to lawmakers says point-blank that "Congress should eliminate federal unemployment insurance." Why? Because they claim the current system, which provides workers only half of their salaries for about six months, "reduces the incentive for the unemployed to seek work."[16] Right, because an ordinary worker living on less than half his/her salary for six months[17] and then being cut off entirely is living on Easy Street.

Others, though, are even more dishonest. President Bush spent his first term running around the country claiming he wanted to increase job training, even as he tried to cut more than a billion dollars out of federal job-training programs.[18] In 1998 the federal government trained about 150,000 jobless workers each year. Today, the government trains about half that number, even though the nation's unemployment rate is up.[19]

Why are these politicians selling American workers down the river? As usual, it is all about money. Our country's trade policies, as noted in the chapter on wages, are sponsored by tens of millions of dollars from corporations who want nothing more than to relocate their factories to the cheapest labor markets, and then be able to sell their products back to Americans, whose jobs they eliminated. And despite the claims to the contrary (examined later in the chapter on unions), Corporate America's contributions to political campaigns regularly dwarf contributions from labor unions, giving them near-total control over the trade agenda.

The motivation to gut unemployment benefits and job training is a little different. There, the cuts are driven to satisfy the tax cut zealots. The less government spends preserving a social safety net for workers, the more government money politicians have on hand to shower their wealthiest campaign donors with new tax cuts. As the *Detroit News* noted in 2004, Bush's job-training cuts "were made as Congress and the administration pushed through more than $600 billion in tax cuts that went primarily to those making more than $288,800." And if you hear someone say tax cuts offset the pain workers felt from cuts to job-training/unemployment insurance, tell that person to get real. "America's working poor have seen any benefits they received from the tax cuts eclipsed by the loss in services," wrote the newspaper.[20]

But the facts don't really matter. When it comes to jobs, there seems to be no amount of overt dishonesty that politicians aren't willing to spew in order to justify Corporate America's abuse of American workers.

LIE: "Free" trade creates good jobs.

Packaging "free" trade as a way to create jobs is about as laughable as Weight Watchers suddenly trumpeting McDonald's Big Macs as a good way to slim down.

In 1993, President Clinton said NAFTA would create thousands of good-paying jobs in America. "Without expanding your customer base, there is no way to create more jobs," he said. "That's what ["free" trade] is about." Many of these better-paying jobs, he told us, would be in the high-tech and information sector, and the customers were supposed to be eager Mexican consumers. Yet Clinton was strangely silent when it came time to explain how these new Mexican customers, often subsisting on $4 a day,[21] were going to afford the new goods America was going to supposedly produce.

HERO: Bernie Sanders, Vermont congressman

BATTLES TO STOP TAXPAYER MONEY FROM SUBSIDIZING THE ELIMINATION OF AMERICAN JOBS

Throughout his career, Independent congressman Bernie Sanders has tried to eliminate massive taxpayer subsidies to already-wealthy corporations that outsource U.S. jobs. One of his targets has been the federal government's Export-Import Bank. During the 1990s, the bank's five biggest corporate beneficiaries received half of the bank's funding, at the very same time these companies eliminated more than one-third of their American workforce. In 2002, he built a bipartisan coalition to support his bill to prevent funds from the federal government's Export-Import Bank from going to companies that eliminate more jobs in America than they do abroad. Though Sanders's legislation was killed, the 2004 presidential election's focus on taxpayer subsidization of outsourcing shows that the congressman's efforts have helped elevate the issue to the national level.

That was the scam. Like most honest observers, Clinton knew that "free" trade isn't about creating good-paying jobs in America. It's about helping corporations who fund politicians' political campaigns eliminate good-paying jobs at home and replace them with low-wage jobs in the developing world. It's about creating a race to the bottom where countries compete to create the worst, most easily exploitable conditions for workers in order to attract corporate investment.

But throw enough money at an issue in Washington and even stark reality can be ignored. William Daley, the official who headed up White House meetings with business lobbyists to push the deal, claimed, "NAFTA is right because it will create more and better jobs for American workers." He then went a step further, mythologizing Clinton. "The very easy political choice for the president would have been to abandon NAFTA," Daley said. "But the presidency is not about easy choices."[22]

What a courageous man that Clinton was. It's just so tough in this era of money-dominated politics for a president to stand with Big Business in selling out America's middle class.

Please.

In reality, experts estimated that Big Business contributed between $50 and $100 million to politicians and lobbying efforts to ram the deal through Congress. NAFTA opponents mustered just $10 million.[23] Clinton, in fact, did make "the very easy political choice": he stood with Big Money.

Daley today works as a high-priced executive for JP Morgan and serves on the board of directors of Merck pharmaceuticals.[24] No doubt his colleagues there are very thankful for his time in public service pushing a trade policy that served their private interests. From the crisp, filtered air of their executive suites and corporate jets, Daley and his friends can laugh off the disastrous effects of the trade policy he pushed. But the rest of America can't.

NAFTA may have created some export jobs in the United States, but those were more than offset by the job losses it brought. The Economic Policy Institute (EPI) reported that by 2000, America had lost roughly 3 million jobs to this "free" trade policy, both through elimination of existing jobs and through jobs never being created that would have been had our trade policy been different.[25] Every state saw trade-related job losses,[26] and, as EPI noted, many "of those lost jobs were high-wage positions in manufacturing industries."[27]

Granted, the public barely heard about the economic devastation of job-destroying "free" trade deals. The media was consumed with the overall jobs numbers improving during the 1990s—even though many of the job gains during that time were either low-paying service jobs, or Internet/high-tech-bubble jobs, which soon burst. It's why at the end of 1997 the *Tampa Tribune* reported that years into the economic "boom" of the 1990s, "average blue-collar American workers are no better off, while the country club crowd is reaping the rewards." A study that year "found the gap between the rich and the middle class is continuing to widen."[28]

Those stats didn't seem to faze Clinton, however. On May 17, 2000, he headlined a fundraiser in Greenwich, Connecticut—one of the richest towns in America and home to the extravagant mansions of many a corporate executive. You could almost imagine Clinton hamming it up with the Great Gatsby over white wine and caviar. Yet back in Washington, it was the eve of the congressional vote on whether to sell out American workers and pass a "free" trade deal with communist China. Kicking those workers in the face, Clinton issued a press release from Greenwich warning wavering members of Congress that "a vote against [the China trade deal] will cost us exports and jobs."[29] Marie Antoinette couldn't have sat there in her gold-plated throne and said "let them eat cake" any more clearly.

The pact passed and the results were the same. In just the first three years, America lost almost a quarter-million good-paying jobs as our trade deficit with China exploded.[30] The corporate-funded Cato Institute tried to spin the disaster, releasing a report called "America's Record Trade Deficit: A Symbol of Economic Strength."[31] It might have been accurate if it was called "a symbol of *China's* economic strength" in using slave labor to eliminate U.S. jobs.[32]

Nothing stops this lunacy—not a burgeoning trade deficit, massive job loss, nothing. At a meeting with corporate executives in 2002—the very time America was hemorrhaging jobs—President George W. Bush demanded Congress pass even more "free" trade legislation. "It is essential that we move aggressively because ["free"] trade means jobs."[33] If only he had added the word *lost* to the end of his statement, he might have finally been telling America the truth.

PATHOLOGICAL LIE: Our government already tries to stop companies from shipping American jobs overseas.

There is no shortage of politicians who publicly declare their desire to preserve American jobs. As the Bush White House spokesman once claimed, "The president views the job of the United States government and its central function as to help protect American jobs."[34]

Yet as we've seen above, that same president continues to push a trade policy that exports American jobs. But even beyond that, our government works in other subtle, more nefarious ways to help Big Money interests eliminate U.S. jobs.

For instance, billions of your taxpayer dollars actually subsidize companies' job-cutting efforts through a multibillion-dollar federal agency called the Export-Import Bank. This is not a private bank, mind you. This is a bank created by Congress and run with taxpayer money. The ostensible function of the Ex-Im Bank is to assist U.S. exporters, with the ultimate goal of improving American competitiveness and creating American jobs. Yet the money the bank spends has almost no restrictions in terms of what it subsidizes—including outsourcing of American jobs. For instance, the bank's five biggest corporate beneficiaries received half of the bank's funding during the 1990s. In that same time, these five companies eliminated more than one-third of their American workforce,[35] while often adding jobs in other low-wage countries. Taxpayer money, in other words, was paying to export American jobs.

One of those companies, General Electric, has been particularly greedy, receiving more than $2.5 billion in loans and loan guarantees from this bank.[36] Yet between 1975 and 1995 GE eliminated more than 150,000 American jobs. And you can be sure some of the taxpayer dollars from the Export-Import Bank are going to the company's top brass: In those same 20 years, GE's executive compensation increased by 950 percent,[37] helping move up CEO Jack Welch's net worth to almost $1 billion.[38]

In 2002, bipartisan legislation was proposed in Congress to prevent these subsidies from going to companies that eliminate more jobs in the United States than they do overseas. Yet with those same five companies spending almost $4 million on campaign contributions to Congress that year,[39] the legislation was voted down. One congressional source actually told reporters that eliminating taxpayer subsidies to companies that slash jobs was "very troubling" to members of Congress.[40] The job cuts weren't troubling. Eliminating taxpayer subsidies for job cutting was.

Most lawmakers, though, weren't that openly dismissive of average Americans in public. Most justified their vote by claiming the bank had been funding mostly small businesses. But statistics showed that at least half and likely up to 80 percent of the Export-Import Bank's budget goes to pad the bottom lines of Fortune 500 companies.[41] Even the corporate-funded think tanks admitted as much. "It's a huge amount of money that goes to the wealthiest corporations," said the Cato Institute's Stephen Moore. "There is no rationale for the government to be involved in this."[42] Except to help Big Business sell out America's workers.

Besides the Ex-Im Bank, there has been spirited public encouragement from political leaders for companies to outsource U.S. jobs. As mentioned above, President Bush actually signed an official White House report trumpeting outsourcing during a serious unemployment crisis. That declaration came even as leading experts predicted the United States would lose more than 800,000 jobs to outsourcing by 2005, and roughly 3.4 million by 2015.[43]

And don't think that Bush's declaration was unintentional. Corporate America is actively rewarding politicians like Bush who help it eliminate U.S. jobs. The *Washington Post* reported in 2004 that the twenty-one large companies that were engaging in wholesale outsourcing had given Bush more than $429,000 dollars in campaign contributions since 1999.[44] That didn't include the $4 million Bush received during a 2000 fundraiser at the home of Cisco Systems CEO John Chambers,[45] the man so focused on eliminating American jobs[46] that he has told reporters he would like to "outline an entire strategy of becoming a Chinese company."[47]

Remember, the executives most focused on eliminating jobs have a lot of money to throw at politicians to make sure the government doesn't do anything that may preserve American jobs. As the nonpartisan Institute for Policy Studies found, CEOs who outsource the most jobs now receive pay raises five times as large as other CEOs. Between 2001 and 2003, the fifty top outsourcing CEOs made more than $2 billion while sending 200,000 jobs overseas.[48] Cisco's Chambers, for instance, made an astounding $48 million in 2003 alone.[49]

Like hungry dogs that follow the smell of a Milk-Bone and will do any tricks to get it, lawmakers eagerly follow this outsourcing cash and do whatever's necessary to get some of it for their campaigns. Take New York Congressman Joe Crowley (D), who has taken almost $300,000 from Wall Street firms in his short career.[50] In 2003, he visited India and attacked legislation being considered in New Jersey that would limit the outsourcing of that state's government jobs. "I don't think this is healthy legislation," Crowley was quoted as saying in business publications. He then insulted thousands of Americans who had already lost their jobs, saying, "Outsourcing results in a win-win situation for both the countries."[51] One year later, Crowley took another trip to India to promote outsourcing, prompting public complaints about the trips from workers.[52] On that trip, Crowley was quoted in Indian newspapers saying he was proud that Democrats were "accentuating the positive" about outsourcing.[53]

Leading state politicians have followed suit. In California, Governor Arnold Schwarzenegger (R) used state funds to hire a consulting company famous for its outsourcing strategies.[54] Two months later, Schwarzenegger vetoed a bill banning taxpayer money from going to companies that would perform work with outsourced labor.[55]

In supporting outsourcing so publicly, Schwarzenegger was merely joining a growing group of state officials who have already done the same. CBS's *60 Minutes* reported in 2004 that at least eighteen states are now outsourcing welfare benefits calls to overseas call centers,[56] and the *Charlotte Observer* reported that forty states outsource calls about food stamps.[57] How truly disgusting: when the unemployed victims of outsourcing now call for welfare, they get to experience firsthand how their tax dollars actually aided their own professional demise.

HERO: Sherrod Brown, Ohio congressman

LEADS FIGHT TO STOP CORPORATE-WRITTEN TRADE DEALS THAT SELL AMERICA OUT

There is nothing more politically risky for a member of Congress than to fight for the interests of ordinary Americans on an issue that the Big Business coalition has deployed its entire army of lobbyists to influence. That's why Representative Sherrod Brown's (D-OH) work in fighting against unfair corporate-written trade deals has been so important—because he shows that there are still some lawmakers trying to shame Congress into doing the right thing. A case in point was Brown's work opposing the Central American Free Trade Agreement (CAFTA)—a bill that deliberately included almost no labor, human rights, or environmental standards, so as to help Corporate America eliminate American jobs and exploit cheap labor abroad. Corraling support from a diverse coalition of grassroots groups, Brown came within one vote of defeating CAFTA, despite the Bush administration and Big Business aggressively pushing for the pact. It was the closest anyone had come to stopping a corporate-written trade deal, showing that with persistence, Congress could one day start standing up for ordinary Americans.

MYTH: If the official unemployment numbers are down, everything is okay.

In early 2004, President Bush gave a radio address bragging that "the nation's unemployment rate fell to 5.6 percent in January, the fourth consecutive monthly decline."[58] The statistic served as his main evidence that the job market was dramatically improving. It certainly seems like solid evidence—the official unemployment number is a statistic released by nonpartisan government researchers, and few believe it is politically biased.

But objectivity is not the problem here. The real hitch is that the official unemployment number is artificially low because you are only considered "unemployed" if you are actively looking for work but can't find a job. The figure does not include those who gave up looking because the economy was so weak they simply couldn't find a job. In fact, as the economy gets weaker and more people simply stop looking for work, the unemployment number can actually start looking better, because there are fewer people being counted, even though the ranks of the unemployed may be increasing. The *Los Angeles Times* reported in 2003 that the true jobless rate is up to 40 percent higher than the official rate cited by politicians.[59] That's why, just weeks after Bush's rosy declaration, Bloomberg News told the real story: "1.6 million Americans have dropped out of the workforce in the past year."[60]

But Bush was determined to make the jobs picture defy reality, no matter what it took. His administration issued a report in 2004 debating whether fast-food jobs should be classified as manufacturing jobs, so as to hide how Corporate America is eliminating good-paying American jobs. Instead of pushing a trade policy or worker-training programs that actually might stop the loss of manufacturing jobs, the White House instead wanted to change the way low-paying jobs are counted to make it seem as if the job market was just as strong as it always has been. The *New York Times* noted how pathetic the idea was: "Counting jobs at McDonald's, Burger King and other fast-food enterprises alongside those at industrial companies like General Motors and Eastman Kodak might seem like a stretch, akin to classifying ketchup in school lunches as a vegetable,"[61] as the Reagan administration infamously tried in 1981.[62]

The only thing worse than doctoring statistics from government reports like this would be to eliminate them altogether. And—surprise, surprise—prominent politicians have tried that as well. During the 1992 recession,[63] the first President Bush terminated the Labor Department's monthly report on mass layoffs (i.e., layoffs of more than fifty people at one time). After the report was restored by President Clinton in 1995,[64] the second President Bush once again terminated it during the 2002 unemployment crisis. The report had become an embarrassing reminder that Bush's claims in 2002 that the job market was improving were actually insulting lies. And it was clear the termination of the report was politically motivated. As the *San Francisco Chronicle* reported, Bush's Labor Department officials made no public announcement of its termination other than "a single paragraph buried deep within a press release issued on Christmas Eve"—a holiday on which almost no reporter is on duty to cover such news.[65]

MYTH: During hard times, Congress will make sure unemployment benefits are adequate.

As tens of thousands of Americans were losing their jobs in the wake of 9/11, the chairman of the House committee that oversees unemployment insurance tried to reassure everyone. "Congress will not turn its back on workers who are in danger of slipping through the cracks," said Representative John Boehner (R-OH). He promised that lawmakers would make sure "that [workers] and their families have adequate relief."[66]

His statement belied both Congress's subsequent actions and its draconian cuts in the recent past. The truth is, America's unemployment insurance system has been gutted. In the mid-1970s jobless workers could receive fifteen months of unemployment benefits. By 2003—two years after Boehner's promise—Congress had cut that to six months. By the end of 2004, just 2.9 million out of 8 million unemployed workers were receiving assistance.[67]

Sure, there were fights to increase these benefits and efforts to hold Boehner to his word. During the 2002 unemployment crisis, Democrats tried to pass legislation temporarily extending unemployment benefits. All they wanted was a measly thirteen-week extension, but congressional leaders and the White House refused, adjourning for the year without passing the measure. Only after public outcry did Bush reverse his opposition and signal he would approve a bill. But even then, he did his best to stiff workers: Bush's bill deliberately refused to provide benefits to more than one million workers who had used up all of their previous federal benefits because the job market was so bleak.[68] This was a particularly devastating blow, coming just as long-term unemployment was becoming a severe problem: one in five unemployed workers in 2002 were out of work for more than six months—the largest percentage in almost a decade.[69]

Nonetheless, in mid-2003, Federal Reserve Chairman Greenspan headed to Capitol Hill to brag about how generous the government is to jobless workers. "Our unemployment insurance system seems to work rather well," he told lawmakers,[70] ignoring the one million workers who were still without benefits.[71] In October, the nonpartisan Center on Budget and Policy Priorities released a report showing that the outlook for jobs was so bleak and unemployment insurance so inadequate that three-quarters of America's unemployed were now running out of benefits before finding a job.[72]

Yet, a month later, House Majority Leader Tom DeLay (R) let everyone know that he would be spearheading the effort to defeat any bills extending unemployment insurance. He callously told reporters he saw "no reason" to pass the legislation.[73] Days later, he was warned by experts that if the bills were voted down, between 80,000 and 90,000 workers would begin losing their benefits each week.[74] He didn't care. He made sure the bills went down to defeat.

Thanks to Congress's refusal to extend unemployment insurance, 3 million workers had exhausted their benefits by the end of 2004—a new record in American history.[75] Apparently, though, this mistreatment wasn't enough. In 2005, President Bush unveiled a budget that not only still refused to increase unemployment insurance but actually gutted other programs that jobless workers rely on — all while pushing new tax cuts for the wealthy. For instance, he proposed cutting the program that aids workers whose jobs have been shipped overseas because of "free" trade agreements[76] (called trade adjustment assistance). This, while he was pushing new "free" trade agreements. Boehner had promised in 2001 that Republicans and the White House "will do everything in our power to help every worker return to work as quickly as possible."[77] Yet their new budget proposed eliminating the government's Employment Service—the program whose sole mission is to match the jobless with jobs.[78]

When asked about these cuts, the typical politician denies they are motivated by a need to find more money to use for tax cuts for their wealthy campaign donors. Instead, the politician claims the cuts are necessary because money is tight. "Many Ohio families understand the constraints of a budget and the tough decisions that sometimes have to be made to meet priorities,"[79] said Ohio representative Deborah Pryce, the fourth-ranking Republican in the House, who helped shepherd the cuts through Congress. She was clearly desperate to justify her support for the cuts to the 170,000 Ohioans who had lost their manufacturing jobs since 2001,[80] and the more than 90,000 who had exhausted their unemployment benefits.[81]

What she didn't tell Ohio families was that the same budgets that supposedly didn't have enough money to help workers included billions of dollars in tax cuts for the wealthiest Americans. For instance, the Bush tax cuts Pryce voted for cost $264 billion in 2004. That's roughly 40 times the cost of extending unemployment benefits for an extra six months[82]—something she voted against.[83] Similarly, Republicans cited the supposed need for frugality in supporting Bush's proposal to cut millions of dollars out of the program that helps unemployed workers find new jobs.[84] Yet that same budget proposed an average of $120 billion in new tax cuts for the wealthy every year for the next decade.[85]

But then, none of this really is a surprise. Jobless workers don't typically have lots of extra cash lying around to hire high-priced lobbyists and buy off politicians the way wealthy fat cats do. In today's corrupt political culture, money to help unemployed citizens survive is money that politicians can hand over to the people they really care about: their big donors.

MYTH: The government is committed to helping workers get job training.

In 2002, Republicans and the Bush administration were panicking. America was losing thousands of jobs every month to the "free" trade policies the federal government had rammed down the country's throat for the last decade. And the midterm elections were approaching. Not a great combination for incumbents running for reelection.

And so in key places like Ohio, which were hemorrhaging jobs, the public started hearing a lot from politicians about how much our government supposedly helps retrain unemployed workers. For instance, Ohio representative Ralph Regula (R), a senior budget writer in Congress, gave a speech in February saying "there is more than enough money currently in our [budget] to fund job-training programs."[86] It was a nice effort to gloss over harsh reality. Three days before Regula's speech, the White House released its budget that proposed cutting more than half a billion dollars out of job-training programs[87]—a massive blow during an unemployment crisis.[88] Those cuts came just weeks after the *Columbus Dispatch* reported that the state was "among the hardest hit" when the Bush administration decided to rescind $110 million that was slated to be spent on job training.[89]

For the cameras, though, the story was different. President Bush soon showed up in Cleveland to reassure folks that the cuts weren't so bad. "The government's willing to pay for reeducation," he said, and "the government's willing to pay for job training."[90] Again, it was smooth spin to cover up the truth. A recent *Dayton Daily News* story before Bush's visit

HACK: Greg Mankiw, chief White House economic adviser

SAYS ELIMINATING U.S. JOBS IS "A PLUS FOR THE ECONOMY"

In early 2004, the American job market was in a severe crisis. Since President Bush had taken office, almost 2 million Americans had lost their jobs, and almost one in ten working-age citizens were jobless. Yet the White House actually issued an official report endorsing Corporate America's efforts to ship American jobs overseas. Worse, when releasing the document, President Bush's chief economic adviser, Greg Mankiw, claimed that outsourcing was "a plus for the economy."

noted that budget cuts to job training had already resulted in dozens of Ohio counties slashing "job-training, education and other, often innovative programs" to help people get new jobs.[91]

By 2004, Bush had slashed roughly $600 million out of job training. On the one hand, that constitutes a massive cut, considering how little the government spends on these programs. But in another respect, it's chump change. According to the *Detroit News*, the job-training cuts in 2004 "were less than 1 percent of the tax breaks received [that] year by those making more than $1 million."[92]

And yet Bush continued to resist any effort to restore the money, even as unemployed workers all over the country were languishing on job-training waiting lists. The *Sarasota Herald-Tribune* reported in 2004 that when asked why job training was being cut during an unemployment crisis, the "Bush administration argues that there's not enough evidence to declare a need for more job-training money and other assistance."[93]

That out-of-touch position, however, didn't stop the White House from publicly feigning concern for the cameras. The day before the 2004 election, Vice President Dick Cheney proudly boasted, "The President and I stand with America's workers." He promised that if they were reelected, "we're going to expand job training to help people find new opportunities."[94]

He and Bush were trumpeting a cynical plan to spend $250 million to help people afford community college. Why cynical? Because, as the *Detroit News* noted, "the administration will pay in part for these programs by cutting existing job-training programs." Meanwhile, Bush was moving forward with his proposal to eviscerate Pell Grants—the federal government's primary grants that help low- and middle-income citizens afford a college education. Though Bush claimed on the eve of the election that he wanted to "expand Pell Grants for low- and middle-income families,"[95] he was actually proposing to cut off 84,000 students from the program entirely, and reduce grants to another million students who rely on them.[96]

Of course, it is not just the Bush administration that has abandoned workers (though the Bush folks may be the most open about it). Over the last twenty-five years, right-wing politicians like Ronald Reagan, George H. W. Bush, and Newt Gingrich hacked away an astounding 84 percent of the funding that used to be spent on job training.[97] These are often some of the most important programs to help people get back into the workforce. In Boston, for example, those who complete training services at the New England Shelter for Homeless Veterans find jobs 90 percent of the time. Yet this program and others like it are exactly the ones that have been on the chopping block—with severe consequences. For instance, a decade ago Detroit's job training served about 13,000 people. Today it can only help about 2,500, and regularly runs out of money before the year is out, leaving the jobless with few avenues back to work.[98]

Solutions

The answer to America's job challenges requires our country to rebuild the social safety net, stop persecuting those who lose their jobs, start preventing the government from subsidizing corporate behavior that undermines the labor market. This is a nonpartisan strategy: some of it requires spending more taxpayer money, some of it requires cutting off taxpayer money from existing programs.

Automatically extend unemployment benefits when the economy goes south. In 2002, Federal Reserve Chairman Alan Greenspan told Congress that the purpose of limiting unemployment benefits "is essentially not to get people involved in long-term unemployment insurance as an alternate to work." The comment was designed to remind the public of the same tired old caricature of the lazy worker living off the government that ultraconservative politicians have been repeating for years in order to justify cuts to unemployment benefits. But even the right-wing Greenspan, in the same testimony, admitted that sometimes "there just are no jobs out there." During periods of "rising unemployment," he said, "I've always been in favor of extending unemployment benefits."[99] Unfortunately, Congress has not followed suit, refusing in 2003 and 2004[100] to extend unemployment benefits to millions of jobless workers who had seen their assistance cut off while the economy was sputtering. So instead of letting the fanatical whims of politicians determine when to cut off jobless workers, we should simply have a formula. When joblessness remains above a certain level—say, 5 percent—benefits should automatically be extended.

Stop taxing unemployment benefits. In the mid-1980s, lawmakers of both parties passed a measure to begin taxing jobless workers' unemployment benefits. The idea was originally proposed by that supposed hater of taxes himself, President Ronald Reagan (apparently, like many of his "tax cutting" disciples, he hated only those taxes that fell on the rich).[101] Summing up the idiocy of this tax, one business consultant told his local newspaper, "It's like the government gives you money with one hand and takes some of it back with the other."[102] Unemployment benefits are already meager. Subjecting these benefits to taxes just makes the plight of the jobless worse—and the tax needs to be repealed.

Make unemployment statistics truthful. The government's monthly unemployment figure clearly underreports how many Americans are jobless. That allows politicians to pretend their corporate-sponsored policies are not creating serious economic problems. It's time to update the way these statistics are tabulated to include the long-term unemployed who have simply stopped looking for work. That would give the public a better picture of what's going on, and make it harder for politicians to keep pretending the middle class is doing just fine when, in fact, it's not.

Make job training as available as public education. There was a time in our history when proposals to provide free primary and secondary education were considered crazy. But creating our public education system was one of the most important factors that helped America ascend to prominence in the twentieth century. Unfortunately, that's not enough anymore. Instead of gutting job training and college education grants and then converting those resources into tax cuts or corporate subsidies, as President Bush proposes, America needs to see these programs as absolute necessities if we are to compete in the twenty-first-century economy. Ultimately, we must make a college education and vocational/job training a right of American citizenship. This is a proposal that even ardent "free" traders could be embarrassed into supporting, if it is packaged correctly. In today's Congress, sellout politicians claim their disastrous trade policies won't hurt Americans, because our workers are the best in the world. Many of them, however, turn around and vote to cut job training and education—the very tools that workers need to compete in the global marketplace. That's like sending troops into battle without providing them basic training. It is wrong.

Stop subsidizing American companies' efforts to ship off our jobs. Government handouts to wealthy corporations are bad enough. But government handouts to corporations that are shipping U.S. jobs overseas are unacceptable. The government needs to follow one simple principle: The taxes paid by Americans should not be used to eliminate our own jobs. We need to audit all federal grants and loans to corporations to see exactly how much taxpayer cash is being handed over to companies that are sending more jobs overseas than they are creating at home. Once a comprehensive list is in hand, Congress should vote on whether to eliminate these grants or not, and whether to instead use the money to give contract preferences to companies that are actually adding jobs in America. Let's put our representatives on record and see whom they stand with—companies that stiff America or the citizens who are getting screwed.

Stop the "free" trade power grab. A growing number of lawmakers in Congress are, thankfully, figuring out that "free" trade is not a winner for America. This realization has a lot to do with pressure from workers who are sick and tired of being kicked around. The problem, however, is that Congress has barely any say in trade policy anymore, after Corporate America helped pass "fast track" legislation in 2002.[103] The law grants the president authority to negotiate the fine-print details of all trade pacts, and forbids Congress from any input other than an up-or-down vote. That's much better for Corporate America—coercing one person to do its bidding is far easier than influencing hundreds of lawmakers who go home and hear their constituents' concern every week. But it's terrible for workers, whose real power is in grassroots numbers. The more input from members of Congress in trade deals, the more likely it is that at least some proworker provisions will get into the fine print of these agreements, especially with the growing revolt against "free" trade brewing in Congress. Fast track must be revoked.

IN ONE of his more famous gaffes, President Bush told an audience in 2002, "There's an old saying in Tennessee—I know it's in Texas, it's probably in Tennessee—that says, 'Fool me once, shame on you. Fool me [twice]—we can't get fooled again."[104] If only that were really true, because when it comes to jobs, our corrupt politicians are convinced they can lie to us as many times as they want—and we'll always be fooled again.

Just look at Bush's behavior over the course of a few months. On December 1, 2003, he gave a speech in Michigan—a state ravaged by job loss during his term. He told the crowd his administration was "laying the foundation for greater prosperity and more jobs across America"[105]— music to desperate workers' ears.

Nine days later, however, the *New York Times* reported that the Bush administration was a "host," "sponsor," and active participant in various "conferences and workshops that encourage American companies to put operations and jobs in China." That's right—the Bush administration was helping to put on lavish events for corporate executives at places like New York's Waldorf-Astoria—events whose sole purpose is to guide companies through the process of selling out American workers.[106]

No matter. The next night at a fundraiser with his big donors in McLean, Virginia, Bush once again told reporters he was focused on laying "the foundation for greater prosperity and more jobs across America."[107] Bush's public message to American workers was clear: Ignore that news about me selling you out, because really, I feel your pain and am working for you.

Two months later, though, Bush was back at it, this time signing his report endorsing outsourcing. The White House spin machine, as usual, was ready. CNN noted just days after the report was issued that Bush was "trying to quell the potential controversy" by heading to Pennsylvania, a state that had lost 85,000 jobs since he took office. "We need to act to make sure there are more jobs at home," he told an audience there.[108]

But three weeks later, on March 2, CNN reported that the President's Export Council had drafted a letter "in which they wholeheartedly endorse outsourcing."[109] The council is a group of the White House's top advisers and corporate CEOs appointed personally by the president to help him make economic policy.[110] Those included CEOs from Bechtel and

HACK: Arnold Schwarzenegger, California governor

USES TAXPAYER FUNDS TO SUBSIDIZE OUTSOURCING

During the 2004 unemployment crisis, California governor Arnold Schwarzenegger (R) used state funds to hire a consulting company famous for its efforts to ship jobs overseas. When asked about the move, the *Sacramento Bee* reported that a "Schwarzenegger spokesman has been quoted as saying the governor will look overseas" for cheap labor. Two months later, Schwarzenegger vetoed a bill explicitly banning taxpayer money from being used to outsource California jobs. Of course, he's not alone. CBS's *60 Minutes* reported in 2004 that at least eighteen states are now outsourcing welfare benefits calls to overseas call centers, and the *Charlotte Observer* reported that forty states outsource calls about food stamps. In other words, when the victims of outsourcing now call for welfare, they get to experience firsthand how their tax dollars actually aided their own demise.

Dell, companies that had been among the top outsourcers in America[111] and who had given the Republican Party more than $1 million since 2000. It also included the CEO of pharmaceutical giant Eli Lilly—a company that had given the GOP more than $1 million since 2000 and was among those firms that the *New York Times* noted have "been ramping up their outsourcing of clinical research" to low-wage countries.[112]

But Bush was back in front of the cameras two days later telling people once again to forget that he was supporting his corporate donors who were eliminating jobs. "We want people who are working to be comfortable that their job is going to be here tomorrow," he told a crowd in Bakersfield, California,[113] which was suffering through double-digit unemployment.[114]

Again, however, it only took another few weeks for the real agenda to shine through. On March 17, the *New York Times* reported that Secretary of State Colin Powell took a trip to Asia "to assure Indians that the Bush administration would not try to halt the outsourcing of high-technology jobs to their country." Experts were predicting that 3.3 million American jobs would be lost to outsourcing,[115] yet the Bush administration's priority was reassuring Big Business that it would do nothing to stop the bleeding and prevent corporate exploitation of low-wage labor.

All of these shenanigans mixed with all of the job losses made the issue of outsourcing a major campaign issue in the summer of 2004. That was the very time Commerce Department analysts were scheduled to issue a damning report about the negative consequences of outsourcing—a report that would once again raise the jobs issue and put President Bush on the defensive. But while the report was mandated to be released in June by recently passed federal legislation, strangely, it never appeared.

A year and a half later, the story of the missing report surfaced after a magazine filed a Freedom of Information Act suit to force its release. According to *Manufacturing and Technology News*, the Commerce report, in fact, had been "completed well before the November 2004 presidential election." However, it "was delayed for clearance by the White House and the Republican-controlled Congress." Why? Because outsourcing was a "controversial subject" and "had become a contentious campaign issue" for Bush, "particularly in the swing states." Worse, when the report did finally resurface, the nonpartisan analysis done by government researchers had been replaced with pro-outsourcing propaganda by Bush's political appointees—propaganda derived from "research conducted by organizations and individuals that have been funded by corporations that benefit from shifting jobs overseas."[116]

As we can see from all of this, when it comes to jobs, there is lying, there is stonewalling, and then there is political rhetoric—a separate and more nefarious form of dishonesty. No matter how dire the situation becomes, all we keep getting is more and more rhetoric—rhetoric about "free" trade creating jobs, rhetoric about government wanting to protect our jobs, rhetoric about outsourcing helping American workers, and worst of all, righteous rhetoric about rhetoric itself.

"Empty talk about jobs," Bush said repeatedly on the 2004 campaign trail, "won't get anyone hired." Every time he uttered the line, you could almost hear the American worker simultaneously laugh and cry. The chuckle came from seeing a politician who had lied so many times before about jobs utter such self-righteous pablum with a straight face, as if it was a *Saturday Night Live* parody, rather than reality.

The tears, on the other hand, were different. They came from the realization that our government is now wholly invested in tricking workers, validating corporate propaganda, and selling us all out.

CHAPTER 4

DEBT

★

THERE'S BEEN a lot of talk lately about how the line separating church and state in America is increasingly blurry. The federal government now doles out taxpayer money to religious organizations, politicians of both parties regularly cite their religious convictions as justification for their political positions, and even the president himself has told people he was put in the White House by God (no joke).[1]

So you might think that with such supposedly devout leaders running our country, there would be strict laws prohibiting companies from charging folks excessively high interest rates on their debts. The Bible, after all, is very explicit in its views on the subject. In Deuteronomy, the Bible says, "Thou shalt not lend upon usury to thy brother." In Ezekiel, we are told the punishment is pretty bad: "He [who] has exacted usury . . . he shall not live . . . he shall surely die."

Tough talk, for sure, and a sign the Supreme Being would heartily endorse statutes that prevent banks and credit card companies from continuing to bilk Americans with exorbitant interest rates and hidden fees.

Lord knows there's a need for such laws. In 2004, the credit card industry made $24 billion from penalty fees[2] alone using some of the most unethical and deceptive tactics imaginable. To pocket late fees, some companies use the fine print to hide the fact that the due date on a bill may not be at the end of a particular day, but at 9 A.M., before that day's mail arrives.[3] Others repeatedly change their post office box numbers, so that your bill arrives at the correct address late, once again meaning penalty fees.[4] Some companies actually charge people extra fees for being responsible and paying off their balances in full.[5] And some simply lie.

In 2000, for instance, San Francisco's district attorney found that Providian was deliberately refusing to credit customers' payments on time so that it could assess millions of dollars of additional late fees.[6] In 2003, New York Attorney General Eliot Spitzer exposed a bank that was tricking low-income citizens into signing up for credit cards without telling them of exorbitant fees.[7]

But even the word of God and a spate of these horror stories is not enough to trump Washington's sacred Eleventh Commandment: politicians shalt obey the credit card industry's every wish. Congress sits idly by, long ago emasculated by Corporate America's hostile takeover, as credit card companies continue to rip off more and more Americans. When lawmakers do act, they only further loosen the regulations that might hold these corporate predators back. For when the credit card industry starts throwing money around, even the most outspoken religious sermonizers in politics suddenly become as quiet as church mice. Why? Because the sheer amount of cash at the industry's disposal is, well, ungodly.

In 2004 alone, the credit card industry pocketed $30 billion in profits.[8] On average, that's about $300 bilked from every household in America.[9] A portion of that vast fortune is used to buy off lawmakers and keep them out of the companies' way. Between 2000 and 2004, the credit card and commercial banking industry donated $103 million to Democratic and Republican candidates for office,[10] much of it targeted to the most influential lawmakers. Credit card giant MBNA, for instance, is President Bush's fifth-largest donor, showering him with almost $600,000 since 2000. The company's CEO was one of the first to throw Bush a major fundraiser, opening up his palatial Kennebunkport summer home in 1999 to raise him $200,000 in one cocktail party.[11]

In Congress, House Financial Services Chairman Mike Oxley (R-Ohio) and Senate Banking Committee Chairman Richard Shelby (R-Ala.) are the two top regulators of the credit card industry. They are also among the top congressional recipients of credit card/banking industry cash.[12]

And the graft isn't limited to campaign contributions. At the 2000 Republican National Convention, for instance, MBNA rented a cruise ship to throw lavish parties for GOP lawmakers. Commercial banks also had their say, throwing a gala for Republican members of the House Banking Committee that was supposed to be regulating their business.

Reporters asked about the propriety of the events, and they were given Kentucky senator Mitch McConnell (R), who was in the process of raising his personal banking industry cash haul to more than $300,000.[13] "We couldn't put on the convention without them," McConnell said, referring not to average people but to credit card companies. Bank lobbyists could barely hide their glee. The galas "will generate positive buzz," wrote one in a memo to bank executives. "Invitations will be eagerly sought and participating sponsors will be remembered."[14]

How right that was. When Bush assumed the presidency and Republicans retained control of Congress in 2000, they remembered all right—and returned the favors. Within weeks, Bush appointed MBNA's senior vice chairman, Lance Weaver, to a special presidential transition team that selected new staff at the Treasury Department, one of the executive agencies that oversees the credit card industry.[15] By 2004, a bank-lawyer-turned-Treasury-official[16] issued an edict invalidating state laws that were cracking down on some of the most abusive credit card practices.[17] (So much for the GOP's support for states' rights.)

But no action was more important to the credit card industry than when Bush and his congressional allies gutted consumer bankruptcy protection laws in early 2005.[18] Under the guise of "reform," lawmakers rammed a bill through Congress that put the hammer down on individual debtors while refusing to regulate abusive lenders.* Despite Americans going broke in record numbers, Congress actually made it harder for people to get temporary protection from creditors. At the same time, lawmakers allowed credit card companies to keep charging astronomical interest rates and threaten low-income debtors with more lawsuits and harassment. Worst of all, lawmakers rejected a series of amendments that would have provided minimal financial protection to the most vulnerable members of society.

For instance, with violence raging in Iraq, lawmakers voted down a bill to provide soldiers with minimum bankruptcy protections from debts incurred when they left better-paying jobs for combat service.[19] Before the debate on the bill, the *New York Times* published a report that found "many military people have become trapped in a spiral of borrowing at sky-high rates that can ruin their finances, distract them from their duties and even destroy their careers."[20] Retired Navy captain Chalker W.

---

*Not surprisingly, the one type of debtor the bankruptcy bill did not crack down on was corporate debtors. Companies like United Airlines, for instance, were still afforded all the bankruptcy protections in the world—including those that allow them to walk away from their pension obligations to retirees while simultaneously increasing executives' pay packages.

HACK: Evan Bayh, Indiana senator

SON OF PRIVILEGE REGURGITATES DISHONEST STEREOTYPES ABOUT WHO GOES BANKRUPT

Indiana senator Evan Bayh (D) told the *Ft. Wayne Journal Gazette* that he supported the corporate-written bankruptcy bill because "people who engage in irresponsible behavior" go bankrupt, and therefore "impose their bad decisions and the cost of that on other people who behave more responsibly." The scapegoating, of course, ignored the fact that most bankruptcies occur because of illness or job loss, not irresponsibility. In Indiana alone, Harvard researchers found 77,000 residents went bankrupt in 2004 because of skyrocketing medical bills. But then, such insulting and dishonest rhetoric isn't a surprise from Bayh, a son of privilege who has raked in more than $290,000 in campaign contributions from the banking interests pushing the bankruptcy legislation.

Brown explained how big a problem that really is: "The last thing you want is a young sailor programming a Tomahawk missile in the Persian Gulf who is worrying about whether his car is being repossessed back home." And yet that's exactly what the politicians in Washington voted for.

Congress also turned a blind eye to victims of identity theft, even as banks were becoming sloppier and sloppier with people's private financial information. On March 1, 2005, for example, Bank of America announced it had lost personal financial data of more than one million customers,[21] exposing tens of thousands of people to possible identity theft. Two days later Florida senator Bill Nelson (D) introduced legislation[22] to exempt debtors from tougher bankruptcy laws if their financial problems were caused by identity theft. But Congress rejected the amendment, essentially saying that banks can lose your information, let your identity be stolen and finances ruined, and then use their own gross negligence as an opportunity to profit from you by raising interest rates, increasing late fees, and unleashing all the other excruciating punishments that come to people who have no bankruptcy protections.

The lawmaker who authored the bankruptcy bill—and fought to stop these amendments—was Representative James Sensenbrenner (R-WI). According to the nonpartisan watchdog group Public Campaign, Sensenbrenner owns nearly a quarter million dollars of stock in the same bank and credit card companies that would benefit from the bill. Yet, instead of recusing himself from working on the bankruptcy issue because of his clear conflict of interest, he did the opposite, authoring the legislation and publicly shepherding it through Congress.[23]

If you thought there was serious opposition to all of this from Democrats—think again. Though claiming to be from "the party of the working class," many Democrats have undergone a nauseating conversion on the road to MasterCard. Just look at their behavior on the bankruptcy bill.

During the Senate debate over the bankruptcy bill, Senator Joe Biden of Delaware acted as credit card companies' personal ambassador, putting his $337,000[24] in campaign contributions from the industry to work. Ultimately, thirteen Democrats provided the key votes to pass the overall legislation.

Never to be outshone by fellow senators in stiffing average Americans, Senator Joe Lieberman (D) joined in the fun. The Connecticut lawmaker, who has taken $267,000 from the banking industry in his career,[25] sent out a press release trumpeting himself as a great defender of the middle class, pointing to his vote against final passage of the bankruptcy legislation.[26] Yet Lieberman's press release conveniently omitted the fact that just hours before his "no" vote, he cast a key "yes" vote that undermined courageous lawmakers who were blocking the bill. This procedural vote (called "cloture"), which Lieberman supported, was widely acknowledged to be the vote that actually passed the bill.[27]

In the House, it was more of the same. Twenty Democrats signed a letter calling for an immediate passage of the bill, euphemistically calling it a "more streamlined bankruptcy system." The lawmakers signing the letter were only months removed from having pocketed a combined $750,000 from the credit card industry in their reelection campaigns.[28] The House's second-ranking Democrat, Maryland representative Steny Hoyer, defended his vote for the bill and acknowledged how screwing the middle class has now become a bipartisan objective. "Every bill is not a partisan bill," Hoyer said before casting his "yes" vote.[29]

Meanwhile, Representative Joe Crowley (D), disregarding his working-class constituents in New York City's Queens and Bronx neighborhoods, bragged in newspapers about organizing a group of corporate lobbyists to pressure fellow Democrats to support the bill.[30] That's par for the course for a member of Congress whose campaign has pocketed roughly $2,500 per month from the banking and credit industries.[31] According to *The Hill* newspaper, Crowley's "efforts were made easier in the absence of official opposition" from other House Democratic leaders. (And yet, remarkably, these same Democrats wonder why most Americans don't think they really stand up for average people.)

Thus, we are left with officially sanctioned theft. Companies now charge up to 650 percent annual interest rates on low-income citizens,[32] driving people further and further into debt. They pilfer billions in fees and control politicians with millions in campaign cash—all to ensure that people like MBNA's CEO get their $250 million salaries.[33]

The real-world effects of this system are tragic. U.S. consumers are now $2 trillion in the hole, with the average household carrying a credit card balance of about $7,500.[34] Each year, roughly 1.6 million Americans are driven into bankruptcy. That's more than 4,000 people every single day, a 150 percent increase from 1989.[35] They are the roadkill on the industry's profit warpath, carcasses who have been picked over for everything they're worth.

It is all part of the transformation of America's financial industry into a thuggish loan-sharking scheme—a transformation aided by government dishonesty.

LIE: If you just pay your bills on time, you won't be punished.

In 2005, the American Bankers Association (ABA) penned an op-ed for *USA Today* to justify its push to gut bankruptcy protection laws. "Those of us who manage our overall debt responsibly and make monthly payments on time are not charged late fees or higher interest rates," claimed then-ABA President Donald Ogilvie. "Those who don't pay their bills on time do wind up paying a late fee, or become subject to a higher interest rate. Seems fair."[36]

He's right—that does seem fair . . . if what he was saying was true.

But it isn't. Credit card companies now routinely raise interest rates and fees for no reason at all—and their actions are officially sanctioned by our government.

In 1978 the Supreme Court decided a bank could charge its cardholders any interest rate allowable in the bank's home state, no matter what the circumstances, and even if you are paying your bills on time. The *New York Times* noted that banks "swiftly moved their credit card operations to places like South Dakota and Delaware that had removed caps on interest rates."[37] Now, when you sign up for a credit card, you are forced to agree to pages of microscopic fine print where companies cement their ability to fleece you in stone. As one standard Visa contract says, "We reserve the right to change the terms at any time for any reason."[38]

Thus, the bait and switch is born. Companies send out 3 to 5 billion credit card solicitations a year[39]—many of which promise super-low interest rates from 0 to 4 percent. But from the moment you sign on, they can raise their rates, often to near 30 percent. According to *USA Today*, at that rate a consumer paying $300 a month on a $10,000 debt would take more than forty-four years to pay it off.[40] And Congress allows this kind of abuse, refusing to pass any laws that punish usury.

Of course, many companies want to preserve the public veneer of fairness, and therefore still claim they only raise rates when customers are late on paying off balances. But even those claims are creatively manipulated.

For instance, three-quarters of companies have adopted a "universal default" policy: if any creditor puts a complaint on your credit report, even if it's not the credit card company in question, you are automatically a candidate to have your credit card interest rates increased.[41] Pay your phone bill late one month, see your MasterCard interest rates skyrocket. Dispute a fraudulent charge on a utility bill and withhold your payment, and Visa can raise the interest rate on your credit card. In one instance, Discover said it was raising its interest rates to near 20 percent if customers had even one late payment on any bill, and then said they would look back on customers' last eleven months of financial transactions (both with Discover and with other creditors) for a late payment that could justify the increase.[42]

And because bought-off politicians refuse to outlaw all of this, software engineer Ed Schwebel's situation is now commonplace. As the *New York Times* reported, he paid his minimum balance every month on time, yet in July 2004, MBNA decided to double his interest rate from 9.2 percent to 18 percent. The company's reason? They simply wanted more money out of him. "I paid the bills the minute the envelope hit the desk," said Mr. Schwebel. "All of a sudden in July, they swapped it to 18 percent. No warning. No reason. It was like I was blindsided."[43]

MYTH: "Bankruptcy queens" have it easy.

During his first run for the presidency, Ronald Reagan repeatedly described a Chicago "welfare queen" who he claimed had raked in more than $150,000 in government handouts and drove around in a fancy Cadillac. The story was patently false—reporters who looked into the case found that the woman had collected $8,000 in extra benefits before being caught and punished.[44] But that didn't matter—the imagery had done its job: namely, to solidify public support for cutting government programs for poor people.

Reagan's dishonest methods were revived in 2005, as conservatives updated the metaphor to create a powerful image of "bankruptcy queens"—a supposed plague of low-lifes who abuse bankruptcy laws and hurt society. As soon as Congress began debating the bankruptcy legislation, out came the bankruptcy queen language, with credit card lobbyists telling newspapers, "Most Americans have seen somebody down the street with two cars, where they go bankrupt and there are no consequences to that, and it really upsets them."[45]

That language was picked up by Iowa senator Charles Grassley (R) when he introduced the bill making it harder for Americans to get bankruptcy protection. Current laws, he said, were being used as a "convenient financial planning tool where deadbeats can get out of paying their debt scot-free while honest Americans who play by the rules have to foot the bill."[46]

As with Reagan's welfare queens, the bankruptcy queen stories are not representative of reality. According to Harvard University researchers, 90 percent of personal bankruptcies are due to illness, medical bills, job loss, death in the family, or divorce.[47] These are by and large not cases of people living large under bankruptcy protections. In Grassley's own state of Iowa, 6,000 out of the 12,000 bankruptcies that occurred in 2004 were the result of medical bills alone, with more than 17,000 Iowans that year living in households bankrupted by medical issues.[48] Again, not quite the loafing "deadbeats" painted by Grassley.

In a *Des Moines Register* article, bankruptcy attorney Nancy Thompson debunked the idea that our country is being plagued by "deadbeat" bankruptcy queens supposedly living the high life courtesy of Chapter 11. And as she noted, "Never once in the 20 years I've practiced have I had a client who really wanted to file for bankruptcy after purposely running up a big debt."[49] She is backed up by the nonpartisan American Bankruptcy

HACK: Jim Moran, Virginia congressman

BAILED OUT BY SPECIAL LOAN, PAYS BACK CREDIT CARD COMPANIES WITH HIS VOTE

In 2002, Virginia representative Jim Moran (D) was nearly $700,000 in debt. Like millions of Americans hammered by exorbitant interest rates, Moran said, "I didn't see any way out." Except Moran is a prominent congressman, so he was able to get himself a special loan from credit card giant MBNA that, according to the *Washington Post,* "permitted him to borrow more money at a lower cost than was standard for the industry." You'd think after his own ordeal, Moran would want to help more Americans get out of the red. Yet, according to the *Post,* "as Moran was negotiating the loan, he also was supporting a bill pushed by MBNA and others in the credit card and finance industry that would make it tougher for people to walk away from debts by declaring bankruptcy." The special loan, in other words, was essentially a payoff from the credit card industry for Moran to push its agenda.

Institute, which estimated that *at most* 3 percent of filers—and almost certainly less—were using the existing bankruptcy laws to get out of paying debts they could afford.[50]

But that didn't stop Corporate America from getting its way when it came to rewriting bankruptcy laws. Egged on by piles of campaign cash, lawmakers publicly parroted the bankruptcy queen language to justify voting down proposals to preserve bankruptcy protections for those who go broke paying for catastrophic medical bills.[51]

Now, months after the bankruptcy bill passed, America is finding out even more ways we got screwed by this atrocity. According to a 2005 study by the Kauffman Foundation, almost one in five Americans who sought bankruptcy protections in recent years had operated a small business just before they went broke. As the *New York Times* noted, though lawmakers promised the bill would crack down "almost entirely on careless consumers who cannot pay credit card bills," the study shows that "the legislation threatens to hobble untold numbers of entrepreneurs and small-business owners" and could "have damaging ramifications for the nation's entrepreneurial culture."[52] That's correct—executives at huge credit card companies will make out like bandits at the expense of not only the poor, the sick, and the bereaved, but also the hardworking citizens who are trying to start their own small business. Yet, incredibly, the "bankruptcy queen" myth lives on.

MYTH: Government handouts are enough to prevent people from going broke.

Supporting the "bankruptcy queen" myth is the fantasy that there are plenty of government programs out there that should prevent you from going bankrupt. One week before Congress finalized its bankruptcy "reforms," Rush Limbaugh regurgitated this corporate line to his listeners: "We got government programs," Limbaugh said. "We got unemployment insurance, food stamps, aid to dependent children, Medicare, Medicaid, Section 8 housing . . . We've got more government programs than anybody can probably catalog." All someone on the verge of bankruptcy has to do, according to Limbaugh, is wise up and get that mythical pot of free money. "People [in the government] go to work there every day, but nobody knows who they are, where they are, where the office is, but we're giving away money in this country left and right, just gotta know how to get it."[53]

Yes, it's true—there is plenty of free money for those who "know how to get it." The problem is, those are usually powerful corporate interests looking for a taxpayer handout, not average citizens. In the last three decades, the U.S. government has spent more than half a trillion dollars bailing out the airline industry, the S&L industry (aka banks), and even the Mexican government.[54]

But for the programs Limbaugh lists, there has been cutback after cutback after cutback. Just take a look:

– Unemployment insurance: In 2005, President Bush proposed a $41 million cut to unemployment insurance grants to states.[55] He also proposed reducing revenues that go into the unemployment insurance fund— a step that could either reduce benefits, or bankrupt the entire system.[56]

– Food stamps (aka food assistance for the very poor): In early 2005, the Bush administration proposed cutting off more than 300,000 people from food stamps.[57] The Associated Press soon reported that a key congressional committee ratified that cut, and a move to cut off school lunches for 40,000 children, even "as the government reported that the number of people who are hungry because they can't afford to buy enough food rose to 38.2 million in 2004." That was an increase of 7 million citizens in just five years—and represents 12 percent of all American households.[58]

– Aid to dependent children (aka child care assistance for welfare recipients who are required to work): In 2003, more than thirty-five states made cuts in these programs for the very poor because the federal government had not provided enough money to keep them solvent. This underfunding came at the same time the White House was passing its second tax cut for the wealthy.[59]

– Medicare (aka health care for seniors): In 2004, the Bush administration announced a 17 percent increase in premiums seniors have to pay for Medicare services.[60]

– Medicaid (aka health care for the very poor): The *Sacramento Bee* reported in 2005 that "just about every state over the past few years has cut off [Medicaid] recipients . . . or begun charging copayments on doctor visits and prescription drugs."[61]

– Section 8 housing (aka rent assistance for the poor): In 2004, President Bush proposed cutting off 250,000 people from their rent assistance, and cutting off another 600,000 by 2009.[62]

And it doesn't stop there. In 2005, the White House slashed $182 million[63] out of the program that gives people heating aid in the winter, even as waiting lists for the program grow. College financial aid? The same thing. Thirty years ago, most of it came in the form of grants, but many of those grants have been reduced, and others have been converted to loans. In 2005 alone, President Bush proposed cutting college financial aid to half a million students.[64] This, at a time when recent college graduates owe 85 percent more in student loans than their counterparts of a decade ago.[65]

Limbaugh's fantasy world where free money is everywhere sounds great, and makes a good case for the credit card industry's effort to eliminate consumer bankruptcy protections. It's true—if everyone who needed help could get it, there really would be no need for bankruptcy protections. But they can't, no matter how many lies are thrown out there to make us think otherwise.

LIE: You have to be irresponsible to go bankrupt.

One of the common myths in America is that only irresponsible people go bankrupt. Bankruptcy protection, this myth says, does not teach low-lifes who go broke a good lesson—it instead lets them be a drag on society. In voting to gut bankruptcy protections, Indiana senator Evan Bayh (D) summed up this argument rather succinctly when he said, "It's not right for people who engage in irresponsible behavior to impose their bad decisions and the cost of that on other people who behave more responsibly."[66]

Bayh, of course, had been handsomely paid to spew that kind of garbage—in his career, he has collected more than $290,000 from the banking industry, according to the nonpartisan center for Responsive Politics. And, in truth, he was only speaking from his own experience: as the son of a senator, raised with all of life's luxuries spoon-fed to him, he is predisposed to see poor people as nothing more than an annoying nuisance, a bunch of "irresponsible" slobs who simply want to "impose their bad decisions" on him and his country club pals.

But consider just a few statistics that Bayh never once had to seriously consider from the confines of his privileged life:

— America's minimum wage is not enough to lift a family of three above the poverty line.[67] Translation: America's 7.3 million minimum wage workers[68] are at constant risk of going bankrupt because they aren't paid enough to survive, no matter how "responsible" they are.

— The average two-bedroom rental apartment requires the typical worker to earn at least $15.37 an hour—roughly three times the minimum wage. Translation: Millions of Americans can barely afford to put a roof over their head, which means that paying for other necessities (food, health care, etc.) puts them at high risk of going bankrupt, regardless of how "responsible" they are.[69]

— Seventy-five percent of those surveyed in Harvard's landmark 2001 study on personal debt had health insurance, but many of them lost cover-

HERO: Paul Wellstone, Minnesota senator

SINGLEHANDEDLY STOPPED CREDIT CARD– WRITTEN BANKRUPTCY LEGISLATION UNTIL HIS DEATH

Until the tragic plane crash that ended his life in 2002, Senator Paul Wellstone (D-MN) had almost singlehandedly derailed the credit card industry's bankruptcy bill year after year. As *National Journal* wrote, "Wellstone could always be relied upon to present the case against the legislation in the most forceful and uncompromising of terms.... [H]e did most of the heavy lifting—babysitting the bill when it was on the floor, raising procedural objections, offering amendments designed to soften the impact on poor debtors." He even went up against his own party's leaders as they "joined with Republican leaders on more than one occasion to quash Wellstone's filibusters" of the bill.

age during their illness, driving them into bankruptcy. Translation: Having health insurance still doesn't prevent being bankrupted by medical bills.[70]

Conservative think tanks and pundits are desperate to distract attention from these facts and from the corruption that has shaped Congress's bankruptcy law. They try to deny these harsh economic realities with the most insulting stories. The Heritage Foundation, for instance, issued a report saying poverty in America was an imaginary creation of "the press, liberal activists and politicians." Its proof? Current living conditions of those in poverty today compare favorably with "tenement living conditions around 1890 in New York City."[71]

Similarly, right-wing author Steve Salerno actually penned a newspaper op-ed piece saying that poverty rates are exaggerated because "at least some percentage of Americans are making money that they'd rather not declare—from drugs, prostitution, gambling and other rackets, outright theft, and so forth."[72] Basically, he's saying that because society has some criminals, that means there aren't real problems with poverty and debt. Incredible.

Back in the real world, the truth is clear: Low wages, poor health insurance, and increasing housing costs are driving even the most responsible, financially cautious citizens into the red. Just look at the story of Deborah Heinrichs. In an article entitled "Destroyed by Doctor Bills," *People* magazine reported on how she suddenly lost her husband to cancer, forcing her into bankruptcy after she tried to keep her family housed and fed. The article also reported on Leanna and Eric Brunner, a couple forced into bankruptcy by the $28,000 they had to spend to save their baby's life after the infant swallowed a shard of plastic that punctured her lungs.[73] And then there is the story of Larry Herman. His hometown newspaper reported that he had to file bankruptcy because he suffered a heart attack, his employer terminated his medical insurance, and he was required to pay for his seven daily medications out-of-pocket.[74]

These are the real stories about bankruptcy in America. Calling these people and the thousands like them "irresponsible" in order to justify corrupt legislation designed to enrich the banking/credit card industry is worse than irresponsible, it's reprehensible.

LIE: Recent bankruptcy "reforms" mean everyone now faces the same consequences.

During the debate over limiting citizens' bankruptcy protections, Senate Majority Leader Bill Frist (R-TN) said the legislation was needed because "wealthy debtors are walking away from debts they can repay."[75]

The problem is that while the bill does crack down on low-middle-income debtors, it has all sorts of exclusive escape hatches for those "wealthy debtors" Frist claims to be concerned with. Here are just a few:

− Anyone who is classified as having primarily business debts isn't subject to the new bankruptcy crackdown. As Harvard's Elizabeth Warren notes, "this means that some high-powered executive who gets sued for malfeasance or who borrows money to invest in diamond mines and loses a ton of money" gets the old, stronger bankruptcy protections, "while some poor guy who has lost his job and run up bills at the hospital will be put through the wringer."

– The bill fails to outlaw so-called asset protection trusts. These euphemistically named rip-off schemes allow the wealthy to shield an unlimited amount of money from creditors. Previously, these trusts were considered so nefarious they were only available offshore.[76] But now they are starting to spring up around the country, and Congress doesn't seem to care.[77] How much cash will be hidden in these schemes? No one knows for sure, but it's a lot. Florida State University expert Adam Hirsch said offshore trusts are already havens for billions of dollars, and new domestic ones "could very well be the same."[78]

– The bill preserves the so-called homestead exemption—a provision that allows people to shield their houses from creditors when they go bankrupt. The original thinking behind the provision was well intentioned: when someone goes broke, at least let them keep a roof over their head. But because Congress refused to limit the size/value of a house that can be exempted, the provision has been perverted into a way for the superwealthy to protect their money. Now, in some states like Texas and Florida, no matter how much your mansion is worth, if you owe money, the banks can't go after the home, as long as you've owned it for more than three and a half years.[79] Picture an executive who loots his company's pension fund being allowed to keep his $20 million mansion, even though he owes workers millions.

– The bill actually goes out of its way to preserve protections for huge companies, while punishing small business. Any business with more than $2 million in debt gets the previous Chapter 11 bankruptcy protections. But small businesses that owe less than that are out of luck. As Warren notes, "they must file a raft of new forms, be subjected to scrutiny from the Justice Department, and meet tight new deadlines." If they can't comply, they are liquidated, and "the bill makes sure bankruptcy judges will not be allowed to make exceptions, no matter how extreme the circumstances."

This says nothing about how the bill permits wealthy corporations to operate under much more lax rules than individuals. As journalist Mark Reutter noted in the *Washington Post*, the new bankruptcy law cracks down on ordinary citizens but "keeps intact the legal system by which corporations can shed certain employee obligations"—a euphemism for companies reneging on their pension, wage, and health care promises to workers. Thanks to the disparity, "federal bankruptcy court has become the venue of choice for sophisticated financiers and corporate managers seeking to pull apart labor contracts and roll back health and welfare programs at troubled companies."[80]

Just look at the auto parts company Delphi. After declaring bankruptcy in 2005, CEO Robert "Steve" Miller demanded huge wage cuts from workers, saying, "They [have to] understand that I haven't got any more money."[81] Yet, as journalist Reutter reported, Delphi was actually sitting on $1.6 billion in cash and had "secured $2 billion in loans and revolving credit from Citigroup and J.P. Morgan Chase bank just before it filed for bankruptcy." In bankruptcy court, it became clear that Miller was trying to use bankruptcy law as a vehicle to shaft workers and enrich his fellow executives. Specifically, at the very same time he was demanding draconian wage cuts for workers, Miller actually petitioned the bankruptcy court to award roughly $90 million in new bonuses to Delphi's senior executives[82]—many of whom had led the company into financial trouble.

What could possibly be the company's justification for proposing such lavish executive bonuses at the very time workers were being squeezed? No joke—the company's official bankruptcy filing that pushed both the worker wage cuts and executive pay package said that "approval of the key employee compensation program will boost employee morale."

But, then, the fact that corporate executives know they can be so brazen is a testament not only to unbridled arrogance and greed, but to the fact that the fat cats know full well that such requests are totally permissible under America's skewed bankruptcy laws. As the *New York Times'* Gretchen Morgenson noted in a 2005 article about Delphi, "When a company jettisons a pension that is underfunded by $11 billion . . . and proposes cuts of up to two-thirds in workers' pay and deep reductions in retiree benefits, you would think that its executives might want to share the pain. [But] all of these facts are irrelevant to the matter at hand: taking care of those at the top." Irrelevant, thanks to our bankruptcy laws.

Ben Stein, the Republican strategist-turned-entertainer, pointed out the nauseating reality of it all in a column. "A bankrupt company enriching its executives even as it destroys its stockholders' equity and demands that its workers revert to spartan living standards?" he asked. "How on earth did the idea come into the head of someone as smart as Mr. Miller that he could get away with enriching those who already have high pay and simultaneously demand that his workers accept poverty or lose their jobs?" Because while bankruptcy laws crack down on Corporate America, they permit corporations and the wealthy to do this kind of thing all the time.

To be sure, before the bankruptcy bill that created these loopholes was voted on and passed into law in early 2005, a few reporters exposed some of the most disgusting provisions and asked top lawmakers about them. When confronted about the asset-protection trusts, for instance, Senator Charles Grassley (R), the chief sponsor of the overall bill, feigned concern. He said through a spokesman that he "is always open to suggestions for closing these loopholes."[83] But when an amendment was brought forward to eliminate the loophole from the final bill, Grassley turned around and led the opposition against the provision, eventually killing it.[84]

Seeing such broad opposition to closing loopholes, Wisconsin senator Russ Feingold (D) decided to go at the bankruptcy bill another way: if the Senate was so determined to preserve state laws in places like Texas and Florida that allow millionaires to protect an unlimited amount of cash in their mansions, he believed lawmakers should also be willing to create a minimum homestead protection as well. After all, in Ohio and North Carolina, state law actually prevents low-income citizens from protecting even their modest homes.[85] Feingold's rationale was simple: If there was no ceiling for the rich, there should at least be a guaranteed floor for the rest of us. He thus proposed a bill to ensure elderly folks the right to protect up to $75,000 of the value of their homes if they go bankrupt. "In many cases, the home may be an elderly individual's only significant asset, representing an entire life savings," Feingold said.[86]

Yet in the same series of votes to reject closing loopholes for the rich, the Senate voted down Feingold's amendment. The superrich got no maximum, the rest of us got no minimum. "Proponents of this bill keep pressing it as designed to eliminate abuse," said Harvard's Warren. "Yet when provisions that permit real abuse by rich people are pointed out, the bill's proponents look the other way."

LIE: Bankruptcy protections threaten credit card profits.

In a nationally televised interview with PBS in 2004, the president of the American Bankers Association (ABA) defended his industry's aggressive push to limit bankruptcy protections, implying that those consumer-friendly protections were damaging the industry's financial viability. "Banking," said the ABA's Ed Yingling, "is not a greatly profitable business."[87]

Surprised, the interviewer pointed out that banking profits had broken records that year, but Yingling insisted that banking is "not an unusually profitable business." When the interviewer noted that MBNA alone

HERO: Elizabeth Warren, Harvard professor

DEBUNKING POLITICIANS' LIES
ABOUT BANKRUPTCY

Though academics are often accused of producing information that has little practical application in politics, Elizabeth Warren has time and again disproved that fallacy. The Harvard law professor has been one of the most tireless and effective warriors in the fight to prevent Congress from rubber-stamping credit card companies' leech-like behavior. It was Warren, for instance, who did the research, published in the journal *Health Affairs*, to prove that most bankruptcies in America are caused by medical bills and job loss—not by lazy people, as bought-off politicians would have us believe. And though Congress ended up passing a draconian bankruptcy bill, Warren continues to methodically debunk credit card industry–owned politicians who continue to devise ways that legalize Big Business rip-off schemes.

had made "one and a half times that of McDonald's," Yingling stuck to his guns, saying with a straight face that "McDonald's didn't do too well last year" (actually, the restaurant chain made roughly $1.5 billion in profits the year before—up 64 percent from the previous year).[88] The interviewer tried again, pointing out that "Citibank is now more profitable than Microsoft [and] Wal-Mart." But still, Yingling wouldn't budge—the illusion of an industry on the brink had to be preserved in order to perpetuate the dishonest rationale for eliminating consumer bankruptcy protections.[89]

Here's the thing: No one wants to put banks out of business, but it is straight-up deception for banks to plead poverty and imply that they will go under unless the government weakens bankruptcy protection laws. In the five years before Congress gutted bankruptcy protections, Harvard researchers found credit card industry profits increased by 163 percent.[90] In fact, the industry was so flush with cash, it paid twenty-three of its top executives almost three-quarters of a billion dollars in total compensation (salary, stock options, bonuses, etc.) between 2002 and 2003. That's about $1 million of interest and penalty fees taken from average Americans and put directly into the pocket of twenty-three executives every single day of those two years, including holidays.[91]

"Does that seem like an industry that is facing a financial crisis or is being taken advantage of by people who are trying to get out from under their responsibilities?" asked Minnesota senator Mark Dayton (D) as he fought to keep bankruptcy protections on the books.[92]

No, especially when you consider that even under the old protections, "most of the credit cards that end up in bankruptcy proceedings [had] already made a profit for the companies that issued them," according to bankruptcy expert Robert R. Weed. "That's because people are paying so many fees that they've already paid more than was originally borrowed."[93]

Credit card industry analyst Robert McKinley put it more bluntly: "The idea that companies are losing their shirts on bankruptcies is a lot of bull," he said before Congress passed the bankruptcy bill. "With these rates and fees, the card industry is a gravy train."[94]

MYTH: The free market—not regulation— will keep interest rates low.

One way to deal with the record-breaking rash of bankruptcies in America is to limit the amount of interest that can be charged to a consumer. Minnesota senator Mark Dayton (D) tried to do just that with his bill to limit interest rates to a whopping 30 percent.

The first line of argument that Big Money interests invariably trot out against capping interest rates is "states rights." Utah senator Orrin Hatch (R), the recipient of $158,000 from the banking industry in his career, exemplified this in arguing against Dayton's legislation.[95] He complained the measure "would preempt many States' usury laws unless the State has a lower interest rate"[96]—as if forcing states to have stronger usury laws is a bad thing. Remember, this was just months after Hatch's White House allies issued regulations invalidating state laws that banned abusive lending practices by credit card companies.[97]

Hatch was ably backed up by Senate Banking Committee Chairman Richard Shelby (R), the second-biggest recipient of credit card industry cash in Congress. Shelby was simply outraged that Dayton wanted to "create a federal usury law"[98]—again, as if that would be a bad thing.

The second, and even more ridiculous argument against interest caps comes shrouded in the concept of "choice" and "competition." The Bush Treasury Department, for instance, claimed that competition between credit card companies keeps rates low for consumers, and therefore no regulation is needed. If consumers don't like the rates they are paying, "they can find another card," said Treasury official Julie Williams in November 2004.[99]

Obviously, Williams has never met destitute soldiers being fleeced by 650 percent annual interest rates, such as those profiled in the *New York Times* just a month later.[100] (She couldn't possibly think those soldiers *chose* that rate, could she?) As New Hampshire's *Concord Monitor* editorial board wrote that autumn, "in the absence of a limit on how much lenders can charge or tough regulation to curb escalating fees and misleading sales pitches, competition doesn't work."[101]

But no matter that the arguments against interest caps are bogus—money talks. Dayton's bill was overwhelmingly defeated, as seventy-four senators voted against it.[102] That included eighteen who, in 1991, had voted for an even tougher bill limiting credit card interest rates to just 14 percent (the measure was eventually killed).[103] Why would those eighteen change their votes on a measure that was weaker than the one they had originally supported? Because in the time between the two votes, the credit card industry sent those eighteen senators $2.3 million in combined campaign contributions.[104] Even the supposedly virtuous Senator John McCain (R), who campaigned for the presidency against the influence of corporate cash, couldn't resist changing his vote after the industry gave him more than a quarter of a million dollars.[105]

Solutions

The debt crisis in American is not a crisis for banks and lenders, who are making astonishing profits, but for average Americans crippled by consumer debts and left without even the last resort of fair bankruptcy laws. The best solutions, therefore, are aimed at helping that consumer, not further enriching the usurers who are bleeding America dry.

Restore bankruptcy protections. Congress should reverse its recent decision to gut bankruptcy protections, and restore them to where they had been for decades. It's that simple.

Create strict laws that control lending to the most vulnerable. In its comprehensive report on the credit card industry, PBS's *Frontline* found that "if a person is close to bankruptcy, they get all kinds of [new] credit card solicitations in the mail."[106] Why? Because the credit card companies know that people close to going broke or just coming out of bankruptcy are the best prey. As ABA president Edward Yingling admitted, "those that use the revolving part of the credit card"—those who are most desperate and can't pay off their bill—"are kind of the sweet spot" for industry profits. Conservative scholar Lawrence Lindsey, who was President George W. Bush's top economic adviser, acknowledged this problem, and said the easiest solution "is for banks and other lenders just to say that they will not lend to anyone who has declared bankruptcy within the last three years."[107] That's a bit harsh, and besides, Lindsey admits "the lenders are not ready to do that"[108] because they are making so much cash under the current system. But he's on to something. Congress should set up rules about how financial companies interact with people on the verge of bankruptcy, or just coming out of bankruptcy. Strict limits on interest rates, fees, and lines of credits granted to these at-risk individuals must be established so that banks' desire to cash in doesn't push the most financially vulnerable citizens over the debt cliff.

Outlaw credit card company behavior that makes them worse than black-market loan sharks. The horror stories of how credit card companies essentially steal money through devious behavior are too many to stuff into one book. The tactics run the gamut, from delaying when they credit your payments so that they can charge you late fees to sending unsolicited cards and then charging stiff penalties if they aren't used enough.[109] Congress must put together a panel of experts to recommend ways to crack down on—and criminalize—all of this kind of nefarious and greedy behavior once and for all.

Make sure that if a customer is playing by the rules, the credit card company plays by the rules, too. Legal restrictions on credit card companies must be in place to govern how much they can raise your interest rates at a given time. They should not be allowed to arbitrarily raise rates by double-digit percentages whenever they want. And they certainly should not be allowed to employ a "universal default" policy that lets them constantly peruse their customers' credit reports and then jack up interest rates if they find a dispute with another creditor. A bill in Congress called the Loan Shark Prevention Act is a solid first step—it would outlaw "universal default." The next step would be a bill regulating how much credit card companies can raise your fees within a given year. If people are paying their credit card bill on time and following the rules, the credit card companies should be forced to follow some rules, too.

Give states back their rights. When Congress passed the so-called Fair Credit Reporting Act, the headline from the December 2003 edition of *American Banker* magazine said it best: "Bush Signs It and the Industry Celebrates."[110] Though the bill's title makes it sound like a great achievement for average Americans, it actually permanently limits states' rights to enact stronger consumer protection and privacy laws. As one expert noted, the bill "prevents the states from enacting any law that restricts the deceptive marketing of credit card offers to consumers . . . limits the authority of states to regulate credit card companies that make mistakes to the credit bureaus, and it prevents the states from ordering the credit card companies not to deceive the credit bureaus."[111] This travesty of a law, mind you, was written by politicians of both parties who bloviate about protecting "states' rights" and "local control," yet usurp that power when it means ordinary people might get some protection from the corporate sharks. The act needs to be repealed and rewritten, to give states the power to protect consumers when the federal government refuses to.

IN 2004, A Cleveland municipal court heard a case that Discover Bank brought against Ruth M. Owens, a fifty-three-year-old disabled woman. She had already paid the bank $3,492 over six years on just a $1,963 debt. Yet she was being dragged into court after the company had assessed her new late fees and finance charges that doubled her remaining balance to $5,564.

When the company took her to court, she wrote the judge a letter. "I would like to inform you that I have no money to make payments," she wrote. "I am on Social Security Disability. . . . If my situation was different I would pay. I just don't have it. I'm sorry."

Luckily, the judge invoked bankruptcy laws and invalidated the debt, saying Owens, had "clearly been the victim of unreasonable, unconscionable and unjust business practices."[112]

Now, though, thanks to politicians' fealty to credit card industry campaign contributions, those bankruptcy protections have been all but eliminated. And the thousands of future Ruth Owenses who are abused by credit card companies will be thrown to the wolves.

CHAPTER 5

PENSIONS

★

YOU PROBABLY have your own special dream about retiring. Maybe you imagine spoiling your grandchildren or playing some golf or driving slowly on the highway and not caring about the traffic jam you are creating. Maybe you even imagine being able to afford a trip to someplace warm during some of those cold winters.

What you probably don't envision is having a corporate lawyer show up at your house and serve you with court papers while you're packing for that trip. And you most definitely don't fantasize about having those court papers say your former employer is suing to terminate the retirement benefits you were promised.

But that is exactly what is happening to more and more Americans in their golden years. As the *Wall Street Journal* reported in 2004, Big Business is filing lawsuits all over America asking "judges to rule that no matter what labor contracts say, they have a right to change the benefits" paid out to retirees.[1] And by "change" they usually mean "cut" or "terminate."

The suits are designed to seize on the inherent weakness of retirees: their age. Companies "have little to lose by trying" to screw the elderly, noted the *Journal*. Why? Because "as such legal cases drag on, the employers save money as some of the retirees, who have to pay growing portions of their health-care costs, forgo costly care, drop out of the plans, or die."[2]

Don't buy the companies' arguments that they are cutting retirement benefits because they are out of cash—it's a lie. Take the railroad car manufacturer ACF Industries, which asked a court to let it change or terminate benefits for 678 of its retirees.[3] The company is owned by Carl Icahn, a man described by *Forbes* magazine as a "corporate raider" who, with more than $5 billion in personal assets, is one of the 100 richest people on the planet.*[4] Yet his company portrays itself as a pauper[5] in order to justify feasting on its workers' retirement benefits.

Or how about the mining company Asarco? In 2003, the company filed a lawsuit to slash the retirement benefits it promised retirees, claiming it was undergoing severe financial distress.[6] Yet as the suit against its workers dragged on into 2004, Asarco's parent company reported more than a quarter billion dollars in profits in just the last quarter of that year.[7] In 2005, more of the same: The Associated Press reported that Asarco's parent company reported "profits that were up 59 percent from the year previous." The company, nonetheless, simultaneously pressed "a three-year wage freeze and reductions in pension and medical benefits" for its workers.[8]

In some respects, workers who get sued are the lucky ones—at least they can argue in court to protect their pensions and retiree benefits. Many don't even have that chance. Some simply get their pensions stolen: In 2004, regulators found more than 1,200 instances where workers' 401(k) money had vanished—that's 37 times the number of instances reported just ten years before.[9]

Others workers are just cut off completely. These are the thousands of people who worked at companies like United Airlines—companies that declare bankruptcy and then terminate their retirees' pensions, even while preserving their executives' multimillion-dollar retirement packages.[10]

And still others are scammed. In 2002, the Associated Press reported that 8 million workers at hundreds of companies saw their retirement plans quietly converted to "cash balance" schemes by corporate executives. These new pensions are often nothing more than a con. Companies essentially back out of their original promise to give workers a lifetime monthly stipend and instead give workers one lump-sum payment. That may sound appealing to workers at first—until they find out that the lump sum is often much smaller than what they would have received in the pension plan they were originally promised. How much smaller? Workers whose pensions were converted to cash balances have lost up to

---

*Icahn is reported to be the real-life inspiration for the Gordon Gekko character in Oliver Stone's *Wall Street*.

50 percent of their promised retirement benefits in some cases. In all, government researchers estimate retirees will lose a combined $200 million a year because of these schemes.[11]

The results are not surprising: America, the richest country on the planet, a country that says it cherishes "family values," is watching more of its elderly go back to work because their pensions have been slashed and they can't pay the bills. A recent study by AARP found that 80 percent of workers near traditional retirement age plan to keep working, with many saying they need the income to survive. In light of pension cutbacks, one AARP official said, "The big unknown for seniors is whether they will have enough money throughout their lifetime. The big worry is that the money will run out before they do."[12]

Aren't our political leaders doing what they can to stop corporate schemes that pilfer workers' retirement nest eggs? Exactly the opposite. Like a getaway car driver in a bank robbery, America's corrupt government is a key part of the heist. For example, when workers questioned the legality of cash-balance scams, President Bush's Treasury Department issued regulations formally legalizing them.[13] When a few gutsy lawmakers offered a bill to overturn those regulations, the Treasury Department issued official talking points against the bill, which were then distributed around Capitol Hill by corporate lobbyists.[14] When United Airlines kicked its retirees in the groin by eliminating their pensions, a federal court gave the move its stamp of approval.[15] And when reporters asked about these abuses, President Bush's Labor Department responded tersely that retired workers "aren't our constituents anymore."[16]

Big Business's hostile takeover of government means this assault on ordinary Americans' retirement isn't about to stop. It's why President Bush rolled out the granddaddy of all pension rip-off schemes: privatizing Social Security. Yes, he had to fabricate a justification for such a radical idea by claiming the program would go "bankrupt without privatization." And yes, it is unclear whether Social Security will ultimately be privatized. But still, no matter whether he succeeds or not, the mere introduction of the concept was a triumph for Corporate America. It showed that when it comes to America's retirement security, politicians today are not only eager to help sabotage private pensions, but also willing to try to sell off the most popular program in American history to Wall Street.

Think about it—Social Security is, bar none, the most successful government initiative passed in the last century. It has lifted millions of Americans out of poverty and has allowed ordinary folks to retire knowing they will get at least something to subsist on. Yet one of America's major political parties has now made privatizing the program—and potentially dismantling it—a legitimate topic for debate. What's the motivation? Simple: cash. The corrupt politicians know that privatization would force Social Security to do the one thing it has never done and was never supposed to do: give away billions of dollars to the same corporate special interests that underwrite politicians' campaigns.

A top University of Chicago economist estimates that Wall Street would stand to make somewhere between $400 billion and $1 trillion in broker fees and skim-off-the-top schemes under President Bush's privatization proposal.[17] That is money taken out of the Social Security system—out of *your* retirement—and handed over to the financial industry. That's why the *Wall Street Journal* said privatizing Social Security "could be the biggest bonanza in the history of the mutual-fund industry."[18] And it is why Corporate America has spent so much cash pushing privatization.

The amounts of money are grotesque: Since 2000, Wall Street firms have given almost a quarter of a billion dollars to politicians.[19] That money flows to people like Louisiana representative Jim McCrery (R), who chairs the House subcommittee that oversees Social Security. He took almost $200,000 from the industry in his last two campaigns for reelection[20]— and he has done everything he can to privatize Social Security.

But buying off politicians is the easy part—manufacturing the lies to mislead the public is what's hard. That is why Big Business has also spent so much cash and effort building up public policy centers that push privatization proposals in the media. Corporate America knows it can launder its destructive agenda through these self-proclaimed "nonpartisan" organizations so that their proposals seem credible. Ultimately, that helps create the public rationale to justify politicians selling their constituents out.

Take the Cato Institute, a group funded by financial services firms like American Express, Citibank, and Prudential Securities.[21] Back in 1996, the institute launched a special Project on Social Security Privatization headed by an advisory board of corporate executives and conservative political operatives. "We're receiving support from the financial community, from the investment community, from the insurance community," bragged one Cato spokesman.[22] Within weeks, it had collected $2 million.[23] By 2001, the *Washington Post* reported that the group was spending millions "to run a virtual war room to promote Social Security privatization."[24]

Similarly, the Heritage Foundation's Web site, which is full of pro-privatization propaganda, boasts about the organization's financial ties to investment firm Merrill Lynch.[25] And the pro-privatization group FreedomWorks is headed by former House majority leader Dick Armey (R)—

who moonlights as a top lobbyist for the mutual fund industry in Washington.[26]

These groups are like a geyser of dishonesty, spewing out a steady stream of steaming hot lies. Cato, for instance, has likened Social Security to "a cancer"[27] and claims the system is in "financial crisis"[28]—even though the government's own data shows that's not the case. The Heritage Foundation, meanwhile, created a calculator purporting to show people how much more retirement money they would earn under a privatized system than they would under the current system. There was just one problem: the calculator grossly distorted the results by underreporting how much people would receive under the current Social Security system.[29]

These lies might not be so frightening if the liars pushing them were marginalized and ridiculed by the political establishment for their dishonesty. Far from it—many of the purveyors of privatization myths are now at the upper echelons of our government, where they can make their agenda a reality. As just one example, take Andrew Biggs, who was the assistant director of the Cato Institute's Social Security privatization project.[30] In 2001, he became a top staffer for the president's special commission charged with proposing new plans for Social Security. That same year, Cato issued a report bragging that the Bush administration's new Social Security privatization plans "mirror Cato's."[31] Shocker. Today, Biggs is even higher up on the food chain. As the head of the Office of Retirement Policy at the Social Security Administration,[32] he finds himself in the perfect place to do Corporate America's bidding and push privatization.

But Social Security is only the most high-profile front in Corporate America's raid on Americans' retirement, as the sharks are also circling state employee pension systems. In January 2005, for instance, California governor Arnold Schwarzenegger (R) announced plans to privatize and dismantle his state's public retirement system. Critics noted that he had pocketed about $6 million from fund managers and other financial interests that would benefit from the idea.[33] Nonetheless, he pushed forward, replacing the head of the pension system's board with an insurance industry executive.[34] And though Schwarzenegger ultimately backed off his proposal, the fledgling effort showed that Big Business is not resting on its laurels.

To be sure, destroying our nation's pension system is no easy task. Americans don't like the idea of being ripped off. That's why Big Business's lies, myths, and half-truths in this debate are among the most well crafted out there. But no amount of deceitfulness can hide the simple

HACK: John Boehner, Ohio congressman

TRIES TO QUIETLY CHANGE LAWS TO ALLOW PENSION RIP-OFFS

During his fifteen years in Congress, Representative John Boehner (R-OH) has pocketed more than $3.5 million in campaign contributions from corporate political action committees. That's roughly $4,500 a week, every week he's been in Congress. And as the chairman of the House Education and Workforce Committee, Boehner has paid Corporate America back for its donations by helping Big Business decimate workers' pensions. In perhaps the best example of this, Boehner in 2005 tried to quietly add language to a bill that would legalize "cash-balance" pension schemes that allow corporate executives to punish older workers by reducing their retirement benefits. Courts had already ruled that these schemes illegally discriminate against older workers. So Boehner tried to undermine those rulings by changing the laws the rulings were based on. To justify his move, he actually said the courts were "jeopardizing generous pension benefits for workers across the country"—a brazen attempt to hide the fact that these pension schemes often mean workers lose up to half of the benefits they were promised.

truth: Pension and Social Security "reforms" are just a euphemism for stealing our retirement nest eggs and using them to line the pockets of corporate fat cats and fund the reelection campaigns of corrupt politicians.

MYTH: Your pension is a rock-solid promise.

One of the ways corporations attract the best workers is to offer them the promise of a solid, guaranteed pension, telling prospective employees they will receive a set monthly stipend in their retirement. To workers, that pension is not only an incentive to take a given job, it is also an incentive to stay at that job, because benefits usually increase the longer one is employed at the company.

These traditional pensions were integral in expanding America's middle class over the last fifty years. Workers considered them a rock-solid guarantee—they were promised a set of benefits up front, which, for the most part, were honored. These were the basic benefits that made sure our grandparents weren't kicked out onto the street simply because they were old and couldn't work anymore.

The problem is that this history makes it seem as if pension promises are rock-solid—as if our laws guarantee that companies can't simply back out of the deal. Unfortunately, that's just not true. Though we would like to believe that corporations are obligated to live up to the pension promises they make, the truth is that they have no such obligation because our bought-off government has no desire to make sure those promises stick.

Consider this fact: corporations are not required to set aside adequate money to actually pay the pensions they've promised to their workers. Let's repeat that because, really, it is so appallingly hard to believe, it needs to be said twice: though your employer may be promising you a nice pension, federal laws actually permit companies to pocket the retirement money that they should be putting aside to follow through on those promises. And boy are they abusing these loopholes to the extreme.

At the end of 2004, the nation's 1,108 weakest private pension plans were underfunded by a total of more than $350 billion. In other words, companies had set aside $350 billion less in pension money than they had promised to their workers.[35] In just the five years between 1999 and 2004, the number of companies whose pensions were underfunded by $50 million or more grew by more than 600 percent.[36]

What happens when workers retire and they ask for the benefits they were promised? Corporate America and our corrupt political system increasingly tell workers to go shove it. For instance, as mentioned above, hundreds of companies have converted workers' pensions into "cash balances," where retirees get one lump-sum payment that can be half of what they were originally promised.[37] Lawmakers, meanwhile, have done all they can to legalize this scheme.

Companies have justified these conversions by claiming cash-balance plans are more flexible, and thus better for younger workers who switch jobs. But as the *Wall Street Journal* reported in 2005, government auditors concluded "that most workers—regardless of age—receive lower retirement benefits when their employers switch from traditional pension plans to cash-balance plans."[38]

Then again, those workers who are screwed by cash-balance pensions are fortunate compared to those who work at companies like United Airlines. There, "loopholes in the federal pension law allowed [the company] to treat its pension fund as solid for years, when in fact it was dangerously weakening," according to the *New York Times*. Company executives kept telling workers they had nothing to worry about, until 2004, when the airline suddenly announced that it owed $72 million to its pension fund, but said it "would not make the contribution" and instead would simply terminate its pension program outright.[39] Again, thanks to pension laws written by bought-off politicians, this move was perfectly legal.

Big companies such as United Airlines like to blame economic problems for their failure to provide retirement security, but the whole point of a traditional pension is to protect retirees from fluctuations in the market. Corporate America is supposed to be socking away money in good times so it can fulfill its promises to workers when things go bad. But that's not happening. From 2003 to 2004, the gap between what companies have in their pension funds and what they have promised workers grew by an eye-popping 27 percent.[40] This jump happened at the same time the economy was improving, and corporate profits were exploding.[41] And as we've seen, it isn't as if those profits are being withheld from pension funds in order to pay for things like better wages or benefits for workers.

So where is the cash going? Some of it is being stolen by greedy executives. Again, as mentioned above, in 2004, the government found more than 1,200 instances where workers' pension money vanished—a 37-fold increase since 1995.[42] That has happened, in part, because Corporate America has done such a good job of buying off politicians who then weaken pension protection laws, cut back on enforcement, or restrict government regulators from cracking down on the abuse. When it comes to pensions, "Worker protections are relatively weak" and "employees often have little recourse," wrote the *Wall Street Journal* in 2005.

Average workers' pension money is also being stuffed into special stashes exclusively for corporate executives. According to a recent study of 500 large companies, more than two-thirds had created supplemental retirement funds for the top brass separate from the rest of the companies' employees. These special plans "usually offer better benefits than traditional pension plans and are sometimes guaranteed regardless of the fate of the company itself," wrote the *New York Times*. And they are hidden from workers. "Unlike a chief executive's salary or stock options," the *Times* wrote, "the cost of these executive pension plans is rarely laid out for shareholders. Instead, the information is usually so deep in a company's regulatory filings that it is difficult to find, let alone calculate." One corporate consultant put it bluntly: "If you wanted to deliver extra compensation and you wanted to do it below the radar screen, you did it through [these schemes]."[43] Yes—all allowed under the law.

The results are predictable. At United, company executives terminated workers' pension plan, while, according to the *Times*, "the $4.5 million worth of retirement benefits for [CEO] Glenn F. Tilton...has remained safe in a special, fully funded trust."[44] At other companies, its the same kind of abuse. It doesn't even matter anymore whether this kind of behavior involves high-profile people who might draw attention to the theft. Just look at Halliburton. There, Vice President Dick Cheney has been given a $20 million retirement package for just five years of service at the company,[45] at the very same time the company is suing its retirees in an effort to reduce their health benefits.[46]

To be sure, executives' efforts to take workers' pension money and make it their own are often publicly justified as reward for executives' service to the company. That argument has often been politicians' public rationale for not passing laws that put an end to the shenanigans. But as *Time* magazine uncovered in 2005, many of these public justifications are based on "phantom employment records"[47] whereby retiring executives are credited for far more years of service than they actually worked. For instance, when John Snow stepped down as head of the railroad company CSX Corp. to become President Bush's treasury secretary, he was given a lump-sum pension of $33.2 million, based on 44 years of employment, even though he had worked at the company for only 26 years. He received this payout just after he had reduced benefits for CSX retirees.[48] Then there was Leo Mullin, former CEO of Delta Airlines, who oversaw the reduction of Delta workers' pension plans. When he left the company, he received a $16 million retirement package based on 28.5 years of employment—which, according to *Time*, was "at least 21 years more than he worked at the airline."[49]

All of this, mind you, is sanctioned by Congress under federal pension rules that lawmakers claim are designed to protect workers. And these rules are still being further weakened.

In 2003, for instance, lawmakers trumpeted a pension "reform" bill as a way to stop corporate abuse and help workers save more for their retirement. But as Deene Goodlaw, one of the nation's foremost experts on pensions, noted, the bill "substantially weakens the rules" that corporations have to follow in paying their retirees and "invites abuse" by shifting the responsibility for following the law away from government regulators and to corporations themselves.[50] That's like letting Jack the Ripper out on probation, and then making him his own probation officer.

If that wasn't enough fox-in-the-henhouse for you, it later came out that many of the key provisions in the legislation were originally written by the ERISA Industry Committee—Corporate America's lobbying organization that focuses on pension policy.[51]

Those are the kinds of details that Big Business doesn't want too many people knowing about—it might make ordinary folks pretty mad. So to prevent any public scrutiny, the corporate toadies who run Congress released the text of the complex ninety-page pension bill at midnight, and told rank-and-file lawmakers that they would be voting on it just hours later in the Ways and Means Committee. The goal was to make sure there wouldn't be enough time for anyone to actually read the bill before it passed. Sensing this, Democrats immediately used a procedural tactic to stall for time, and then retreated to a private room to discuss strategy.[52]

But even that was not okay. The Ways and Means Committee chairman, Representative Bill Thomas (R), one of Big Business's go-to guys, panicked and then did his best chest-thumping-Third-World-dictator impression by deploying an armed team of Capitol police to try to prevent the Democrats from even meeting (how dare they have the nerve to actually want to read the legislation before voting on it!).[53] The bill ultimately passed with barely a peep. The message was clear: With a government owned and operated by Corporate America, there is no room for deliberation, especially when it may threaten executives' ability to raid workers' pensions for themselves.

MYTH: The government guarantees your pension even if Corporate America rips you off.

On Labor Day, 1974, President Gerald Ford signed legislation he promised would "finally give the American worker solid protection in his pension plan."[54] The bill created the Pension Benefit Guaranty Corporation (PBGC)—an agency that was supposed to insure your pension plan when/if your employer went bankrupt and terminated the retirement benefits you were promised.

Today, workers are given much the same assurances: "When companies fail and can't make good on their retirement promises," said Labor Secretary Elaine Chao in 2005, "the PBGC steps in and guarantees these workers a basic benefit."[55]

This rhetoric naturally leads lots of workers to believe they don't have to *really* worry about Corporate America abandoning retirees—which is exactly the point. Keep the public in the dark about everything, make us think there's nothing to worry about, and it will be too late for us to do anything once we realize what's really going on.

But violins playing on the deck of the *Titanic* didn't really make passengers ignore their sinking ship—and hot air from paid-off government con artists can't hide the truth. What rarely gets mentioned is this: when your employer bails out on you and forces the PBGC to pay your pension, you can only receive up to about $45,600 a year in retirement benefits.[56] If you had been banking on more because that's what you were promised, sorry, you are out of luck.

Why are there such strict limits? It has to do with how the PBGC is funded. Just like you are legally obligated to pay to insure your car, corporations are supposed to be required to pay premiums to the PBGC to insure their pension plans. Those premiums are supposed to fund the PBGC, so that when corporations go bankrupt, taxpayers aren't left having to pick up the tab.

But the important phrase is "supposed to": politicians have made sure loopholes exist to let Corporate America avoid paying those premiums. In 2004, for instance, companies avoided paying roughly 80 percent of the PBGC premiums they were "required" to pay.[57] The *New York Times* reported in 2005 that "companies have so many ways of tweaking their pension calculations that they almost never have to make the special catch-up contributions" they are supposed to make when their pension plans are reaching a crisis.[58]

As just one example, the Labor Department reported in 2005 that Bethlehem Steel had paid just $60 million to the PBGC. That's not an annual number—that's $60 million in the company's entire history, despite the fact that it employed thousands. When the company ultimately terminated its pensions, PBGC was forced to pick up a $3.7 billion tab for its workers.[59]

That kind of thing, spread across many industries, has left the PBGC with a massive $23 billion deficit[60]—a deficit that means the PBGC must limit benefits in order to stay afloat. And experts estimate that if Big Business is allowed to continue evading its responsibilities, the PBGC will be entirely out of resources by 2021.[61] As the *Detroit News* reported, for the one million workers whose pensions have already been dumped onto

PBGC, that could mean the "system won't be able to pay all the lifetime benefits that it owes" to them.[62]

As with all of these shell games, it is in Corporate America's best interest to keep everything secret, which is why, in 2005, one congressional investigation found "dramatic" differences between the information released to the public and information that only government regulators are allowed to see. Data shows that corporations are only telling the public about half of the pension underfunding that goes on.[63] Did government regulators who know the real story warn retirees that they might be facing benefit cuts? No, because, amazingly, politicians made sure federal law actually prohibits those government regulators from warning retirees until it is too late for them to plan their finances for the upcoming tragedy.[64] These are regulators paid by your tax dollars, who are supposed to be working for you, but are prevented by law from letting you know your employer is about to rip you off. Only when you are already being fleeced can they tell you what you already know.

To understand how crazy this is, just think about it in simpler terms: Imagine opening a savings account at a bank that promised to guard your money, and promised that your money was insured by the federal government against theft. Then imagine that the bank started draining cash from the account while giving you false balance statements that hid the theft. Then imagine that when the police found out about the situation, they were barred from warning you until there was no money left to your name. Finally, imagine that when you asked the government to make good on the insurance policy backing up your savings, it couldn't afford to give you back all your money, because it was refusing to collect insurance premiums from the same bank that stole from you in the first place.

That's what's happening on a grand scale to thousands of America's retirees—and it is all perfectly legal, thanks to industry-owned politicians who wrote the laws endorsing this behavior.

MYTH: Social Security is in crisis and going bankrupt.

"Social Security's a joke, and everybody knows it," said the twenty-two-year-old Texas worker. "By the time I retire it's not going to be around."[65]

That sentiment, captured by the *New York Times* in a 2005 interview, was surely music to Corporate America's ears. It speaks to the success of

HACK: Jim Nussle, Iowa congressman

USING CHAIRMANSHIP TO SPREAD FEAR-MONGERING LIES ABOUT SOCIAL SECURITY

Iowa representative Jim Nussle (R) is chairman of the U.S. House Budget committee, and in that role he is supposed to speak credibly about fiscal issues. Yet in 2005 he said that "by the year 2042, the entire [Social Security] system, in fact, by most people's definition of the word *bankrupt*, would be bankrupt." It was a lie designed to scare people into supporting a Social Security privatization scheme that would give away billions of taxpayer dollars to Wall Street. But the lie was not surprising, considering Nussle had taken more than $180,000 from the financial services industry during his political career. The truth is that the system will be very far from bankrupt in 2042. According to Social Security's own actuaries, if Congress does absolutely nothing, Social Security will still be able to pay 74 percent of its full benefits after 2041—far from "bankrupt." Robert Ball, Social Security commissioner under both Democratic and Republican presidents, told the *New York Times* in 2005 what's really going on: "What they're saying is not true. The program is not going bankrupt."

its PR campaign aimed at misleading Americans into believing that Social Security's demise is a foregone conclusion and thus the program must be privatized.

That PR campaign's loudest spokespeople have been corrupt politicians. Nearly every bought-off lawmaker looking for campaign contributions from Wall Street has loudly supported privatizing Social Security. And they all repeat the same two talking points to publicly justify their position. The first is designed to create a sense of emergency, as when President Bush told Congress that when it comes to Social Security, "the crisis is now . . . You may not feel it. Your constituents may not be overwhelming you with letters demanding a fix now, but the crisis is now."[66]

Yet no one—not even the most extreme or corrupt politician—

disputes the fact that Social Security will pay out full benefits for at least the next thirty-five years. According to Social Security's own actuaries, the system will provide full benefits until 2041.[67] The only dispute is from congressional researchers, who project that Social Security will be able to pay full benefits until 2052.[68]

When confronted with this reality, the president's allies on Capitol Hill have tried to change the subject, lie about a "crisis," or both. California representative Bill Thomas (R), whose committee oversees Social Security, actually lied about the lies, claiming "The president never said [Social Security] was in a crisis."[69] Pathetic.

The second talking point repeated by corporate parrots on Capitol Hill claims that Social Security will be completely broke. "By the year 2042, the entire system, in fact, by most people's definition of the word bankrupt, would be bankrupt," said the Budget Committee chairman, Representative Jim Nussle (R-IA),[70] a reliable corporate ally who has taken more than $180,000 from the financial services industry during his political career.[71]

In referring to "most people," Nussle was surely including the *American Heritage Dictionary*. But that venerable book defines *bankrupt* as "totally depleted" — which is far from what Social Security will be, even thirty-plus years in the future. According to Social Security's own actuaries, if Congress does absolutely nothing, Social Security will still be able to pay 74 percent of its full benefits after 2041.[72] The only serious questioning of those calculations comes from Congress's own nonpartisan researchers, who contend the system is actually more solvent than even that. They say Social Security will be able to pay 78 percent of its benefits after 2052.[73] Robert Ball, who was a Social Security commissioner under both Democratic and Republican presidents during the 1960s and 1970s, made it pretty clear: "What [privatizers] are saying is not true," he said. "The program is not going bankrupt."[74]

So, to review: the only disagreement among nonpartisan experts is about when Social Security will start paying three-quarters of its benefits — thirty-five years from now or forty-five years from now. That time frame hardly warrants the term *crisis* or *bankrupt*.

Luckily, polls in mid-2005 showed Americans fundamentally understood this truth and weren't buying the dishonest alarmism. But instead of fessing up to the dishonesty, Bush began taking his rhetoric into the stratosphere of lies — where the facts are so thin even the timid Washington press corps gags and coughs up the truth.

For instance, Bush started saying there's nothing left in the Social Security trust fund except "an empty IOU, a piece of paper."[75] That sounds really frightening—until you realize he is using scary-sounding euphemisms to describe some of the safest investments in the world. As the *New York Times* pointed out, Bush never mentioned that "those IOU's are Treasury securities backed by the full faith and credit of the United States," and "the government has never defaulted on its obligations"[76] to pay these IOUs—ever. Put another way, calling these bonds worthless pieces of paper is about as ridiculous as calling a 5-carat diamond a worthless piece of gravel.

Then again, since the very beginning of his political career, Bush has been willing to lie about Social Security. According to the *Texas Observer,* Bush in 1978 "warned that Social Security would go bust in ten years unless people were given a chance to invest the money themselves"[77] (aka privatization). You may have noticed that never happened. Congress made some changes to Social Security in the early 1980s to shore up the system, but privatization was never seriously considered. And as you probably know, Social Security did not go bust in 1988.

Why are we seeing such a serious push for privatization again today? It's obvious: Big Business needs a public rationale to dismantle Social Security. Desperate to start skimming off billions from ordinary Americans' retirement, these liars will say or do anything to create a sense of urgency that would build public support for the system to be radically altered.

MYTH: Privatizing Social Security will "fix" the system.

Let's say that even after reading the previous section, you still believe Social Security is in "crisis," is going "bankrupt," and therefore requires some sort of radical change. Are you really sure privatizing the system would "fix" it? Hopefully not—because you shouldn't be.

Certainly, Wall Street and its political allies want you to believe that privatizing Social Security will automatically mean a huge windfall for the existing Social Security system. In 2000, then–presidential candidate George W. Bush said privatization "will help save Social Security."[78] In 2005, when Bush began pushing his scheme, White House press secretary Scott McClellan insisted that privatization is the critical part of a plan that "fixes the hole in the safety net for future generations."[79] Utah senator

Robert Bennett (R) went even further, stating flatly, "Personal accounts are a long-term fix" for Social Security.[80]

But if we assume that by "saving" or "fixing" Social Security these politicians mean extending the system's long-term solvency and maintaining benefit levels, then we can assume they are deliberately lying. Here's why:

— In January 2005, the *New York Times* reported that while the Bush administration was claiming that a privatized Social Security system "would substantially exceed what the current program can actually pay . . . other analysts, including the Congressional Budget Office, have reached a different conclusion." Specifically, these nonpartisan experts said retiree benefits under a privatized system are "likely to be less than actual benefits under the current system."[81]

— In February 2005, the nonpartisan Center on Budget and Policy Priorities (CBPP) analyzed data from Social Security actuaries and proved that privatization would actually accelerate Social Security's problems. Whereas the current system would stop paying out full benefits in 2042, a privatized system would stop paying out full benefits in 2031.[82] That report was followed up by another one in May that pulled no punches: Privatization "would accelerate the date on which Social Security begins to have a cash-flow deficit as well as the date of insolvency."[83]

— In March of 2005, Republican[84] David Walker, the federal government's comptroller general,[85] told Congress that privatizing Social Security would "exacerbate" Social Security's problems and would mean that the system's "insolvency date would get closer," not farther away.[86] Walker was an expert—before serving as the government's top auditor, he had served as one of President George H.W. Bush's top appointees overseeing Social Security.[87]

Why would privatization be so bad for the Social Security system? Because, as the White House has been forced to admit, privatizing Social Security would cost at least $750 billion in "transition costs."[88] As CBPP notes, that means "diverting large sums from Social Security to the [private] accounts"[89]—depleting the current system of its resources.

This is why, after such rosy proclamations about privatization "saving Social Security," President Bush in mid-2005 was embarrassed into admitting privatization "doesn't fix the system."[90] Yes, he still kept trying to convince the public that it does—but the cat is out of the bag: privatization doesn't fix anything. It makes things worse.

LIE: Real-world examples prove Social Security privatization works.

Galveston, Texas, and Chile don't have all that much in common. The former is a midsize Texas city on the Gulf of Mexico, the other is a South American country. Yet both have taken center stage in the push to privatize Social Security, because both have privatized their own retirement systems.

The claims about these two locales are simple: the two supposedly enacted programs that succeeded in boosting retirees' income, and therefore a privatized Social Security could do the same.

Conservative blowhard Sean Hannity was a big cheerleader pushing this tall tale. On his March 5, 2005, TV show about Social Security, Hannity asked, "You know what I love?" Someone might have cut him off right there and said, "Yourself?" But no, Hannity insisted he loved that "the president is going to have a barnstorming tour, sixty cities. It means something to him, and he's putting the weight of his presidency behind [Social Security privatization] because he knows it's been successful in Galveston, Texas. He knows it's worked in Chile, and he knows it will work here."[91]

The message appeals to Americans' can-do patriotism: If others can do something successfully, so can we (notice, this argument never gets heard when discussing others' success in providing health care to all citizens, better wages, etc.). It is undoubtedly a convincing argument—until you take a peek at what really happened in both places.

Chile's story is rather simple: Before 1981, Chile had a traditional pay-as-you-go pension system like the current Social Security program, where contributions went into safe government bonds. Then Chile's politicians switched it over to a private system, where workers' retirement money was put into the stock market. President Bush has long held up Chile as a model of success, saying during a 2001 press conference that "Members of Congress could take some lessons from Chile, particularly when it comes to how to run our pension plans." He then turned to the Chilean president and said, "Our Social Security system needs to be modernized, Mr. President, and I look forward to getting some suggestions as to how to do so, since you have done so, so well."[92]

"So, so well?" Really?

It is true that raiding workers' hard-earned savings and putting it in

HERO: Ellen Schultz, *Wall Street Journal* reporter

EXPOSING CORPORATE AMERICA'S PENSION RIP-OFF SCHEMES

Few issues are more complex than pensions. With intricate formulas and shell game tricks, Big Business has made an art out of hiding, obscuring, and distorting what it is actually doing with workers' retirement money. Pension reporting, therefore, is a particularly difficult field of journalism, which explains why most newspapers never seriously cover the subject, even though it affects millions of Americans. Yet there is one reporter, the *Wall Street Journal*'s Ellen Schultz, who has stuck to the subject like a junkyard dog. Far from a partisan, Schultz has objectively exposed some of the most questionable pension rip-off schemes Corporate America has crafted. She reminds readers of what a journalist is supposed to be: not a pundit, not a glory-seeking bloviator — but a tough investigator who has mastered her niche so as to not be spun by the usual corporate and political propaganda.

the stock market did slightly boost Chilean corporations. But it also decimated the retirement benefits of millions of ordinary citizens. According to the *New York Times*, "many of the claims initially made on behalf of [Chile's] privatized system proved exaggerated or inaccurate." Ultimately, Chilean workers' private accounts fell prey to investment firms' skimming fees off the top. According to the World Bank, up to a third of a Chilean workers' retirement money went to paying such charges. For many of the country's retirees, that means they will get barely half of what they would have received if their pensions hadn't been privatized.[93] "It is absolutely impossible to think that a system of this nature is going to resolve the income needs of Chileans when they reach old age," admitted Chile's minister of labor and social security.

Facts, though, don't get in the way of Big Business's mythmaking. President Bush has assured Americans that his Chilean-style privatization scheme is "going to make sure you're not gouged."[94] He promises "there's going to be government oversight to make sure that people are treated fairly"—as if we should believe that. After all, this is the same guy whose definition of "government oversight" was sitting by in 2001 as Enron bilked electricity ratepayers,[95] pretending not to notice in 2003 when Halliburton was caught overcharging the government,[96] and twiddling his thumbs in 2005 when oil companies jacked up gas prices to fleece consumers.

But his claims are amplified by an army of Wall Street–sponsored think tanks. For instance, the Cato Institute, funded by financial services companies, actually employs the founder of Chile's disastrous system, José Piñera, as the cochairman of its influential Project on Social Security Privatization. That's about as appropriate as making singer Michael Jackson the president of the Boy Scouts of America.

In his new job, Piñera regularly backs up Bush's pro-privatization rhetoric by publishing articles repackaging privatization as a panacea. Meanwhile, the Cato Institute uses a well-oiled publicity machine to promote Piñera as "the architect of [Chile's] successful privatization of its pension system."[97] Can you imagine the Boy Scouts trumpeting Jackson as "the architect of the Boy Scouts' successful sex education system"? No of course you can't—you'd either laugh out loud or call the police. But the equivalent passes for serious public policy in Washington.

The Galveston story is much the same. In 1981, the city and two other Texas counties opted out of the rock-solid, guaranteed benefits of Social Security and put their public employees into a system of private retirement accounts.* In subsequent years, the Galveston system has been meticulously sugarcoated in an intense propaganda campaign to convince people it has been a screaming success. Texas congressman Kevin Brady (R), a recipient of almost a half million dollars of campaign cash from the financial sector, claimed Galveston retirees get "about twice [the] retirement paycheck as Social Security would have provided."[98] Similarly, the private investment manager who designed the system claimed, "In every case we ever looked at, people end up better off in our plan."[99]

Apparently, they didn't talk to people who actually lived under the plan. Because if they did, they would have found the exact opposite in many cases. "I didn't come out ahead," one longtime Galveston court clerk told reporters in 2005. "My chief deputy did not come out ahead. My bookkeeper did not come out ahead. I personally don't know anyone who has retired who came out ahead."[100]

---

*Such opting out was later made illegal, in 1983, though the counties were exempted because their privatized systems were already up and running.

Similarly, a twenty-three-year Galveston county worker said, "I get around $460 per month now, but under Social Security, I would have gotten $1,000. They are putting this up to be a model for the rest of the country. Some model."[101]

When government auditors researched the system, they came to much the same conclusion. Galveston's low-wage workers retiring today "generally would have qualified for higher retirement incomes had they been under Social Security," said a 1999 report from the Government Accountability Office. Additionally, "Many median wage earners, while initially receiving higher benefits under the (Galveston plan), would have eventually received larger benefits under Social Security."[102]

True, some higher-income workers have done better. But a study by the Social Security Administration found that after twenty years of retirement, Social Security would provide more benefits to all retirees than the Galveston system.[103]

After analyzing the situation, Syracuse University professor Eric Kingson summed it up: The privatization plans in Chile and Galveston that are being held up as models by politicians on Wall Street's payroll "won't work for most people and would destroy Social Security for the vast number of Americans who depend on it."[104] Exactly.

LIE: **There are no ideas—other than privatization— to shore up Social Security.**

Have you ever pretended that your cell phone's reception went out when in fact you just didn't want to talk to the person on the line? Most of us have done it, or have at least considered doing it. Yes, it is dishonest, but in the grand scheme, it is a pretty minor infraction.

The same cannot be said for corporate-owned politicians' imitation of this trick on a grand scale. Since they started their latest push for Social Security privatization at the beginning of 2005, these hacks actually pretend not to hear anyone else's alternative proposals—even as they say they want to hear alternatives.

"Democrat leaders propose nothing," said Republican Party chairman Ken Mehlman in 2005. "No plans, no solutions, no proposals to save [the] Social Security system."[105]

"If you've got a good idea, bring it forward," demanded President Bush in 2005, as if no one had proposed anything other than privatization. "I don't care if it's a Republican idea or a Democrat idea, independent idea, Texas idea, any kind of idea: Bring it forward."[106]

But that's the thing—other rational proposals to shore up Social Security have been out there for years. But because they don't shower taxpayer cash on Big Business, many politicians don't want to acknowledge them. In today's Washington, unless an idea is crafted, vetted, and hand-delivered to lawmakers by a corporate sponsor, it's not considered a legitimate alternative.

For instance, two months before Bush made it seem as if there were no other Social Security plans out there, the *Washington Post* ran a front-page story detailing a proposal by Wisconsin representative David Obey (D) and former Social Security commissioner Robert Ball that would preserve full Social Security benefits through 2078, according to Social Security's own actuaries.[107]

Among other things, their bill would dedicate all revenues brought in from inheritance taxes on multimillion-dollar estates to Social Security. It would also raise the income levels that Social Security taxes are applied to—a concept endorsed even by conservative South Carolina senator Lindsey Graham (R), a Bush supporter.[108] Currently, you pay Social Security taxes on income up to about $90,000 a year. Any income above that is shielded from payroll taxes that fund Social Security, which means lower-income and middle-income families pay a higher portion of their income in payroll taxes than the very wealthy. As Graham said, the wealthy should accept raising the cap "with the whole idea that you're helping people less fortunate than you"—a novel concept to the greedy sharks in Washington.[109]

There was also legislation by Minnesota representative Martin Sabo (D) that would force the government to pay higher interest rates on the treasury bills in the Social Security Trust Fund. Put another way, Sabo's bill would simply mandate the government pay more into the system. The rap on this concept, of course, is that it isn't serious, because it demands more money without prescribing exactly where to find it. But as the *Minneapolis Star Tribune* pointed out, "The president's privatization plan does exactly the same thing." Specifically, "the White House acknowledged . . . that it would borrow at least $700 billion over the next decade to finance the transition to private accounts, a sum that is almost certainly bigger than the obligations entailed by Sabo's plan."[110]

Even if Bush only wanted alternative proposals that put some Social Security funds into the stock market, they were already out there. In 1999, New York representative Jerry Nadler (D)[111] authored a bill to allow an independent board to invest a chunk of the Social Security Trust

Fund into a fixed formula of conservative stock market funds. A similar bill was proposed by Oregon representative Peter DeFazio in 2001.[112] Again, actuaries agreed that both proposals would allow Social Security to pay out full benefits for seventy-five years.[113]

The difference between the Nadler/DeFazio proposals and Bush's is that an entire portion of the Social Security Trust Fund would be invested as a whole, instead of millions of individual citizens' investing relatively small sums of money on their own. Why is the former better? Because it would virtually eliminate the huge broker fees that would be paid to Wall Street under Bush's plan. Additionally, it would make sure any stock market risk would be shared by all retirees, so as to prevent any one citizen from seeing his/her retirement funds decimated by a bad investment.

But that's not what Corporate America wants to hear, so their bought-and-paid-for political allies pretend the proposals don't exist, knowing the media is too lazy to take five minutes to actually research the issue and report it accurately. For instance, after one Bush speech on Social Security, CNN's Judy Woodruff claimed Americans "see the Democrats not even willing to come halfway, not even willing to engage in a conversation" about Social Security.[114] Woodruff seemed to have no idea that maybe — just maybe — that misperception existed because people like her in the media refused to cover Democrats' engagement. But then, her crack reporting was exactly what the White House wanted, because with that kind of "journalism" it seems as if Bush's corporate-backed privatization plan is the only legitimate idea out there.

Solutions

Solving the pension and Social Security squeeze requires us to block out the corporate hypemen trying to convince us that there's a crisis — one that requires pensions to be cut and our Social Security system radically changed, all to the benefit of Big Business's bottom line. Sure, our retirement system has some challenges facing it, but they can be fixed, as long as we have a government that isn't trying to assist those who want to rob us blind.

Be rational about Social Security—and don't try to privatize it. Though Social Security is most definitely not in "crisis," there is a credible argument to be made that we should shore it up, if only to be prudent. But if that's the goal, privatizing the system does exactly the opposite. The whole idea that we need to throw America's most successful retirement program to the wolves on Wall Street in order to "save" it is nothing but a ploy to liquidate the system and pad Corporate America's bottom line. There are a number of well-crafted proposals out there to shore up the system. Lawmakers from both parties were able to come together to strengthen Social Security in the 1980s with a rational plan, and they should be able to do the same today.

Make sure as many retirees as possible get their full pension when they are dumped. When a company dumps its pension plan onto the federal government's Pension Benefit Guaranty Corporation (PBGC), most retirees should be able to receive all the pension benefits they were promised up to a certain point. Today, that point is roughly $46,000—and for many middle-class workers who put in thirty or forty years at their company, that is not even near what they were promised. Though there still needs to be a cap to prevent executives from getting multimillion-dollar pensions after they run their companies into the ground, the cap needs to be raised so that the vast majority of ordinary workers still get their due. To make sure taxpayers don't have to pick up the tab, companies will need to contribute more to the PBGC—and they should not be able to continue getting out of making their required payments, especially when they are reporting profits.

Let retirees know when a train wreck is coming. If federal regulators get wind that a company's pension plan is severely underfunded, they should be legally obligated to let the public know about it, instead of legally obligated to keep their mouths shut. Corporate America naturally doesn't want any disclosure laws at all—companies know that if they can keep their pension shell games under wraps, there will be less public pressure to bear on them to shape up. But this desire to keep people in the dark can ruin lives. Too often, retirees aren't able to plan in advance of their pension being decimated, and more and more of the elderly are thus being forced to go back into the workforce to make ends meet.[115] This has got to stop. The least we can do is give our nation's retirees the right to be warned of the oncoming train wreck before they get run over.

Outlaw cash-balance conversions that don't give workers a choice. Every year, the federal government hands out billions in tax breaks to companies that maintain their traditional pension plans.[116] These breaks are incentives for companies to keep their retirees' benefits intact, and that's fine. What's not fine is continuing to give these tax breaks to companies that force their long-standing employees into "cash balance" schemes that slash benefits and don't give these employees the choice to remain in the pension plan they were originally promised. Bipartisan legislation[117] has already been written to terminate these tax breaks if a company doesn't give its workers a choice—it must be passed.

When the plane is going down, don't let executives use golden parachutes. In a 2005 report on the state of America's pension system, the *New York Times* laid out one of the big problems in a single succinct sentence: "At a time when millions of American workers have seen their pension plans pared back or shut down, and millions more are being asked to bear the risk of managing their own retirement savings, departing chief executives are making out better than ever."[118] Many of these executives pocket lavish retirement benefits at the same time they are pleading poverty and dumping workers' pensions onto the federal government's insurance program—an insurance program that often slashes a retiree's benefits. Executives shouldn't be allowed to have these golden parachutes for their retirement when the rest of the company's retirement system is going down the drain. Legislation by California representative George Miller (D) would prohibit companies that dump their worker's pensions from adding cash to their executives' pension plans.[119] This would provide an incentive for executives to try to save their workers' pensions, because if they fail, they will see their own retirements suffer.

Don't let corporations rip off their workers' retirement nest eggs as a way to cut costs. When Oxford Automotive corporation tried to slash its retirees' pensions, the *Detroit News* reported that a union representative of these retirees "wonders why Congress can pass a bankruptcy bill to make sure individuals pay all their debts, but they haven't addressed corporations walking away from their pension obligations?"[120] It is a good question with an easy answer—eliminating bankruptcy protections for ordinary people while letting Big Business ignore its debts helps Corporate America's bottom line, even if the policies are hypocritical. And because Congress has refused to pass stronger pension laws, this double standard is being stretched to the limit. Companies are being allowed to regularly cut or eliminate the pensions they promised workers as just another way to increase their profits. Congress must step in and pass legislation that would, first and foremost, make sure companies are setting aside the pension money they are promising their workers. The bill should also create regulations that only allow a company to get out of fulfilling its pension obligations if it can concretely prove it had done

HERO: Warren Gunnels, congressional staffer

TRENCH WARRIOR DEFENDING WORKERS' PENSIONS

If you've worked on Capitol Hill, you have probably heard of Warren Gunnels. He's probably left you twenty voice-mails, sent you thirty e-mails, and gotten up in your face at a committee hearing or two. In the process, he has also probably bullied, begged, cajoled, or coerced you into getting the lawmaker you work for to do something— anything—to protect workers' pensions. As the pension expert in Representative Bernie Sanders's (I-VT) office, Gunnels is one of the most tenacious advocates fighting the various rip-off schemes Corporate America has proposed in recent years. In one particularly nasty battle over a proposal to legalize schemes that reduce older workers' pensions, Gunnels commissioned a report showing what would happen to lawmakers' own pensions if their pensions were treated in the same way. The move helped embarrass Congress into outlawing the schemes. And though outmanned and outgunned in his fight, Gunnels shows that even in our nation's capital, where corruption is often rewarded, there are little-known warriors fighting the good fight every day.

everything possible to avoid screwing its retirees. Companies would have to prove they explored alternatives, such as reducing CEO pay packages, eliminating executive perks, and minimizing multimillion-dollar golden parachutes. As Representative Miller said, "The termination of an employee pension nest egg should be the last resort, not simply another way to cut your labor costs."[121]

ON DECEMBER 9, 2002, President Bush announced that he was replacing his treasury secretary with one of America's most powerful CEOs, John Snow of the CSX Railroad Corporation. During the announcement,

Bush lamented that "many Americans have very little money left over after taxes" and that "some struggle under a weight of debt that makes it difficult to save for retirement." He pledged, "My administration will make specific proposals as how best to address these challenges."[122]

Within twenty-four hours, he did release specific proposals—but ones that made the situation worse for workers. Specifically, the administration made public new rules to legalize "cash-balance" pensions—the schemes that allow Corporate America to severely reduce workers' pensions under the guise of offering them "flexibility."

At a public event that day, reporters wanted some explanation of the new policy, considering it would affect millions of workers. But when a reporter asked, "Mr. President, can we ask you about your pension guidelines, sir?" Bush retorted, "No," and then abruptly left the room.[123] It was clear why he didn't want to answer any questions—because it would quickly become painfully obvious that he was once again helping Big Business step on ordinary Americans. As CBS News reported that night, "Corporations love cash balance plans. By restructuring pension contributions, they save tens of millions of dollars every year . . . older workers nearing retirement often lose substantial income."[124]

But Corporate America couldn't let that truth just hang out there, which is why the Associated Press soon reported that "White House spokesman Ari Fleischer said criticisms that cash balance plans hurt older workers are 'not valid.' "[125]

It was one of those insulting statements by a government mouthpiece where both the liar and those being lied to knew it wasn't true. Many of the 8 million workers who had seen their pensions converted to cash-balance schemes[126] had already watched their retirement benefits slashed by up to 50 percent. Yet the government was denying that basic fact.

At this point, fights in Washington usually end, with most seeing the situation as Big Business just confidently stomping out another minor brush fire—but not this time. A group of tenacious lawmakers who had fought pension rip-offs had a novel idea: They would draft legislation saying that if Congress rubber-stamped the president's efforts to legalize cash-balance schemes, on the very same day, congressmen and senators would see their own pension plans converted to those same cash-balance schemes. If, as Bush and his allies said, cash-balance pensions were so great, did not hurt workers, and did not reduce benefits, then there would be no opposition.

Of course, that was the catch—every politician in Washington knew these pension plans were rip-off schemes, even as they were telling Americans how great they were. And the nonpartisan Congressional Research

Service only confirmed that reality in starker terms: It found that converting Congress's pension system to a cash-balance scheme would destroy the retirement benefits of almost every lawmaker in Congress—especially those who had been trying to legalize these schemes. House Majority Leader Tom DeLay (R-TX)[127] and House Speaker Dennis Hastert (R-IL),[128] who led their party in opposition to pension-protection bills, would lose about 60 percent and 70 percent of their pensions, respectively.

When the legislation to convert Congress's pension moved forward, the bill's author, Representative Bernie Sanders (I-VT), said the choice for these and other corrupt politicians in Congress would be simple: "If they think a cash-balance plan is good enough for American workers, why don't they convert their own pensions?"[129]

It was a good question—and one Congress made sure never to answer. On the floor of the House, Hastert, DeLay, and other allies of Corporate America used parliamentary rules to prohibit the bill from even being voted on. "Members of Congress will not reduce their own pensions," an outraged Sanders said. "But they are prepared to force millions of American workers to lower their benefits."[130]

It was no use—the bill was blacklisted and killed, with House leaders making sure it would never see the light of day in a committee hearing or on the House floor again. These shills who were trying to legalize Big Business's rip-off schemes knew that if they went on record voting against Sanders' bill, they would be admitting the phoniness of all their pro-worker rhetoric about how great cash-balance schemes are. And as even the most junior politician in Washington knows, if you get caught deliberately trying to trick the public about one retirement policy, things might snowball. It could quickly become obvious that all the justifications for Social Security privatization and pension "reform" are just more lies designed to hide the one important truth: that Congress is working hand in hand with Big Business, every day, to rip off America's retirees.

CHAPTER

HEALTH CARE

★

SOMETIMES YOU just have to step back and wonder how society has become so desensitized to truly awful news. On the local news, reports about casualties in Iraq quickly fade into the sports highlights and then the weather. On the network news, we see earthquakes in far-off places killing thousands, and then, seamlessly, it is on to the interview with Paris Hilton or Ben Affleck. When the news reports involve sudden natural catastrophes or the deaths of soldiers and luckless civilians in another part of the world, our desire to stick our heads in the sand of celebrity bullshit makes a perverse sort of sense.

But our apathy is mystifying when the catastrophe is unfolding right here at home. The health care crisis in this country can only be called a full-blown catastrophe—one in six citizens have no health insurance at all. That's no small matter: as *The New Yorker* reported in 2005, "the death rate in any given year for someone without health insurance is 25 percent higher than for someone with insurance,"[1] which is why experts agree thousands of Americans die each year because they are uninsured.[2]

Yet, incredibly, the health care crisis rarely takes center stage in our media or our political debate. In the all-too-rare instances when the crisis is covered, it is treated like a subject as remote and unfathomable as a tsunami on the other side of the world. Stories about people whose lives are ruined as they are denied access to medical care and thrown off their insurance plans are considered just another boring fact of everyday life.

In December 2004, for instance, the *Los Angeles Times* told us that while California governor Arnold Schwarzenegger's new budget included no new taxes, it "relied heavily on cuts to health care programs for the poor and elderly."[3] The story made it seem as if the move was just another mundane and acceptable budget tactic.

Two days later, the *New York Times* noted that several states were trying "to deny [health] benefits to poor children." One state, for example, refused to cover the "most basic necessities prescribed by a doctor for a 16-year-old boy with spina bifida." The story was buried on page 24, as if it were barely worth even noting.[4]

The next month, the local paper in Columbia, Missouri, reported that as one of his first acts as governor, Matt Blunt would be eliminating health care coverage for roughly 90,000 of his state's most destitute citizens.[5] These are 90,000 real live people now at risk, mind you, not just statistics. A few Democratic lawmakers protested the move, but they were ignored. Yet at the same time Blunt was citing budget constraints to justify the health care cutbacks, he was pushing a series of new corporate tax cuts.[6] Meanwhile, the Associated Press reported that Blunt's allies in the Missouri legislature decided to "dedicate millions of dollars for professional sports facilities around the state."[7] The whole thing was presented as boring fine print of another complicated budget, instead of a four-alarm outrage.

The media has spouted off a lot lately about how much right-wing politicians supposedly care about "moral values," yet this is the kind of gross immorality those same politicians say we should just accept. Ultraconservative religious leaders demand a "culture of life," yet are largely silent about the culture of death that corrupt politicians have allowed the health insurance profiteers to impose on our society. The media follows the politicians' lead. We saw twenty-four-hour coverage of self-righteous politicians supposedly trying to save the life of Terri Schiavo, the Florida woman in a persistent vegetative state. We saw almost no coverage of those same politicians attempting to gut the health care program, Medicaid, that financed many life-support services for Schiavo and thousands of others.[8]

We are, in short, being conditioned to believe that there is no health care crisis, even as the crisis unfolds right before our eyes. And don't kid yourself—it is a crisis. We live in the wealthiest country in the industrialized world, yet millions of our fellow citizens have no health insurance whatsoever. In the face of that travesty, Corporate America and its political allies are training us to accept it all as an immutable fact of life—as if that's just the way it is and always will be. We are told that the current private, for-profit health care system that has created these atrocities is "the best in the world," even though about 85 million Americans were forced to go without any health care coverage sometime between 2003 and 2004.[9] We are told that any changes to the system will hurt medical quality, even though there is almost no concrete evidence to back that up. We are told that there simply isn't enough money to make sure every citizen gets some basic level of health care, even as our government passes more tax breaks for billionaires that gut the treasury.

How is it that government and media have settled into complacency when the system is so bad for so many? You guessed it—someone is making a fast buck off the status quo. In 2003, health insurance companies (HMOs) nearly doubled their profits from just a year before, adding $4.7 billion to their bottom line, for a total of more than $10 billion in profits.[10] That year, top executives at the eleven largest health insurers made a combined $85 million.[11] In the first three quarters of 2004, HMO profits increased by another 33 percent.[12] The sheer numbers behind these profits are staggering: In 2004 alone, the four biggest health insurance companies reported $100 billion[13] in revenues. That's $273 million a day, every day, 365 days of the year.

That's the kind of cash that allowed the health industry to spend more than $300 million on lobbying in 2003,[14] and another $300 million on campaign contributions to politicians since 2000.[15] The industry's political agenda is pretty simple: use that compaign cash to keep the government out of health care at all costs, even if it means more and more Americans go without any health care at all.

To make its arguments, the industry and other Big Money interests involved in health care buy off high-profile ex-politicians and make them their spokespeople. Take Marc Racicot, one of Corporate America's favorite tools. Once a popular Republican governor of Montana, he left public service to become an Enron lobbyist,[16] then became chairman of the Republican National Committee,[17] and then headed President Bush's reelection campaign. Now, looking again to cash in, Racicot has taken a job as the $1-million-a-year public shill for the American Insurance Association—the insurance industry's chief lobbying group in Washington, which has aggressively worked to keep the government from enacting pro-consumer health care policies.[18] Racicot's direct access to the president will undoubtedly serve him well in his new role.

Another reliable industry whore is former House speaker Newt Gingrich (R). In the health care realm, Gingrich is best known for killing President Clinton's universal health care proposal. That, and having a rather questionable bedside manner: two of Gingrich's ex-wives admit he sought divorces almost immediately after they were diagnosed with life-threatening illnesses.[19] These days, Gingrich is the head of the so-called Center for Health Transformation—a Washington front group for the health industry. He told the *New York Times* his group believes "you have to put the moral dimension first"—as if his organization was just a do-gooder group looking out for the average American. The *Times*, though, quickly pointed out that the for-profit group's members are "mostly corporations" who "pay yearly fees of up to $200,000" to Gingrich's organization for legislative expertise—expertise that helps them push their profit-at-all-costs agenda.[20]

To be fair, those lucky enough to have health insurance can often be apathetic toward the health care crisis because we are conditioned to think it won't affect us. Because they can currently afford coverage, some believe they don't have to worry about the health industry's undue influence over the political system. That is false comfort. Our government not only refuses to do what's necessary to expand health care, it sits back and does nothing as Corporate America quietly shifts more and more of the cost of health coverage onto workers. Big Business and its political apologists claim that corporations are strapped for cash and have no choice but to balance the books on the backs of average workers. That argument is as laughable as Warren Buffett's showing up for a handout at his local soup kitchen. Since 2000, employers have raised employee health premiums three times faster than they have workers' wages,[21] even though corporate profits have exploded.[22]

Just look at some of the recent fights between workers and corporations over health care. In 2004, GM pled poverty, then tried to wriggle out of its contract obligations and convince workers to accept worse health care. Yet GM was sitting on a $20 billion cash surplus, while company CEO Richard Wagoner Jr. received a $2.5 million bonus on top of his $2.2 million in salary that year.[23]

Then there is Wal-Mart—the company that pulls in about a quarter trillion dollars a year.[24] In recent years, a spate of news stories has been written about how thousands of Wal-Mart workers and their families are forced to apply for meager government health care assistance, thanks to the company's refusal to provide adequate health care benefits. But instead of improving employee health benefits, Wal-Mart has done exactly the opposite, publicly denying its nefarious behavior and trying to further shaft workers.

As the *New York Times* reported in the fall of 2005, Wal-Mart's top executive who oversees employee benefits claimed, "Our benefit plan is known today as being generous," even though more than half of the company's employees have no health benefits at all. Her sky-is-not-blue comments came after she sent an internal memo to the company's board of directors proposing "numerous ways to hold down spending on health care and other benefits." One recommendation said Wal-Mart should consider "hiring more part-time workers," whom the company would not have to provide health care benefits to. Another supported a policy "discouraging unhealthy people from working at Wal-Mart" because people who get sick cost more to insure.[25]

Americans are not stupid—polls show ordinary people understand that there is a severe health care crisis in our country right now.[26] Yet few politicians are willing to pay anything more than lip service to the issue. Most opt just to spit up gross distortions that prevent any honest discussion of the issue. Those distortions are hand-me-down excuses honed by the health care industry's lobbyists and PR machine for years. They are designed to make you feel that the system can never be improved and that gross health care atrocities are just the American way. The goal is to make sure corporate profiteering is never scrutinized for what it is: a plague on America's health care system.

LIE: Americans don't want government involved in health care because that would be bad.

Old pros in Washington know one of the easiest ways to kill a good idea is to invoke Americans' fear of a slow, bloated bureaucracy. Government—you remember, that wholesome old friend who paves the streets, picks up the trash, sends Grandma her Social Security check, and, by the way, *we voted into office*—is made into Government-zilla, a huge 70-story-tall fire-breathing monster ruining everything in its path. The White House press secretary, Scott McClellan, invoked Government-zilla in 2004, when he attacked President Bush's opponents for wanting "a government-run system [where] taxpayers will pick up more of the tab" for health care.[27] Republican National Committee Chairman Ed Gillespie, previously head of a firm that lobbies for health care companies,[28] declared that "the American people have rejected a government-run system of national health care."[29]

The language is an effort to scare people. The health industry and its bankrolled politicians believe that anything described as "government-run" will bring up images of a heartless, Soviet-style monolith of paper-

HACK: Newt Gingrich, former Speaker of the House

CASHES IN AFTER FIGHTING AGAINST EXPANDING HEALTH CARE

During the 1990s, House Speaker Newt Gingrich (R-GA) made his name killing most major proposals to expand Americans' access to health care. Now, out of government, Gingrich is heading the so-called Center for Health Transformation—a Washington front group for the health insurance industry. He told the *New York Times* in 2005 that his group believes "you have to put the moral dimension first"—as if he was working for just another do-gooder organization looking out for the average American. The *Times*, though, quickly pointed out that the for-profit group's members are "mostly corporations" (including drug and health insurance companies) who "pay yearly fees of up to $200,000" to Gingrich for his legislative expertise pushing their profit-at-all-cost agenda.

work, waiting lines, and bureaucrats—like something out of a Kafka novel. And they are correct, nobody wants that kind of Government-zilla involved in health care.

There's just one problem for them—most Americans are seeing right through the fearmongering.

According to a nationwide ABC/*Washington Post* poll in 2003, Americans by a 2-to-1 margin, 62 to 32 percent, prefer a universal health insurance program "run by the government and financed by taxpayers" over the current private system.[30] This is not weak support either: the poll showed four in five Americans said it is more important to provide universal health care, even if it means raising taxes, than to hold down taxes and leave some citizens with no coverage.[31] Those numbers were similar to other nationwide polls on the same issue[32]—and they are long-standing. In 1945, when President Harry Truman tried to create a national health care program, 75 percent of Americans supported the idea.[33]

Doctors, too, are chiming in with support. In 2003, the prestigious *Journal of the American Medical Association* published a proposal for government-sponsored universal health care that was endorsed by more than 8,000 physicians (including two former surgeons general).[34]

Even parts of the business community support government intervention. For instance, Ford, GM, and Chrysler all endorsed Canada's system, where the government funds health care for all citizens.[35] Similarly, a poll of Michigan small businesses found that 63 percent supported creating a universal health care system, even it required tax increases.[36] The health insurance industry, you see, is not only gouging patients—it is gouging employers who provide health care benefits to workers.

Still, everywhere you turn there is a politician deriding any proposal to use the power of government to expand health care—a testament to the power and influence of the health care industry over the political system. "When government writes the checks when it comes to health care, they start writing the rules when it comes to health care," said President Bush during the 2004 campaign. "And when they start writing the rules when it comes to health care, they start making decisions for you when it comes to your health care, and they start making decisions for the doctors when it comes to health care."[37]

Sadly, the media report this drivel with little question, even though it would only take one question to deflate Bush's entire argument: If "government-run" health care is so terrible, as he and the health care industry claim, wouldn't Americans hate Medicare? The answer is yes, but they don't—the "government-run" program is widely considered one of the most popular in American history. In fact, polls show that America's elderly, who are covered by the program, are far happier with their health care than the rest of America. That's not a surprise—those of us not on Medicare have to survive in the shark-infested waters of the private, for-profit system that Bush and others say is so wonderful.[38] In other words, our government's own track record shows there's nothing inherently wrong with government involvement in health care. On the contrary, Americans seem to like having the government involved, because it guarantees a minimum standard of coverage, not subject to the for-profit whims of some HMO executive who denies us care in order to pocket a few extra bucks.

What's particularly hilarious about the anti–government health care rhetoric from politicians is that they enjoy some of the finest health care in the world—and they get it from a "government-sponsored" system. Bush, for instance, is treated at the National Naval Medical Center—a "government-run" and "government-sponsored" institution that just happens to also be a world-class medical center. Same thing with Vice President Cheney, who has railed on the concept of a "government-run health care system that dictates coverage."[39] But as a member of Congress, as secretary of defense, and as vice president, he reaped the benefits of having "government-run" health care expertly treat his heart condition. Same thing in Congress. In fighting against universal health care proposals, Texas senator Phil Gramm (R) declared that Americans "won't want and will never tolerate a government-run health care system."[40] Yet he tolerated "government-run" health care for himself almost his entire working life as a politician.[41] And let's be clear—none of these folks renounced or refused to accept their "government-sponsored" health care, nor did they complain about the treatment they were getting from the government.

What these hypocrites really want is a generous government-run health care system for themselves but a private, profit-at-all-cost system for everyone else, even if it means it is so inefficient and expensive that millions of citizens have no insurance at all. That way, politicians get the best of both worlds: excellent, government-guaranteed health care for themselves, and a private health care system for everyone else that—no matter its inadequacies and failures for the average American—generates huge profits and thus massive campaign contributions.

HALF-TRUTH: America has the best health care system in the world.

In 2003, Fox News aired an interview with Chris Viehbacher, a top executive from the pharmaceutical giant GlaxoSmithKline. When asked whether his company was worried that expanding Medicare might cut into the health industry's profits, he responded with one of the most oft-cited reasons for opposing any reform: "This is the best health care system in the world," he said, implying that any changes to the current system might threaten that status.[42]

Viehbacher wasn't entirely lying. For an exorbitantly paid executive at a company that made more than $12 billion in profits that year,[43] America's health care system really is the best in the world, just as it is for other executives, CEOs, fat cats, and professional politicians.

But that's the problem—health care in America is only as good as what you can afford. No matter whether a drug industry executive or the president of the United States tells you "we have the best health care system in the world," the fact remains that America has a survival-of-the-richest system, where it is only the "best" for people who can fork over the cash. For the rest of us, the real story is quite different:

— Studies by the nonpartisan Families USA and Kaiser Family Foundation found that 82 million Americans went without health insurance at some point during 2002 and 2003. Excluding Medicare recipients, that's about one-third of the nation's entire population—and an increase of 7 million from the same study the year before.[44] Almost 20 percent of Americans report being forced to postpone seeking medical care—often because they can't afford it. Of these, more than a third said the delay resulted in a temporary disability that included significant pain and suffering.[45] And in case you drank the right-wing Kool-Aid and thought all uninsured people had no health coverage because they were lazy, think again: 20 million adults who have jobs have no health insurance.[46] By contrast, every other major industrialized country on Earth has a universal health care system that covers all citizens.

— According to the *American Journal of Public Health,* 889,000 deaths could have been prevented from 1991 to 2000 if African-Americans had received, on average, the same health care as whites. To put that in perspective, that's like experiencing the same number of deaths every two weeks as occurred on 9/11—for nine straight years.[47] While racism and other factors play a role, much of that disparity is due to the fact that African-Americans, as a group, make less money, and thus cannot afford the same care in the survival-of-the-richest health care system.[48] Again by contrast, every other major industrialized country has a universal health care system where everyone has access to a minimum level of basic care.

You could argue that these depressing statistics only debunk the "best health care in the world" argument in terms of coverage, but not in terms of quality of care. But even on that score, the argument doesn't hold up. Just look at the cold hard facts, as outlined by author Malcolm Gladwell in a 2005 article for *The New Yorker:*

Americans spend $5,267 per capita on health care every year, almost two and a half times the industrialized world's median of $2,193; the extra spending comes to hundreds of billions of dollars a year. What does that extra spending buy us? Americans have fewer doctors per capita than most Western countries. We go to the doctor less than people in other Western countries. We get admitted to the hospital less frequently than people in other Western countries. We are less satisfied with our health care than our counterparts in other countries. American life expectancy is lower than the Western average.... The United States spends more than a thousand dollars per capita per year—or close to four hundred billion dollars—on health-care-related paperwork and administration, whereas Canada, for example, spends only about three hundred dollars per capita.[49]

This is the story the health industry profiteers and the D.C. elites on their payroll don't want told, but it's the story regular people all over America know a lot about. It is why in 2000 the United Nations' World Health Organization ranked the United States' overall health care system a dismal thirty-seventh in the world. That's behind even countries like Morocco and Costa Rica[50]—countries considered so undeveloped and impoverished, we send them our Peace Corps volunteers as charity.[51] Yet objective experts say our health care system is worse than theirs.

The ranking makes sense, really. America may have the best doctors and facilities in the world, but that doesn't mean we have the best health care *system,* because those doctors and facilities are of absolutely no value to the growing millions who can't afford to use them. When the UN's health experts looked at this picture as a whole, they saw two things: a group of fortunate people who can afford the terrific health care we hear so much about from corporate executives, politicians, and insulated pundits; and then millions of uninsured and underinsured people who have Third World–level health care—that is, slim to none. Average those two together and suddenly the hot air about America having "the best health care system in the world" is exposed for what it is—a dishonest rationale for not reforming the system.

LIE: America can't afford universal health care coverage because it is too expensive.

In 2004, Senate Majority Leader Bill Frist (R) was asked whether America could afford to provide health care to all its citizens. Since he was the first surgeon to head the Senate, some were hoping Frist would address the situation optimistically. Instead, he said "it is impossible to get everybody covered," citing the fact that his home state of Tennessee was supposedly "going bankrupt" trying to achieve universal coverage.[52]

The mind reels at how someone like Frist could claim the government does not have enough money to deal with health care. His comment, after all, came just a few years removed from his family being forced to pay $1.7 billion in criminal and civil fines for trying to rip off Medicare[53] while running the nation's largest for-profit hospital chain, HCA.* Evidently, the Frists believe that there is plenty of health care money lying around to be stolen by well-heeled con artists. But when it comes to health care money for covering ordinary people, well, that's a different story.

The issue came up again in the 2004 presidential debate, when President Bush attacked Senator John Kerry's (D) universal health care proposal. Kerry "wants everybody to be able to buy into the same plan that senators and congressmen get," Bush said derisively, as if the idea of having us common folk get the same health care as the elite was too disgusting for Bush to stomach. He continued by saying that such a proposal "costs the government $7,700 per family. If every family in America signed up, like the senator suggested, it would cost us $5 trillion over ten years." He wanted us to believe the numbers were too huge to ever consider affording, and thus that Kerry was a liar. "It's an empty promise," Bush said. "It's called bait and switch."[54]

But the slimy politician who was engaging in a bait and switch was Bush. The government's own health care experts admit that if we continue allowing Bush's campaign donors in the health insurance industry to profiteer as they have been, the country will be forced to spend not $5 trillion but $20 trillion on health care over the next decade.[55] America, you see, already spends roughly $5,500 per person on health care every year, according to the nonpartisan Congressional Budget Office.[56] That's per person, not per family, meaning for a household of three, we're spending $16,500 per family every year. Compare that with Kerry's plan that Bush said would cost $7,700 per family per year and $5 trillion over ten years, and all of a sudden Kerry's universal health care plan looks like a bargain.

That's because it is a bargain compared with our current system. According to a study by top experts in 2005, "the United States wastes more on [private] health-care bureaucracy than it would cost to provide health care to all its uninsured."[57] That's right—wastes. As the World Health Organization noted in a separate report, 15 cents of every dollar Americans spend on private health insurance goes to administrative expenses. The term "administrative expenses" is a euphemism for the costs incurred by Corporate America's quest for profits: that's everything from filling out

---

*Frist was later the target of an SEC investigation after he sold his HCA stock in 2005—right before the stock price plummeted. Frist claimed the stock was in a blind trust, but the *Washington Post* uncovered evidence that the trustees of the "blind" trust had contacted Frist at least fifteen times about his HCA stock holdings before he sold his holdings. See note 53.

and processing insurance paperwork to padding HMO executives' salaries. By contrast, when the government spends money on public health care programs like Medicare, those administrative expenses consume only about 4 cents of every dollar.[58]

That is one of the big reasons America has the embarrassing distinction of being the wealthiest country on Earth, spending the most on health care on the planet,[59] yet having roughly 15 percent of citizens completely uninsured.[60] It is also why a universal system where the government is the single payer for everyone's health care would eliminate most of that bureaucracy and redundancy, save Americans a huge amount of money, and still be able to extend high-quality coverage to everyone. For instance, the universal health care proposal put forward by 8,000 doctors in 2003 would save about $200 billion a year.[61] That roughly matches a report during the same year showing that if American "administrative" health care costs were limited to Canadian levels, our country would save more than $280 billion a year.[62]

But let's say you don't want a "single-payer" system like much of the industrialized world has. Let's say you just want government to pay for extending private health insurance coverage to the 45 million uninsured Americans.[63] Even that idea is affordable. According to the nonpartisan Kaiser Family Foundation, such an endeavor would cost about $69 billion a year.[64] By contrast, the wealthiest 5 percent of Americans are getting an average of $75 billion a year from the Bush tax cuts.[65] Repeal most of those tax cuts and there's your money for universal health care. Sure, politicians and pundits in Washington paint that as some crackpot idea, but it's not—Americans overwhelmingly support it. A 2003 poll by the Pew Research Center found "two-thirds of the public favors the government guaranteeing health care for all citizens even if it means repealing most of the recent tax cuts," and further, even if it means raising taxes.[66]

Remember, none of these proposals even take into account the amount that many businesses would save with a universal health care system. Consider General Motors. "In 2003 its costs of building a midsize car in Canada were $1,400 less than building the identical car in the United States," wrote former *Washington Post* reporter Morton Mintz, now head of the Investigative Journalism Fund. "Such savings are no mystery. Canadian companies pay far less in taxes for health coverage for everyone than the premiums they would pay" to private health insurance companies in America. In fact, if our country doesn't create a universal health care system soon, we could start seeing some severe economic consequences—consequences like those we saw in 2005, when Toyota turned down hundreds of millions of dollars of U.S. taxpayer subsidies and announced

HACK: Bob Ehrlich, Maryland governor

TAKES WAL-MART CASH, VETOES BILL FORCING BETTER HEALTH BENEFITS FOR WAL-MART EMPLOYEES

In 2005, the *Washington Post* reported that Maryland lawmakers passed a bill to force companies "with more than 10,000 employees to spend at least 8 percent of their payroll on health care benefits—or put the money directly into the state's health program for the poor." The commonsense move was targeted at Wal-Mart, which provides so few benefits to employees that states are having to pick up a bigger and bigger tab for low-income health programs. In response, Maryland governor Bob Ehrlich (R) held a photo-op with one of Wal-Mart's top executives and vetoed the measure, a clear payback for Wal-Mart's financial contributions to Ehrlich's political campaigns. Just months before the veto, in fact, Wal-Mart held a fundraiser for Ehrlich. Clearly, the company got its money's worth.

plans to open up a factory in Ontario, Canada. Why? Because, as officials noted, "Canadian workers are $4 to $5 cheaper to employ partly thanks to the taxpayer-funded health-care system in Canada."[67]

That's correct—the existence of government-sponsored health care is giving other countries an edge over the United States in attracting new jobs. As one top Canadian business executive said, even with higher taxes his country's universal health care system is proving to be "an economic asset, not a burden."

"In an era of globalization, we need every competitive and comparative advantage we have," he said. "And the fundamentals of our [universal] health care system are one of those advantages."[68]

The only industries a universal health care system in America would hurt are the big HMOs, the insurance companies, and the drug companies, all of which continue to rake in obscene profits from the status quo. In the current everyone-for-themselves system, they can dictate high prices because citizens are not organized into large blocs that can negotiate lower prices. People are divided, and so the health industry conquers. A universal system, however, would allow the government to demand huge discounts on behalf of everyone. The billions in health industry profits and "administrative costs" that line health industry executives' pockets and make their way back to politicians as campaign contributions would be put to use actually treating sick people.

LIE: Limiting jury awards will automatically bring down health care prices.

Fresh off an election cycle where his campaign raked in $3.2 million from the insurance industry, President Bush visited Madison, Illinois in early 2005 to pay back the industry for its financial support. Corporate-funded think tanks call the town a "judicial hellhole"[69] because 700 medical malpractice lawsuits were filed there between 1997 and 2003,[70] and Bush was there to spread more corporate lies.

"To make sure our health care system works the way we want it to work," Bush said, "we've got to address the root causes of rising medical costs." Pharmaceutical industry profiteering? HMO scams? Not according to Bush, who blamed the problem on "junk lawsuits: and doctors' "constant risk of being hit by a massive jury award." According to Bush, that is what "drive[s] up insurance costs for all doctors." And, he said, "when insurance premiums rise, doctors have no choice but to pass some of the costs on to their patients. . . . That's the effect of all the lawsuits. It affects your wallet."

His answer to this "problem" was simple: limit citizens' right to seek legal redress against health care providers when they are harmed. If your surgeon absentmindedly cuts off your leg, or your doctor poisons you, sorry, pal—your president says you should only be able to seek damages up to about $250,000. That way, he claims, insurance companies will have to pay out less in damages for the doctors they cover, and they will suppposedly pass on those savings by charging doctors less for malpractice insurance. Doctors will then lower their prices to patients. It is trickle-down health care economics.

Bush's argument seems mildly logical at first, but when looked at closely, it's as structurally sound as a house of cards. There are so many feeble lies involved, the whole thing comes tumbling down after about two minutes of analysis.

First, Bush and the insurance industry regularly claim that "junk" malpractice suits are increasing, meaning insurance companies are supposedly being forced to pay out more in legal fees to defend their physician clients. That is wholly misleading. The Kaiser Family Foundation found in 2005 that the number of malpractice claims per doctor has actually declined over the last twelve years.[71] In fact, even the industry-funded American Tort Reform Association—whose sole goal is to limit citizens' legal rights—was forced to admit that the much talked about "lawsuit crisis" simply does not exist. "There is no question that it is very rare that frivolous suits are brought against doctors," the group's legal counsel told the *Los Angeles Times* in 2004.[72]

Bush and the insurance industry also claim that jury awards in malpractice cases are out of control, meaning insurance companies are supposedly being forced to shell out far more than ever in damages. Again, that assertion becomes a laughingstock after modest investigation. In 2005, the *New York Times* reported that a newly released nonpartisan study showed that "net claims for medical malpractice paid by 15 leading insurance companies have remained flat over the last five years." Yet in that same time period, when less money was going out the door, "net premiums have surged 120 percent."[73] As just one real-world example of this rip-off, consider Washington, D.C.'s largest medical malpractice insurer. Between 2000 and 2004 the company saw its total paid claims decline by 9 percent, yet raised its premiums on the city's doctors in the same time by 51 percent.[74]

So to review: The whole argument for tort "reform" is based on the claim that if insurance companies pay out less in legal fees, they will pass those savings on to doctors and patients. But the data shows that the opposite is happening: the insurance industry is charging higher premiums, even though its legal fees (generated by "junk" lawsuits and jury awards) are not increasing. As a 2005 study by Missouri's former insurance commissioner reported, "over the last five years the amount the major medical malpractice insurers have collected in premiums has more than doubled, while their claims payouts have remained essentially flat." In all, these insurance companies increased their premiums by 21 times the amount their payouts increased.[75]

And that gets us to the most important question: Where is the extra cash going?

Right into the insurance company's pockets, that's where.

According to ISO, a leading industry analyst, insurance company profits rose 29 percent in 2004 to a record $38 billion.[76] That followed 2003, in which the industry's profits rose by almost 900 percent.[77] In all, insurance companies are sitting on almost $400 billion in cash.[78]

Yet even with the industry sitting this pretty, it has spent $200 million on campaign contributions to politicians since 1994, with one goal: get Congress to eliminate victims' legal rights completely, while allowing Corporate America to keep doctors' premiums high—a perfect strategy to maximize their bottom line.

The only thing standing in the industry's way is the truth. Insurance companies' exorbitant profits coupled with data showing their legal fees are flat prove that litigation is not driving up health care costs—insurance industry greed is. That explains why industry executives, desperate to fabricate a rationale for their price gouging, publicly claim that malpractice insurance companies are actually losing money. But that's another lie. According to data from the National Association of Insurance Commissioners, malpractice insurance companies made 6 percent annual profits between 1994 and 2003—a healthy clip.[79]

Still, these companies go to great lengths to hide their profiteering. For instance, studies by the Foundation for Taxpayer and Consumer Rights showed that insurance companies actually cook their books to make it seem as if they are paying one-third more in legal fees and payouts than they actually do.[80] But no amount of cooking can hide the truth: these companies are ripping off America's doctors and patients alike.

If after reading all this data you still don't believe that corrupt politicians' efforts to limit victims' rights is all about profits and not about lowering health care costs or doctors' premiums, then just look at the consequences when these politicians have passed the insurance companies' tort reform agenda into law.

In 2003, financial analysts at Weiss Ratings found that states that had limited jury awards saw doctors' insurance premiums rise 19 percent more than states that had not limited jury awards.[81] Let's repeat that, because it is so damning: In states that had limited victims' legal rights, insurance companies actually raised their premiums more quickly than in states that had not limited victims' legal rights.

The specific examples also provide a good picture:

− The state of California passed a series of laws in 1975 that capped damages victims of medical malpractice could receive. Thirteen years later, insurance companies were charging doctors 450 percent more for malpractice coverage.[82]

− In Ohio, the *Cincinnati Enquirer* reported in 2004 that "more than a year after [the state's] malpractice cap took effect, doctors are paying more for coverage than ever."[83]

– In Texas, the nation's largest malpractice insurance company, GE Medical Protective, actually raised physicians' premiums by 19 percent just six months after Texas enacted a cap on malpractice awards.[84]

At one point in 2005, the insurance industry was actually asked about its profiteering, and its unwillingness to lower rates even in states that had limited victims' rights. The response was—surprisingly—quite candid. "We have not promised price reductions with tort reform,"[85] said the industry's spokesman. Exactly—because those reductions never come. All that comes are bigger insurance industry profits, more campaign contributions, and more proposals to further limit citizens' legal rights.

In 2002 and 2004, the nonpartisan Congressional Budget Office (CBO) tried to explain this reality to federal lawmakers who were considering a bill to limit victims' legal rights. There is "no statistically significant connection between malpractice tort limits and overall health care spending,"[86] CBO said in 2002 when Congress debated insurance industry-written legislation. When it came up again in 2004, CBO reported that "even a reduction of 25 percent to 30 percent in malpractice costs would lower health care costs by only about 0.4 percent"—that is, almost nothing.[87] Because, again, when you limit victims' rights, all you do is let the insurance industry pocket more profits—not bring down the cost of health care.

MYTH: Government involvement in health care will mean rationing, while private insurance doesn't.

In 2004, the nonpartisan group Families USA was asked to testify before a House committee on the issue of health care. The organization is well known and well respected for its work trying to get Congress to pass laws guaranteeing every American a minimum level of health care.

But of course, the hearing was only a formality, really. Congress has no intention of listening to much of anyone who doesn't come bearing a very large check. Nonetheless, the political goons in the employ of the big health and insurance companies understand that in even the most mundane situations in Washington, the truth must be squelched at all costs. So it was no surprise when amidst the boring proceedings, fireworks started.

Michigan congressman Mike Rogers (R) apparently had heard enough about America's health care crisis, especially after he and his comrades in Congress had spent so much time trying to distract the public's attention from the problem. In the middle of the testimony by Ron Pollack, Families USA's executive director, Rogers snapped. "Just so I understand your organization," Rogers said. "You support rationing [and] limited pharmaceutical use?"

It was a nice tribute to McCarthyism—couch an outrageous, unfounded accusation in a seemingly innocent question. Pollock denied the charge. But it didn't stop there. Like a rabid, drooling pit bull snarling at a passerby, Rogers barked, "You support rationing health care for American citizens and limiting the ability for them to have access to pharmaceutical treatment in order to keep costs down."[88]

Rogers might well have screamed "Communist!" had his time not run out. Why was he so aggressively hurling out deceptive accusations during seemingly innocuous testimony? Because he was just doing the job he'd been paid to do: over the previous four years, Rogers had collected $270,000 in campaign contributions from the health care industry,[89] making him just another expensive cog in the health industry's spin machine. That machine has been quite effective over the years in one of its most important goals: portraying any proposal for government-sponsored health care as a dangerous precursor to "rationing."

Rogers is not alone—his claims are parroted by almost every single politician shilling for the health care industry. In 2000, it was New York congressman Rick Lazio (R) who said plans during the 1990s to expand healthcare "would have led to health care rationing."[90] A few years later, President Bush somberly warned us that "government-sponsored health care would lead to rationing."[91] And Montana senator Conrad Burns (R) feigned outrage that Saddam Hussein "controlled his people by rationing, even in health care."[92] That's right, not only is Saddam a mass murderer, but he presided over a country that—gasp!—rationed health care. God forbid that should ever happen here, right?

Except that it does happen here, all the time. We are led to believe that because we have a private, for-profit health care system, we don't have health care rationing in America. That such an incoherent line of reasoning has even been publicly pushed is a tribute to how dishonest our health care debate really is. Just stop for a moment and think about it: *the whole point of for-profit health insurance companies is to ration care* and limit amount of coverage its patients get in order to make money. Even the Supreme Court admits that. In 2000, the justices issued a unanimous opinion noting that the existence of HMOs means "there must be rationing and inducement to ration" care.[93] The ultraconservative *Washington Times* admitted the court made very clear that "it is the point of any

HMO to ration care and within its prerogative to delay tests, avert expensive consultations or refuse experimental care."[94]

This isn't just rationing of noncritical health services. In 2001, for instance, the *Sacramento Business Journal* ran a piece headlined "Medical Rationing." The story uncovered evidence that senior citizens who were receiving cancer treatment were being priced out of their chemotherapy by an HMO that had arbitrarily decided to raise its rates. "For many seniors on fixed incomes, the choice is to die or take a shot at physical survival and life in poverty," wrote the magazine. "This is how the free market rations healthcare. . . . We have the specter of an HMO effectively turning out the elderly to die."[95]

Similarly, a study in 1999 found that about nine out of every ten physicians said that some of their patients had been denied coverage for services that the physician had ordered during the past two years. Between one-third and two-thirds of doctors said that denial of care resulted in a decline in their patient's health.[96] This wasn't optional care that was being denied. Critical care was being rationed and held back from a substantial number of patients because their insurance companies refused to cover them.

Of course, this is not the dreaded *government* rationing of health care, it is *corporate* rationing of health care. But then, why is that any more acceptable to politicians?

Because when Corporate America rations care, it means billions more in profits for wealthy executives, and millions more in campaign contributions for lawmakers. As the Gallup polling organization noted in a 2003 analysis of health care issues, in America "decisions about the prioritization and rationing of healthcare may be driven not by need or quality, but by profit." That's why, despite concerns about how HMOs profiteer and deny coverage to ordinary folks, "much of the healthcare legislation now in Congress proposes to increase private-sector HMO participation"[97]—participation that results in more rationing, and more profiteering.

Beyond just the sheer corruption and deception of all this is the insulting pretense that these politicians actually care that health care rationing is going on in the first place. They say they oppose a government-funded health care system because it would result in rationing. Yet they are the very same people who actually write the policies that force the government to ration.

Yes, the same corporate apologists in Congress who deride rationing are the people who have eliminated funding for veterans' health services to the point that thousands of veterans wait well over six months for basic care (aka: rationing).[98] The same right-wing political ideology that purports to despise the evils of rationing had no problem denying a destitute

HERO: Deborah Ortiz, California state senator

CRAFTS BILL FORCING INSURANCE INDUSTRY TO JUSTIFY HEALTH CARE PREMIUM INCREASES

In 2004, California state senator Deborah Ortiz (D) crafted a bill that would have required HMOs to submit an application for rate increases to the state's insurance commissioner, much as the auto insurance industry must do in many states. Rate increases deemed excessive or unfair would be denied. Unfortunately, health insurance companies spent $1 million on lobbying in the 90 days before the bill got a hearing, and it was eventually voted down. But Ortiz's legislation serves as a model for other states looking to stop health care industry profiteering.

sixteen-year-old boy on Medicaid the assistance he needed to help him afford what his doctor prescribed for his spina bifida (i.e., rationing).[99] The same politicians who say they don't want government to ration health care unveiled plans in Missouri to eliminate existing health care assistance to workers with disabilities (translation: rationing).[100]

In short, politicians criticize government rationing even though they are responsible for it. The truth is, government programs are not inherently bad at providing health care, nor do they automatically ration care. Government programs are as good or bad at providing health care as they are given adequate money to do their jobs. Notice, you never hear politicians complaining that the health care benefits they receive from the government are inadequate or rationed. That's because, unlike programs for veterans or the poor, lawmakers make sure to fully fund their own health benefits.

Why, then, if these politicians say they hate rationing, do they refuse to make sure all government programs have enough funding to prevent rationing?

Part of it goes back to budget constraints: if, like today's politicians, your highest priority is cutting taxes for your wealthy campaign donors and making sure your own personal health care benefits are lavishly funded, you lack enough money to ensure that the other government health care programs can prevent rationing.

The other part, however, surely has something to do with creating a rationale to preserve the current private health care system—a system that permits profiteering by big corporations who fund political campaigns. If the minimal emergency health care that the government provides to the extremely poor is inadequate, withheld, and rationed, Americans can be convinced their only choice is between a flawed, underfunded government nightmare or sticking with the private, for-profit system. It's a false choice, of course, but it is perfectly calibrated to justify the private health care industry and its massive profits.

MYTH: We don't need serious health insurance reform because most people who are uninsured "choose" to be uninsured.

At a town hall meeting with senior citizens in 2000, Montana Senator Conrad Burns (R) voiced one of the biggest myths out there about health care in America. Asked about the roughly 50 million Americans who did not have insurance (including one in five in his own state[101]), Burns said that "most of them elect to be uninsured."[102]

Burns, who has taken $277,000 from the health industry during his career,[103] was soon challenged by his opponents to produce a list of people who "elect to be uninsured." The senator declined. Why? Because his claim was false. As Montana's state government found in its landmark health care study just four years later, "Being uninsured is not voluntary, with 90 percent of the uninsured reporting being unable to buy health insurance after paying for food, clothing, and shelter."[104]

Sadly, Burns is just one example of powerful politicians who make this claim. His argument is a well-crafted, oft-repeated lie. It is a story line designed by the insurance industry to perpetuate the myth that America's health care crisis is driven by citizens' stupid or irresponsible choices. The more this fairy tale is told, the more attention is deflected from the real cause of the problem: The health industry's profiteering, Corporate America's overall wage cutting, and corrupt politicians' acquiescence to both.

The truth is, most uninsured Americans have no health coverage not by choice, but because they can't afford it. Just take a look at the stats:

− In a landmark national survey of the uninsured in 1993, nearly six in ten said they were without health coverage because they could not afford it. Another 22 percent said they were uninsured because they were unemployed, or their employer didn't offer coverage. And here's the most important point: only 7 percent said they could afford insurance but chose not to have it.[105]

– Of the 82 million Americans who were uninsured at some point between 2002 and 2003, more than half came from families making below 200 percent of the official poverty line. That was $37,320 for a family of four—not exactly a lot. Not surprisingly, nearly two-thirds of people in families below the poverty line were uninsured. As the nonpartisan group Families USA reported, "The likelihood of being uninsured decreases considerably as income increases."[106] Wow, who woulda thunk it?

The insurance companies and the bought-off politicians know these facts—and don't necessarily deny them. Instead, they play an Orwellian semantics game whereby the words *choose* or *elects* are substituted for "not able to afford." Had the Families USA report been written by the insurance industry, it might have said "the likelihood of choosing not to have insurance decreases considerably as income increases."

To understand in real-world terms how dishonest this spin really is, consider the Idaho hairdresser interviewed by Harvard researchers in their book *Uninsured in America*. She makes $900 a month in a beauty salon that offers her a pretty meager health insurance plan: she pays $200 a month for a $1,000 deductible. As *The New Yorker* magazine noted, "she could 'choose' to accept health insurance, but only if she chose to stop buying food or paying the rent." Yet when she doesn't buy her employer's insurance because she can't afford it, she is classified as "choosing" to be uninsured.[107]

Politicians have employed truly nauseating tactics to perpetuate this myth. For instance, at a hearing about health policy in 1999, congressmen heard testimony from a woman whose family earns about $12,000 a year and could not afford health insurance—something they desperately needed, because the husband had recurring cancer. At one point, the woman mentioned that she had read something about the health facility in her community on a website. Minutes later, Representative Tom Coburn (R) had the floor. In the previous four years, he had taken $221,000 from the health industry,[108] so he went on the attack. "We had a great example [of] somebody here that makes $12,000 a year, who has Internet access in her home," he said. "She *chooses* to have that, but *chooses* not to have health care coverage. So the question is, What are their priorities?"

First and foremost, the woman never said she had the Internet (or even a computer) in her home—she was probably using a public facility such as a library. But more important, typical Internet access cost about $150 for a year at the time, while health insurance cost thousands. Yet Coburn was publicly attacking the woman and trying to claim that because she had used the Internet, she was "choosing" to go without health insurance. Worse, when Coburn was criticized for his dishonest tactic, he refused to back down, saying, "We all have discretion with the money that we have. Some discretion is used to buy certain things. Others have the discretion to buy health care."[109]

As disgusting and dishonest as this rhetoric is, the media has often regurgitated it as fact. A *Washington Post* article about a 1997 research paper is typical. The headline read "More Employees *Decline* to Pay for Health Plans, Boosting Number of Uninsured." Notice: *decline*—instead of *can't afford.* The article then said "increasing numbers of Americans are *choosing not to buy* health insurance even when their employers offer it"—*choosing not to buy* instead of *unable to buy.* Finally, in the worst example, the *Post* said that "the proportion of workers who are offered insurance through their jobs has increased" and that the study is the first to explore how much of the growing health care problem "is due to *changing choices* made by employees, rather than by the companies for which they work." Again, a reiteration of a dishonest story line: irresponsible people are just deciding not to be insured, even though benevolent companies are trying to fix the problem.

Only until halfway through the article is there any mention that the reason the uninsured rate is rising is "largely economic"—and not because of "choices." Lower-paid workers were overwhelmingly the ones "declining" to pay for health care benefits. And the overall rise in the ranks of the uninsured was occurring "during a period in which insurance premiums rose by 90 percent, four times the increase in wages." Additionally, "fewer employers [were] paying the entire price of those premiums."

That is the real story of America's uninsured, whether Corporate America and its political allies "choose" to believe it or not.

Solutions

Politicians want us to think that solving the health care crisis is as impossible as winning a game of solitaire with only fifty-one cards in the deck, so as to keep us feeling hopeless. But as you'll see, the solutions are pretty straightforward and don't require huge giveaways to the big insurers. It's getting Corporate America and corrupt lawmakers to stop dishonestly stacking the deck that's the hard part.

Extend traditional Medicare to all citizens. Fact: Thousands of Americans suffer and die each year because they can't afford adequate health care. Fact: Even if you don't care about those people, the for-profit health care system is hurting our country by forcing us to spend billions of dollars on an inherently wasteful system, thus creating a huge drag on our economy that affects everyone. One solution is a universal health care system where the government is the single payer. A shorter name for this is "Medicare for Everybody." As economist Paul Krugman notes, "The great advantage of universal, government-provided health insurance is lower costs." Medicare, Krugman notes, "has much lower administrative costs than private insurance." In all, he points out "the savings from a single-payer system would probably exceed $200 billion a year, far more than the cost of covering all of those now uninsured."[110] Medicare is one of the most popular programs in American history. The only reason we don't have Medicare for everybody is that the private insurance companies know such a system would be the end of their legalized profiteering, and they have thus spent millions of dollars on lobbying and campaign contributions to prevent such a reform. How many more people have to die before Congress acts? How many more billions of dollars does our country have to waste before we do what we obviously need to do?

Create minimum health care standards. Short of a universal, single-payer health care system, our government must create minimum health care standards that Big Business must meet, the same way we have minimum wage standards. Just consider Wal-Mart, the wealthiest company in the world, to understand how important this policy really is. Wal-Mart spokespeople and right-wing pundits would have you believe that the company treats its workers terrifically. Yet, because the company refuses to provide health care benefits to many of its workers, Wal-Mart employees are the single largest recipients of government-funded low-income health care assistance in states all over America.[111] Put another way, because there are no minimum health care standards that companies must meet, Wal-Mart is allowed to skimp on health care and rely on state and local governments to pick up the health care tab for its workers. This has to stop. Large, highly profitable corporations must be forced to provide at least some amount of health care benefits to their employees, or reimburse taxpayers for the health care costs their negligence incurs. And before you say that idea is "too liberal," remember it was the Republican

House Speaker in Idaho (not exactly a "liberal" and not exactly a "liberal" state) who announced his interest in this very proposal in 2005.[112] "Rather than taxpayers subsidizing the wealthiest family in the world," he said, referring to the Waltons, "maybe the wealthiest family in the world ought to reimburse Medicaid." Exactly.

Regulate health insurance prices like any other utility. Because you are legally required to have car insurance, most states regulate the rates auto insurance companies can charge you. The rationale for the regulation makes perfect sense: if you are required to buy something, companies should not be permitted to charge you whatever they want for it. It's equally true that some services—even if not officially mandated by the government—are absolutely critical: electricity and water, for instance. And in those cases, government regulates what companies can charge, so no one is left at the mercy of the profit motive when it comes to life's essentials. And really, what's more essential than health care? We all need health insurance, but our government does very little to regulate the prices that insurance companies can charge consumers. That is simply wrong. In 2004, California lawmakers offered legislation to do this but were defeated on a close vote. During the debate, the lobbyist for one major health insurance company claimed, "We are a very low-profit industry,"[113] apparently ignoring the billions in profits the health insurance is making every year.[114] (In fact, just a few months later, that lobbyists' same company reported doubling its profits from just one year before.)[115] The industry fought the California bill by claiming it must be able to freely raise premiums so as to cover rising medical costs. But a 2002 study found that insurance premiums in California increased 250 percent more than medical costs that insurance companies have to pay for,[116] meaning the increases were just fattening the health industry's bottom line. Enough is enough: Health insurance prices should be regulated like any other utility to stop this kind of profiteering.

Regulate malpractice insurance prices for doctors. Politicians continue to claim they want to lower doctors' malpractice insurance rates even if, as shown, they only say that to justify enriching the insurance industry. But if we take them at their word, then there is a very clear way for them to lower malpractice insurance rates: they would stop talking about limiting victims' rights (which as we've seen, has little to do with insurance prices) and start talking about regulating malpractice insurance companies. In 1988, California voters approved a referendum placing limits on how much insurers could charge doctors. The results were stark:

According to the Foundation for Taxpayer and Consumer Rights, "medical malpractice rates in California began to fall immediately . . . within three years of the passage of insurance reform, total medical malpractice premiums had dropped by 20.2% from the 1988 high."[117] That's the kind of thing every state needs to do—rather than focusing on protecting the insurance companies.

THE INSTITUTE of Medicine is not some radical fringe outfit. It was created by Congress to be the chief, nonpartisan adviser to the federal government on all matters related to health care.[118] That's why its announcement in 2004 was so stunning:

"Lack of health insurance causes roughly 18,000 unnecessary deaths every year in the United States," the institute said. Therefore, "By 2010, everyone in the United States should have health insurance. . . . [The institute] urges the president and Congress to act immediately by establishing a firm and explicit plan to reach this goal."[119]

It was a shrill call to arms from deep in the heart of the establishment itself. The health care system, which is supposed to preserve and protect human life, is allowing thousands of Americans to die unnecessarily every year, and America's top medical experts were sounding the alarm.

Reporters naturally asked for reaction from the federal government's Department of Health and Human Services—a department whose official mission is to "protect the health of all Americans and provide essential human services, especially for those who are least able to help themselves."[120]

You would think that mission would mean a favorable reaction to the institute's demands from the agency. But then, that would mean you forgot President Bush had installed former Wisconsin governor Tommy Thompson as the health and human services secretary. In Thompson's last political campaign in Wisconsin before being appointed secretary, he accepted $216,000 from the insurance industry.[121]

Thus, his answer: Universal health insurance in America by 2010, said Thompson, was "not realistic."

"I just don't think it's in the cards," he said.[122]

His admission was, at least, honest. Making sure ordinary people are able to get adequate health care really isn't in the cards in our corrupt political system. The same politicians in Washington who preach about the "culture of life" and "moral values" are too addicted to health care industry cash to care about people who can't afford to see a doctor.

HERO: Marcia Angell, former editor of the *New England Journal of Medicine*

LEADS PHYSICIANS IN FIGHT FOR UNIVERSAL HEALTH CARE IN AMERICA

As the former editor of the *New England Journal of Medicine*, Marcia Angell is one of the most highly respected voices among physicians. That's why it was such a big deal when she penned an op-ed in the *New York Times* pushing for a single-payer, universal health care program. "Many people believe a single-payer system is a good idea, but that we can't afford it," she wrote. "The truth is that we can no longer afford not to have such a system. We now spend more than $5,000 a year on health care for each American—more than twice the average of other advanced countries. But nearly half that amount is wasted." The next year, she led a group of almost 8,000 physicians in supporting a detailed proposal for such a single-payer system. Continuing her work at Harvard University, Angell has been critical in drawing attention to the need for serious health care reform in America.

What's in their deck of cards is clear: more tax breaks for the wealthy, as 18,000 Americans die unnecessarily each year at the hands of our profit-at-all-costs system; more billion-dollar federal contracts for Halliburton, as one in six Americans can't afford health insurance; and more government handouts to already-wealthy drug companies, as the government cuts back programs for the truly destitute.

We do not have a government dedicated to "protecting the health of all Americans," as we are told. We have a bunch of bought-off frauds pretending to care about ordinary Americans but really only interested in protecting the health of one thing: the health care and insurance industries' bottom lines.

CHAPTER 7

PRESCRIPTION DRUGS

★

TURN ON the television for more than five minutes and you will inevitably see an advertisement for a new drug. The ads portray happy people living life to the fullest, amped up on whatever fix the company is hawking. Purple pills falling from the sky, middle-aged Viagra fiends chasing after their wives, Cialis-stoned seniors salivating on Sunday morning—it is horny and healthy America brought to you by our friendly neighborhood pharmaceutical industry.

But the images are an illusion: We're not going to look as good as those TV people when we're older, we're probably not going to have the sex drive, and, most important, we're not going to be able to afford the pills. Because behind this drug-crazed Nirvana is an industry that has one thing and one thing only on its mind: making huge amounts of money, and making sure the American government helps pharmaceutical companies squeeze every last dollar out of the general population, no matter what the cost to society.

Here's the real story you don't see on TV: at the same time drug industry fat cats are bathing themselves in cash, more and more Americans are unable to afford their medicines. While seniors are skimping on their pills to save money, a 2001 study showed the average pharmaceutical executive rakes in more than $780,000 a year,[1] with drug company CEOs often making millions more.[2] While American taxpayers pay for roughly a third of all research costs for drugs, we are rewarded for our investment by being charged the highest prices in the world for medicine. At the same time, desperate citizens take buses to Canada in search of lower prices, bankrolled politicians push to crack down on drug importation while refusing to mandate lower prices in the United States.

The results of this rip-off scheme are stark: Drug prices are rising at almost four times the rate of inflation[3] as Congress sits and twiddles its thumbs. In 2003, Americans spent $179 billion on prescription drugs—up more than $17 billion from the previous year. Pharmacists are forced to simply turn away seniors who can't afford their medications. As one pharmacist told his local news station, "They start crying in front of me, telling me they cannot afford [their prescriptions] and it breaks my heart."[4]

And the problem is now spreading like wildfire through the economy. Businesses large and small are being forced to either pay more for their employees' drug coverage or drop their health care benefits altogether. For instance, in 2002 high drug prices forced General Motors to cough up $1.4 billion to cover its employee and retiree prescription drug coverage.[5] That's $1.4 billion from one company straight into the drug industry's coffers. Thanks in part to this profiteering, one in ten firms in 2003 completely eliminated health care for their future retirees, and almost three-quarters forced existing retirees to pay more for their benefits.[6]

Though drug companies deny they profiteer, they have inadvertently admitted their price gouging ways. In 2004, Novartis pharmaceuticals, one of the world's biggest drugmakers, actually sent a memo to its own employees asking them to refrain from using their health insurance to purchase brand-name medicines. The reason? The drug company was having trouble paying the astronomical drug prices in the United States. "Every major company in the U.S. has felt these increases and, as a result, many corporations are reducing or restricting their benefits coverage for employees," complained Novartis's CEO Paulo Costa, as if his company was the helpless victim of spiraling drug costs and not one of the perpetrators. Worse, Novartis asked employees to start using more generic medicines—apparently forgetting that Novartis and the pharmaceutical industry as a whole have been fighting tenacious court battles to protect their patents and prevent lower-cost generics from reaching pharmacy shelves.[7]

You might expect such price gouging and subsequent pleas of poverty to come from a cash-strapped industry that was just getting by. But the drug industry is one of the most profitable industries in America. In 2002, the top ten drug companies made more than 18 cents in profit for every $1 of sales—eight times the average profit margin for all other Fortune 500 companies.[8] The next year, these ten companies made $35.9 billion in profits—more than the combined total profits of the other 490 companies on the Fortune 500 list.[9]

It is this ocean of money that has made sure Congress sits by while a public health crisis unfolds. Each year, as seniors fork over more of their Social Security checks to drug industry executives, a portion of those enormous profits are recycled back into the political system. Since 1997, the industry has spent nearly $478 million lobbying the federal government—and remember, that's $478 million at the same time the drug industry says it can't afford to lower drug prices.[10]

That cash has bought the industry 675 well-heeled lobbyists in Washington[11] to make sure it always gets its way. In military terms, that is the equivalent of a battalion[12]—only this is a battalion of mercenaries fighting tooth and nail for the drug industry's bottom line.

The arsenal at the lobbyists' disposal brings up notions of the Empire from Star Wars—instead of star destroyers, each drug company has its own well-funded political action committee that, over the last decade, has blasted more than $100 million into the political system in the form of campaign contributions.[13] That's more than $27,000 a day, seven days a week, for ten years—all to America's leading political figures.

Instead of Darth Vader, drug companies have CEOs who double as top campaign fundraisers. In the last election alone, fifteen pharmaceutical/health products executives[14] were among President Bush's Pioneers and Rangers—those who personally raised him more than $100,000 and $200,000, respectively.

Instead of storm troopers, the pharmaceutical industry has operatives who go in and out of government jobs to do their dirty work. For instance, President Bush installed one of the drug industry's top lobbyists, Ann-Marie Lynch, to a key position at the Department of Health and Human Services (HHS). The *Denver Post* reported that as a lobbyist, Lynch had "fought congressional attempts to cap prices for drugs." And soon after her appointment to HHS, the government office she headed issued an official report criticizing drug price controls.[15]

There's more.

Bush made an Eli Lilly lobbyist the White House's top health policy adviser,[16] who then let the pharmaceutical industry write sections of the administration's Medicare bill to make sure it gave away billions to the drug companies, without securing lower prices.[17] Bush also appointed an

Eli Lilly vice president to head the White House's budget office.[18] The administration subsequently tried to pass a bill shielding Eli Lilly from lawsuits brought by families whose kids had been hurt when the company blew off scientific warnings[19] and allowed mercury into its childhood vaccines.[20]

And Bush even appointed Eli Lilly's former CEO, Randall Tobias, to be the State Department's Global AIDS coordinator, heading up a new $15 billion fund to fight AIDS in the developing world. Within a year it was clear why Tobias had been chosen for the job. The Associated Press reported that Tobias made sure that the fund "can only buy brand-name drugs, usually [from] American [companies], shutting out cheaper generic medicines." In other words, the AIDS fund was being manipulated to put drug industry profits first.[21]

Backing up these storm troopers, of course, is the Death Star: the Pharmaceutical Research and Manufacturers of America (PhRMA)—the drug industry's all-powerful Washington trade association. The organization is now headed by former Republican congressman Billy Tauzin, who took the multimillion-dollar job just one year after he authored the House version of the Medicare bill.

Known as the most powerful organization in Washington, PhRMA watches over everything, and when challenged, has the power to blow even the most important legislation to smithereens. Sure, PhRMA presents itself as an innocuous representative of "companies that are devoted to inventing medicines that allow patients to live longer, healthier, and more productive lives."[22] But under the veneer is a sophisticated political attack machine that employs every weapon—no matter how dishonest and unethical—to get its way.

For instance, when bills arose in 2000 to force drug companies to lower their prices, PhRMA created a front group called Citizens for Better Medicare[23] to air $30 million in attack ads against lawmakers who supported the legislation. Representative Rosa DeLauro (D), a drug industry critic, pointed out just how fraudulent the group really was. "These are not citizens [and] they are not for a better Medicare." No matter. The group soon tried to confuse and manipulate seniors, airing ads "enticing twenty-somethings to call their grandparents and urge them to lobby" against lower prices, according to the *New York Times*.[24] The legislation was defeated.

In 2002, though, the public still wanted lower drug prices. PhRMA responded by directing $20 million worth of spending on congressional races, while getting one of its front groups to kick in another $17 million

HACK: Tom Scully, administrator of Medicare

"WAIVER" HELPS HIM GET JOB WITH DRUG INDUSTRY AS HE WAS CRAFTING MEDICARE LEGISLATION

Under the law, top government officials are not allowed to solicit job offers from industries they are supposed to be regulating. The point is to prevent government regulators from doing something in their official capacity that might help them get a high-paying private sector job afterward. Enter Medicare chief Tom Scully. In 2003, the *St. Petersburg Times* reported that "while [Scully] was deeply involved in drafting the new Medicare legislation . . . he also discussed job offers with firms that have a financial interest in the bill." How was he allowed to do this? He got a so-called ethics "waiver"—a piece of paper from his friends in the White House that said he could ignore the law. Ultimately, Scully landed himself a high-paying job as a health care and pharmaceutical lobbyist just weeks after he made sure the new Medicare bill was passed—a bill that gave away billions to the health care and pharmaceutical industries, which he subsequently went to work for.

for a television ad campaign featuring actor Art Linkletter defending Republicans who favored an industry-written plan.[25]

The result is a political system that behaves like a wholly owned subsidiary of America's drug industry—and everyone knows it. As one local Missouri newspaper lamented, "You can almost see the dummy sitting in the ventriloquist's lap. Every time the government has had an opportunity to help consumers, it has instead protected the drug industry's interests."[26] That's right, when Big Pharma gets involved, all principled pretense is shoved to the side: Congress's "free" traders become protectionists, its penny-pinchers become spendthrifts, and its small-government populists become corporate welfare queens—all to make sure the average American keeps padding Big Business's bottom line.

SCARE TACTIC: Lower drug prices will mean less innovation.

Any effort by Congress to lower drug prices in America is inevitably met with alarmism by the drug industry. "Price controls stifle innovation," said PhRMA's now-retired president Alan Holmer, "They delay the availability of important new medicines to patients."[27] Arizona Republican senator John Kyl, inspired by the $143,000 he's taken from the pharmaceutical/health products industry,[28] took the argument one step further. Instead of talking about how high drug prices prevent thousands of citizens from getting the medicines they need, he claimed lower drug prices would be the real health hazard. "If America were to adopt price controls," Kyl said, "countless lives that could have been saved will not be."[29]

Kyl is not alone in making such an absurd argument with a straight face. He is joined by a chorus of industry-financed organizations in Washington. For instance, the Progressive Policy Institute, which has taken money from the likes of Pfizer and Merck,[30] says, "Republicans have rightly opposed U.S. price controls for Medicare prescription drugs."[31] The pious Senator Daniel Patrick Moynihan (D-NY), who pocketed more than $77,000 from the drug industry in his final reelection campaign,[32] said that if America tried to control drug prices "a period of enormous innovation, very recent in the history of medicine, will come to a close."[33]

The argument sounds pretty good, if the industry really was plowing most of its revenues back into researching and developing new drugs. But it isn't. As the watchdog group Public Citizen reported in 2002, most major drug companies devote twice as much of their budgets to advertising and "administrative costs" (read: executive salaries and profits) as they do to R&D.[34]

The secret the industry would rather you not know is that you the taxpayer, not the drug companies, have underwritten much of the nation's meaningful research and development. Through the National Institutes of Health (NIH), taxpayers are funding about one-third of all biomedical R&D.[35] From 1955 to 1992, for example, 92 percent of drugs approved by the FDA to treat cancer were researched and developed by the NIH.[36] And that doesn't include the massive drug industry tax credits our government shells out. Between 1990 and 1996, drug companies received $27.4 billion in R&D tax credits—and the amount has only grown since.[37] These are tax credits, mind you, to companies that are already raking in record-breaking profits.

Though the pharmaceutical industry loves to air commercials showing their earnest, white-coated scientists peering at beakers and saving lives, the *New England Journal of Medicine*'s Marcia Angell notes, "The innovative drugs come almost entirely from publicly funded research done in universities and government labs"[38]—not from drug companies. In fact, much of the R&D done by the drug industry itself is devoted to copying already commercially successful medicines rather than creating new ones. Thus, we see a proliferation of Viagra pawn-offs like Cialis that makes huge profits in rich countries, and a dearth of drugs to cure or control afflictions like malaria,[39] a disease that kills thousands every year in poor tropical regions.

These facts, of course, don't stop some of the most ardent corporate sellouts in the U.S. Senate. Take Louisiana Senator John Breaux (D), who between 1998 and 2004 took $145,000 from the drug industry.[40] In 2004, he not only criticized the idea of price controls in America but actually blamed price controls in other countries for America's high prices. "The rest of the world is sticking it to us," Breaux bellowed at a Senate hearing, saying Congress must use its power not to lower prices at home but to force other countries to allow price gouging. American allies aren't going to act, he complained, "unless there's some huge hammer someone's putting over their heads."[41]

Breaux expects the public to believe that if other countries raise their prices, drug companies out of the goodness of their hearts will lower their prices in America. The argument is either inanely naïve, or a deliberate lie. If European prices suddenly went up, what incentive would the drug companies have to lower prices in America? None. Instead, they would just pocket more cash, as Breaux well knows.

To bolster their claims that lower prices would hurt R&D, politicians claim drug companies can't even afford to do research and development in places like Europe, where medicine costs less because of price regulation. But as Princeton University's Uwe Reinhardt notes, "The truth is that R&D spending [as a percentage of drug industry revenue] is equal or higher in Europe than here"—even though the European market has price controls. For instance, the price-controlled British drug industry spends about 20 percent of its revenues on R&D.[42] In America, drug companies spend just 14 percent.[43]

In reality, the jihad against lower drug prices is motivated not by a concern for R&D, but by pure greed. Industry-backed politicians may claim higher prices mean more R&D and thus better health care. But in the face of all the evidence that refutes this theory, it's clear the debate is all about money. Higher prices mean higher executive salaries and more campaign contributions. Those contributions make sure the power of Congress is used not to protect the consumer but to make sure every ordinary citizen on Earth pays astronomical prices for medicines.

The proof is everywhere you look. In 2000, for example, an anonymous U.S. senator added a provision extending the patent for Claritin to a massive unrelated bill. The allergy drug was making Schering-Plough roughly $2.7 billion a year thanks to patents that prevented a cheaper generic version from being produced. When the nonprofit Seniors Coalition offered a $1,000 reward to anyone who would reveal the identity of "Senator Anonymous," Utah's Senator Orrin Hatch (R) stepped forward and admitted he was the perpetrator.

As the chairman of the Senate Judiciary Committee that oversees patents, Hatch is perennially among the top recipients of drug industry cash and perks. In fact, at almost the very same time he was trying to extend Claritin's patent, Hatch was using Schering-Plough's private jet for his presidential campaign travel. Additionally, Hatch's son and former chief of staff were employed by Schering-Plough's lobbying firm.[44] The Center for Responsive Politics, a nonpartisan watchdog, said "Orrin Hatch's relationship with Schering-Plough is one of the most blatant things we've seen in terms of whether money plays a role in what happens on Capitol Hill."[45]

The same kind of thing happened three years later during the debate over a new Medicare bill. Democrats proposed letting federal officials use Medicare's bulk purchasing power to negotiate lower prices for prescription drugs from drug manufacturers. It seemed like a simple idea—if you're buying medicine for millions of Medicare recipients, those big-volume purchases can be leveraged to negotiate discounts. It's the same rationale that companies like Costco and federal agencies like the Department of Veterans Affairs use to secure discounts of up to 50 percent off the regular price of goods they purchase. In fact, almost every other industrialized nation on the planet does this kind of thing to save money.[46]

But to politicians who don't think the drug industry's 18 percent profit margin is enough, money trumps everything. House Majority Whip Roy Blunt (R-MO) bragged to reporters about allowing industry lobbyists to set up a "war room" in his Capitol office to make sure the final Medicare bill was exactly what the drug companies wanted.[47] Republicans soon slipped in a provision prohibiting federal officials from negotiating lower prices. In response, some lawmakers tried to find out whether the prohibition would mean the final bill would cost substantially more. But the White House threatened to fire the government's top health care actuary if he admitted the truth, and told lawmakers the bill would actually cost hundreds of billions of dollars more than the White House said it would cost.[48] (Congressional investigators later found the threats to be a likely illegal abuse of power—but did nothing about it.)[49]

Taxpayers got screwed in the deal, but those doing the screwing made out like bandits. The drug industry will make hundreds of billions of dollars off the final legislation—including an additional $139 billion just from the provision that bans Medicare from negotiating lower prices.[50] Those profits will surely trickle down to people like John McManus, the House Republicans' chief health policy expert who was hired as a PhRMA lobbyist four months after the Medicare bill passed.[51]

They will also line the pockets of people like Tom Scully, who left his position as Medicare administrator to become (surprise!) a lobbyist for the drug industry right after the bill was signed.[52] Scully actually went the extra mile and got his corrupt behavior rubber-stamped by his higher-ups: Months before leaving government service, he convinced his White House cronies to give him a euphemistically named ethics "waiver." What's that, exactly? A piece of paper that said Scully could ignore regulations barring him from negotiating a job from the drug industry he was supposed to be regulating as a government official.[53]

Presidential candidate Senator John Edwards (D-NC) tried to raise public awareness of this unethical behavior. "This is an all-too-familiar example as to why we need to stop this revolving door," he said on the campaign trail. Feigning indignation, Iowa Republican senator Chuck Grassley responded by claiming he wanted an investigation into Scully's behavior,[54] but Grassley's grandstanding ended when he realized that his top health policy adviser was following Scully to the same ritzy lobbying firm.[55] Montana Democratic senator Max Baucus, Grassley's counterpart on the Senate Finance Committee, could have pushed an investigation, too. But his chief of staff (now a registered PhRMA lobbyist)[56] was setting up his own pharmaceutical lobbying shop as the bill's ink was still drying.[57]

But don't blame any of these people alone for their corruption. They are part of the larger cabal in Washington that is so divorced from reality it believes lying about the connection between drug prices and drug R&D is acceptable, and that institutionalized bribery is the only possible way to operate. As John McManus asked upon becoming a pharmaceutical lobbyist, "What am I supposed to do? Dig ditches?"[58]

HYPOCRISY: Taxpayers shouldn't get a return on their investment.

One of the arguments most often used by the drug industry to fight price controls is capitalism. They argue that if they take the risk of investing huge amounts of money into a new drug that might not ever come to fruition, they should reap a big payoff if and when they do develop a successful product.

It seemed only fair, then, for the same rationale to be applied to taxpayers. During the 1980s, Congress required drug companies to offer medicines developed at taxpayer expense at a "fair and reasonable" price to Americans. The law said that since taxpayers take a financial risk by investing in this research, taxpayers should reap a benefit—namely, the right to affordable prices for drugs the public paid for.

Apparently, though, what's good for the drug industry isn't good for the rest of us. In 1995, the Clinton Administration repealed the "reasonable pricing" rule,[59] effectively encouraging drugmakers to price-gouge even on medicines taxpayers paid to develop. Soon, drugs developed at taxpayer expense were being sold to Americans for the highest prices in the world.

According to a 1998 exposé by the *Boston Globe,* Biogen charged more than $11,000 a year for a supply of the multiple sclerosis drug Avonex, even though it was developed with $4.6 million in government aid. As one multiple sclerosis patient who couldn't afford the medicine said, "They take my tax dollars, it benefits the companies, and I don't get any use out of it."[60]

Johnson & Johnson marketed the anticancer drug Levamisole to Americans at 100 times its cost to produce, despite the drug being developed with an $11 million NIH grant.[61] According to ABC News, the price gouging for the medicine was so obscene that low-income colon cancer patients were being forced to turn to the black market to buy a livestock medicine that consisted of ground-up Levamisole. That livestock medicine, which was exactly the same as the human medicine, was being sold to farmers for 6 cents a dose, but that price was only available legally for farm use. For human consumption, the price was far higher, even though it was the exact same product, meaning colon cancer patients had to risk their luck by breaking the law to afford the medicine they needed. If the medicines were exactly the same, why was the company selling the medi-

HACK: Orrin Hatch, Utah senator

TRIES TO ANONYMOUSLY GIVE THE DRUG INDUSTRY A GIFT

In 2000, an anonymous U.S. senator inserted a provision in a massive bill that extended the patent for Claritin, the allergy drug that was making Schering-Plough roughly $2.7 billion a year. The patent would allow the company to prevent competition and keep charging high prices for the medicine. When the nonprofit Seniors Coalition offered a $1,000 reward to anyone who would reveal the identity of "Senator Anonymous," Utah's senator Orrin Hatch stepped forward and admitted he was the perpetrator. As the chairman of the Senate Judiciary Committee, which oversees patents, Hatch is regularly among the top recipients of drug industry cash. At almost the very same time he was extending Claritin's patent, Hatch was using Schering-Plough's private jet for his presidential campaign. He was also probably working with Schering-Plough's lobbying firm Parry & Romani, where his former chief of staff and his son both worked. The Center for Responsive Politics, a nonpartisan watchdog, said, "Orrin Hatch's relationship with Schering-Plough is one of the most blatant things we've seen in terms of whether money plays a role in what happens on Capitol Hill."

cine for human use at a higher price than for farm use? Because "a sheep farmer probably would not pay $6 a pill," said Johnson & Johnson's CEO. Left unsaid was the fact that someone dying of cancer might, even if it means skimping on bare necessities.[62] Thus, the difference in prices.

Similarly, Abbott Laboratories jacked up the price of its key AIDS drug Norvir by 400 percent in one year,[63] despite the drug having been developed with $3.2 million of federal money.[64] When Abbott faced questions about its move, the company's CEO said, "Abbott is absolutely committed to ensuring that . . . not a single patient goes without Norvir because of the repricing." Yet he refused to reverse the price hike.

Activists then petitioned the government to invoke a 1980 law that authorizes other companies to manufacture lower-priced, generic copies of taxpayer-financed drugs to address emergency "health or safety needs."[65] Not surprisingly, the petition was rejected.

There are countless other examples. As the *Boston Globe* found in its 1998 report, 45 of 50 top-selling drugs were the product of government research subsidies totaling nearly $175 million—and you can bet almost all of these drugs were sold to Americans at exorbitant prices.[66]

In response to the situation, Representatives Bernie Sanders (I-VT) and Dana Rohrabacher (R-CA) have repeatedly offered legislation reinstating the reasonable-pricing rule, attempting to shame Congress into doing the right thing. In 2000, they actually got close. In a debate on CNN, Sanders hammered Ways and Means Committee chairman Bill Thomas (R-CA) for his opposition to the reasonable-pricing rule. Thomas, the House's top recipient of drug industry cash, was backed into a corner. "I agree with you that where taxpayer dollars are invested in research, taxpayer dollars should get a fair return on any profit from that research," he said. "There is no reason why [taxpayers] shouldn't get a fair return on their investment just like the pharmaceutical companies when they spend their own money." Thomas then told Sanders on-air, "Bernie, see me on the floor and we'll work on your legislation."[67]

But when Sanders tracked down Thomas after the debate, the chairman refused to support the legislation, and when the bill came to the floor, Thomas fought it tooth and nail. But it wasn't enough. The House passed it.

No worries for the drug industry, though. When the legislation was considered by the Senate, it was voted down, with eight Democrats joining all the Republicans to protect the drug industry's profits. The next year, the same thing happened. The bill was initially tacked on to a larger piece of legislation and passed by the House. But when the final legislation was negotiated between House and Senate lawmakers behind closed doors, it was stripped out. Drug industry shills smugly claimed the reasonable-pricing bills were defeated because there was "compelling evidence that taxpayers are getting a significant benefit from the relationship between industry and NIH."

"[There is] a payoff of 15 times taxpayers' NIH investment," claimed one PhRMA spokesman.[68]

Try telling that to the fixed-income cancer patient whose taxes were used to develop drugs and who then couldn't afford the exorbitantly priced medicine those taxes helped finance.

RED HERRING: Drugs from other industrialized countries are unsafe.

In the 1960s and 1970s, many draft-age men headed to Canada to avoid military service during the Vietnam War. Today that same generation is older, but they are once again heading north—this time to avoid the pharmaceutical industry's price gouging.

Using buses and Internet pharmacies, roughly 2 million Americans[69] are now getting their prescriptions filled in Canada. There, prices for brand-name medicines are up to 80 percent cheaper[70] than in the United States, mostly because the Canadian government has laws that prohibit pharmaceutical industry profiteering.

Those who head to Canada to buy prescription drugs are technically violating U.S. law. Though the North American Free Trade Agreement (NAFTA) was supposed to permit the free importation of every commodity, the pharmaceutical industry made sure to pay off enough lawmakers to preserve federal laws specifically forbidding consumers from importing one product: medicine.[71]

The public rationale for this drug importation ban is "safety." As PhRMA's Alan Holmer claimed, drugs made abroad "greatly increase the risk that America's medicine supply would be corrupted" by unsafe counterfeits.[72]

The first problem with this argument is its sheer hypocrisy. Why is it okay to freely import vegetables from other countries that caused mass hepatitis outbreaks in Pennsylvania in 2004, but not okay for consumers to import lower-priced medicines they needed?[73] Why can big food-processing companies still import beef from Canada after discoveries of mad cow disease there,[74] but low-income seniors can't import more affordable cancer drugs to treat their illness?

The second problem with the safety argument is that the drug industry is already importing medicine into the United States from all over the world.[75] While trade law prevents average citizens from buying medicine from abroad, it permits drug companies to import those medicines themselves.[76] This loophole was designed so that drug companies can set up manufacturing plants in lower-wage countries to save on overhead costs and then import the finished products back into the United States for sale to consumers at inflated prices. Apparently, safety is only a concern when it means lower prices for ordinary people, and cost savings are only important when they pad Big Business's bottom line.

Of course, while these first two examples of hyprocrisy are valid, they would still be moot if there really is evidence to back up the claim by Bush's Food and Drug Administration (FDA) officials that imported medicines "expose the public to significant potential health risks."[77] That rationale is invoked as the trump card by President Bush. He said in 2004, "What I don't want to do is be the president that says we'll allow for importation, and all of a sudden drugs that are manufactured somewhere else come in over the Internet and it begins to harm our citizens."[78]

Sounds like a pretty strong argument, right? Wrong. As Minnesota Republican governor Tim Pawlenty said in pushing to legalize imports, "My first response to that [safety argument] is show me the dead Canadians. Where are the dead Canadians?"[79]

He's right. If drugs from Canada and other industrialized countries are so unsafe, why haven't there been mass casualties in those countries? Better yet, where are all the dead Americans who have already evaded the law and driven to Canada for cheaper medicines?

The answer is, they don't exist. As Knight Ridder newspapers reported in 2003, "FDA officials can't name a single American who's been injured or killed by drugs bought from licensed Canadian pharmacies."[80] Similarly, Canada's health ministry reported that it "does not have any information that would indicate that any Americans have become ill or have died as a result of taking prescription medications purchased from Canada."[81] It is why, under pressure, President Bush suddenly forgot his politically motivated opposition to drug imports and said in 2004 that the United States would try to buy flu vaccine from Canada to deal with a domestic shortage[82]—because there really is no safety concern.

Even some drug executives are now coming clean about the lie. Peter Rost, a vice president of Pfizer who oversaw the company's European operations, first blew the whistle in 2004. "The safety issue is a made-up story," Rost said. "The real concern about safety is about people who do not take drugs because they cannot afford it."[83] He noted that country-to-country importation has been done in Europe for two decades, and in that time he "never, not once, heard the drug industry, regulatory agencies, the government, or anyone else express any concern related to safety."

For his willingness to speak out, Rost was investigated by Pfizer officials, and harassed by the company's lawyers in a brazen effort to shut him up.[84] But he refused, hitting the campaign trail in 2004 to face down corrupt politicians who continued parroting the drug industry's lies. In

HERO: Peter Rost, vice president of Pfizer

EXPOSES LIES USED TO PREVENT CONSUMERS FROM BUYING LOWER-PRICED MEDICINE

The pharmaceutical industry has for years claimed that allowing Americans to buy lower-priced medicines in Canada or Europe would be "unsafe." Though the industry has no proof, its lobbyists continue to use this red herring to defeat bills to allow drug importation. But in 2004, a top drug industry executive blew the whistle. Peter Rost, vice president of Pfizer, told reporters, "The safety issue is a made-up story." He noted that country-to-country importation has been done in Europe for two decades and in that time he "never, not once, heard the drug industry, regulatory agencies, the government or anyone else express any concern related to safety." For his willingness to speak out, Rost was investigated by Pfizer officials, and harassed by the company's lawyers in a brazen effort to shut him up. But he refused to stand down. Rost courageously penned a *New York Times* op-ed where he said, "Americans are dying without appropriate drugs because my industry and Congress are more concerned about protecting astronomical profits for conglomerates than they are about protecting the health of Americans."

North Carolina, Rost attacked congressman Richard Burr (R) for voting repeatedly against allowing Americans to buy cheaper medicines from abroad. "Mr. Burr is the No. 1 recipient[85] in the House and in the Senate of money from the drug companies," Rost said. "Guess who he's beholden to?"[86] Rost then penned a *New York Times* op-ed where he said, "Americans are dying without appropriate drugs because my industry and Congress are more concerned about protecting astronomical profits for conglomerates than they are about protecting the health of Americans."[87]

You might think these facts would lead a "scientific" agency like the FDA to conclude that prescription drug importation is, in fact, safe. But then that wrongly assumes that the FDA considers only scientific data, not the pharmaceutical industry's desire to maximize profits. As Ohio congressman Sherrod Brown (D) noted, "There's a trend at the FDA now where they're supporting drug company efforts on a whole host of issues. You can see a prejudice toward the drug companies in the way they've talked, the way they position themselves, the statements they have made."[88]

Remember, this is an agency whose chief counsel until 2004 was Bush appointee Daniel Troy, a former Pfizer lawyer. According to sworn affidavits,[89] Troy held at least fifty round table meetings at FDA with drug industry executives to tell them it was FDA's goal not to help warn citizens of safety threats, but instead to "control the flow of risk info" to the public.[90] It is also an agency that, according to whistleblowers, helped drug companies suppress evidence that the painkiller medication Vioxx posed a serious public health risk. Instead of sounding the alarm early, FDA officials made phone calls to editors of a top medical journal in an attempt to stop the publication of an article about Vioxx's dangerous side effects.[91] Safety, it seems, is only relevant when it protects drug industry profits.[92]

Then–FDA Commissioner Mark McClellan's behavior during the debate over the new Medicare bill exemplifies the corruption. As lawmakers from both parties tried to include provisions in the bill to legalize drug importation, McClellan gave speeches all over Washington claiming drugs from Canada were unsafe. When Republican senator John McCain (AZ) demanded McClellan come before Congress and explain his lies, McClellan refused. "Dr. McClellan has done a great disservice by trying to frighten our citizens into believing that drugs imported from Canada are somehow hazardous or dangerous," McCain said.[93]

But McClellan was ultimately successful—Congress bought into his dishonest scare tactic, and stripped out the provisions permitting importation from the final bill. McClellan soon received an award from the American Council on Science and Health—a group that gets its funding from the likes of Abbott Laboratories, Bristol-Myers Squibb, Eli Lilly, Merck, and Pfizer—all companies that lobbied against legalized drug importation.[94]

Emboldened by its victory in 2003, the drug industry is becoming even more brazen. In 2004, four of the biggest pharmaceutical companies took steps to limit medicine supplies to Canada, essentially telling Canada either it must stop selling medicines to Americans who drive over the border or it will see its own drug inventories choked off.[95] Under this blackmail scheme, Canada has been forced to crack down on its own drug exporters.[96] The move came just as Bayer won a lawsuit in European court that allows them to limit drug supplies to EU countries that legally export medicines at lower prices.[97]

The tactics are also playing out on a local level. In California, major drug companies helped pay for Governor Arnold Schwarzenegger's (R) trip to the Republican National Convention.[98] In return, Schwarzenegger vetoed state legislation to begin a pilot drug importation program.[99] In New York, when Mayor Michael Bloomberg (R) began pressing the federal government to legalize importation,[100] PhRMA put former New York mayor Rudolph Giuliani (R) on its payroll. Giuliani had long been a friend to drug companies—as a potential Senate candidate in 2000, he raked in almost $100,000 from pharmaceutical executives.[101] PhRMA knew Giuliani could be counted on to pocket their money, and use his 9/11 prominence to publicize reports reiterating safety red herrings.[102]

Even brute force and intimidation tactics are showing up. In early 2004, federal agents stormed a Minnesota Senior Federation's bus returning from a Canadian pharmacy. Though drug reimportation is still technically against the law, authorities for years had refused to actually arrest or physically intimidate seniors coming across the border with their medicines. Apparently, the policy is changing.

"The FDA agents came on the bus like Gestapo agents," said sixty-eight-year-old Dick Johnson, who was on the trip. Despite concerns about border security in the post-9/11 world, the authorities weren't looking for terrorists or chemical weapons—they were hunting down lower-priced medicines, as if that was the true national security threat.

"They were in black uniforms, similar to police uniforms," Johnson said, describing a scene out of some Third World police state. "They said they wanted to see what we had. They started at the back of the bus and looked at everybody's purchases. They actually went into our bags, physically looked at the bottles, looked at you, and then moved on to the next person." Though the FDA later tried to apologize for its actions, Johnson said, "I don't think it was an accident that the FDA came on the bus, because they knew exactly what we were doing, they knew our intent. To me, it was orchestrated to scare a bunch of seniors."[103]

Just a few months later, it became clear Johnson was only half right—the effort is not to scare just seniors but to dishonestly scare all Americans. One day after Senator John Kerry (D) held a town meeting to trumpet his support for legalizing drug importation, the Bush administration invoked terrorism to justify its opposition. Sending out its FDA commissioner, the administration claimed "cues from chatter" indicated al Qaeda would try to attack Americans by contaminating imported prescription drugs. It was an explosive allegation—and it was patently untrue. "We have no specific information now about any al Qaeda threats to our food or drug supply," admitted the Department of Homeland Security when pressed for details.[104] In other words, the government was once again desperately using the safety red herring to protect pharmaceutical industry profits, not average Americans.

LIE: Recent changes to Medicare will improve health care for seniors.

For the average citizen watching the political process through the eyes of inane reporters and pundits, it can be very hard to tell fact from fiction. But there's one good axiom to guide you through it all: usually, the bigger the bill or issue that is being dealt with, the more politicians are lying to you and doing their Big Money donors' bidding.

Thus, the debate in 2003 about the president's plan to add a prescription drug benefit to Medicare really ended up being one symphony of dishonesty. The first lie came from the Bush administration's top Medicare official, Tom Scully. He promised lawmakers that there were provisions in the president's preferred bill that tried to keep companies from eliminating drug benefits many were already providing, and prevent them from dumping retirees into the new, less generous Medicare benefit. The White House noted that the bill included $71 billion in subsidies to companies for this purpose, as long as companies didn't reduce the quality of their drug benefits below what would be offered by the government.[105] "Nobody's going to lose their retiree coverage in this bill," Scully said. "It's actually getting a little better."[106]

Less than two months after that declaration, the *Wall Street Journal* reported that the Bush administration had slipped "a little-noticed provision" into the bill helping Corporate America to do exactly what Scully promised the bill wouldn't do: severely reduce the drug benefits companies were already offering to their retirees. There was also a twist: companies could reduce the benefits while still receiving the massive government subsidies.[107] That's right, your employer could pocket a government handout for agreeing not to cut your benefits, and then turn right around and cut your benefits.

The provision was pushed by the so-called Employers' Coalition on Medicare—a front group made up of big corporations that had given

President Bush and the Republican Party more than $47 million since 2000.[108] A few months later, government data showed that Big Business would reduce or eliminate health benefits for almost 4 million retirees and dump them into the less generous Medicare plan.[109] Scully had no need to worry about being punished for his lie. As mentioned before, he took a job with a health industry lobbying firm almost immediately after the Medicare bill was signed into law.[110]

The second example of dishonesty came when the White House tried to hide the true cost of the Medicare bill—and the true recipients of the payoff. Many rank-and-file Republican and Democratic lawmakers were concerned that because the bill had no provisions to bring down the price of drugs and restrict insurance industry profiteering, it would end up being a budget-busting giveaway to pharmaceutical companies and would fail to improve health care in America. So California representative Bill Thomas (R), the bill's author, took to the House floor to defend the legislation by declaring, "We need to be sensitive to taxpayers." He said, "This bill is really all about a fair deal. . . . There are going to be 140 million taxpayers who are going to be pleased."[111]

No one should have trusted him—as the author of most major health legislation in Congress, Thomas has been the recipient of roughly $2.7 million in health and pharmaceutical industry campaign cash.[112] Some lawmakers wanted better proof than just a promise from an industry-lobbyist-in-congressman's clothing like Thomas. So they asked to speak directly with the government's top health care actuary, Richard Foster, about the cost of the bill. They were prohibited: the Bush administration threatened to fire Foster if he talked, because they knew he would admit the bill cost billions more than Thomas or the White House was admitting.[113] In fact, the legislation was such an embarrassing giveaway to the drug and HMO industry that Republican leaders ultimately held the vote on it in the middle of the night in order to avoid media scrutiny.

Four months after that vote, in March 2004, the truth came out: reporters uncovered e-mails showing that Foster warned the Bush administration that the bill, promoted by the White House as costing $395 billion, would actually cost billions more.[114] Among the more odious provisions inflating the cost are those that steer "at least $125 billion over the next decade in extra assistance to the health care industry and U.S. businesses,"[115] according to the *Washington Post*. As the headline of one of Wall Street's leading newsletters blared, "HMOs Look to Fatten Up on Medicare Reform."[116] And because the bill specifically prohibited the government from negotiating lower drug prices when purchasing medicines for Medicare beneficiaries, it ended up unnecessarily giving away tens of

HERO: James Love, director of the
Consumer Project on Technology

**EXPOSES HOW THE DRUG INDUSTRY USES FINE
PRINT TO SCREW ORDINARY AMERICANS**

Patent and copyright law is not a very accessible
discipline. For most people, even the thought of the subject
is a cure for insomnia. But not for James Love of the
Consumer Project on Technology. He understands better
than anyone how the pharmaceutical industry has used
patent and copyright law to hurt consumers and keep
medicine prices artificially high. Love has been a thorn
in the drug industry's side, providing key testimony to
Congress and documenting on his website (www.cptech
.org) exactly how the industry has bought off America's
domestic patent policies and international trade policies to
specifically protect its own bottom line. He continues to be
a crucial resource for the courageous lawmakers and
activists trying to stop pharmaceutical profiteering.

---

billions of dollars to the pharmaceutical industry. By 2005, the cost estimates rose even more: with President Bush safely reelected, the *Washington Post* reported that the White House admitted the bill's price tag will
ultimately be more than $1.2 trillion.

That astronomical cost might have been easier to swallow had the bill
dramatically improved America's health care system. But that gets us to
the third batch of lies, the ones where politicians started giving Americans false hope. Not only were lawmakers denying that the Medicare bill
was designed exclusively to enrich their campaign contributors in the
health and drug industries, they began trying to convince seniors that
their health care problems had been solved. "[The bill] strengthens and
improves Medicare [and] gives health care security to our seniors," said
Senate Minority Leader Bill Frist (R). President Bush called it nothing
less than "the greatest advance in health care coverage for America's seniors since the founding of Medicare."[117]

But as Families USA reported one year later, provisions hidden in the law's fine print—no doubt fine-tuned by corporate lobbyists—put "approximately half of America's Medicare beneficiaries at risk of being worse off than they are today."[118] Not only did the bill provide a financial incentive for corporations to eliminate retirees' existing drug coverage, but the White House was cutting off food stamps and eliminating Medicaid's key low-income benefits[119] to destitute citizens who applied for the new Medicare benefit. The bill had become a giant shell game designed to rip off the poor.

Make no mistake about it: this was a huge giveaway of taxpayer money for almost no benefit to taxpayers—all covered in a thin veneer of lies. It was, in short, as if Congress packaged up a bag of garbage in pretty wrapping paper and a bow, and then gave it to the American people as a present, expecting us never to figure out what was inside.

Solutions

No one wants to put the pharmaceutical industry out of business. Drug companies play an important role in the world's health care system. But in recent years, their quest for profits has led these companies to play a more destructive role in preventing medicines from getting to the people who need them. That is why our government must step in and make sure the drug industry's profit motive stops drowning out every other societal need. Drug companies should be able to make a healthy profit, but there's a difference between healthy profits and unhealthy profiteering. And the latter is particularly unacceptable when it means that people are denied the medicines they need.

Restrict profiteering. In almost every other industrialized country on the globe, society has created rules to make sure drug companies are not allowed to profiteer. America should do the same. One model can be found in Canada. There, if a pharmaceutical company wants the government to enforce exclusive patent rights on a particular drug, the company has to agree to price ceilings that both ensure profitability and prevent the gouging of consumers.[120] It seems a logical trade-off: instead of simply giving away patent protection for free, as the U.S. Congress currently does, America could have new laws that require drug companies to pony up something in return for their patents. Namely, fairer prices. Another model comes from Britain, where the government simply says drug companies cannot make more than a certain amount of profits.[121] Whatever the policy, the broader point is for our government to start standing up for ordinary people whose savings are being fleeced and whose lives are being endangered by the drug industry's profiteering.

Repeal laws that give away billions to drug companies. Congress should also repeal and then radically reform the recent Medicare prescription drug "benefit," which gives away billions to the drug industry and Corporate America without giving seniors real help. Just look at this rip-off: for $1.2 trillion, America got a bill that is so intent on padding drug industry profits, it will end up actually raising drug costs for one in four seniors, according to the Associated Press.[122] Those who do get a "benefit" have to pay $670 in new premiums and deductibles before they get anything, and what they get is pretty paltry. For instance, someone who spends $1,000 a year on medicines winds up saving just $143.[123] And those "benefits" are going to quickly disappear, as monthly premiums and deductibles are scheduled to rise.[124] As one expert said, "When the bill is fully implemented and medicine prices rise, [seniors] will pay more out of pocket than they do now."[125]

Prevent companies from persecuting American consumers. How about we save the $1.2 trillion giveaway in the Medicare bill and instead pass a simple law that forces drug companies to charge seniors no more than the average price they charge consumers in other industrialized countries? This legislation, already written by Maine representative Tom Allen, would save seniors 40 percent on their medicines without creating the bureaucracy and headache of a whole new entitlement program.[126]

Let Medicare negotiate lower prices, as every other business is allowed to do. Politicians always talk about trying to make the government behave like a business, saving costs and becoming more efficient. Why, then, would they ban Medicare from using its market power and volume purchases to negotiate lower drug prices for seniors? After all, most large corporations in America, when buying materials in bulk, negotiate lower prices from their suppliers. The three lines in the law restricting Medicare cost taxpayers $17 billion a year, or almost $2 million every hour.[127] A 2005 study by the nonpartisan watchdog group Families USA showed that if Medicare was allowed to negotiate with drug companies like other government agencies and businesses, it could purchase drugs for recipients at roughly half the price. That's your hard-earned taxpayer money that could be saved—but because the government prohibits Medicare from negotiating lower prices, it is being given away for no good reason to the drug industry. That has to change.

If we're going to bribe companies, at least get something in return. Congress must put some requirements on companies who profiteer off people's health care. The Medicare bill, for instance, gives corporations up to $940 per retiree[128] if they continue their existing drug programs, and if those drug programs are equal in value to the new benefits Medicare will provide. That is essentially a bribe, only it's worse: little-noticed loopholes made sure companies still get the subsidy even if they force their retirees to pay higher premiums,[129] and can ultimately avoid meeting Medicare's level.[130] How about rules that say companies only get the subsidy if they don't shift more costs onto their retirees, and only if they provide a benefit that's better than Medicare's bare minimum?

If taxpayers invest in the research and development of a drug, don't let companies reward us with the highest prices in the world for the final product. Instead of spending Americans' hard-earned tax dollars on drug research, and then giving that research away for free to drug companies, the federal government must start demanding fair prices in return. That means before any taxpayer-funded research is given away, drug companies would have to sign contracts prohibiting them from offering the final product at an excessive price. This would end the system whereby drugs developed at taxpayer expense are sold to American taxpayers at the highest prices in the world. This was the strict law of the land under Presidents Reagan and Bush I. It should be the law again.

Let Americans buy medicines at world market prices. We need to make drug importation legal, as it is in almost every other industrialized nation on Earth. As the above discussion points out, it is dishonest to say importation is unsafe. It is also unpatriotically insulting. As Pfizer's Dr. Peter Rost said, "It is outright derogatory to claim that Americans would not be able to handle reimportation of drugs when the rest of the world can do this."[131] Under intense questioning from House lawmakers in 2004, FDA Commissioner Lester Crawford was forced to agree. He said that yes, the United States could set up a safe, reliable, government-regulated system of importation for just $58 million a year.[132] To put that number in perspective, lawmakers in 2004 spent $15.8 billion of taxpayer money on wasteful pet projects—things like studying catfish genomes, protecting North Dakota sunflowers from birds, and buying President Bush his very own yacht.[133] The government that year also spent about $80 million on radio, television, and direct-mail ads promoting the Medicare bill.[134] Instead of using that money on pet projects or on propaganda about a bill that gives away billions to the drug industry, the government could use the cash to actually implement an importation system and lower drug prices.

UNDOUBTEDLY, pharmaceutical executives and their pals in Congress will forever argue against lower prices, no matter how many citizens are forced to go without the medicines they need. They will claim that any price reductions will hurt their bottom lines—as if their profit margins should take priority over people's health. But even this profit perspective is suspect. An April 2004 study by Boston University researchers[135] found that because lower-priced medicines would allow more citizens to buy medicines they previously could not afford, drug companies could actually see their profits rise.[136]

It's the old volume method: lower prices mean more sales, which means more profits—especially when you consider that the actual cost to manufacture more pills at a factory is often relatively small.[137] However, this would require the drug industry and corrupt politicians to actually change their current methods, which are harming Americans but are also guaranteeing high profits and huge campaign contributions. Such a change, then, is unlikely, especially considering Congress is too bought off to actually act. Still, the concept is compelling because we know it works. When he was responsible for Pfizer sales in Northern Europe (where country-to-country importation is legal), Dr. Rost doubled his sales in two years not by hiking prices and gouging consumers, but by lowering them and expanding his customer base. "As a drug company executive, I care about profits," Rost said. "I proved that it is possible to do good business with lower prices."[138]

If only more drug executives—and politicians—were so honest . . .

CHAPTER 8

ENERGY

★

THERE ARE certain truths that the average onlooker might assume are not up for debate, even in the seedy world of politics. The Earth is round. Water is wet. The sun emits light. Humans need air to breathe or they die. The A-team's B. A. Baracus doesn't like to fly on planes. Phillies pitcher Mitch Williams singlehandedly blew the World Series in 1993 and forever crushed the hearts of millions of sports fans (okay, so maybe the last two are a bit personal to the author of this book, less universally agreed upon, and known only to a smaller audience).

Yet one of the most elementary truisms in the world today is still apparently up for debate by corrupt politicians and their industry backers. And it shows that with enough money, even the most basic facts can be bought for a price in the political arena.

"The world is not running out of oil," says Charles DiBona, the energy industry's longtime top spokesman in Washington. "In fact, it will never run out of oil."[1]

Such a proclamation from such a powerful person might have raised eyebrows in other parts of America, prompting folks to whisper that the guy was "losing it." But in Washington, it was accepted as "fact," just another piece of black-is-white propaganda that denies all geologic data and common sense in pursuit of a corrupt public policy.

Here are the real facts: Oil is finite, meaning it will run out. Experts believe a supply crisis is coming sometime in the next twenty to forty years. As *National Geographic* noted in 2004, "Humanity's way of life is on a collision course with geology [and] the stark fact that the Earth holds a finite supply of oil." Experts believe that, whether five or thirty years from now, supply "will ultimately top out, then dwindle."[2]

This is a problem especially for America. Even though our country represents just 5 percent of the world's population,[3] the Bush administration admits we consume 26 percent of the world's daily oil production. And if you think we can drill our way out of the problem here at home, remember, the administration also quietly admits we sit atop just 2 percent of the world's petroleum reserves.[4]

Despite this troubling reality, our laws actually encourage more and more energy consumption, in large part because rhetoric like DiBona's is peddled as truth by lobbyists and bankrolled politicians in the halls of power. Instead of energy conservation, we get tax breaks encouraging us to use more.[5] Instead of regulating energy prices, we get Enron-backed deregulation schemes. Instead of getting America off its oil addiction, we get promises that more drilling into a supposedly infinite petroleum reservoir is the answer.

The reason we keep pursuing this clearly misguided policy is obvious—the energy industry and the politicians it bankrolls are making a killing off average consumers. Between 2000 and 2004, America's oil companies stuck consumers with about $250 billion in price increases, and increased oil industry profits by up to $80 billion.[6] In 2004 alone, oil executives used massive price increases to double their annual compensation packages to an average of roughly $16 million a year—by far the highest median for any industry in America.[7] And remember this the next time you fill up and get gouged at the gas pump: a nice chunk of what you just paid is being used to buy complicity from the political leaders who are supposed to be protecting you from being fleeced. Between 2000 and 2004, for instance, the oil and gas industry gave the Republican Party $67 million—that's $1,900 an hour, twenty-four hours a day, seven days a week for four straight years[8]—all to make sure that government looks the other way when you get ripped off.

And *ripped off* is the right term for what's going on, both on a macro level, in terms of how much the energy industry is bilking from consumers, and in the specific tactics energy companies are employing to bleed people dry. Look at how Enron gamed the market to fleece as many consumers as possible. The company deliberately shut down power plants[9] in order to create energy shortages that drove energy prices up and pilfered billions from consumers. And there was no remorse. On the contrary, audiotapes uncovered by CBS news caught Enron traders laughing in 2001 about jacking up prices to milk as much cash as possible from ratepayers. "I want to see what pain and heartache this is going to cause," said one Enron trader, chuckling as he engineered price increases in Nevada. "I want to f—k with Nevada for a while."[10]

The efforts to bilk consumers continued well after the Enron demise. In 2004, for example, Dallas-based TXU Energy in 2004 notified 27 percent of its customers they would be charged higher rates if they had credit ratings below a certain level.[11] In the months leading up to the announcement, TXU had dug into its customers' financial history, including bills that had nothing to do with electricity.* The move would mean that lower-income citizens with the least ability to pay would be charged higher rates. Though the company was ultimately embarrassed into backing off, it was a reminder about how energy industry greed—unrestricted by any government oversight—can run roughshod over society.

And that's what it is—unrestricted, unapologetic greed. As consumers struggled to pay higher and higher energy prices in 2005, energy industry executives had the nerve to publicly worry about having too much money. As *Fortune* magazine reported in 2005, Exxon's CEO wasn't fretting that middle-class people were getting squeezed. He was worrying about "the headache of what to do with all that cash" that was coming in because of high prices. His company had "a cash hoard of more than $25 billion" on hand, and was accumulating more than $1 billion a month—pilfered right from average consumers.[12]

These oil executives don't have to worry about government regulators cracking down on their behavior, because many of those regulators were actually handpicked by energy companies in the first place. For instance, Pat Wood, who chaired the Federal Energy Regulatory Commission (FERC) during the Enron crisis, was given his position after Enron CEO Ken Lay submitted his name to the White House.[13] Lay was an official member of Bush's energy advisory team during Bush's transition into the White House,[14] no doubt making sure the Energy and Commerce Departments were stocked with industry-friendly regulators. He helped put in place people like assistant energy secretary Vicky Bailey, who was previously president of a subsidiary of Cinergy Corp.,[15] and commerce undersecretary Kathleen Cooper, who had been ExxonMobil's chief economist.

And you can bet President Bush's other appointees had the energy

---

*The move was reminiscent of how credit card companies use "universal default" to justify charging you higher interest rates if you have paid an unrelated bill late—a move made for no other reason than to bilk the most defenseless consumers.

industry's interest in mind, too. According to the Center for Public Integrity, the top hundred Bush appointees "collectively had most of their holdings in the energy sector," owning approximately $144 million worth of energy stock. In other words, the regulators' own personal fortunes were directly related to their letting the industry fleece average Americans.[16] So was Bush's campaign bank account: forty-eight oil and gas industry executives were either Bush Pioneers or Rangers—people who raised him more than $100,000 or $200,000 each.[17]

Where have the Democrats been, you ask? Some of them have tried to cry foul, but all too often the party's top leaders are in bed with the industry. For example, when details of the Enron scandal came out, Connecticut senator Joseph Lieberman (D) was heading the committee that was to investigate the matter. The problem was, Lieberman and the political organizations he was affiliated with had taken thousands of dollars from Enron.[18] Meanwhile, his former chief of staff was an Enron lobbyist.[19] Not surprisingly, Lieberman "balked" when it came time to press the Enron investigation, slow-walking the probe by taking "more than three months from the time he announced his committee's Enron investigation to finally hand the [Bush] administration a subpoena," according to the *Washington Monthly*. It was plenty of time to make sure the Enron investigation remained as confined and as innocuous to Corporate America as possible.[20]

The state level is no less corrupt. Take former Montana governor Marc Racicot (R). In 1997, he helped pass corporate-backed legislation deregulating his state's energy industry.[21] That legislation allowed the state's largest power company to liquidate all its assets[22] and rip off thousands of Montanans who had invested their retirement nest eggs in company stock. When Racicot's term ended three years later, not only did he not apologize for the havoc he had wreaked in his home state, he cashed in on the catastrophe, signing up to be a paid Washington lobbyist for Enron, which was pushing more deregulation.[23] Think that insulting sellout kept him from a future in politics? Think again. A few short years later, Racicot was appointed head of the Republican National Committee.

The hostile takeover of our government by these energy industry whores is designed to make sure the fleecing of ordinary Americans is allowed to continue, and things like stricter fuel efficiency standards, alternative sources of energy, and industry regulation that could save consumers money are never a public policy priority. So what if the average family is forced to spend about $1,000 more a year on gasoline and home heating oil than they were in 2000?[24] So what if Americans could save up to $45 billion a year with better fuel efficiency standards?[25] So what if America is forced to rely on autocratic dictators like the Saudi royal family for our energy?[26] In Washington, those concerns are secondary, because the energy industry has a huge amount of power (no pun intended).

According to the Center for Public Integrity, the oil and gas industry has spent more than $440 million over the past six years on politicians, political parties, and lobbyists in order to protect its interests.[27] The industry is so influential, it actually had Congress pass a law creating a National Petroleum Council—a federally chartered panel of oil executives specifically tasked with influencing the secretary of energy.[28]

But it doesn't stop there. Oil companies are some of the most generous donors to public policy research organizations, which in turn churn out a steady stream of pro-industry reports for lawmakers to use when defending industry interests. When the industry's top spokesman makes the inane statement that the world "will never run out of oil," he's quickly backed up by a truckload of slick talking points, press releases, and policy papers that make the claim seem legitimate. For instance, as President Bush in 2002 was pushing new tax incentives for oil company drilling, former Reagan official Bruce Bartlett penned an article in the *National Review* claiming "the world will never run out of [oil]." The article noted that Bartlett was now employed as a top official for the National Center for Policy Analysis (NCPA)—but it didn't mention that NCPA has pocketed tens of thousands of dollars from ExxonMobil. Nonetheless, Bartlett's rhetoric was promptly amplified by Rush Limbaugh to 20 million listeners as objective fact. Similarly, the libertarian CATO Institute, which receives grants from Chevron and ExxonMobil[29] has issued a report claiming "fossil-fuel resources are becoming more abundant, not scarcer."[30] Then there is Ed Fuelner, president of the Chevron/Exxon Mobil/Shell-funded Heritage Foundation,[31] who wrote an op-ed saying cars "clear our air"[32]—proof that he's either never seen the Los Angeles skyline, or, more likely, is deliberately lying. Meanwhile, Heritage's media spinoff, Townhall.com,[33] published an op-ed from right-wing pundit John Stossel headlined "In Praise of Price Gouging" during the 2005 energy crisis. As more and more Americans were struggling to pay their skyrocketing energy bills, Stossel argued that "price 'gougers' save lives."[34]

But with the White House headed by two oilmen, this kind of nonsense has substituted for public policy. Within months of taking office, Vice President Cheney convened a secret task force to solicit oil executives help in writing federal energy policy. That Cheney was heading this

HACK: Ed Fuelner, president of the Heritage Foundation

SAYS AUTOMOBILES "CLEAN OUR AIR"

Ed Fuelner, president of the Chevron/ExxonMobil/
Shell-funded Heritage Foundation, penned an op-ed
in 2004 disparaging Earth Day, and claiming that
automobiles actually help the environment. Cars "clean
our air," Fuelner wrote. He said that we should be thankful
for auto pollution, because "let's not forget what autos
replaced: horses." That's right, he said cars were better for
the envirnonment than horses because horses meant that
"our streets were filled with manure [which] was itself a
dangerous form of pollution." Of course, Fuelner never
went on to explain how cars "clean our air" or how he
could possibly allude to a claim that manure is a worse
form of pollution than cancer-causing smog from
automobile exhaust.

panel while still receiving compensation from the oil company Halliburton was ignored.[35] What mattered was paying back the industry that gave
the Bush campaign more than $4.5 million.[36]

Much of the task force's recommendations were subsequently signed
into law when Congress passed the 2005 energy bill—and they were a
classic effort to pay wealthy corporations to do what the government
could have mandated for free. Instead of legislation toughening fuel-
efficiency laws to save consumers billions at the gas pump, the bill was
nothing more than a series of multibillion-dollar tax breaks for oil and gas
companies. According to the nonpartisan government watchdog group
Public Citizen, one provision actually provides hundreds of millions of
dollars for a new energy project headed by former executives at Enron,
the company that just years before had stolen millions from its stockholders and employees, but was apparently still looked upon favorably by the
president, thanks to its massive donations to his political campaigns.[37]
The bill also repeals a seventy-year-old law that prevents overconsolida-
tion in the energy industry. It was a law that prevented the Enrons of the

world from owning too much of America's energy system so that one company's rip-off schemes couldn't ruin the entire country.[38]

To the oil industry's delight, the Bush administration also started pushing federal budgets that simultaneously cut funding for alternative fuel[39] and hybrid engine research,[40] while creating a new, $100,000 tax write-off for people who purchase gas-guzzling Hummers.[41]

Even serious crises bring no divergence from the energy industry's agenda. During the 2000–2001 West Coast energy crisis, when Enron was fleecing billions from consumers[42] and laughing about it, the White House refused to support temporary price caps and successfully pressured allies on Capitol Hill—including those from the West Coast—to vote them down.[43]

Sure, there were some heroic efforts by earnest lawmakers. In 2003, for instance, the Associated Press reported that Senator Maria Cantwell (D-WA) introduced a simple bill that would "have made illegal the unethical practices used by Enron and other marketers."[44] But it was quickly defeated after Senate Energy and Natural Resources Committee chairman Pete Domenici (R-NM) rallied opposition. Despite proof that Enron had robbed billions from unsuspecting consumers in California and the Northwest,[45] Domenici stood on the Senate floor and publicly denied that the company had engaged in any market manipulation. Arrogantly referring to himself in the third person, Domenici said, "The senator from New Mexico has done everything he could to try to find out what the real experts say caused it, and none of them say it was manipulation that was at the heart of the problem of prices going outlandishly high on the West Coast."[46]

That's the kind of stark lie that could only come from a Senator like Domenici, who had taken more than $1 million from the energy industry over his career.[47] In truth, three months before, the Federal Energy Regulatory Commission (FERC) issued its official report, noting on the very first page that "significant market manipulation" was a major factor in the price crisis.[48] The New York Times noted that FERC officials "said investigators had found an 'epidemic' number of efforts to manipulate gas prices."[49] Are we really to believe that Domenici, the chairman of the Senate Energy and Natural Resources Committee, hadn't talked to FERC, the primary regulatory agency overseeing the energy industry? Are we really to believe that he hadn't also consulted California's top energy officials, who had lived through the Enron nightmare? No, of course no one believes that. That means before he made his dishonest declaration, Domenici was well aware of the FERC report, and he was well aware that experts at places like San Diego Gas & Electric said "the root cause of the runaway power bills [was] wholesale price manipulation by a handful of power generators," according to the *San Francisco Chronicle*.[50]

Of course, there are scores of other examples where bought-off politicians like Domenici knowingly parrot Corporate America's lies in order to justify policies that screw ordinary citizens. But there is no better place to see the raw power of the oil industry in particular than in President Bush's behavior immediately after 9/11. The country had just been attacked by terrorists primarily from Saudi Arabia[51]—the same country that makes its money by selling oil to America. It was, perhaps, the one time in American history where a leader could have transcended the power of the oil companies and called for a serious energy-conservation and fuel-efficiency program to get us off of Mideast oil.

Yet there was none of that. Instead, Bush's big domestic initiative was a declaration telling Americans to "do your business around the country . . . fly and enjoy America's great destination spots. Take your families and enjoy life." That was it. Go shopping and don't think about how our government's energy policies endanger America by tying us so closely to unstable despotic regimes. In the entire first month after the attacks, in fact, Bush uttered the word *oil* just once—and only in reference to his pre-9/11 energy bill, which was just a dressed-up package of tax breaks for the industry. That is the power of the energy companies—keeping a president of the United States silent during an emergency; preserving the oil-driven relationship between America and the country that produced terrorists who had just killed 3,000 innocent people; and using a spate of lies to justify making Americans fork over more of their hard-earned money to Corporate America.

MYTH: Low supplies and high prices of crude oil have been the only reason energy prices have risen in the last few years.

Whenever the oil industry raises its prices, it cites supply-and-demand, claiming low supplies and steady demand naturally drive up costs. That argument may hold some water in the future, when the Earth's supplies of crude oil do dwindle (and see below—they *will* dwindle). But right now, short-term physical supplies of crude oil are fairly steady. That means that in recent years the supply-and-demand argument has been used as a cover for sheer profiteering. As mentioned above, between 2000 and 2004 American oil companies stuck consumers with about a quarter-trillion dollars in price hikes.[52] Those might have been justified if physical supplies of crude oil had dwindled, and the industry's overall profits had stayed roughly even. But they didn't[53]—crude supplies remained relatively constant, and the price spikes resulted in a $50 to $80 billion increase in after-tax windfall profits for the industry.[54]

In October 2004, Consumers Union took a look at the situation, and found that in the first nine months of that year, oil companies' profits increased by a whopping 35 percent. The watchdog group found that the price increases that created those profits came more from higher charges for refining the crude oil into gasoline, rather than from higher prices for the raw crude itself (i.e., supply).[55] Why would those refining charges increase? Because federal regulators have allowed the oil industry to pursue its goal of deliberately reducing refining capacity to create artificial bottlenecks in supply. Those bottlenecks then drive up the overall price of gasoline. And make no mistake about it—the moves have been deliberate. "If the U.S. petroleum industry doesn't reduce its refining capacity," said a 1995 internal Chevron memo, "it will never see any substantial increase in refinery profits."[56]

The government's complicity in this has been bipartisan. For instance, President Clinton's regulators at the Federal Trade Commission (FTC) approved 413 mergers in the refining industry worth about $265 billion. He was topped by President George W. Bush, whose regulators approved another 520 mergers worth $178 billion in just his first three years in office.[57] But that apparently wasn't a fast enough clip. So, in 2004, Bush nominated ChevronTexaco lawyer Deborah Majoras to head the FTC.[58] Today, five of the largest American oil companies control 48 percent of domestic oil production, 50 percent of refining, and 62 percent of the retail gasoline market.[59]

What does this consolidation mean for the average person? Artificially higher prices.

At the gas pump it is most obvious. As the FTC reported after fuel prices rose in 2001, oil firms were using their monopolistic market shares to intentionally withhold or delay oil shipments as a way to artificially limit supply and to keep prices up—a practice the FTC euphemistically referred to as "profit-maximization."[60]

In 2005, gas prices rose again—and again profiteering—not supply-and-demand—was the root cause. California provides a clear case study. Petroleum industry analyst Tim Hamilton released a report documenting how between January and April 2005, gas prices in the Golden State jumped 65 cents per gallon. This occurred even though "no public evidence exists of substantive increases to oil companies in the cost of a) producing crude oil; b) refining oil into gasoline or diesel; or c) transport-ing the refined products to market." Where did the money go? Straight into the oil companies' pockets—Hamilton discovered that at exactly the time consumers were hit with the 65-cent-per-gallon increase, oil refiners increased their profits by 61 cents per gallon.[61] In other words, the higher prices were not because of less supply of crude but because the industry simply decided it wanted to bilk consumers.

After the 2005 hurricane season, oil industry executives have tried to claim that natural disasters and the damage to oil pumping/refining infra-structure on the Gulf Coast were really the reason that gas prices contin-ued to rise. But as PBS reported, "the price of gas increased three times as much as [the price of] crude in the month leading up to Katrina." That's correct—the profiteering was already occurring well before any of the storms, meaning the industry's scapegoating of Mother Nature was delib-erately dishonest hot air.

This profiteering has also gone beyond just the gas station. Audio-tapes discovered by the *New York Times* proved that Enron deliberately shut down a power plant providing energy to California homes and busi-nesses in order to exacerbate that state's energy crisis in 2001. "We want you guys to get a little creative and come up with a reason to go down," said one Enron trader to the power plant operator. He agreed, saying, "O.K., so we're just coming down for some maintenance, like a forced outage type of thing"—and then the two laughed. The next day, Califor-nia called a power emergency, prices spiked, and rolling blackouts hit up to a half-million consumers.[62]

These crooks don't have to worry about government regulators step-ping in. The industry's $67 million in campaign contributions and annual $50 million in lobbying expenses make sure the market manipulation is allowed to continue.[63] It's why every call by the few courageous political leaders for a crackdown on oil industry collusion has been met with over-whelming opposition in Washington, D.C.—because such a crackdown would offend the Big Money interests who are cashing in.

MYTH: Drilling will lower prices and make us more secure.

There is no better indication that an argument by Corporate America and corrupt politicians is dishonest than when they invoke patriotism and national security to try to quell opposition. And fewer issues try to tug harder at Americans' security fears than the debate over whether to allow drilling in Alaska's Arctic National Wildlife Refuge (ANWR).

The drumbeat for drilling in this pristine coastal plain has been going on for years. In 2000, Robert Ebel of the Center for Strategic and International Studies invoked the national security red herring at a U.S. Senate hearing. The energy-industry-executive-turned-supposedly-objective expert[64] asked, "Should the world's sole superpower be put in a position where it literally has to travel, hat-in-hand, to exporting countries to ask for increases in supply to bring prices down?"[65] In 2001, FreedomWorks, a think tank backed by the heirs to Koch Oil Industries,[66] said that allowing drilling "could curb dependence on foreign oil [and] ease future gas crunches."[67] That was followed by Chevron/ExxonMobil/Shell's Heritage Foundation, which said that more drilling "will increase U.S. energy independence."[68]

By 2005, this baloney was passing for legitimate fact on the floor of the U.S. Senate.

Senator John Thune (R-SD), just months removed from using $260,000 of oil/gas industry cash for his election campaign,[69] said drilling in ANWR "will reduce America's dependence on foreign sources of oil, strengthening our economic security, strengthening our energy security, and strengthening our national security."[70]

There is no question that getting America off foreign oil is a critical national security challenge. But the whole idea that drilling in ANWR solves that challenge for the long term is ridiculous on its face. In reality, the government's own economists acknowledge that if drilling in ANWR is allowed, America would go from importing 62 percent of our oil to importing 60 percent[71]—a far cry from "curbing dependence on foreign oil."

That's because there's relatively little oil to be drilled. A 1998 study by government scientists estimated that ANWR might hold 10.4 billion barrels of recoverable oil.[72] That is less oil than the United States consumes in six months.[73] By comparison, the National Academy of Sciences told Congress in 2001 that increasing cars' fuel economy standards by 45 percent (as current technology already can) would save 25 billion gallons of oil annually by 2015.[74]

Even if, after these facts, you still somehow believe drilling in ANWR will seriously increase domestic production, that doesn't mean it would lower energy prices for consumers. The oil-industry-funded Cato Institute openly admits that. "Even if all the oil we consumed in this country came from Texas and Alaska, every drop of it, assume we didn't import any oil from the Persian Gulf, prices would still be just as high today," said Cato's Jerry Taylor in a moment of candor. "And the main reason is that domestic prices will rise to the world price." In other words no amount of new domestic oil production is going to stop the price gouging.[75] By contrast, experts report that modest investments in energy efficiency could save consumers $45 billion annually by 2010.[76]

But that doesn't stop the misguided policy. In 2003, the U.S. Senate voted down a measure to increase automobile fuel-efficiency standards,[77] and then in 2005, passed a bill allowing drilling in ANWR.[78] Thirty-eight senators, many of whom claimed they want to get America off foreign oil, actually voted against the former and for the latter—proof positive that all they really care about is making their energy industry donors happy.

Admittedly, you may not care much about the debate over drilling because it seems as though it will take place on some far-off tract of forest in the middle of nowhere. But drilling very well could be coming to a neighborhood near you. The *New York Times* reported that one of President Bush's Texas advisers indicated that allowing drilling in ANWR is just a first step toward drilling in other places. "If you can't do ANWR," said Matthew R. Simmons, a Houston investment banker for the energy industry and a Bush adviser in 2000, "you'll never be able to drill in the promising areas."[79]

Places like the California and Florida coast are now being discussed as new drilling locations, as is the pristine Rocky Mountain front in Colorado[80] and Montana.[81] Congress has even talked about allowing oil drilling under the Great Lakes. To understand how ludicrous it is to even talk about that, consider the following statistics: Scientists say there are only about 500 million barrels of oil under the lakes[82]—that's less oil than the United States consumes in a month.[83] To get this pittance, drilling proponents want to allow oil companies to risk contaminating the largest freshwater source in the world—a serious concern, considering just one quart of leaked crude oil can contaminate up to 2 million gallons of drinking water.[84] The oil industry may say that spills are rare, but you don't have to go back to the *Exxon Valdez* to know that's not true. Just look at what's happened near the lakes already: Michigan's inland wells leaked oil or gas at least eighty-nine times in 2001 alone.[85] To most, the risk of ruining a huge natural resource just to get a trivial amount of another natural resource may sound absurd. But that's the logic of Washington, where oil money alchemizes the absurd into legitimate topics for Congress to consider.

HACK: Pete Domenici, New Mexico senator

***LIES ABOUT EXPERTS, PUBLICLY DENIES ENRON
MANIPULATED THE MARKET***

In March 2003, the Federal Energy Regulatory
Commission (FERC) issued a report about its investigation
into Enron and energy price gouging. On the very first
page, FERC noted that "significant market manipulation"
played a major role in the situation. As the *New York
Times* reported on the findings, "electricity and natural
gas prices were driven higher because of widespread
manipulation and misconduct by Enron and others." FERC
officials, noted the *Times*, "said investigators had found an
'epidemic' number of efforts to manipulate gas prices." Yet
three months later, Senator Pete Domenici (R-NM),
chairman of the Senate Energy Committee, gave a speech
on the Senate floor claiming "none of [the experts] say it
was manipulation that was at the heart of the problem of
prices going outlandishly high." It was the kind of stark lie
that only $1 million in energy industry campaign
contributions to Domenici could have bought.

MYTH: **Don't worry, the energy bill will lower
gas prices, and wasn't just a pointless giveaway
to the energy companies.**

In May 2004, Illinois representative Ray LaHood (R) held a press
conference at a gas station in Peoria to trumpet the industry-written energy bill that President Bush was pushing in Congress. The local newspaper reported the story under the headline "GOP Has Gas Price
Solution," noting that LaHood "said his party has crafted an energy bill
that will reduce gas prices."

"As you can see, [gas] is well over $2 here. That's a lot of money," said LaHood, the recipient of $151,000 in campaign contributions from energy/natural resource industries.[86] "It really infringes of the budgets of the average citizens." To fix that problem, he said, "We need a good energy bill in this country."[87]

The next year in Nebraska, it was the same thing with Senator Ben Nelson (D). There, the *Grand Island Independent* newspaper blared the headline "Nelson: Passing Energy Bill Could Lower Gas Prices." The Democratic senator, who had taken $201,000 from the energy/natural resource industries, said, "If we pass an energy bill, that might positively affect the price of gasoline."[88]

The motive was obvious—make the public believe the president's energy bill would bring down the price of gas, and the public would probably ignore the fact that the bill was really just a massive taxpayer giveaway to already-wealthy energy companies at a time of record budget deficits. There was just one hitch: the promises of lower prices were lies.

A month after Nelson's comments, President Bush was forced to acknowledge this reality, admitting in a speech that his "energy bill wouldn't change the price at the pump today."[89] He did try desperately to argue that the bill would have a long-term positive impact for consumers because it would supposedly diminish demand for petroleum, but even some experts in his own party weren't buying it. Take Republican representative Sherwood Boehlert (NY), chairman of the House Science Committee. As the *New York Times* reported, "In Mr. Boehlert's view, the bill would not reduce oil consumption by a single barrel by 2020."[90] The *Chicago Tribune* reported that even Jerry Taylor from the ultraconservative Cato Institute said "Congress probably would be better off passing no energy bill" rather than the Bush bill. "It will waste money to no good effect," Taylor said.[91]

To preserve support for the bill in the face of his admission that it would do nothing for gas prices, Bush knew he needed to prevent the public from finding out how much of a giveaway it was to the energy industry. So he publicly talked tough about the bill's supposed fiscal austerity. "Energy companies do not need taxpayer-funded incentives to explore for oil and gas," he said, as if his legislation was free of giveaways like that. But as Bloomberg News reported, the bill included provisions to make sure that "ExxonMobil Corp. and ConocoPhillips among other oil and gas producers get incentives to drill"—incentives given to these already-wealthy companies paid for by billions of taxpayer dollars.[92]

LIE: Only a tiny group of "radical environmentalists" support government efforts to raise fuel efficiency.

One of the ways Big Business and its political cronies marginalize arguments against their agenda is to make their opponents seem like a small fringe group. When it comes to lowering energy prices and raising fuel efficiency, out come the stereotypes of the long-haired Birkenstock-wearing tree huggers, the "radical environmentalists whose real agenda is to hobble industrial civilization," according to the right-wing *Washington Times*.[93]

When legislation was brought forward in 2001 to force cars to get better gas mileage, out came the same stereotype. "We're going to beat back the radical environmentalists . . . on overregulating the auto industry," House Majority Leader Tom DeLay (R) said to the delight of his energy and auto industry campaign donors. He then engineered the bill's defeat.[94] The next year, the Senate had a debate about whether to raise fuel efficiency standards or simply open up more public land to oil drilling. Senator Ted Stevens (R-AK) attacked those who supported raising fuel efficiency standards, saying, "a real problem is the people who really take advantage of the nation when we are evenly divided, the minority of the population—2 percent—which represents these radical environmentalists."[95]

Who are these "radical environmentalist" crazies? Do they really represent a minuscule 2 percent of America? Nope, not even close. According to a March 2005 national poll by the nonpartisan Opinion Research Corporation, "a strong majority (66%) of Americans agree that it is patriotic to buy a fuel efficient vehicle that uses less gasoline and, therefore, requires this country to import less oil from the Middle East." In case you thought these were all liberal tree-hugging Northeasterners, the poll also found that "about three out of five conservatives agree that buying a fuel-efficient vehicle is a patriotic act, as do 67% of those who follow NASCAR."

But maybe these people want to buy fuel-efficient vehicles but don't think the government should intervene? Wrong again. Of those surveyed, "89% agreed on the importance of government action to reach the 40 mile per gallon fuel efficiency level for U.S. vehicles." That includes "83% of conservatives, and 85% of NASCAR fans."[96]

The people who are the "radicals" are the corrupt politicians and the oil industry lobbyists. It is *their* fringe views that are out of the mainstream, not ours.

MYTH: Conservation and energy efficiency won't help folks avoid being gouged.

One hundred days into the Bush administration's first term, Vice President Dick Cheney gave a speech on energy policy. The former Halliburton CEO used the opportunity to reinforce one of the oil industry's favorite myths. "Conservation may be a sign of personal virtue," Cheney said. "But it is not a sufficient basis for a sound, comprehensive energy policy."[97]

At the time Cheney gave the speech, he was putting the finishing touches on his task force report that downplayed energy conservation and encouraged more drilling and more reliance on fossil fuels. The report was so skewed toward the oil industry's priorities, in fact, that folks started asking Cheney who helped him write it. He refused to answer. But ultimately, the *Washington Post* reported that government auditors found that he "collaborated heavily with corporations" and "relied for outside advice primarily on 'petroleum, coal, nuclear, natural gas, electricity industry representatives and lobbyists,' while seeking limited input from academic experts, environmentalists and policy groups."[98]

Cheney's criticism of conservation was, of course, a calculation. As vice president, he was still receiving a salary from Halliburton and still held hundreds of thousands of shares of stock options from the company.[99] As *USA Today* columnist DeWayne Wickham wrote at the time, Cheney was "returning the favor by fashioning an energy policy that will fatten the bottom line of Halliburton and many of the nation's other energy companies [by] trying to scare Americans into supporting an energy plan that panders to our gluttonous consumption of fossil fuels and stuffs the coffers of energy companies."[100] The less conservation and the more oil that is consumed, the higher the prices for oil and the more profits roll in for Halliburton and other oil companies.

But attacking conservation was not only a payback to big money interests, it was dishonest. Scientists at the Department of Energy were just completing a comprehensive, three-year study showing that if the White House backed a serious conservation agenda, it could dramatically reduce energy consumption—and thus energy prices—throughout America. Though President Bush promised that decisions about energy policy would be "based upon sound science,"[101] his administration was deliberately ignoring its own researchers, who found that a government-led efficiency program could reduce the growth in electricity demand by between 20 percent and 47 percent. That would be 20 to 47 percent off things like your home energy bill and your gas bill—a little fact Cheney and his oil industry pals conveniently forget to mention when they downplay conservation.[102]

LIE: Our government already does everything it can to encourage conservation.

At the same time politicians tell us that conservation is essentially pointless, they also contradict themselves by bragging about how much the government is already supposedly doing to support conservation. At a campaign rally in June 2004, for instance, President Bush said he understood that "we need to encourage conservation and develop alternative sources of energy." He later claimed that one of his priorities as president was to "encourage conservation."[103]

It's great rhetoric, especially with gas prices climbing. But it's a bunch of crap. In his first four budgets as president, Bush proposed more than $350 million worth of cuts to alternative-energy and energy-efficiency programs.[104] These are programs that, for instance, help families insulate their houses to save energy—programs that, according to experts, now save consumers up to $25 billion a year.[105]

But energy companies aren't happy with their political cronies just cutting efficiency and conservation programs. They want government policies that encourage wastefulness—and that's what they got when, in 2003, the White House actually passed a provision to encourage more fossil fuel consumption. Specifically, the White House slipped a line into its tax-cut bill that allowed folks to deduct from their taxes up to $100,000 on purchases of vehicles weighing more than 6,000 pounds. These are behemoths like the Hummer H2, the Lincoln Navigator, and the Cadillac Escalade—SUVs that get some of the worst gas mileage on the road. The provision, which can ultimately save a wealthy consumer thousands after the write-off,[106] was such an incredible taxpayer subsidy for the rich to increase their consumption of oil that auto dealers around the country began a special advertising blitz about the windfall. One advertisement from Dugan & Lopatka, an accounting firm in Wheaton, Illinois, read, "Write-Off 100% of Your New SUV? Yes, If It's Under $100,000!"[107]

Now, it's true—even Congress can be embarrassed into reversing itself. And in 2004, Senator Don Nickles (R-OK), normally a staunch oil industry ally, made a big deal about his amendment to roll back this egregious tax subsidy. "The senator thought this was bad tax policy," said Nickles's spokeswoman, as if her boss had suddenly seen the light. "He saw this as a pretty obvious loophole that needed to be closed."[108]

But as the *Detroit News* noted, the Nickles legislation still allowed many SUVs to "qualify for a hefty discount." Not only could consumers still qualify for a $25,000 SUV deduction, they could get "bonus depreciations." Thus, even after Nickles's bill, "a business owner purchasing a Hummer H1, with a sticker price of $106,185, would be able to deduct $60,722."[109]

To put all this in perspective, consider our government's attitude toward hybrid gas-electric cars—the most fuel-efficient vehicles on the road. At most, you can get a $3,400 tax deduction when you buy one.[110] In other words, at a time when gas prices are skyrocketing, the government provides a tax subisdy for the most fuel-inefficient cars that is many times bigger than what it provides for the most fuel-efficient cars. Worse, as part of the 2005 energy bill, lawmakers limited the number of hybrid tax credits that can be awarded.[111]

As this tax credit disparity has encouraged more gas guzzling, federal regulators have also tried to stop states that encourage consumers to buy cars that are more fuel-efficient. In California, for instance, the Bush administration stalled a plan to immediately allow hybrids on special, lower-traffic highway lanes.[112] On the traffic-congested West Coast, this idea was considered a major enticement for consumers to buy more efficient vehicles. But when it comes to keeping America addicted to oil, states' rights are secondary to the energy industry's wishes.

In mid-2005, as gas prices approached $3 a gallon, there was another blow—this time on fuel-efficiency standards. The *Financial Times* reported that in "the first revision of fuel-economy requirements in three decades," federal regulators decided "to give US carmakers even less incentive to build small, fuel-efficient minivans and sports utility vehicles." Though politicians trumpeted the announcement as welcome news for a country experiencing an energy crisis, critics exposed the truth: the rules would actually encourage "carmakers to build bigger vehicles that qualify for the least rigorous fuel-economy standards."[113]

LIE: We don't need to conserve because the Earth will never run out of oil.

As noted in the beginning of this chapter, top spokesmen for the oil industry, oil industry-funded think tanks and right-wing media celebrities promote the idea that the Earth "will never run out of oil"[114] as a rationale for policies that encourage oil consumption. But America pretending the Earth will never run out of oil is like a drunk pretending his bottle of scotch will never run dry. We're both deliriously trying to avoid dealing with a very bad hangover when reality finally hits us in the face.

Seriously, it's hard not to laugh at the sheer idiocy of people who justify public policies that encourage energy consumption by claiming the Earth will never run out of oil. Oil is finite. By definition, we can and will run out of something that is finite, especially if we keep consuming it the way we do. As the *Wall Street Journal* reported in 2004, "oil consumption is outpacing the industry's discovery of new reserves." While there has been no physical shortage of crude oil yet (and thus the short term price spikes we've experienced are sheer profiteering) at our current rate, there are about forty years left of proven oil reserves in the Earth, according to the petroleum industry's own data.[115] "[A shortage] will probably happen in the next ten to twenty years," Professor David Goodstein, a physicist at the California Institute of Technology, told CNN. "And it may have already begun."[116] Even some experts working in the oil industry itself quietly admit as much. The head of exploration for a major oil company told the *New York Times*, "You can certainly make a good case that sometime before the year 2050 conventional oil production will have peaked."[117]

Remember, we Americans can't just factor in our own gluttonous oil consumption when looking at the future. Two of the most populous countries in the world, China and India, only consume about a barrel of oil per person per year. But their economies are growing rapidly. If and when they reach even one-quarter or one-third of the United States's twenty-five barrels consumed per person per year, the world will require 50 percent more oil production—bringing on the end even sooner.[118]

It's true, denying this reality, as the energy industry spends so much time doing, creates a simple justification for America's careless gas guzzling. That keeps the profits rolling in, makes sure the oil industry campaign contributions continue flowing, and prevents consumers from

HERO: Brian Schweitzer, Montana governor

DEVELOPING RENEWABLE, ENVIRONMENTALLY FRIENDLY ENERGY SOURCES IN AMERICA

It's never easy to take on the big energy companies, especially as a first-term governor. But that's exactly what Montana governor Brian Schweitzer did. In his first five months in office, he signed two major pro-consumer energy bills. The first requires energy companies to produce at least 5 percent of their electricity from renewable sources (solar, wind, fuel cells, etc.) by 2008, and at least 15 percent by 2015. The second requires nearly all gasoline in the state to be blended with 10 percent ethanol—a renewable fuel made from corn or wheat in America. Now, Schweitzer is building support for his plan to use well-established technology to convert Montana's massive taxpayer-owned coal reserves into billions of barrels of fuel. The ultra-low-emissions conversion process, known as Fischer-Tropsch, creates a combustible fuel that is cleaner than any burned today in cars or jets because it removes the sulfur, mercury, and arsenic while sequestering the carbon dioxide. Schweitzer's efforts show that with some leadership, America can start getting itself off foreign oil and on to domestic sources of clean energy.

feeling guilty about driving ever-more-inefficient vehicles. But it also leaves America dangerously unprepared for the inevitable future.

In 2005, a team of Energy Department consultants warned that peaking oil production will ultimately "result in dramatically higher oil prices, which will cause protracted economic hardship in the United States and the world."[119] Already, higher prices brought on by oil industry gouging has had a ripple effect throughout the economy. The *Christian Science Monitor* reported in 2005 that because of high energy prices, "air travelers on international routes are now seeing huge fuel surcharges, the cost of a bunch of grapes is up a few cents, and economists expect to see costs increase on an array of manufactured goods from televisions to toasters."[120] Just think of what it will be like when the supplies really start running dry.

MYTH: Energy efficiency would eliminate jobs.

Whenever a proposal comes along that would save consumers money by raising fuel-economy or energy-efficiency standards in America, there's always a virulently antiunion congressman who suddenly postures as the champion of the workingman. For instance, when in 2004 Massachusetts senator John Kerry (D) proposed raising Corporate Average Fuel Economy (CAFE) standards (the government's minimum fuel-efficiency requirements for automobiles), it was Speaker of the House Dennis Hastert who lamented that it was "a proposal to kill more than 100,000 United Autoworker jobs."[121] The union-hating Hastert, who opposes every union priority from minimum-wage increases to pension protection, suddenly tried to transform himself into the populist union guardian.

But it isn't as if he really cared about those jobs—he was just clumsily trying to mask his subservience to the energy industry. This is a man, after all, who has one of the poorest voting records on union issues in Congress but has pocketed more than a half-million dollars from energy industry executives during his career. So it's clear whose bidding he's doing, and it's likely he knows his job numbers are fabricated.

As the American Council for an Energy-Efficient Economy reported, raising fuel-economy standards won't kill jobs, it will create 244,000 of them.[122] This is not some tree-hugger outfit, mind you—this is a group funded, in part, by the U.S. Department of Energy.[123] Their researchers found that investing in energy efficiency creates almost twice as many jobs as investing in oil drilling, because the latter is one of the least labor-intensive industries around. Specifically, while oil production creates just three direct jobs per million dollars of investment, energy efficiency investments support almost twenty-seven jobs for the same amount of money.[124]

These are not theoretical numbers. Just look at Sacramento in the 1990s: After spending $59 million on energy-efficiency technologies, the city government saved $45 million on power, created 880 jobs, and increased regional income by $124 million. Hardly a jobs killer.[125]

Not raising efficiency standards, as Hastert and the oil industry desire, would actually be the real jobs killer in the long run. As the University of Michigan reported in 2004, America could actually lose a huge number of jobs if it doesn't enact stricter fuel-efficiency standards. Japan's dominance in making more efficient cars "could result in a loss to the United States of as many as 207,000 jobs and $2.8 billion per year in federal tax receipts" by 2009, researchers concluded.[126] Not a pretty sight.

RED HERRING: Fuel efficiency kills people.

Lots of things in this world kill people. Cancer, murderers, watching too much of *The O'Reilly Factor*, gang violence, terrorism, smoking... and now, according to the oil companies, fuel efficiency.

Yes, it's true—even as Americans are seeing more of their paychecks eaten away by high energy costs, the energy industry and its think tanks continue to push the myth that making cars more fuel-efficient endangers lives. "Expert" Sam Kazman is a case in point. He works for the so-called Competitive Enterprise Institute, an oil industry front group that has taken in more than $1 million from Exxon since 1998.[127] He wrote a 2003 op-ed in the *Atlanta Journal-Constitution* opposing any increase in government's CAFE standards that regulate fuel efficiency standards. "CAFE kills people," he wrote. "It causes vehicles to be downsized, since lighter, smaller models use less fuel." And because he claims "smaller cars are less crashworthy than similarly equipped large ones, the result is higher traffic deaths."[128]

This kind of rhetoric deftly and dishonestly plays on people's fears. As Kazman admits in his article, once people hear the claim that fuel efficiency will put them at risk, "their support for higher standards plummets." But the claims about safety are totally out of touch with reality. According to the *New York Times*, a government panel made up of industry consultants and executives (and no environmentalists)[129] found in 2001 that "new engine technologies can produce fuel-efficiency savings without compromising safety."[130] Two years later, researchers at the University of Michigan and the Lawrence Berkeley National Laboratory came to similar conclusions, finding that most cars are as good as or better than the average SUV at protecting their own drivers, and far more protective than the average pickup truck.[131]

What Kazman and the oil industry don't want you to know is that often bigger vehicles have a much higher chance of rolling over than regular cars. According to the government's top safety experts, SUVs' rollover rates are almost three times higher than passenger cars[132]—a key statistic, considering that rollovers cause more fatalities than any other kind of motor vehicle accident (about one-quarter of all car deaths each year).[133]

But it doesn't take statistics to know the safety argument is a red herring. Take the words of Jeffrey W. Runge, the chief of the National Highway Traffic Safety Administration (NHTSA) under George W. Bush—a president not exactly unfriendly to the oil industry. In January 2003, the *Los Angeles Times* reported that Runge "stunned" Corporate America "in a speech by declaring that sport utility vehicles are not safe enough and consumers should reconsider buying them." Runge was an especially credible voice—before serving in government, he was an emergency room physician where he treated 30,000 people, a third of them injured in car accidents.[134]

This, of course, says nothing about how dangerous SUVs are to other drivers on the road. According to the NHTSA, SUVs are nearly three times as likely as cars to kill other drivers[135]—and that rate can be far higher among some of the most popular SUVs. PBS reported in 2002 that the Ford Explorer, for instance, "is sixteen times as likely as a typical family car to kill occupants of another vehicle in a crash."[136]

Why? Because without strong fuel-efficiency standards reducing the size of *all* cars, there exists a wide disparity in vehicle sizes on the road. It is the size disparity between giant SUVs and normal passenger cars that is the safety threat, not the size of more fuel-efficient passenger cars unto themselves, as corporate shills would have you believe.

Just put the debate into real-world terms. Imagine the difference between a Cadillac Escalade hitting a Honda Accord and a Ford Taurus hitting a Honda Accord. The former collision is likely to be far more fatal because the Escalade has a better chance of tipping over and killing its driver, while the size disparity between the vehicles is likely to kill the Honda driver. It's the reason that, according to the *New York Times*, the same federal panel made up of consultants and executives admitted "that safety may actually be improved if automakers are forced to reduce the bulk of the largest sport utilities and pickups."[137]

Nonetheless, fuel-efficiency standards remain taboo in Washington. A smaller-sized vehicle fleet in America may be safer, but that fleet would also be more fuel-efficient, and that would mean less profit for the oil industry. As the watchdog group Public Citizen reported in 2003, "SUV owners collectively paid almost $9 billion—$350 each—more for gasoline in 2002 in the United States than they would [have] if SUVs were as fuel-efficient as the average car." That "translates into 151 million extra barrels of oil consumed in the United States in 2002"—a windfall for the oil industry.[138]

Thus, the fear mongering about fuel efficiency continues. Just look at what happened in 2002 when Senators John McCain (R-AZ) and John Kerry (D-MA) offered legislation to raise fuel-economy standards as a way to get America off Mideast oil in the wake of the 9/11 attacks. The bill was defeated when Senator Kit Bond (R-MO), who has taken almost $300,000 from the oil industry,[139] once again played the safety card, claiming mothers and children would be particularly at risk. "You can see the golf carts going down the highway to soccer practice, maybe two kids in each golf cart," Bond said with a straight face on the Senate floor, absurdly equating smaller cars with golf carts. The safety red herring lives on . . .

Solutions

The solutions to our energy problems can be found in increasing efficiency and conservation and preventing price gouging—moves that will be all but painless, as long as you're not an energy executive or a member of the Saudi royal family.

Raise fuel efficiency standards immediately. Improving fuel-economy standards for all passenger vehicles from 27.5 to 40 miles per gallon, and for light trucks (including SUVs and vans) from 20.7 to 27.5 miles per gallon would save the United States 54 billion gallons of oil between 2005 and 2012.[140] It would also save consumers hundreds of billions of dollars. The technology exists to make this a reality—we could, for instance, make every car a hybrid. But the only way that will happen is if a law forces auto companies to do it.

Create fuel-efficiency standards high enough to make *all* cars lighter. "People that choose to drive small cars are jeopardizing their family's safety," said one Hummer driver, epitomizing the fear-based attitude of so many car buyers today. "Just because you drive a skateboard in front of my Hummer doesn't mean I'm more at fault because I chose to escalate the auto arms race."[141] Because Corporate America and corrupt politicians have been so effective in scaring people into adopting this totally ridiculous way of thinking, there is no way to stop people from buying bigger and bigger cars out of irrational fear. That is, unless the government steps in. Fuel-economy standards need to be high enough not only to reduce our oil consumption but also to seriously limit how large *all* cars are, so as to lessen size disparities and make our roads safer. Sure, we should make special rules to allow larger vehicles for businesses and farms that genuinely need them—but those who really *need* SUVs are, by far, the exception and not the rule in America. Making our overall fleet of vehicles smaller and thus more fuel-efficient must become a national priority.

Buy out the profiteers. During the 2001 California energy crisis, Los Angeles was one of the few cities where citizens weren't gouged by exorbitant prices. Why? Because the city government owned the power companies and was thus able to insulate citizens against corporate profiteering.[142] This example highlights how communities can protect themselves by moving to publicly owned power. The movement is already spreading. In Montana, a state that was scarred by energy deregulation, five cities in 2005 made a bid to buy out the state's largest energy company.[143] The same kind of thing can be done all over America.

Dramatically increase how much we spend developing alternative-energy and energy-efficiency technology. In 1997, a group of scientists and retired energy executives told the White House that doubling the amount the federal government spends on alternative energy and energy-efficiency technology would provide a 40-to-1 return on investment. That means investing an additional $1 billion from our $2 trillion federal budget, for a return of up to $40 billion in reduced energy costs for American consumers—not a bad deal.[144] But in another favor to its oil industry donors whose profits might be threatened by efficiency/renewable programs, the Bush administration has reduced funding for many of these key initiatives.[145] Those reductions need to be reversed, and our government must embark on a major push to develop these new technologies. This is not a Republican or Democratic idea. As the *Washington Post* reported, a "who's who of right-leaning military hawks" joined in 2005 with environmental advocates to lobby Congress to spend $12 billion to cut oil use in half by 2025.[146] They know that other countries are spending serious money developing new sources of energy and that if we lag behind, America will be at an economic and military disadvantage when oil supplies dwindle. If we invest now, however, we can stay ahead of the game.

Make every car in America a flexible-fuel vehicle. After the oil crisis in the 1970s, at least some countries figured out that they could start using alternative fuels like ethanol (the alcohol-based fuel derived from corn) to reduce their dependence on unpredictably priced Mideast oil. In Brazil, for example, ethanol-based fuels are dominant, and according to Cox News Service, they are "available at approximately 50 percent of the cost of fossil fuel."[147] We can make the same kinds of fuels in America, quite cheaply. But like Brazil,[148] we must use public policy to make sure new cars are "flexible-fuel vehicles" equipped to use both gasoline and ethanol-based fuels. As experts have testified to Congress, the flexible-fuel capability comes almost at no extra cost to the car buyer.[149] A federal law forcing all vehicles to be flexible-fuel-ready would be a major step toward getting America off foreign oil and onto a cheaper product that can be made right here at home. The benefits could be huge: Experts note that combining new hybrid systems with this flexible-fuel technology could ultimately produce an engine that gets up to 500 miles per gallon—no joke.[150]

Don't rob Peter to pay Paul. President Bush has bragged about creating a program to research a hydrogen-powered car. It's a good idea, except for the fact that he is having the government pay for that program by reducing energy efficiency R&D and eliminating the key program to develop more affordable, fuel-efficient gas-electric hybrid vehicles.[151] The move was particularly devious, though not surprising from a former oilman: most experts believe developing a hydrogen-powered car will take at least fifteen to twenty years,[152] while improving the fuel efficiency of existing vehicles through hybrid technology could happen right now, saving consumers money immediately. By eliminating hybrid research and using the money for hydrogen, Bush effectively put off serious fuel-efficiency improvements for two decades—a boost for the oil industry but a negative for society as a whole. This is stupid. There's no reason both the hydrogen and the hybrid programs shouldn't be funded at the same time. One is critical for our present situation; the other could provide huge benefits in the future.

Institute a windfall profits tax. In 1980, Congress enacted a tax on the excess profits oil companies were raking in through their price-gouging ways.[153] Though the industry used campaign cash and lobbying clout to engineer the tax's repeal in 1988, it can and must be reinstated. This is not a radical idea—a national poll released in September 2005 found four out of five Americans—including 76 percent of Republicans—support such a tax.[154] Implementing it would be easy. A panel of economic experts could determine what constitutes a healthy profit margin. Profits above what is considered fair (and "fair" can be generously defined while still falling short of the industry's insane profits) would be subjected to a steep tax whose revenues would be used to better fund programs that help consumers. These include energy-efficiency initiatives

HERO: Jeffrey Runge, head of the National Highway Traffic Safety Administration

DEBUNKED MYTH THAT GAS-GUZZLING SUVS ARE SAFER THAN CARS

Corporate America has for years argued that SUVs, because of their size, are safer than regular cars. The argument has been one of the most effective public rationales in preventing the government from creating higher fuel-efficiency standards that might reduce SUVs' size and overall production. So it was big news in 2003 when Jeffrey Runge, the Bush administration's top traffic safety expert, courageously deflated that myth. As head of the National Highway Traffic Safety Administration (NHTSA), he gave a speech telling consumers that SUV rollovers—often caused by the vehicles' excessive size—should be a major concern, and that he personally wouldn't drive the roughly one-third of all current SUVs that receive low marks for rollover safety. The speech effectively deflated the entire argument that SUVs are safer than more fuel-efficient cars.

and low-income energy assistance. Oil executives rail about price controls. That's fine. But they should pay a price for ripping people off.

Punish blatant market manipulation. Capitalism, supply-and-demand, and the natural laws of economics don't work if corporations are permitted to use monopolistic power to game the system. The Enron scandal should have been enough to make that clear. Congress should make it illegal for companies to intentionally withhold energy supplies from the market for the sole purpose of engineering shortages that drive prices up. But that is only half the solution because it is an after-the-fact punishment aimed at deterring misbehavior. Congress can also take proactive steps by requiring energy companies to increase the size of their storage facilities and hold a much larger amount of reserve in that storage. That way, if companies try to create artificial shortages, Congress can order those reserves released so as to recalibrate the market.[155]

Regulate the regulator. Antitrust laws are on the books for a reason: to allow society to prevent mergers that are not in the nation's best interest. For too long, those laws have gone unused, as regulators at the Federal Trade Commission (FTC) approve more and more consolidation in the energy industry—consolidation that results in price gouging. The FTC needs to reassert itself and more closely scrutinize—and slow down—oil industry mergers. If it doesn't, Congress must intervene and force the agency to do its job. It can start by creating restrictions on who can be appointed to the FTC. Nominees should be required to have at least three years between when they worked for a company with major business before the FTC and when they are appointed to the FTC itself— otherwise, they shouldn't be able to be appointed. That would prevent future presidents from appointing people like ChevronTexaco's lawyer to head the agency, as President Bush did.

ON MARCH 31, 2005, the stock market lit up with a buzz. Goldman Sachs, one of the largest investment banks in the world, had released a report predicting U.S. oil prices were in the early stage of a "super spike"— meaning prices could go from about $50 a barrel to more than $100. The prediction was motivated by a host of converging factors: China's demand for oil was increasing, world oil supplies were not growing as fast as they had been, and U.S. consumption was staying strong—in part, because corrupt politicians were ensuring that energy efficiency remained on the back burner. For the average American, it was bad news.

But bad news for regular people is often great news for profiteers. Energy stock prices shot up, with speculators eagerly trying to get on board the gravy train before it left the station.[156] Oil executives no doubt smiled as they saw the value of their own portfolios rise. It meant more in their pocket, and more hush money for politicians in Washington.

By September, gas prices were hovering around $3 a gallon—again, bad news for consumers, but good news for the oil profiteers. That month, the *Boston Herald* reported that "ExxonMobil's profits are likely to soar above $10 billion this quarter. . . . That's $110 million a day, and more net income than any company has ever made in a quarter."[157] That's correct— more profits than any company in American history.

True, governors soon embarrassed the Bush administration into initi-
ating a price-gouging investigation.[158] But it was really just a formality.
Why? Because the White House made sure the Federal Trade Commission would be the agency conducting the probe.[159] That's the same Federal Trade Commission headed by a former ChevronTexaco lawyer,
thanks to President Bush.[160] And that meant the investigation, as usual,
would go nowhere.

It is this vicious cycle that every American should be worried about.
The more the energy industry games the market, raises prices, and sucks
cash out of consumers' pockets, the better it is for the industry's bottom
line, and for the government officials on the oil industry dole. The simple
truth is that the interests of those in power are directly opposed to the interests of most Americans. And no matter how many myths, lies, and half-
truths try to hide or justify the energy industry's price gouging, we will
always be stuck with that very simple reality, until we demand change.

CHAPTER 9

UNIONS

★

IN 2003, THE Labor Department chose chocolate tycoon Milton Hershey for induction into the Labor Hall of Fame.[1] According to historians, Hershey's managers were famous for organizing antiunion gangs to beat "with clubs, pipes, blackjacks and fists" strikers who were fighting to form a union at his factory.[2]

It was the equivalent of someone giving Jayson Blair a Pulitzer Prize for accurate reporting, or Keanu Reeves an Academy Award for dramatic acting in his portrayal of Ted in *Bill & Ted's Excellent Adventure*—and it was an unabashed boot in workers' eye. But that was precisely the point. It spoke volumes about a government that still dishonestly aids, abets, and valorizes Corporate America's efforts to destroy the American labor movement.

Corporate America's hostile takeover of government can perhaps be seen most clearly in how politicians today treat one of American workers' most basic rights: the right to organize themselves and fight for their economic rights. This right has always been under attack by moneyed interests, but only recently has bashing workers become a trophy sport among politicians, who now seem to go out of their way to flaunt how much they despise workers' rights.

Consider the actions of a few top politicians in their first days in office. These are the days when they are trying to set the tone for their time in office, and their actions in this period are designed to send a broad message about what they believe are their top priorities.

So it was really quite a reflection of the hostile takeover when President Bush marked his first weeks in office with a series of high-profile orders aimed specifically at weakening unions. As seen in previous chapters, America was and is facing all sorts of massive economic challenges, yet the supposedly "compassionate" conservative President decided that he wanted to lead off his term by bashing workers.

One of his orders prohibited government agencies from targeting federal contracts to companies that employ union workers (the practice had been used as a way to provide a financial incentive for companies to allow union workers, who make better wages).[3] Another permitted corporations to hide expenditures they make on secret campaigns to intimidate workers who are trying to form a union.[4] And another repealed a regulation prohibiting your taxpayer dollars from going to companies that repeatedly violate labor laws.[5]

In the states, others followed his lead. Missouri governor Matt Blunt's (R) very first act as his state's chief executive in 2005 was repealing collective bargaining rights for 30,000 state workers.[6] It wasn't extending health care, or raising wages, or feeding the poor—it was stripping average workers of their rights.

In Indiana, it took newly elected governor Mitch Daniels (R) just two days in office to do the same thing and eliminate collective bargaining rights for 25,000 of his state's workers. As a former corporate executive, Daniels seemed to salivate at the chance to stiff workers, not only eliminating their union rights, but also canceling a previously negotiated contract that protected their health care benefits and workplace standards.[7]

To be sure, this open animosity toward unions is one of Corporate America's oldest traditions. For most Americans, the only inevitables are life, death, and taxes. For the average corporate executive and bought-off politician, that list is bigger. There is also golf with friends at the country club, luxury junkets on private jets, and, most important, aggressive efforts to violate workers' union rights. To these privileged few, persecuting workers is as American as baseball and apple pie.

There are countless examples of this persecution, but what happened in New York City in the winter of 2005 is perhaps the best and most recent display of open animosity toward unions by those in power. The New York city and state governments were trying to cut transit workers' pensions, and when the workers' union went on strike, all hell broke loose, as the city ground to a halt. But instead of suddenly realizing the value of the union workers and backing off the pension cuts, billionaire New York Mayor Michael Bloomberg was seemingly blinded by a hatred for unions likely developed as a longtime corporate executive. He called the union "selfish" and said it was acting "thuggishly" for having the nerve to fight for workers' economic rights.

But it was Bloomberg and state officials who were the real selfish thugs. As the *New York Times* reported, they were trying to enact $20 million worth of cuts to union workers' pensions even though the transit system had $1 billion surplus. That $20 million was a relative pittance to the city, but huge for blue collar workers. Even worse, just weeks before the strike, Bloomberg and state officials had given away about $1.5 billion in taxpayer-financed bonds to Goldman Sachs, one of the wealthiest investment banks in the world. Yes, you read that correctly: In November 2005, New York's top politicians held a pompous groundbreaking ceremony with Goldman Sachs executives to hand them $1.5 billion in taxpayer-financed bonds for construction of a palatial new headquarters. One month later, the very same politicians were apparently so blinded by their hatred for unions that they were refusing to cough up $20 million to preserve thousands of workers' pensions.

Why should you, an ordinary American, care about all of this? Why are union rights as important to a discussion of pocketbook issues as any other issue? Because unless you are a superwealthy fat cat, the existence of unions is integral to your economic well-being—whether you are in a union or not. For union members themselves, the benefits of unions couldn't be more stark. "By every available measure, union members are better-clothed, better-fed, better-paid and better housed than nonunion workers with comparable jobs," notes University of Alabama Professor Glenn Feldman. "They enjoy better and fuller access to health care and prescription drugs. They have safer and more dignified workplaces and a great deal more recourse when employers violate the most basic standards of justice and equity."[8]

Want a real-life example of what those union benefits really mean? Just look at the Enron debacle. Though you didn't hear about it in the traditionally anti-union media, one of the big stories coming out of the scandal was about the power of unions to protect workers. While thousands of nonunion workers saw their pensions decimated by politically connected corporate rip-off artists, those who were in a union survived. As AFL-CIO president John Sweeney noted in 2002, "Some 1,000 employees of Enron subsidiaries who are members of the Sheet Metal Workers Union didn't lose a dime in pension dollars because they were protected" by contract guarantees they had secured from their employers through their union.

But what about nonunion members? Why should you care about union issues if you aren't in a union? Because unions help all workers. Don't believe it? Next time you enjoy a night at home with your family or a relaxing weekend, remember—it was the union movement that helped end the system that forced people to work twelve-hour days, seven days a week for almost no pay. And that's not all, as Feldman points out. "A majority of the MBA students I have taught can enumerate with childlike glee the Christmas list of goodies that awaits them once they go out and take a real job," he wrote. They get "sick pay, overtime pay, vacation pay, health insurance, disability insurance, good wages, safety standards, pension benefits, prescription drug coverage, and more—without ever once realizing that it is unions to whom they owe a massive thank-you for setting the industrial standard."[9]

Those benefits, however, are being eliminated as Big Business and politicians persecute unions, and do everything they can to keep the public in the dark about the benefits unions offer. Corporate America and its allies in Congress have spent the last few decades spreading all sorts of lies about unions to make people forget about the labor movement's positive effect on America's past and present. The ultimate goal is to make the public see unions as monolithic monsters instead of what they really are: just a collection of ordinary workers banding together to protect their basic common rights.

Why such vitriol against unions by the powers that be? Because executives, lobbyists, and bought-off politicians understand that with the hostile takeover of our government complete, unions are one of the few remaining institutions capable of preventing Corporate America from abusing workers with low wages, bad benefits, and poor working conditions. In fact, Big Business has understood this for years. At the turn of the century, workers could be shot or lynched by companies for trying to join a union and improve their conditions—and government often either looked the other way, or sent troops to help . . . the company.[10] Today things may be a bit less violent, but the paradigm is the same: corporations and their political allies still publicly bash unions and fight unionizing efforts with a seething vengeance.

Just look at the facts. Cornell University researchers found that 20,000 workers a year are fired or discriminated against just for trying to exercise their legal right to unionize.[11] Union busting is so pervasive, it has become a sport all unto itself, with Corporate America devoting huge amounts of money specifically to screwing workers. In 2005, for instance, one of Wal-Mart's top executives claimed that he was given a half million dollars of company money to fund antiunion activities that he said included illegal spying and threats.[12]

That kind of money has created its own cottage industry of white-collar thugs who specialize in persecuting workers. The *New York Times* reported in 2003 that there now exists "a little known but thriving business in which law firms and consultants work with corporations to beat back unionization efforts." The national law firm Jackson Lewis, for instance, actually describes itself as "committed to the practice of preventive labor relations." That's a euphemism for gangster-like behavior. As the *New York Times* reported in 2004, one company under Jackson Lewis's tutelage was forced to pay millions in damages for gross violations of labor law during a union drive. In the court proceedings, the whole business of "preventive labor relations" was shown to be nothing more than bare-knuckled intimidation, including sending unmarked envelopes of cash to buy the services of thugs who threaten pro-union workers.[13]

Technically, much of this behavior is illegal. But you wouldn't know it if you looked at the government agency that is supposed to be enforcing the law. The National Labor Relations Board (NLRB) has been packed with antiunion appointees straight out of Corporate America's ranks, and the agency is now a laughingstock. It can take up to a decade for a worker whose rights have been violated to have his/her grievances addressed.[14] Think of an agency as irritatingly slow and incompetent as the DMV— only the unresponsiveness is deliberate so as to prevent workers from getting their due.

The politicians are even worse—they aren't just unresponsive, they openly hurl insults at workers. For instance, then-secretary of education Rod Paige actually called the nation's biggest teachers' union "a terrorist organization."[15] Similarly, after 9/11, House Majority Leader Tom DeLay (R-TX) said unions present "a clear and present danger to the security of the United States at home and the safety of our armed forces overseas."[16] He didn't care that many of the police, firefighters, and emergency workers who died during the terrorist attacks were card-carrying union members. What he cared about was trying to paint workers who fight for their rights as enemies of America.

A few years later, Georgia Congressman Charlie Norwood (R) one-upped DeLay. As the chairman of the House Subcommittee on Work-

HACKS: Matt Blunt, Missouri governor; Mitch Daniels, Indiana governor

DURING FIRST DAYS IN OFFICE, REVOKED COLLECTIVE BARGAINING RIGHTS FOR WORKERS

In January 2005, Matt Blunt (R) and Mitch Daniels (R) were sworn in as governors of Missouri and Indiana, respectively. On his very first day in office, Blunt revoked collective bargaining rights for 30,000 state workers. Daniels waited until his second day in office to do the same thing, while also canceling a previously negotiated contract that protected workers' health care benefits and workplace standards.

force Protections, he is supposed to be defending American workers and making sure their rights are protected. Instead, he authored a 2005 op-ed calling unions "enemies of freedom and democracy" who supposedly support the same "tyranny that Americans are fighting and dying to defeat in Iraq and Afghanistan." Seeming to rationalize physical violence, he said unions' support for this tyranny is a "justification for why we still need the Second Amendment" allowing Americans to own guns.[17]

You might be wondering how lawmakers can get away with such vitriol, especially when we are led to believe unions are ultrapowerful political puppeteers that use huge amounts of money to control politicians. The answer is what you rarely hear in our political debate: Corporate America, with its endless resources, is able to spend far more on campaign contributions and lobbying than unions. As just one example, look at the 2004 election cycle. Business interests gave almost $100 million to members of the two congressional committees that oversee labor laws in America. In that same time period, unions mustered barely $7 million to those same politicians.[18] That gross discrepancy, which runs throughout the political system, means politicians of all stripes can bash workers as much as they want. In fact, as the numbers show, they are given a huge financial incentive to do so by the true big money donors—Big Business—that control politics.

Corporate cash buys not only executive orders and angry rhetoric but a barrage of other antiunion efforts from lawmakers as well. There have been initiatives, hilariously called "Paycheck Protection" bills, that would cut off the revenues unions use to coordinate campaigns for higher wages;[19] there have been administrative rules that make it harder for workers to organize;[20] and there have been overt threats by the Bush administration to "use any means necessary" to prevent workers from exercising their legal right to strike when they are abused.[21] That's a sad reminder of how far our government has come from the days when a Republican named Abraham Lincoln once famously said, "I know that in almost every case of strikes, the men have just cause for complaint."[22]

Much of this hateful atttitude toward workers has been channeled into witch hunts. In 1996, for instance, right-wing columnist Robert Novak cheered on an effort by Republicans to tie "Washington union bosses" to "alleged affiliations with organized crime." Echoing the McCarthyist tactics of years past, Novak noted that then–House Speaker Newt Gingrich (R) was heading up a "GOP committee task force on the labor movement" designed exclusively to initiate a "major assault" on unions. The move was so extreme, one Republican congressman assailed his own party's leadership for an "antiunion attitude that appeals to the mentality of hillbillies at revival meetings."[23] That concern was summarily ignored.

Though the efforts of these extremists ultimately didn't amount to anything substantive, the message had been sent. Workers were essentially warned that when they join a union they are no longer doing so under the protection of their government. Quite the opposite: they now run the risk of having their lives destroyed by corrupt politicians willing to exploit government power for Big Business's antiunion agenda.

Sadly, these and other intimidation efforts have worked. Union membership is smaller now than at any point in American history, with less than 13 percent of workers belonging to a union. That is the lowest unionization rate in the industrialized world.[24] Not surprisingly, this decline in union membership has been accompanied by stagnating wages, worse health care coverage for workers, and less pension security than in recent decades. Companies know that with fewer unions, they can get away with ripping off more of their workers.

Pundits and others reciting the corporate line say that declining union membership means people simply don't want to be in a union. But polls show that's not true. What's really going on, says Harvard professor Richard Freeman, is an increase in "the level and effectiveness of management opposition to unionism." During the last three decades, Corporate

America "turned against unions and collective bargaining to a degree not seen anywhere else." Virtually all companies that face union efforts "engage in expensive, aggressive campaigns to persuade and pressure workers to reject unions." And while "unfair labor practices ... such as firing union activists skyrocketed to rates five or six times" what they had been, government looks away and instead joins in spreading lies about unions at every turn.[25]

LIE: Unions hurt union members.

In its arsenal of antiunion weapons, Wal-Mart has a pamphlet for its employees called *A Manager's Toolbox to Remaining Union Free.*[26] It looks like just another company guidebook—harmless and boring. But within this antiworker screed is the core of Corporate America's efforts to paint unions as toxic to workers.

Unions "are a business, a big business, that needs to make money," says the handbook. "However, unions do not make or sell products. So where do they get their money? Out of the pockets of their members!"[27] The message is clear: Unions exist only to rob workers, so workers should vehemently oppose joining a union.

Wal-Mart is not alone. There are thousands of other antiunion companies that make exactly the same case, and worse. We are expected to believe not only that unions' only goal is to steal money but also that unions' whole reason for existence is to hurt workers. As one right-wing economics professor in California wrote, "the effect of many union activities and union-backed policies is to harm most American workers." He added that "much of what [unions] do and promote injures the vast majority" of workers in order to "protect [unions'] own vested interests."[28]

If this patent dishonesty was limited just to Big Business and academics in their ivory towers, it would not be so alarming. But it is now regularly regurgitated by political leaders who are supposed to be representing ordinary Americans. For instance, take then-Congressman Joe Scarborough (R-FL). He appeared on CNN in 2000 to decry unions for supposedly "being able to steal money from employees."[29] A newspaper later reported that local politicians had put wording in one Florida county's legal code "that says unions would not help workers, and the county would oppose unions by any lawful means."[30]

Or how about Representative Charlie Norwood (R)? In 2005, he depicted union leaders as "thugs who are currently trying to steal worker's rights."[31] He also claimed unions have "failed to provide any real value" to workers.[32] And then there was President Bush's first nominee to be U.S. secretary of labor. Despite the position requiring a person to specifically represent the interests of workers, Bush nominated extremist firebrand Linda Chavez—a person who had opposed the concept of a minimum wage[33] and had publicly disparaged the labor movement by claiming "union members are hardly representative of the American working public."[34] She later wrote a book saying unions "claim to represent working men and women" but they "have actually caused millions of union members to lose their jobs."[35] Not corporate "free" trade policies that carelessly shuffled jobs overseas or draconian and merciless corporate downsizing, mind you. Unions.

To be sure, there have been corruption scandals involving unions. But that's no different from just about every other sector of the economy. Just as you can't say all businesses are completely corrupt because of Enron, you can't say that all unions are corrupt because of a few scandals (more on this later).

The real effect of unions on society is found in the concrete facts—not in the rhetoric of hyperventilating extremists:

— The average worker who belongs to a union receives about one-quarter more in total compensation than a nonunion worker.

— 89 percent of union workers have access to health care benefits from their employer, compared with just 67 percent of nonunion workers—and employers typically pay a bigger share of union workers' health care premiums than nonunion workers' premiums.[36]

— More than two-thirds of union workers have short-term disability coverage, compared with only about one-third of nonunion workers.[37]

— Unionized workers receive 26 percent more vacation time and 14 percent more total paid leave (vacations and holidays) than nonunion workers.[38]

As mentioned earlier, the benefits of unions are not limited to union members. The nonpartisan Economic Policy Institute reported that union influence has resulted in an 8.8 percent wage increase for the average nonunion high school graduate.[39] For the average wage worker who makes about $33,000 a year,[40] that's an extra $3,000 thanks to unions.

How is this possible? Two reasons. First is what's called the "union threat effect": In highly unionized industries, nonunion companies will often meet higher standards in order to prevent workers from becoming unhappy and unionizing. Second, EPI notes "unions have set norms and established practices that become more generalized throughout the economy."[41] Many benefits such as pensions, health insurance, and decent wages were first provided to union workers and then became more generalized (though, as we have seen, not universal).

But there's a flip side: The more corporations and politicians try to demonize and eliminate unions, the more all workers are harmed. It's why the nonpartisan Council on Foreign Relations reported that the decline in union membership "is correlated with the early and sharp widening of the U.S. wage gap" between the very wealthy and the rest of us.[42]

LIE: Workers don't want to join unions.

When you see or hear Big Business purporting to understand and sympathize with the desires of average workers, you should immediately feel a pang of distrust, because it is usually a sign that you are about to be doused in a steaming pile of bullshit. When it comes to unions, this tactic usually materializes in the form of corporate hacks explaining low union membership—and justifying antiunion behavior—by claiming workers simply don't want to join unions.

The tactic is pervasive. As the *Los Angeles Times* noted in 1999, "Employers and organized labor critics say that many workers don't want to join unions [because] they say many workers have been turned off by unions' ineffectiveness."[43] John Lehman, a former Wal-Mart manager, told PBS exactly how that "turning off" happens in the real world. "I used to stand up in front of my workers and lie to them," he said. "I used to say the talking points, that the union's a cult: 'You don't want to join a union. It's a cult. Why pay someone to speak for you? You can speak for yourself.' "[44]

Corporate executives have been very public about using this rationale to ignore already established unions in their midst. For instance, the *Boston Globe* reported in 1999 that the CEO of the New Balance shoe company "balked at negotiating a contract with workers in his Lawrence (Massachusetts) distribution center because he says many of his workers don't want to have to join the union" that workers voted for and created at the company.[45]

HACKS: Rod Paige, secretary of education; Charlie Norwood, Georgia congressman

LIKENED UNION WORKERS TO TERRORISTS

In 2004, Education Secretary Rod Paige actually told governors that he believes America's biggest teachers' union is "a terrorist organization." He was followed up a year later by Georgia congressman Charlie Norwood (R), who likened unions to "enemies of freedom and democracy" that use the same "tyranny that Americans are fighting and dying to defeat in Iraq and Afghanistan." This from Norwood, the chairman of the House Subcommittee on Workforce Protections—the panel that is supposed to be defending, not attacking, American workers.

In the 1990s, researchers at Harvard and the University of Wisconsin looked at the situation. Can declining union membership be explained by a mythical hatred of unions by ordinary workers? No, according to the results of their polling. The researchers found at least 42 million workers in America want to join a union[46]—more than double the 16 million currently unionized workers in this country.[47] In 2002, the AFL-CIO commissioned a poll to see if those results were accurate. The union found that 50 percent of all workers not already in a union would join a union immediately if they had the chance.[48] In 2005, another nationwide poll found the number grew: 53 percent of nonunion workers said they would vote to form a union at their workplace if given the choice.[49]

Citing the fact that only 13 percent of workers are unionized, Corporate America's lobbying arm in Washington usually insists that the poll numbers are wrong. "The fact is that when employees are given a free choice of whether to join a union, a vast majority have refused," said one antiunion lobbyist after the 2002 poll was released.[50] It was a perfectly calibrated answer, using just enough hazy language to seem accurate.

He is right that many workers have voted against joining a union, but very often that is because they aren't really being "given a free choice"— Corporate America basically has a gun to workers' heads warning them that a vote to join a union will result in all sorts of harassment, intimidation, and frightening consequences. A 1991 poll found that almost four in five workers said it was likely "that nonunion workers will get fired if they try to organize a union"[51]—a fear that, as mentioned above, Cornell researchers found to be well grounded. It's why Professor Charles Morris, one of the nation's leading labor experts, concluded that "a substantial number" of companies "deliberately use employment discrimination against employees as a device to remove union activists and thereby inject an element of fear in the process of selecting or rejecting union representation."[52]

In 1999, Harvard and University of Wisconsin researchers found that more than half of all managers said they would oppose any unionization effort in their workplace. That opposition is also often based in fear: one-third of managers said that allowing their workers to unionize would hurt their advancement in the company. Many of them are correct: when the researchers told business leaders that 15 percent of managers in non-union companies said they would welcome unionization efforts, the executives wanted to know who those managers were "so we can get them fired immediately."[53] And thanks to corrupt politicians who have gutted labor laws and reduced enforcement of workplace protections, those kinds of tactics are being used all the time.

Remember, these threats against unions are normally backed up by larger threats by employers of mass layoffs. A 1997 report for NAFTA administrators found that companies threaten to close up shop—and eliminate all jobs—in half the instances when workers try to form a union.[54] In other words, "free choice" in joining a union is rarely, if ever, a reality.

The Bush administration has lent a helping hand to these sorts of union-busting activities. In 2002, for instance, Bush repealed a federal regulation that allowed government agencies to prevent taxpayer money from going to contractors that had violated federal labor laws.[55] The rule had originally been issued by President Clinton in 2000 after a government study found that in one year alone, 261 federal contractors with 5,121 health and safety law violations received $38 billion in contracts. That's more than one out of every five federal contract dollars going to companies that ignore workers' rights.[56] Yet instead of cutting off this cash, Bush kept the spigot on, effectively endorsing companies' misbehavior.

Congress, too, could have done something—and some lawmakers tried. In 2003, lawmakers from both parties introduced the Employee Free Choice Act, which would have cracked down on companies that deliberately intimidate workers when they tried to form a union. Despite almost half of all House members cosponsoring the bill, corporate lobbyists made sure it was never even permitted to be brought up for a vote.[57]

MYTH: Labor law gives unfair advantages to labor unions.

The term "labor law" might make you believe that the statutes governing workers are designed exclusively to protect the rights of labor unions.
It's a myth that's naturally been perpetuated by Corporate America, which
wants the public to believe business is being persecuted by unions.

"Washington has created rules that benefit unions—to the disadvantage of most other groups," wrote *Investors Business Daily,* Corporate
America's rag sheet. "Indeed, organized labor has been the recipient of
special privileges granted by federal law for much of the last century."[58]

"Federal, state and even local laws give special legal privileges to
labor union officials," said Stefan Gleason, of the National Right to Work
Legal Defense Foundation[59]—a euphemistically named front group
funded by corporate interests including, among others, the Walton family
of Wal-Mart fame.[60]

It's true, labor laws do recognize unions' right to collectively bargain
on behalf of workers. But since their passage during the Great Depression, these laws have been so utterly weakened as to be rendered nearly
completely useless. Forget about wage and pension protections—those
were long ago gutted and left for dead. Forget about the free right to
strike—that's been severely limited, too, with very specific restrictions allowing the president to legally bar workers from striking and to make
sure unions can't exert too much pressure on Big Business. Forget even
about first amendment rights to free speech—laws actually bar striking or
picketing union workers from asking workers in other unions to join
them in solidarity.[61] Corporate America has cut through all that flesh and
is now down to the bone, sawing into the most basic, minimum legal protections for workers who want to organize into a collective unit.

According to Cornell University researchers, one out of four employers illegally fires at least one worker during a union election campaign,
three out of four hire antiunion consultants, and eight out of ten force
workers to attend antiunion lectures.[62] In this climate, what happened at
EnerSys battery factory in South Carolina has become commonplace. According to the *New York Times,* evidence showed the company engaging in
behavior usually reserved for Third World dictatorships. That included
"firing the top seven union leaders, spying on workers, refusing to bargain,
and ultimately closing the 500-worker plant to retaliate against the union."[63]

It is true that even under today's pathetically weak labor laws, this behavior is technically illegal. But laws are only as strong as their enforcement. With corporate-owned politicians running the show, labor law enforcement has become an oxymoron, and the National Labor Relations Board (NLRB) has become a punch line. Within months of assuming office, President Bush packed the agency with appointees straight out of Big Business's ranks, effectively transforming it into the scalpel that helps Big Business completely amputate all of our union rights.

For instance, Bush appointed Robert Battista chairman of the NLRB, despite Battista's record as the management attorney for the Detroit newspaper chain that had become infamous for union busting in the 1990s.[64] He also appointed William B. Cowen, the former chief attorney for Institutional Labor Advisors, a company that advises corporate clients on how to put the squeeze on unions.[65] And he appointed Michael Bartlett, who was the labor specialist at the notoriously antiunion U.S. Chamber of Commerce. Bartlett is so opposed to the existence of unions, he bragged to one newspaper that the merciless firing of unionized air traffic controllers in the 1980s was a good example of an employer "standing up for their rights."[66]

Under this leadership, the NLRB has gone out of its way to crush unions. In 2003, the agency formally endorsed a lawsuit brought by Bartlett's old employer, the Chamber of Commerce, that would strike down a California law preventing companies from using your taxpayer dollars to bust unions.[67] Specifically, the legislation prohibited companies that do business with the state from using the taxpayer money they pocket to intimidate, persecute, or otherwise harass workers who want to organize.[68]

By 2005, the *New York Times* reported that the NLRB had "made it more difficult for temporary workers to unionize and for unions to obtain financial information from companies during contract talks." The agency also "ruled that graduate students working as teaching assistants do not have the right to unionize at private universities, and it has given companies greater flexibility to use a powerful antiunion weapon—locking out workers—in labor disputes."[69]

But getting corrupt politicians to appoint ideological lunatics is only one of the ways Corporate America influences the NLRB. Starving the agency for resources is the other way. NLRB is chronically (and deliberately) understaffed, meaning it is constantly overloaded with cases. "Even when the NLRB finds that employees have been illegally fired, they rarely return to their jobs," wrote two of the nation's leading labor law experts in 2003.[70] That's because it takes years to litigate any dispute. As former Michigan Congressman David Bonior (D) recounted, when six workers were fired in 1992 from their factory jobs after voting to form a union, it took the NLRB eleven years to order the company to provide back pay. And even then, the company used additional delaying tactics, meaning the workers still have not received their due.[71]

With no real cop on the beat, corporate persecution of workers is on the rise. In the 1950s, for example, the annual number of documented cases in which workers were punished by companies for union activities was in the hundreds. By 1969, that number hit 6,000. And by the end of the 1990s, it was over 20,000.[72]

The nonpartisan Human Rights Watch issued a report in 2000 summing up the situation best. Even as America tells other countries to clean up their act and respect individual rights, the report found here at home among workers "freedom of association is a right under severe, often buckling pressure."[73] It sounded straight out of a State Department report criticizing one of the world's repressive regimes. Only, thanks to our own corrupt government, it describes everyday reality for millions of workers in the United States.

MYTH: Unions are all-powerful political forces that unduly influence Congress.

Imagine if your local middle school basketball team had an upcoming game against the NBA All-Star Team. Then imagine if, before the game, the 7 foot, 300 pound Shaquille O'Neal complained to your local newspaper that he feared he would be outplayed by the gangly, prepubescent 5'8" adolescent who would be guarding him. You would think you were reading a joke, right? You would laugh, right?

Yet whenever an election rolls around, we see this same kind of ridiculous propaganda vomited up by Corporate America's politicians and pundits, as they make wild claims about the influence of labor unions on the political process. In 1996, House Speaker Newt Gingrich said "union bosses [are] deeply involved in trying to buy the election."[74]

During the 2000 presidential campaign, Senator John McCain (R) flew around on corporate jets[75] owned by companies with business before the Senate committee he chaired. It was a gross display of how Corporate America owns our elections. Yet while McCain did acknowledge the generally corrosive influence of money on politics, he went out of his way to single out "the labor bosses [who] go down with the big checks"[76] as the

HERO: Dan Cantor, founder and director of New York's Working Families Party

BROUGHT TOGETHER UNIONS AND GRASSROOTS GROUPS TO CREATE A TRUE POLITICAL FORCE

Tired of being pushed around by politicians of both parties who sell American workers out, New York political organizer Dan Cantor was among those who in 1998 broke the mold. In that year, key unions and grassroots groups formed the Working Families Party (WFP), with Cantor as the founding executive director. The party is laser-focused on electing candidates who will stand up for ordinary citizens' economic concerns. Because New York allows one party to cross-endorse the nominee of another party (helping to avoid the "spoiler" and "wasted-vote" dilemmas), the WFP has strategically used its endorsements to help good Republican and Democratic candidates and pressure bad ones. And under Cantor's leadership, WFP has been wildly successful. As the *New York Times* reported after the 2004 elections, WFP has "established itself as an emerging political force statewide." Not only has it succeeded at the polls, it has been instrumental in making its agenda a reality. For instance, WFP was widely credited with playing a pivotal role in getting New York's Republican State Senate to override Republican governor George Pataki's veto of a minimum-wage increase—no small accomplishment. The WFP shows just how positive a force unions can be in fighting for the economic interests of all citizens.

prime culprits ruining our democracy—not the corporate cronies who were flying him all over the country.

In the 2004 election, the rhetoric got even hotter, as Bush's former labor secretary nominee, Linda Chavez, published a book claiming unions "wield extraordinary political power at all levels of government—federal, state, and local." Unions, she said, have "corrupted not only the electoral process but also our system of governing. And we're all paying the price."[77]

Remember the metaphor: Shaquille O'Neal publicly fretting over playing your local middle school's junior varsity center. Because that's how hilarious this rhetoric really is.

Yes, unions spend millions of dollars on all sorts of campaign activities: registering voters, getting people to the polls, advertisements—you name it, unions do it, and they would happily plead guilty to charges of political activism on behalf of workers.

But all those efforts are positively dwarfed by the amount Corporate America spends influencing elections. According to a 2001 report by the nonpartisan watchdog group Public Campaign, "for every one dollar contributed by labor unions business interests gave $15." When looking at just individual contributions to lawmakers, the gap is even more pronounced: "Business executives out-contributed labor leaders and staff by a factor of 1,000 to 1."[78]

Politicians are well aware of this reality, but do everything they can to perpetuate the myth of the Big Labor bosses controlling politics because it helps them deflect attention from their corporate paymasters. Their most practiced routine of rhetorical acrobatics was exemplified by Mississippi senator Trent Lott (R) in 2001, who told one side of the story, and then distorted that story completely. First, the one-sided back flip: The same month Public Campaign issued its report, Lott told reporters that unions "spent more money in last year's campaign than either party" (he provided absolutely no evidence). Then, the distortion: Lott said that meant that labor money "tilts the scales tremendously."[79] What he didn't say was that Corporate America spent *way, way, way* more than either party or the labor movement, meaning the scales were tipped not to workers but to Big Business.

But don't Democrats rely on more labor money than corporate money? And wouldn't that at least mean the Democrats are controlled by union money? The *Wall Street Journal* took a closer look at that question in 2001. The newspaper found that 80 percent of the Republican Party's 2000 campaign resources came from corporate sources—no surprise. But the paper also noted that while Democrats received "strong support from labor organizations and their members . . . more than 70% of the Democratic total also came from businesses and their employees."[80] To repeat, even Democrats, who Chavez claims are "in the pocket" of "leftist labor unions," relied on double the amount of money from business interests than they did from unions.

In 2004, there was little difference. Labor scraped together about $60 million for campaign contributions, while business poured in $1.5 billion. That's a 20-to-1 ratio.[81] In terms of contributions to unregulated political committees (called 527s), it was the same. Unions spent about $100 million, while single-issue/ideological committees (often heavily funded by Big Business) spent more than $430 million.[82]

But it isn't just campaign contributions where workers are outspent. Between 1997 and 2000, Corporate America spent an astounding $9.7 billion lobbying Congress.[83] That's about 4.5 million worth of lobbying for every single member of Congress every single year.[84] In that same four-year period, unions were able to muster less than $100 million for lobbying, meaning they were outgunned by more than 50 to 1.

MYTH: Unions are responsible for companies' financial problems.

The typical media coverage of labor disputes goes something like this:

A corporate executive pleads poverty for his company, claiming he needs to "renegotiate" the preexisting contract with the union that represents the company's workers. That "renegotiation" inevitably includes massive wage and health care benefit cuts. The public is told that if workers don't accept the cuts, the company will go belly-up—leading us to believe that the union's success in securing decent wages and benefits for its members is the reason the company is in trouble in the first place. This all fits perfectly into the overall portrayal of unions as evil, overly powerful monsters whose only goal is to bleed companies dry.

What rarely gets reported by the media or regulated by politicians, however, are the unethical and dishonest shenanigans that run counter to this one-sided story line. We rarely hear how these same executives pleading poverty often not only refuse to take the same pay cuts they are demanding from workers, but actually give themselves pay increases. We rarely hear how the company that is supposedly going bankrupt is actually sitting on a hidden pile of cash—some of it being used for vicious antiunion activities.

Consider three examples that prove this happens all the time:

– In 2005, Northwest Airlines executives demanded $176 million in wage and benefit cuts from its mechanics union, pleading poverty. Yet when those mechanics reacted by going on strike, the *New York Times* revealed that in the months leading up to the demand for wage/benefit cuts, "the airline had spent more than $100 million to hire and train 1,500 substitutes" for the striking mechanics—$100 million, that is, on activities designed to undermine the union. While no one denies that Northwest was having serious financial troubles, no one asked a simple question: If the company was supposedly in such severe financial straits that worker pay/benefit cuts were required, how did executives have $100 million of company money to throw around for these antiunion activities?[85]

– In 2005, executives at Ford and GM started making it known that they wanted its workers' union to agree to wages/benefit cuts because the companies had hit a financial bump in the road. But buried in a *Business Week* story like a needle in a haystack was the truth. "Both companies also have huge cash hoards," the magazine noted. "$20 billion at GM and $23 billion at Ford." What's more, the magazine reported that Ford and GM "execs aren't sharing in the pain they are prescribing for workers"— a major red flag for dishonesty. The magazine pointed out that when Chrysler pled poverty and secured wage cuts in 1981, "Chrysler canceled its [stockholder] dividend, top execs took a 10 percent pay cut, and then-Chairman Lee A. Iacocca worked for a dollar that year." But in 2005, "both GM and Ford still pay a dividend, and GM CEO G. Richard Wagoner Jr. got a $2.5 million bonus for 2004—on top of his $2.2 million in salary."[86]

– In 2002, US Airways went to its unions and asked for massive wage cuts. Understanding that the company was in serious trouble, the unions agreed. Yet just months later, the supposedly strapped-for-cash company doled out $6 million in bonuses to top executives—the same executives responsible for landing the airline in Chapter 11 bankruptcy in the first place.[87]

Again, no one is saying that companies never have a legitimate need to ask for wage/benefit concessions from unions when things really go south—and many times, unions agree to those concessions for the sake of keeping companies in business. The problem is that our corrupt political system has created no legal prohibitions against executives who do not tell the whole truth about the situation. They are allowed to deceive, distort, and lie in order to create a dishonest, blame-the-union rationale for their real agenda: squeezing workers and pocketing more cash for themselves.

LIE: Corruption requires unions to be under more scrutiny than corporations.

"The Bush administration is rapidly expanding audits of the nation's labor unions, citing a need to ferret out and deter corruption," the *New York Times* reported breathlessly on April 17, 2005. "Pointing to embezzlement of hundreds of thousands of dollars . . . Labor Department officials say the number of audits fell too far in the 1990's."[88]

Five days later, the Associated Press reported that the very same Bush administration was "weighing revisions to companies' [financial] reporting requirements" after "legions of companies complain[ed] that the rules are too burdensome and need to be eased."[89] By "revisions" it was clear the administration meant weakening post-Enron corporate financial disclosure laws.

It was the perfect example of how politicians are more than happy to create one set of standards for ordinary Americans and another set for the wealthy and powerful. Unions, they were telling us, are menacing, mafia-esque organizations that need a crackdown. Think Al Capone. But corporations, we are told, are honest and clean. Don't think Enron's Ken Lay.

Certainly, all this might be justified if union corruption were as big a problem—or bigger—than corporate corruption, which is exactly what Big Business wants you to think. But the numbers tell a much different story:

– In 2005, the Bush administration justified increasing audits of unions because it said there was an "embezzlement of hundreds of thousands of dollars" by two union leaders.[90] Yet three weeks before its announcement, the White House barely made a peep when the IRS issued a report showing that tax cheats are stealing $300 billion a year from the federal government.[91] Bush had made his nonchalant attitude toward the tax matter clear a year before, saying "the really rich people figure out how to dodge taxes anyway."[92]

– In 2003, investigators discovered that directors of a union-owned insurance company (Ullico) may have broken laws in a stock trading scandal that netted them $6 million.[93] The famously antiunion *Washington Times* reported that Republicans, "armed with 80,000 subpoenaed documents,"

HERO: Joshua Noble, Wal-Mart employee

TWENTY-ONE-YEAR-OLD LED BATTLE TO UNIONIZE THE MOST ANTIUNION COMPANY IN THE WORLD

Wal-Mart is the largest and wealthiest company in America, employing more than one million workers, and pulling in more than a quarter-trillion dollars a year. Yet because the company has spent years preventing unionization, workers are almost entirely powerless to demand the company pay better wages, even though Wal-Mart's wages are so low many employees are often forced to go on welfare. Enter Joshua Noble, a twenty-one-year-old Wal-Mart employee in Loveland, Colorado. In late 2004, he led a majority of his coworkers to sign statements supporting a union. Almost immediately, Wal-Mart executives flew in a special team of antiunion consultants to spread lies about unions. By the time the official vote on whether to create a union occurred three months later, Wal-Mart had gotten its way and crushed the union drive. But the damage had been done: Noble's high-profile campaign let American workers know that even the most powerful company on the globe could be challenged, and that with enough organization, workers will be able to one day obtain the rights they deserve.

said "they have a narrative that emulates the stock-price manipulation that brought down Enron."[94] To be sure, the scandal was no laughing matter. But comparing it to the Enron scandal is nothing short of hysterical. Enron swindled $60 billion from investors[95] and extorted billions more from ratepayers during an energy crisis it deliberately created—all while executives pocketed tens of millions of dollars from manipulated stock sales and showered politicians with thousands[96] to get them to look the other way. The Ullico scandal "emulates" Enron in the same way an eight-year-old T-ball player "emulates" Babe Ruth or a blade of grass "emulates" an oak tree.

▬ In 2002, Bush's Department of Labor filed a lawsuit against a group of union leaders, claiming they mismanaged their members' pension fund by investing a portion of it in a Florida hotel.[97] The lawsuit didn't claim the union leaders stole money—just that they failed "to prudently manage and invest their members' pension funds." After two years of harassment, the union leaders agreed to pay $11 million to settle the case (even though Knight Ridder reported that far from a bad investment, industry experts said it had turned out to be quite prudent).[98] Contrast this with the administration's attitude toward companies that deliberately try to rip off their workers' pensions. When IBM tried to slash its older workers' pensions, for instance, the Bush Treasury Department issued rules claiming the move was perfectly legal (it wasn't).[99] When United Airlines told workers the company would not honor their pensions, the Bush administration did nothing. It didn't sue the company, it didn't complain about the company failing "to prudently manage" workers' pensions—nothing.

Labor expert Nathan Newman notes that what's really amazing is just how clean the labor movement is in comparison with Corporate America. "Think about it," he wrote. "Out of the hundreds of billions of dollars invested by various union officials in different funds all over the country" antiunion forces have come up with relatively small scandals. "If anything, the fact that [a few officials] at Ullico couldn't even get away with stealing these relatively petty amounts speaks pretty well to union corporate accountability controls, controls obviously far better than the corporations plunged into bankruptcy because of money gone and unrecoverable."[100]

Yet the enforcement hypocrisy continues to this day. In 2004, the White House used the union corruption argument to justify new accounting rules for unions that are so complex and burdensome, many experts believed they were designed solely to usurp unions' time and energy—and in many cases make them spend triple what they currently do on bookkeeping. According to the *Hartford Courant*, "virtually every dollar spent by the union, and the time allotted by much of the staff, must find its way onto an expanded U.S. Department of Labor form—and it must be placed in a category according to what type of activity it represents." The paper added, "It's hard to see how this is anything other than administrative terrorism foisted on working people and their representatives."[101]

These rules contrast with the supposedly tough corporate "reforms" Bush bragged about after the Enron scandal. All they did was set new standards for how companies must do their internal accounting, instead of subjecting these companies to the same morass of public reporting that unions are now subject to. In fact, in 2001, Bush actually reduced the amount of public reporting for companies, signing an executive order eliminating existing regulations that made companies tell the public how much they were spending on antiunion activities.[102] As one union leader noted, "If for-profit corporations had to have the same level of disclosure [as unions], there would be a general meltdown on Wall Street."[103]

And that brings us to the real purpose behind the vilifying of unions in the first place. Antiunion politicians aren't really concerned about cleaning up a problem, because let's face it—the problem of corporate corruption dwarfs union corruption. As Newman notes, what they want to do is make unions look like Tony Soprano–run mafias by highlighting tiny scandals "that amount in dollar terms to less than one dollar for every ten thousand dollars involved in Enron alone." They can then use that false image of unions to silence labor leaders who are fighting against Corporate America's extremist agenda on behalf of ordinary workers.[104]

LIE: Antiunion bills are designed only to "protect paychecks."

The most nefarious legislative efforts are always draped in the most altruistic language, and "paycheck protection" is no exception. For years, Corporate America's closest allies in Congress have used this phrase to describe bills that would force union leaders to get the written permission of every one of their thousands of members before using union money to push the union's political agenda.

These politicians, of course, depict themselves as defenders of the common man. Mississippi senator Trent Lott (R) pushed "paycheck protection" because he said he was concerned with the "inappropriate use of union dues for campaigns all across the country without the members' permission."[105] Similarly, Representative Bill Thomas (R) justified his support by saying "all we're asking is that . . . people whose money is going to be used [for politics] have a right to say whether or not they agree to it."[106]

Sounds pretty fair—until people started wondering why these new rules would apply only to unions, and not corporations. If union leaders have to get explicit permission from their members to use resources for politics, shouldn't corporate executives have to do the same with their millions of stockholders? Aren't stockholders entitled to the same "protection" of their money?

Yes, if the goal is really to "protect" average people. No, if the real goal is exclusively to neuter unions by tying up their political resources in red tape—which, of course, it is. It's why in 1998, the *National Journal* reported that "paycheck protection" advocate Senator Don Nickles (R-OK) said he would "vigorously oppose" attempts "to require prior written consent of shareholders before corporations can fund political activities."[107]

When questions started to boil about the hypocrisy, Kentucky senator Mitch McConnell (R) took charge. Instead of displaying a stubborn attitude as Nickles had, he pretended to play ball, having his allies draft amendments to make it seem as if yes, corporations would be included in the proposed restrictions. He then went on Fox News to say the bill, "which we call 'paycheck protection,' includes corporations."[108]

Fair enough, right? Not really. As *Slate* reporter Tim Noah discovered, the amended "paycheck protection" legislation gave Big Business "a huge loophole" that was deceptively crafted to make sure the stockholder provisions were meaningless. As Noah said, "If the loophole hadn't been there, you can be sure Fortune 500 companies would have been out in force lobbying against it."[109]

Thankfully, these federal measures were rejected, at least temporarily protecting unions' ability to press their agenda in the public arena. But that hasn't stopped efforts at the state level. In 1998, Grover Norquist of the corporate-funded Americans for Tax Reform led a drive to enact "paycheck protection" bills in state legislatures.[110] He was using huge amounts of money from wealthy corporate donors[111] to push something he claimed was all about protecting average workers. What a joke. As Norquist admitted a year before, the effort was really all about destroying workers' political voice. If these antiunion bills passed and "if 10 percent of union members [refused to give permission]," Norquist told a magazine, "It would crush labor unions as a political entity."[112] Exactly—and that is, unfortunately, the point of "paycheck protection" proposals.

Solutions

Unions have served too important a role in our country's history to be sacrificed at the altar of corporate greed. Especially in an era when government is a wholly owned subsidiary of Corporate America, unions are one of the few strong voices left to defend ordinary Americans' economic interests. The union "problem" today is not that they are too powerful. It is that they—and the workers who rely on them—are under a vicious, relentless attack. Here are some solutions:

Pass the bipartisan bill that protects workers' rights. The only way workers can guarantee themselves a union is if they petition the NLRB to hold an official election. By design, those petitions can take weeks or even months to be processed by the deliberately understaffed and unresponsive agency. That delay allows companies to wage bitter campaigns against the union drive, with hired mercenaries employed by the company to intimidate, spy on, and fire workers who support the union. The tactics, unfortunately, work. According to a study of 400 union election campaigns in 1998 to 1999, more than a third of workers who voted against union representation said their vote was a response to corporate pressure.[113] But a bipartisan bill in Congress called the Employee Free Choice Act would authorize what's known as a "card check" system where, if enough workers sign a form indicating their support, a union can be formed immediately. The card check system is superior to the NLRB election system because it allows workers to decide on their own time, in private, and without corporate pressure whether they want to unionize. Workers should be entitled to this kind of freedom from harassment. The bill should be passed.[114]

Hold companies to the same standards as unions. Federal law requires the government to immediately get a court order limiting union activity if there is evidence that unions are engaging in illegal strikes/boycotts. But those same court-ordered limits are not required of companies when there is evidence they are illegally threatening, intimidating, or harassing workers who are exercising their rights to unionize. The standard needs to be made the same.[115]

Make companies that violate the law pay for it. Under the current system, illegally firing workers who are trying to form a union is often a good business decision. Federal "authorities" (if you can even call the pathetic NLRB that) regularly let the legal process drag out for years, and often only force the offending company to pay back wages. That can be quite a good bargain for Big Business, if it means keeping their entire workforce from unionizing and demanding better wages/working conditions. The only way to stop these illegal tactics is to hit companies where it hurts: in the pocketbook. Companies should be forced to pay a much larger punitive penalty when they are found guilty of illegally firing workers who are trying to unionize. Money talks—and a punishment for illegal behavior must be financially painful enough for corporations to see a deterrent.

Prohibit taxpayer cash from going to corporate criminals who persecute workers. President Bush's executive orders have uniformly favored his big corporate donors over unions. The most egregious of them is the directive allowing federal contracts to go to companies that have violated federal laws protecting worker rights. If a company repeatedly ignores basic laws protecting workers, taxpayers should not be subsidizing that company. Period.

Force corporations to disclose as much as unions. Labor expert Nathan Newman notes that unions today must submit "hundreds of pages listing the salaries and compensation of every [union] officer and employee, down to the clerical staff." And that was before the Bush administration cited bogus corruption charges to create even more red tape. "Can you imagine what would be said if [politicians] were demanding similar disclosure from every corporation?" he asked.[116] Actually, it's not that hard. Just a few years after Congress passed its weak, post-Enron disclosure laws for corporations, the *New York Times* reported that "business representatives gathered in Washington at an all-day round table discussion held by federal regulators and complained" about the cost of new reporting requirements. They were complaining even though there were "continuing revelations of potential fraud, criminal prosecution of fraud and convictions on fraud charges." Yet, by the end of 2005, the SEC began taking steps to formally weaken the new disclosure laws.[117] Remember, these new laws aren't even close to as tough as the existing laws governing unions—especially after President Bush repealed regulations forcing companies to disclose their expenditures on antiunion activities.[118] The system needs to be uniform, with Corporate America and unions governed by the same exact rules. Forcing unions to spend resources recording and disclosing every last transaction at the same time corporations are allowed to conceal most of their financial information is about as fair as forcing one poker player to have all his cards face up on the table while everyone else holds theirs close to the vest.

TO REALLY understand just how vicious a war our government is waging on workers' union rights, take a look at how your taxpayer money has been spent. Between 2001 and 2005, the Bush administration cut more than $100 million out of the government agency that is responsible for enforcing overtime, minimum-wage, and child labor laws.[119] This is an agency that most of President Bush's corporate campaign donors hate, as it is supposed to be the cop that keeps companies in line. By taking away that cop's resources, Bush had quietly reduced its ability to do its job, even though there was more and more evidence that workers needed stronger, not weaker cops on the beat.

At the very same year these cuts were proposed, the White House added $74 million to the budget of the agency whose primary purpose is to investigate labor unions.[120] Even though Bush had already created new layers of disclosure rules for unions,[121] he apparently wasn't satisfied that American workers were being harassed enough.

The moves alone were disgusting, but the fact that they were simultaneous was even more appalling. Through its budget decisions, the White House was bragging that our government now values harassing unions more than it does making sure basic federal protections for workers are enforced. Even more troubling, the administration was letting that fact be known at the very time when the public was hearing more and more stories of workers being abused and mistreated by Corporate America.

As mentioned before, hostility toward workers from moneyed interests is no shock—that's been around for years, as have specific antiunion policies. What's troubling is just how open today's politicians are in their hostility. The fact that they no longer see any reason to hide their hatred of workers' rights means the hostile takeover of our government has advanced well past just the buying and selling of specific policies. We are now in an era where Corporate America is using its influence over corrupt lawmakers to redefine what the government's entire job is—and that should frighten us all.

CHAPTER 10

LEGAL RIGHTS

★

THERE ARE few more disgusting forms of human behavior than a bully picking on a sick or weak person. For example, it would take a pretty awful human being to attack mine workers that are dying from exposure to asbestos. Weakened by terrible diseases like asbestosis and cancer, these are some of the most defenseless people around.

So it was naturally quite nauseating when the president of the United States—the most powerful man in the world—made attacking these sick workers and their families a centerpiece of his February 7, 2005, State of the Union Address. Far from offering words of condolence, or a tribute to their courageous work ethic, President Bush hammered the workers for having the nerve to exercise their legal rights—in this case, their legal right to demand health care resources from the companies that had harmed them.

"Our economy is held back by irresponsible class actions and frivolous asbestos claims," Bush said to a round of applause from onlooking lawmakers. That's right—it's not held back by abusive corporations who send people to their grave. It's not held back by greedy executives who refuse to help the workers whose lives they've destroyed. According to Bush, it's held back by "frivolous" asbestos claims, as if the people filing the claims tried to get deathly ill just so they could initiate a court case.

Five days after Bush's speech, prosecutors disclosed their indictment

against one of the biggest natural resource companies in America. According to the Associated Press, prosecutors said the company "knew a
Montana mine was releasing cancer-causing asbestos into the air and
tried to hide the danger to workers and townspeople."[1] Prosecutors noted
that more than 1,200 people became ill and some died. In all, almost
10,000 people now die every year because they were exposed to asbestos.[2]

Did the Bush administration change its tune? Was there an apology
for those insensitive State of the Union comments? Far from it. Hours
after the indictment was issued, Vice President Dick Cheney, whose own
company, Halliburton, had also been the target of asbestos claims, went
on the attack. He gave a speech deriding "frivolous lawsuits from trial
lawyers."[3] Two days later, Bush told a crowd, "We need to have tort reform so that these frivolous and junk lawsuits" from victims can be eliminated.[4] His allies on Capitol Hill soon introduced legislation to ban
workers from filing lawsuits against companies that exposed them to
asbestos—a bill that would save the chemical/mining industry up to $20
billion in damages they likely would have had to pay to victims.[5] The legislation sent a clear signal back to Corporate America that stiffing victims
was A-OK by those in the government. Not surprisingly, the Associated
Press reported a few months later that mining company W.R. Grace sent
a letter to 870 people sickened by asbestos-related illnesses "saying they
no longer have asbestos-related disease, or may not be as sick as they
thought," and thus must accept cuts to their health care benefits.[6] If these
victims thought about suing, well, the Bush administration had been clear
in its intention to thwart their efforts.

The whole episode shows us just how sophisticated Corporate America's propaganda cycle really is—and how, because of the hostile
takeover, politicians have become just another appendage of that propaganda machine. After all, there are few accomplishments more incredible
than getting America's most powerful politicians to openly attack sick
people, try to limit their legal rights, and then sit back and watch while
Big Business abandons victims—all in order to pad corporate executives'
bottom line.

In ages past, these efforts might have been hidden in the secret confines of the smoky backroom. Politicians might have wanted to avoid
being associated with trying to limit their constituents' rights. Today, however, Big Business has used its clout to give us the spectacle of tort
"reform"—the public euphemism for legislation aimed at limiting the
average person's legal rights. The goal is to restrict your ability to file
lawsuits against corrupt companies and cap the damages a corporation
can be forced to pay for its misbehavior. It is a goal Corporate America

has pursued for years. The more restrictions on a citizen's legal rights, the less huge companies have to pay someone when they screw him/her over.

Why is this an important economic issue? Because your right to file a lawsuit against a company is one of the only deterrents that prevent Corporate America from mistreating you. That is critically important especially now, when, as we've seen, our government often refuses to adequately enforce the law. Your boss may want to skim cash off the top of your paycheck, and he knows he might be able to sneak the move past government regulators because they are either nonexistent or bought-off. But your boss also knows you have a right to sue, which may give him pause before he tries to pick your pocket. Your phone company may want to add illegal fees to inflate your bill, but it also knows you can sue. It's the same all the way down the line.

Sure, it's not a perfect system, and few ordinary citizens want to have to sue or even threaten to sue. But Americans' legal right to fight back in court is one of the last and most critically important defenses against corporate greed. As one of the government's top regulators at the Securities and Exchange Commission (SEC) admitted after the Enron scandal, lawsuits "are a big part of the existing deterrent in the country today" against corporate abuse. In fact, as the regulator noted, "Private lawsuits probably have a much greater impact, even [more] than the SEC, on the behavior of company executives and auditors."[7]

Of course, that's not the candor the public has come to expect in discussions of our legal rights. Big Business and corrupt politicians have packaged the corporate agenda in populist rhetoric—as if preventing citizens from fighting back in court is good for the average Joe. As Bush says, "We must protect workers and small-business owners from the frivolous lawsuits."[8] It's the *Communist Manifesto* turned on its head. We're told "Workers of the world, unite ... unite to limit your own legal rights."

Undoubtedly, it has taken quite a big chunk of change to buy off enough politicians to move such an offensively greedy agenda through Congress. But there is plenty to go around, as a wide array of companies have a financial interest in bills that prevent them from being called onto the carpet in court. The corporate money is targeted precisely to influence the most important legislators. Just look at the top contributors to lawmakers on the House and Senate Judiciary committees—the panels that craft the details of tort "reform" bills. In 2004, business interests that stood to gain from tort reform gave these lawmakers an eye-popping $54 million. That was almost double the amount that groups that opposed the legislation (such as lawyers and unions) could muster.[9]

The U.S. Chamber of Commerce plays a particularly prominent role pushing tort "reform." In 2004 alone, the group spent $53 million exclusively on lobbying. That was "more than any lobbying entity has ever spent in a single year," according to *The Hill* newspaper.[10] Its four-year record told the same story: More than $140 million on lobbying between 2001 and 2004. That was ten times what the supposedly all-powerful trial lawyers spent in the same time.[11]

Much of the Chamber of Commerce's cash is funneled into its Institute for Legal Reform—a front group created exclusively to lobby for limiting citizens' legal rights. The institute tries to keep its funding sources secret and hide behind the perception that the Chamber of Commerce represents local mom-and-pop businesses. But the watchdog group Public Citizen documented in 2003 that it was being underwritten by a handful of big insurance and manufacturing conglomerates—industries with a big financial stake in limiting citizens' legal rights.[12]

The money has done its job. In 1995, Congress passed a bill limiting stockholders' right to file lawsuits against company executives when they cook the books or otherwise violate the law. When President Clinton courageously vetoed the bill, then–Democratic National Committee Chairman senator Chris Dodd (CT) led the successful fight to override him, earning himself a quarter of a million dollars in accounting industry campaign contributions.[13] As one market analyst noted after the Enron scandals, the measure "paved the way for corporate chieftains basically to lie without fear of being sued."[14]

Ten years later, Congress acted again, passing a bill limiting citizens' right to file class-action lawsuits. These are the suits on behalf of large groups of people who have been wronged by big companies. Think of the multibillion-dollar suit against the tobacco companies. Once again, both Democrats and Republicans joined together to pass the legislation.[15]

The fight is also happening in the states. Some states have limited punitive damages—the large cash payouts companies are ordered to pay as punishment for their malicious behavior, and which serve as the best deterrent to corporate misbehavior.[16] Other states prevent citizens from seeking damages from more than one company, even if they have been harmed by more than one company.[17] And still other states limit the amount of "noneconomic" damages that can be awarded to a citizen. This is compensation for pain and suffering, so that, for instance, a worker who loses his arm because of a faulty factory machine can force the company to fork over more than just his back wages.

But even that is not enough. Every year, Congress and state legislatures consider even more extreme legislation that is ultimately aimed at one

HACK: Mary Landrieu, Louisiana senator

AFTER $227,000, SWITCHES VOTE TO SUPPORT ELIMINATING CITIZENS' LEGAL RIGHTS

In 2003, Senator Mary Landrieu (D-LA) provided a critical vote delaying legislation limiting citizens' right to fight corporate abuse in court. Yet according to *Congressional Quarterly*, right after her vote she let business lobbyists know that "if they want a Democrat to work with them, I'm willing to, but I've got to have certain assurances." Two years and $227,000 in corporate political contributions later, Landrieu switched her position and voted for the bill.

thing: completely curtailing an average person's right to fight back against corporate abuse.

To be sure, no one denies there are people who abuse the system with frivolous lawsuits. And Big Business has been quite successful at distorting cases to make them seem frivolous. It's why everyone knows about the woman who won a punitive judgment against McDonald's after spilling hot coffee on herself, while almost no one knows that McDonald's had previously received more than 700 reports of often severe burns caused by the 190-degree coffee it was serving (liquids over 130 degrees can cause third-degree burns).[18]

But as the data shows, this "lawsuit crisis," for the most part, doesn't exist. It is a story line woven with all the same threads of dishonesty that come with a political system focused solely on protecting corporate profits, not ordinary people.

MYTH: America is suffering through a lawsuit crisis.

"A woman throws a soft drink at her boyfriend at a restaurant, then slips on the floor she wet and breaks her tailbone," wrote Mort

Zuckerman, publisher of *U.S. News & World Report,* in 2003. "She sues. Bingo—a jury says the restaurant owes her $100,000!"

He wasn't finished. "A woman tries to sneak through a restroom window at a nightclub to avoid paying the $3.50 cover charge," he wrote. "She falls, knocks out two front teeth, and sues. A jury awards her $12,000 for dental expenses."

Zuckerman's piece was called "Welcome to Sue City, U.S.A."[19]—and it had one thing in mind: perpetuating Corporate America's myth that our country is currently suffering through an intolerable flood of lawsuits that can only be cured by laws that limit ordinary citizens' legal rights.

Thankfully, the *Washington Post* caught Zuckerman in what was a flat-out lie. "The cases of the soda-slipping Pennsylvania woman and the window-wriggling Delaware woman are fabricated," noted the paper. "No public records could be found for them."[20]

But for every lie that is caught, you can bet there are scores that go unchallenged, helping Big Business create a perception of crisis that simply does not exist.

How do they get away with it? First and foremost, repetition. Every time you hear a corrupt politician, right-wing pundit, or corporate lobbyist talk about lawsuits, you inevitably hear a version of what conservative commentator Tucker Carlson said in 2004: "Everybody knows lawsuits are out of control."[21] The more it is said, the more it becomes the conventional wisdom, parroted by the media, no matter how untrue.

Then comes the exaggeration of the rare frivolous lawsuits, and crazy-sounding torts. Though these cases usually get thrown out by the courts, Big Business and its political allies seize on these examples and exaggerate them in an effort to create the perception that America's legal system is being wholly abused. But the real facts about lawsuits tell a completely different story. As the *Los Angeles Times* reported in 2005, America is being flooded with "an anthology of legal urban legends that have circulated widely on the Internet, regaling millions with examples of cluelessness and greed being richly rewarded by the courts. These fables have also been widely disseminated by columnists and pundits who, in their haste to expose the gullibility of juries, did not verify the stories and were taken in themselves." Experts note that despite most of these tales being false, "their wide acceptance has helped to rally public opinion behind business-led campaigns to overhaul the civil justice system by restricting some types of lawsuits and capping damage awards."

The hard statistics tell the same story—there is no tort "crisis." According to state court and population data, tort lawsuits decreased by roughly 15 percent between 1992 and 2001 when adjusted for population growth.[22] In 2003, the U.S. Justice Department released a report showing that the number of torts that went to trial dropped by almost half, from 1992 to 2001.[23] In fact, as CNN reported in 2005, "only 3 percent of tort cases actually make it to trial."[24]

Meanwhile, for every rare instance of an outrageous lawsuit, there is an equally ridiculous law passed that you never hear about that exempts a different special interest from legal liability. In Indiana, for instance, if your family member dies, and you later find out that he/she has been buried in the wrong place or the body parts have been mishandled, a state law says the mortician isn't legally accountable. Want to donate your spoiled meat to charity and use it as a tax write-off? Head to Idaho, Illinois, New Mexico, or Tennessee. There, lawmakers grant you legal immunity if that meat harms or kills the people who eat it. And if you are thinking about going to a tanning salon, make sure it's not in Colorado. Laws there say you can't hold a tanning salon liable if its machines accidentally broil you to a crisp.[25]

Unfortunately, the media have largely taken the side of those who want to limit citizens' legal rights and exempt corporations from legal responsibility. As media critic Steve Brill told the *Washington Monthly* in 2004, "I had gone back through the archives of *Time* magazine, and every ten years, *Time* declared a 'litigation crisis.' But there was no crisis." Why do journalists parrot the lies? "Reporters are basically lazy" and don't want to dig into the real data, said Brill. Instead, they use the sensationalist exaggerations as headline grabbers. "You can always find a ridiculous lawsuit to make the system look crazy," he said.[26]

Thus, with no one holding our political leaders' feet to the fire, the most shamelessly dishonest myths keep being repeated. As mentioned in the health care chapter, President Bush traveled to Madison County, Illinois in 2005 to reiterate his call for legislation limiting citizens' legal rights. The county is regularly called a "judicial hellhole" by corporate-funded front groups pushing tort "reform."[27] Bush claimed that because 700 lawsuits had been filed there between 1996 and 2003, people "see firsthand what happens when the system gets out of control."[28]

What he didn't say was that just 14 out of the 700 cases resulted in a verdict—with most cases not going to trial, or being thrown out. Just six of the cases that did go to trial favored plaintiffs.[29] In other words, the system largely worked on its own to get rid of the "frivolous lawsuits."

But then, curbing "frivolous" lawsuits really isn't the point of those who push tort "reform." Stopping *all* lawsuits—no matter how valid—is the real goal. Corrupt politicians use the term *frivolous* or *junk* every time they say "lawsuit"—but that's not what they care about. They are focused on creating a public rationale for new laws that prevent you from fighting back when a corporation violates your rights. As one political strategist told the *Washington Post,* limiting people's legal rights is all about "pleas[ing] everybody from the Chamber of Commerce to the drug companies to the realtors . . . you name it."[30]

LIE: Limiting class-action lawsuits is designed to help ordinary people.

In an age when our government has reduced or eliminated most major restrictions on Corporate America's irresponsible behavior, class-action lawsuits are the last haven for the abused citizen. These suits are really very simple: groups of people who have been wronged by their employer or by a company's faulty product come together to seek legal redress in court. Instead of filing hundreds of individual suits that might clog the courts, they file one suit on behalf of all the victims. That allows abused individuals who might not have the money to legally protect themselves in court to band together and pool limited resources.

Class actions, mind you, have been some of the most famous cases in American history, resulting in positive social change. *Brown v. Board of Education,* the case that ended segregation in schools, was a class action.[31] So was the historic case against Ford for producing Pintos that were exploding and killing people.[32] And they are being used today by some of the most abused people in America—workers whose wages have been stolen by employers, mine workers afflicted with preventable disease, and employees who have faced sexual discrimination.

Knowing all this, you can understand Corporate America's desire to limit or eliminate citizens' class-action rights. These lawsuits force companies to either behave or pay a big price in the form of a massive judgment. Fewer class actions means more corporate abuse and license for Big Business to cut corners and rip off consumers/employees.

Enter Congress, which is more than happy to take the side of the moneyed interests. Using the most nefarious language, politicians on the take shamelessly claim that restricting people's legal rights is the best way to help ordinary Americans. It is sort of like the ridiculed wartime oxymoron that you have to burn a village down to save it.

"To protect small businesses and workers," President Bush said in 2005, "we need to change the way we handle class-action lawsuits." By that he meant eliminate them altogether. He said these suits "hurt the honest workers"[33]—an insult to low-wage workers who were, at the time, pressing a high-profile class-action suit against Wal-Mart, charging the company with cheating them out of their paychecks.[34]

Bush continued on to tell the crowd that "all the lawsuits . . . affect your wallet" because he claimed companies are forced to defend themselves, and therefore raise prices to recover those costs. But he didn't mention that class actions often result in lower prices for all consumers—not just the ones who file the suits. Consider just a few random examples:

– FleetBoston started charging consumers a $35 annual fee on a credit card it billed as "no annual fee." Consumers filed a class-action suit in 2002, forced the company to repay them and eliminate the fee.

– MCI started secretly charging customers as much as $2.87 for a one-minute call, even after the company widely advertised a rate of five-cents-a-minute. Consumers filed a class-action suit in 2000, were repaid, and forced the company to uphold its rate promises.

– Anyone who has bought a home knows how confusing all the fees are during the process. In 2002, consumers discovered that a major bank was charging up to $500 more per transaction than allowed. They filed a class action, and forced the company to reduce the fee.[35]

And remember—these class actions don't just take the company in question to the woodshed. They create an industry-wide chilling effect on similarly abusive behavior. You can bet that credit card companies thought twice about doing what FleetBoston did, phone companies reconsidered doing what MCI did, and banks hesitated before devising another fraudulent fee rip-off on a mortgage transaction.

Sadly, though, they won't have to hesitate as much anymore. A few months after Bush's speech, Big Business got its wish. The White House rammed a bill through Congress that severely limits the right of citizens to file class-action suits. Actually, *rammed* is the wrong word—the bill sailed through our money-drenched Congress with wide bipartisan support.[36]

The bill specifically forces most class actions to be filed only in federal court. That doesn't sound so bad, until you consider that it probably means many tough state laws will be rendered useless. Why? Because federal courts often allow federal law to preempt or invalidate state statutes that are critical in protecting citizens against corporate abuse.

Meanwhile, victims will have to wait far longer—and spend more money—to litigate their cases, because the federal court system is

HACK: John Stossel, ABC News "reporter"

RAILS ON PEOPLE WHO FILE LAWSUITS AFTER FILING A LAWSUIT HIMSELF

ABC hilariously bills John Stossel as a "reporter," even though he is widely known as one of the most rabid right-wing ideologues in America. Stossel has earned that reputation, in part, from his attacks on people who file lawsuits—especially those who sue for pain and suffering when they are abused. He has called these and other plaintiffs "parasites" who "feed off the productive members of society." Yet it was Stossel who filed a high-profile lawsuit for his own pain and suffering when a pro wrestler slapped him during an interview. And it was Stossel who bragged to a newspaper that he sued "for as much as I could get," ultimately pocketing $200,000.

understaffed, underfunded, and overburdened. As the *Los Angeles Times* editorial board said, the bill means "defrauded retirees, swindled consumers and patients harmed by drugs or faulty pacemakers would probably have to wait years longer for redress—if they received it at all."[37] It's why the U.S. Judicial Conference—the group that represents federal judges—opposed the legislation. Even though the bill gave more power to federal judges, the organization knew it was way too extreme.[38]

While proponents talked about how much the bill would help average folks, you could almost hear corporate executives high-fiving when Bush signed the bill. Jackson Lewis, the law firm (mentioned in the previous chapter) that specializes in helping companies screw workers, excitedly noted on its website that the legislation means "state overtime class actions may now be removed to federal court." Because of that Jackson Lewis also reported that "employers may begin to benefit from the more stringent federal class action rules."[39] Similarly, because federal courts are already so overburdened, one financial analyst gloated that "the practical effect of the change could be that many cases will never be heard."[40]

This is why Corporate America had lobbied so intensely for the legislation. Between 2000 and 2003 when the class action bill was initially introduced, for example, at least 100 major companies and business organizations unleashed at least 475 lobbyists to promote these class-action "reforms." These weren't amateurs either: almost one-third of the lobbyists had some kind of "revolving door" connection from having previously worked inside the government. The U.S. Chamber of Commerce actually set up a separate foundation to employ 45 lobbyists on its own. It joined with other business groups to spend more than $22 million in one year influencing members of Congress on the issue. Even more money was spent directly on campaign contributions: the 29 corporations and business groups that lobbied most actively for class-action legislation slathered $50 million in campaign contributions on lawmakers between 1998 and 2002.[41]

The corruption that surrounded the debate over the bill was particularly sickening. For instance, in an October 2003 debate over the issue, Louisiana senator Mary Landrieu (D) provided a critical vote to delay the legislation, positioning herself as a consumer champion. Yet *Congressional Quarterly* reported that she was "sure to be targeted by business lobbyists." They didn't have to do much work—she quickly let it be known her vote was negotiable. "If they want a Democrat to work with them, I'm willing to," she said. "But I've got to have certain assurances."[42] The money poured in. In 2003 and 2004 alone, she raked in more than $227,000 from corporate political action committees.[43] When the bill was up for consideration again in 2005, she voted for it.[44]

LIE: Self-described "tort reformers" actually believe in tort reform.

There is nothing like the hypocrisy of a corrupt politician or political operative who says he wants a standard for everyone but himself. And when it comes to tort reform, the advocates of limiting citizens' legal rights are among the biggest hypocrites out there.

Take Pennsylvania senator Rick Santorum (R). As a House member in 1994, he authored a bill to prevent juries from awarding plaintiffs any more than $250,000 for "noneconomic" damages.[45] Within months of becoming a senator, in 1995, he gave a speech on the floor of the Senate to declare, "We have a much too costly legal system. It is one that makes us uncompetitive and inefficient, and one that is not fair to society as a whole. While we may have people, individuals, who hit the jackpot and win the lottery in some cases, that is not exactly what our legal system should be designed to do."[46]

Four years later, however, Santorum supported his wife's $500,000 lawsuit against her chiropractor. At the trial, the senator took the stand to offer testimony aimed at convincing jurors to compensate his family for the very "noneconomic" pain and suffering that his legislation had aimed to stop.[47] When reporters asked Santorum about the naked hypocrisy, he refused to answer the questions himself, instead shoving out his spokesman to claim that "the legislative positions that Senator Santorum has taken on tort reform and health care have been consistent with the case involving Mrs. Santorum."[48] Apparently, Santorum has a far different definition of "consistent" than most Americans.

Then there is George W. Bush. Since his time as governor of Texas, he has been on a tort "reform" rampage. One of his first acts as an elected official was to use a special procedure called "emergency status" to expedite tort "reform" legislation through the Texas legislature.[49] He ignored government data showing punitive damage claims had dropped in his state.[50] He also brushed aside a nonpartisan report exposing Bush's own conflict of interest in the matter. Specifically, the report showed that as many as three-quarters of the companies Bush personally owned stock in were companies that would be protected by his legislation.[51] Not surprisingly, the measures he ultimately signed were some of the most extreme limits on citizens' legal rights in any state.

As president, Bush has been the same. He's traveled all over the country deriding "junk" and "frivolous" lawsuits. Yet in 1999, it was George W. Bush who sued a rental car company over a fender-bender involving his daughters in which no one was hurt. The accident was so minor, the police weren't even called. Additionally, Bush's own insurance company would have covered the repair cost, making a lawsuit entirely unnecessary.[52] That wasn't good enough for Bush, though. He tried to sue the driver, too.[53]

This kind of hypocrisy isn't just limited to bought-off politicians. For instance, take corporate-backed[54] advocacy groups like Texans for Lawsuit Reform and Citizens Against Lawsuit Abuse, who helped Bush push through his tort "reforms" as governor. According to Austin's leading newspaper, their goal was to have "state law rewritten to reduce lawsuits, protect businesses and lower awards." Yet the newspaper also noted that top board members of the two groups had themselves filed about eighty civil lawsuits since the late 1970s.[55] One of those board members was the plaintiff in a $100 million lawsuit proceeding at the very same time that board member was pushing bills to limit such lawsuits. His support of the bill was no act of self-sacrifice, though—because his suit was already filed before the bill passed, it wasn't affected.[56]

Then there is right-wing "journalist" John Stossel of ABC News. He bills himself as an objective reporter but is widely considered one of the most untrustworthy and partisan figures on television.[57] Not surprisingly, he is regularly given awards for his dishonest work by archconservative corporate-funded think tanks.[58] Those embarrassing accolades come, in part, from Stossel's willingness to attack people who file lawsuits, thus perpetuating Corporate America's spin. He has gone on the air to call those who fight for citizens' legal rights in court "parasites" who "feed off the productive members of society."[59]

"We all have pain and suffering in our lives," Stossel has said. "And if each time we hang onto it until we get some kind of compensation, society can't work."

Funny, though—it was Stossel who earlier in his career filed a lawsuit for his own pain and suffering after a professional wrestler slapped him during an interview. "I had ear pain for sometime afterward," Stossel whined to the *Providence Journal-Bulletin*, trying to justify his hypocrisy. "But in fact, as soon as I got paid, my ear pain diminished." What a coincidence. Did he limit the damages he sought, as many tort reformers demand? "I asked for as much as I could get," he said, ultimately pocketing a fat $200,000 settlement.[60]

What does this hypocrisy show? A few things. First, when it comes to legal rights, corrupt politicians, operatives, and pundits—many who play up their "I'm just a regular guy" image—are actually elitists who want to play by different rules than everyone else plays by. Second, these tort "reformers" don't even really believe the merits of their own corporate-written arguments, because in their personal lives, they are as ready to exercise their legal rights as the people they vilify. Third (and perhaps most vomit-inducing), we see that these powerful people are so corrupt, they have no problem insulting the public with this kind of hypocritical behavior, as long as corporate cash keeps coming in.

MYTH: Greedy citizens are behind the supposed problem of "lawsuit abuse."

We've all heard it before: rich trial lawyers and greedy citizens are responsible for abusing America's legal system by filing a glut of "frivolous lawsuits." Because of these parasites, we're told, honest people are suffering.

In 1996, it was Republican presidential candidate Bob Dole who pushed this myth. "These frivolous lawsuits are putting businessmen and businesswomen out of business," Dole said. "They're costing millions and millions and millions of dollars and putting people out of business." Now it's George W. Bush, who said in 2002 that honest businesses are "falling prey to frivolous lawsuits, all designed to make trial lawyers even wealthier."[61]

This is all used, naturally, as a justification for limiting individuals' legal rights. There's just one problem: businesses—not individuals—are responsible for most lawsuits.

That's right, despite there being 281 million citizens in America and just 7 million businesses, corporations "file about four times as many lawsuits as individuals represented by trial lawyers," according to a 2004 report by the watchdog group Public Citizen. Corporations, in fact, were 69 percent more likely to be sanctioned for frivolous cases than individuals represented by trial lawyers.[62]

The National Center for State Courts did its own analysis of seventeen key states and found that between 1993 and 2002, personal tort cases dropped by 5 percent, while contract disputes—typically brought by corporations[63]—increased by 21 percent in the same time. As Public Citizen notes, these contract disputes account for "more than 10 times as many lawsuits as are filed by injured consumers in products liability and medical malpractice actions, combined."[64]

The hypocrisy is everywhere. Insurance companies, for example, have spent millions of dollars lobbying for legislation that would restrict citizens' legal rights and cap damages that can be awarded to individuals. The fewer rights an average person has in court and the lower the cap on damages, the less the insurance company has to pay out for the corporate clients it insures.

Yet insurance companies are simultaneously some of the most litigious corporations in America. In Cook County, Illinois, alone, insurers file over 8,000 lawsuits a year. According to Public Citizen, filing lawsuits is so important to insurers that their lobbyists tried to have insurance companies exempted from their own model tort "reform" bills.[65]

Vice President Dick Cheney personifies this dishonesty. In May 2004, he gave a speech at Wal-Mart's corporate headquarters in Arkansas where he said "junk lawsuits are cluttering the courts, weakening our economy, hurting employers and workers."[66]

It was surely music to Wal-Mart executives' ears, as the company was

HERO: Frank Clemente, director of Public Citizen's Congress Watch

TIRELESSLY DISPROVING BIG BUSINESS'S LIES ABOUT TORT "REFORM"

It is a thankless task to fight for citizens' basic rights when almost all of Corporate America is aligned against you. But that's what Frank Clemente and Public Citizen's Congress Watch do when it comes to defending citizens' basic legal rights. The nonprofit organization has been one of the most effective watchdog groups in debunking Big Business's lies about the American legal system. For instance, it was Congress Watch that proved corporations—not greedy citizens—are responsible for most frivolous lawsuits. And it is Congress Watch that tries to let Americans know how citizens' legal rights keep corporate abuse in check.

facing a series of lawsuits from its employees over sex discrimination,[67] and violations of workplace/wage laws.[68] And the rhetoric certainly sounded good—except for one hitch: Cheney railing on lawsuits is about as credible as Wilt Chamberlain preaching abstinence.

In just the five years that Cheney served as Halliburton's CEO, the corporation was involved in 151 court claims it filed in fifteen states. That's an average of 30 lawsuits per year under Cheney's leadership. Though Halliburton makes billions each year, no lawsuit seemed too small or "frivolous" to the company under Cheney, as it sued some debtors for as little as $1,500.[69]

Certainly, this kind of hypocrisy is appalling. But that's not the half of it. At the very same time that lawmakers are lying about who is actually filing lawsuits and claiming they want to stop "lawsuit abuse," they are actually granting corporations special privileges to file even more lawsuits. For instance, the North American Free Trade Agreement (NAFTA) quietly established special courts where foreign companies can sue U.S. federal and state governments for compensation when laws protecting health, labor, or environmental standards cut into corporate profits.

One company, for instance, sought nearly $1 billion from California (more than 1 percent of the state's entire budget) as compensation for a state law that prohibited the use of an environmentally hazardous gasoline additive. In all, Big Business has used these special tribunals to force American taxpayers to hand over $1.8 billion. Where is the outcry from corporate-backed politicians who say they are concerned about "frivolous lawsuits"? Nowhere. Instead of eliminating these special privileges for corporations, the Bush administration is pressing for more NAFTA-style trade agreements, creating the potential for even more of these outrageous lawsuits.[70]

MYTH: Jury awards and lawsuit costs to the economy are out of control.

In 2003, Vice President Dick Cheney said, "We need a cap of $250,000 on noneconomic damages, and we need reasonable limits on punitive damages." He declared that "the time has come for Congress to set reasonable limits on the litigation culture," because jury awards to citizens who file lawsuits were out of control.[71]

Two months later, *Newsweek* pathetically regurgitated Cheney's rhetoric. In a cover story called "Civil Wars," the magazine breathlessly claimed "an onslaught of litigation" was costing the U.S. economy "an estimated $200 billion a year," as greedy individuals were supposedly abusing "a system that allows sympathetic juries to award plaintiffs not just real damages . . . but millions more for the impossible-to-measure 'pain and suffering' and highly arbitrary 'punitive damages.' "[72]

Both Cheney and *Newsweek* had financial motives in pushing these claims. Cheney had made a career out of raking in campaign cash from companies that have been pushing to limit jury awards. Similarly, *Newsweek*'s parent company had been repeatedly sued by individuals and the federal government[73] for employment discrimination, with courts forcing the magazine's owner to pay millions for such misbehavior.[74] The lower the jury awards, the less *Newsweek* would have to pay in the future.*

---

*Unfortunately, *Newsweek* refused to mention these conflicts of interest in its story. The magazine also had the nerve to quote Philip K. Howard, a top attorney from its own defense law firm, attacking citizen lawsuits. The magazine then glowingly referred to him as a "legal reformer" who is trying to "save Americans from a legal system gone mad." See *The Lawyer*, 11/22/04; Gloria Cooper, "Darts & Laurels," *Columbia Journalism Review*, 4/04; Stuart Taylor Jr. and Evan Thomas, *Newsweek*, 12/15/03.

But bias is one thing, lies are another. According to the Bush administration's own Justice Department in April 2004, the median jury award in all tort suits was $37,000 in 2001—down from $65,000 in 1992.[75] That's a far cry from the "millions" we're told are regularly doled out. Same thing with punitive damages. They were only awarded in 6 percent of all trials,[76] and averaged just $50,000.[77] That's actually an outrage— punitive damages are intended not as compensation to a victim but as punishment to big companies so they don't misbehave again, meaning punitive-damage rulings have to be big in order to make an impact. For many large companies, $50,000 is barely a rounding error.

These numbers tell the same story even in places like the famous Madison County, Illinois, where President Bush claimed in 2005 "there is a constant risk of being hit by a massive jury award." Yet between 1996 and 2003, only four wrongful death cases there involved awards above the $250,000 cap Bush and Cheney were pushing. "When they talk about awards and judgments and things of that nature, they're just not here," said one local lawyer.[78]

And what about that $200 billion number? Like *Newsweek*, President Bush claimed that "the cost to our economy of litigation is conservatively estimated to be over $230 billion a year."[79] Is that really how much lawsuits are costing our country every year? No, and there's nothing conservative—or accurate—about that number at all. It is a grossly inflated figure fabricated out of thin air by an insurance industry consulting company called Tillinghast-Towers Perrin (TTP). The figure is so deliberately inaccurate, the nonpartisan Congressional Budget Office investigated it. Researchers found that TTP simply added up the total amount the highly profitable liability insurance industry spends every year and then deceptively peddled it as the cost to society of all lawsuits. Those "costs" included, for instance, the insurance industry's huge administrative expenses and its executives' multimillion-dollar salaries.[80]

Solutions

To the degree that there is lawsuit abuse—and there certainly is some of that—there are ways of reforming the system without stripping citizens of their legal rights. That's something Big Business doesn't want to hear. Corporate executives want to throw out not only the baby and the bathwater, but the tub itself and the entire bathroom. That's both dangerous and unnecessary.

Prevent limits on jury awards—especially punitive damages.
Blanket limits on how much juries can award to victims of corporate
abuse are obscene. They prevent juries from using discretion in awarding victims what they need to get their lives back in order. It's not as if
jury awards are out of control. As previously mentioned, the median
jury award in tort suits is $37,000—and that's down more than 56 per-
cent since 1992.[81] Ending limits on punitive damages is particularly important. These are the awards above and beyond what individuals get
for their tribulations. They are the punishments that make sure the
guilty company does not do what it did again. That means in many cases
punitive damages have to be large in order to make a company get the
point. If they are too small, the company will know it can continue such
misbehavior, and simply chalk up the verdicts as minor costs of doing
business. That does no good. Think about it this way—let's say you are
running late for an airline flight and have to park your car in a hurry.
And let's say it costs $10 a day to park in the lot that's far enough away
that you might miss your flight, while the penalty for parking illegally in
the lot right in front of the terminal is only $10.25 a day. You would
likely park illegally and break the law because it would make financial
sense to you. In this case, the benefits of breaking the law (convenience,
making your flight, and not losing your $300 plane fare) likely outweigh
the benefits of behaving legally (in this case, saving 25 cents a day).
That's the same thing that happens when punitive damages are limited.
Companies can often have a financial incentive to abuse people, because
the cost to them if they get caught—reduced punitive damages—are less
than the amount they make by misbehaving.

Better fund the court system. The state and federal court system is
overburdened, understaffed, and poorly funded. That isn't good for anyone, as it drags out court cases for years. In 1999, for instance, there were
more than 17,000 cases pending in federal court for more than three
years.[82] That leaves victims of corporate abuse having to spend more
money on prolonged litigation, and more time waiting for justice.

**Increase punishments when the rare frivolous lawsuit comes
to court.** In 2003, Fox News network filed a lawsuit against Al Franken,
claiming the comedian's use of the term "fair and balanced" violated the
company's supposed trademark on the phrase. "This is an easy case," said
the federal judge in court. Fox's suit was "wholly without merit, both fac-
tually and legally," he said, and then he dismissed the case.[83] It was the

classic—albeit rare—frivolous lawsuit. Unfortunately, Fox News faced no serious punishment for wasting the court's time, and no sanctions for forcing Franken to spend money defending himself. That is wrong. In the uncommon instance that a judge finds a case to be truly frivolous and "wholly without merit," there should be tough penalties against the lawyers who bring the suit. That in no way means we should adopt corporate-written legislation to limit people's right to bring lawsuits and exercise their legal rights. But it does mean that at least some deterrent to frivolous lawsuits needs to exist. In 2004, some Democrats proposed a three-strikes-and-you're-out rule. If a lawyer is sanctioned by judges three times for filing frivolous cases, he/she would be banned from bringing any suit to court for the next decade.[84] That's not a bad start.

Prevent hiding the most important information in court. In 2000, nine-year-old Gus Barber was killed by a bullet from a Remington rifle that accidentally went off because of a problem with the gun's trigger. When Gus's father, Rich, looked into the situation, he learned that Remington had previously settled dozens of lawsuits arising from these problems[85]—but had forced victims' families to accept gag orders preventing them from talking about the product's deadly flaw.[86] In effect, the company could continue producing dangerously defective products because courts were authorizing settlements that hid the severity of the problem. That deliberately prevented bigger lawsuits from arising that might have created a financial incentive for the company to clean up its act. Make no mistake about it—these kinds of gag rules are pushed by corporations and then authorized by courts all the time. So in 2005, the Montana legislature passed a law preventing judges from sealing information about products that have harmed people.[87] It is a good law that leverages the threat of legal action to deter companies from cutting corners and manufacturing dangerous products. It should be replicated all over America.

Allow tougher state laws to apply. With Big Business's success in moving class-action cases to federal court, many state laws could now be ignored or overridden in the legal process. These are laws that, for instance, protect consumer privacy, set workplace standards, and prevent discrimination. If Congress won't simply repeal the recent class-action bill, then federal judges should at least be given the power to apply these important state protections in the class-action cases they will now be hearing. Such a proposal was offered in the Senate,[88] but Corporate

HERO: John Conyers, Michigan congressman

CRAFTS ALTERNATIVE BILLS THAT SHOW
CORPORATE AMERICA'S TRUE INTENTIONS

Elected in 1964, Michigan representative John Conyers (D)
is the second most senior member of the U.S. House. As
ranking Democrat on the Judiciary Committee, he has been
at the forefront in protecting citizens' legal rights. Conyers
has crafted reasonable, commonsense alternatives to the
corporate-backed bills which would restrict citizens'
ability to seek legal redress when they are harmed. For
instance, when the insurance industry pushed a bill to
limit malpractice awards, Conyers crafted an alternative
that would have weeded out frivolous cases and also
regulated insurance industry profits so that doctors stop
getting ripped off with excessively high premiums. Though
voted down, Conyers's bill highlighted how Big Business's
agenda has almost nothing to do with frivolous lawsuits,
and everything to do with limiting citizens' legal rights in
the name of profits.

America would have none of it, and its allies voted it down.[89] That legislation needs to be revived and passed.

IN 2004, THE chairman of one of the world's largest insurance companies, Maurice "Hank" Greenberg, gave a speech to business executives in
Boston. His company, AIG, has been vigorously lobbying for legislation
to limit citizens' legal rights. The company's financial interest in tort "reform" is not hard to understand—AIG insures other corporations against
damages when those corporations get sued. The fewer court cases AIG's
corporate clients have to deal with, the less AIG has to pay out to victims of
corporate malfeasance, and the more the company can pocket in profits.

Greenberg's speech was mostly mundane, until he started talking
about lawsuits. Dealing with ordinary people who are fighting for their

rights in court, he said, is "like fighting the war on terrorists." He continued by saying trial lawyers are "terrorists."[90]

The comments were undeniably offensive, especially considering the American Association of Trial Lawyers was, on a pro bono basis, in the process of representing 1,700 families of 9/11 victims in their efforts to receive aid from the 9/11 victims' compensation fund.[91]

But even beyond the crass nature of the remark was the hypocrisy. Greenberg is the head of a company that has made headlines terrorizing innocent families when they dare to exercise their legal rights. For instance, in 2001 a nine-year-old girl was sexually molested by a child care employee of one of the insurer's hotel clients. Despite the employee being convicted in criminal court, AIG tried to intimidate the victim's family when they filed suit against the hotel for hiring the criminal in the first place. AIG's thugs "have done everything they can to ruin these people," said Ernie Allen, president of the National Center for Missing & Exploited Children. "This has been scorched earth."[92]

Then again, you can understand why a person like Greenberg felt so personally affronted by lawsuits that might undercut his company's profits: he was making millions each year[93] as AIG's CEO at the same time the company was being investigated for cooking its books.[94] The more money AIG was ordered to pay out in court when its clients misbehave, the more uncomfortable book cooking might have been necessary to keep Greenberg's salary nice and fat.

It would be one thing if this profit-at-all-cost attitude was confined to sharks like Greenberg (who was ultimately charged with "deception and fraud" by New York State regulators[95]). But we now have politicians turning that attitude into legislative reality through tort "reform." They may couch those initiatives in populist language, but no rhetoric can hide the fact that there really are only two things that protect average people from corporate greed: law enforcement by government regulators and lawsuits. Clearly, as shown in previous chapters, our government is not enforcing the laws that protect workers, the environment, and families. So, at the very least, average folks need to have the right to sue companies for violating those laws. Otherwise, there is literally nothing stopping a company from doing whatever it wants—no matter how awful—to pad its bottom line.

That's why, especially now, the push to limit people's legal rights is so dangerous—because it is happening at the very same time Corporate America's political allies are systematically hobbling government's ability to protect people. As just one example, take the Occupational Safety and Health Administration (OSHA), the agency that enforces workplace laws. In 2005, Congress refused to increase OSHA's budget, even though data showed more Americans are dying in workplace injuries every year (roughly 5,500[96]) than have been killed on 9/11, in Iraq, and in Afghanistan combined.* The agency was desperate for more resources—previous cuts had so gutted OSHA that it would take 108 years to inspect every worksite under its jurisdiction.[97] But that was the point—corporations didn't want regulators stepping in and forcing them to spend more money complying with the workplace safety laws.

In this kind of deregulated environment, the threat of legal action is the average person's last line of defense. For example, had there been adequate law enforcement from the government, Wal-Mart workers might not have needed to file lawsuits[98] against the company when they believed their wages were being pilfered. But the Bush Labor Department had made a secret deal with Wal-Mart to give the company advance notice before federal regulators investigated such allegations—advance notice that could potentially let the company hide illegal behavior.[99] When a proposal was floated in the House of Representatives to terminate this deal, it was voted down, with 212 Republicans and 22 Democrats joining hands to stiff workers.[100] Worst of all, the *Wall Street Journal* reported that "the federal government agreed not to pursue any criminal charges against Wal-Mart executives" even as documents "suggested that at least three executives" at the company knew a major subcontractor was violating wage laws.[101] If citizens' legal rights are limited, there is simply no way to fight back against these and other abuses.

Sure, it may make headlines to criticize "greedy trial lawyers" and call them "terrorists." And yes, tort "reform" may sound great on the campaign stump. After all, how many people really *enjoy* lawsuits? But without them—or the threat of them—there is simply no way for average citizens to defend themselves.

---

*As of mid-2005.

CONCLUSION

★

IF YOU'VE made it to this point, you decided to take the red pill. How do you feel? Depressed? Angry? Outraged?

It is okay to feel all these things and more—seeing the effects of the hostile takeover is disturbing, to say the least. It's that same gutshot state of shock one probably experiences when discovering a spouse has been unfaithful. A sixth sense had already let you know something bad was going on, but you didn't really believe it until you came home one night to find clothes strewn all over the house and him/her in bed with someone else. Only this time when you pull back the sheets, you see that it's your government and Corporate America embraced in a sweaty blaze of visceral glory.

Sadly, just catching them in the act is not about to stop the affair. In fact, the hostile takeover is only getting more intense. How do we know? Because it is getting more public. As recently as five or ten years ago, there was still a desire to hide the fact that government had become just another corporate-owned entity. Today that fact is not hidden, it is flaunted.

For instance, as this book was being written, the *Salt Lake Tribune* reported that Utah senator Orrin Hatch (R) publicly auctioned off a "day with the Senator." No joke. Those who attended a fundraising event with

Hatch were asked to bid for a day's worth of access to him—a good buy for anybody having business with the government, as Hatch is one of the most senior and powerful members of Congress. When two big donors got into a bidding war and the price hit $10,000, Hatch happily agreed to accommodate both and have two days of access, netting a nice $20,000 for his state's Republican Party.[1]

It's true, politicians have long sold access, but in the past, the quid pro quo was hidden. Today it's right up in our face, out in the open, as if Washington is one big legalized brothel. Corporate America may have always had a wide selection of politicians to pay off for a nice quickie, but now Big Business and its political allies are opening the shades so that all can watch the screwing of American democracy.

Perhaps the best example of this crass outlook could be seen during the 2005 indictment of Representative Tom DeLay (R) on money-laundering charges. At his first court hearing, DeLay might have considered trying to hide how close he was to the Big Money interests that had bought his votes for so long. Instead, he actually flew to the proceedings on a jet owned by the R.J. Reynolds tobacco company, which had also given DeLay $17,000 for his legal defense.[2] Then with a straight face—as if not even comprehending the hypocrisy of his own behavior at that moment—DeLay called charges that he allowed corporate dollars to improperly influence the political process "contrived and baseless."[3]

This behavior, of course, is a result of a promiscuous atmosphere where almost nothing is considered too outrageous—not even open shilling for convicted criminals. For example, few even batted an eye when the *Wall Street Journal* reported in 2005 that despite Enron illegally ripping off billions from consumers, "the Chamber of Commerce is challenging the Justice Department's efforts to secure long prison terms for five individuals convicted of conspiracy and fraud in the Enron scandal."[4] Understand what that means: just a few years after Corporate America apologized for one of the biggest scandals in American history, it was publicly using its most prominent lobbying organization to get the perpetrators off the hook.

But then, getting criminals off is a last resort—Corporate America has done its best to make sure criminals don't get caught in the first place. The best way to do that is make sure the authorities are anything but impartial—exactly the goal when Big Business convinced the White House in 2005 to nominate Representative Chris Cox (R-CA) to head the Securities and Exchange Commission, the chief agency that regulates of American business.

The move was like appointing a pimp to head up the local police department's antiprostitution efforts. Cox, a former corporate lawyer turned politician, is most famous for writing the law that actually permits corporate executives like Enron's Ken Lay to avoid consequences when they mislead their employees and shareholders.[5] Legal experts have called Cox's signature legislation Corporate America's "license to lie"[6]—and with Cox heading the SEC, you can bet that license will be used.

When it can't install its brethren in positions of power, Big Business has displayed an increasingly dizzying—and creative—array of tactics to ensure that politicians remain subservient. For instance, Corporate America has shown it can be family-friendly, as long as you're a politician presiding over important corporate legislation. In 2003, the *Los Angeles Times* reported that "these days, when a corporation or interest group wants support from a key member of Congress, it often hires a member of the lawmaker's family." In all, "at least 17 senators and 11 members of the House have family members who lobby or work as consultants" to corporations that often "rely on the related lawmakers' goodwill" for government policies that enrich those corporations.[7] Big Business's motivation in hiring relatives is downright mafia-like: Even if these lawmakers wanted to suddenly do the right thing and stop selling America out, they couldn't, because to do so would directly imperil their families' finances.

Don't think for a second that these relatives are hired because of their policy experience—they are hired because of their blood connections and often have no expertise at all. For instance, take Chester Trent Lott Jr., son of U.S. senator Trent Lott (R). He was hired to lobby for telecom giant BellSouth. His experience? "Running a string of pizza franchises and playing polo" and "having earlier dabbled in country music," according to the *Los Angeles Times*. Even though BellSouth "already had a stable of seasoned communications lobbyists," they hired Lott because he could bring something that no one else could: blood loyalty from one of the most powerful senators on the committee overseeing telecommunications policy.[8]

These conflicts of interest are so severe, you might think even the most corrupt politician would avoid them, for fear that they might be discovered by their constituents. But then, you forget that these politicians know that 99 percent of the time they won't be caught by the lazy/cynical media. In the rare instance that they are caught, they can buy reelection with the corporate cash they amass by selling out. And most important, if they play the game and engage in these conflicts, they have a lucrative career waiting for them when they decide to leave public office. As the *Washington Post* reported in 2005, nearly half of all congressional lawmakers now become highly paid lobbyists when they retire, openly selling off their government experience to the highest bidder.[9] The payoff is huge: The *Post* notes that starting salaries for lobbyists "have risen to about $300,000 a year for the best-connected aides" and can be far higher for former lawmakers.[10]

Louisiana senator John Breaux (D) shows how when lawmakers now leave office, the whole thing resembles professional sports—only instead of players, it's politicians who are being auctioned off. Like an all-star free agent, Breaux hired a high-powered attorney "to negotiate his career options" even before he left the Senate, according to *The Hill* newspaper.[11] Corporations looking for Breaux to shill for them considered him "one of the biggest catches," and he soon became the subject of a "bidding war" between two top firms.[12] For Big Business, there was much to covet about Breaux—he had long been comfortable using his office to whore for the most odious corporate malfeasance. According to the *Los Angeles Times*, that included assisting his son-turned-lobbyist John Breaux Jr.'s efforts to make sure an oil company was allowed to keep spewing toxic sulfur dioxide all over Breaux Sr.'s small-town Louisiana constituents.[13] By early 2005, *Roll Call* newspaper reported that "lobbyists estimate that Breaux could be collecting $4 million a year" after signing with one of Washington's most exclusive firms.[14] You could almost imagine him inking the deal and then donning a jersey—only instead of a sports team insignia, there would be a corporate logo on his chest.

The effects of these supercharged sellouts are obvious. "We've got a problem here," said Allan Cigler, a political scientist at the University of Kansas. "The growth of lobbying makes even worse than it is already the balance between those with resources and those without resources."[15] Sadly, that's exactly the point. The more permissive the system of legalized bribery, the more a handful of very wealthy corporations and individuals can get Congress to ignore the rest of us.

But lobbying abuse is only one example of how the revolving door between business and government is spinning like some supercharged turbine. There are many others, including a redoubled effort by Corporate America to infest the insides of government with its vermin. Take the case of Philip Cooney. Before heading up George W. Bush's White House Council on Environmental Quality, he was a lobbyist for the American Petroleum Institute—the lobbying group for the same oil and gas industry that bankrolled Bush's campaign,[16] and the same oil and gas industry that is regulated by the White House office Cooney was heading up. As a White House official, Cooney was caught in 2005 doctoring reports from government scientists in order to hide how oil emissions increase global warming.[17] But far from being sanctioned for his behavior, Cooney was instead given a pat on the back and soon rewarded with a job offer from ExxonMobil.[18]

This infestation is now reaching into the judicial branch of government as well. Big Business knows that to own the court system is to own the referees—and that's worth a lot, especially when so many issues about government's ability to regulate business are decided by judges.

Look at the National Association of Manufacturers (NAM)—the organization that represents some of the largest corporations in America. When a Supreme Court slot opened up in 2005, NAM bragged to the *Wall Street Journal* about "creating a committee of executives to screen the business rulings of prospective nominees" and forwarding those findings to politicians on Capitol Hill who would be voting to confirm the next justice.[19] The *Washington Post* soon noted that corporations "told the White House that they plan to bankroll large-scale efforts to promote" a nominee who fits their qualifications, which, not surprisingly,[20] meant nothing more than a nominee willing to strike down any laws that protect consumers or workers.

When President Bush nominated corporate lawyer John G. Roberts to the Supreme Court in 2005, the fruits of Big Business's efforts were on full display. Here was a nominee to the highest court in the land who had all of two-and-a-half years' experience as a judge. Yet U.S. senators from both parties roundly praised him as well qualified. Why? Because, according to his close associates, Roberts had been Big Business's "go-to lawyer" for years,[21] and, according to the *Washington Post,* "rules that govern conflicts of interest would allow [Roberts] to hear Supreme Court cases involving those same companies" he represented as a corporate lawyer.[22] In an earlier era, that kind of nominee might have raised serious questions. But in today's political system, where both parties are drenched in corporate money, Roberts's expertise shilling for Big Business is exactly the kind of thing that forges bipartisanship. Despite the fact that nearly half of all Supreme Court cases today deal with business issues,[23] both parties made sure the debate over Roberts's nomination largely focused on social issues. Republicans and Democrats seemed to do everything possible to ignore Roberts's economic outlook and ideology before confirming him overwhelmingly.[24]

If the hostile takeover of the court system isn't enough, check out how Big Money interests are now starting to use charities to buy off politicians. The Associated Press reported in 2005 that Senate Majority Leader Bill Frist (R-TN) set up an AIDS charity and then used the money it raised to siphon "nearly a half-million dollars in consulting fees to members of his political inner circle." The story noted that the major donors to the charity—and thus to the political aides working in the halls of power—"included several corporations with frequent business before Congress, such as insurer Blue Cross/Blue Shield, manufacturer 3M, drug maker Eli Lilly, and the Goldman Sachs investment firm."

SO WILL this downward spiral ever end? Is our government destined to be owned by Big Business forever, or can we start taking it back? The answer is that it depends. There is good news and bad news about whether we can turn back the hostile takeover.

BAD NEWS: Politicians of both parties are embracing the hostile takeover.

The first piece of bad news is that the current crop of politicians from both parties is doing its best to help expand the hostile takeover. The Republicans, for instance, loosened prohibitions on corporate lobbying by retiring top government officials just in time for a spate of Bush cabinet secretaries to retire at the end of 2004.[25] Similarly, when in 2005 serious allegations of improper corporate vote buying arose against top congressional leaders, the GOP moved to emasculate the Ethics Committee, which is supposed to enforce rules prohibiting such activity. Ultimately, Republicans actually removed their own committee chairman, Representative Joel Hefley (R), because he had had the gall to actually start investigating the charges.[26] And then, of course, there was the Republican vote-buying scandals surrounding GOP lobbyist Jack Abramoff. Instead of admitting their corrupt ways and advocating for serious reforms, Republicans pretended to be shocked—just shocked!—about the whole thing, as if we're expected to believe it was an isolated incident and not, as the *Washington Post* noted, "the biggest corruption scandal to infect Congress in a generation."

Democrats, meanwhile, are busy sidling up to Big Business in preparation for the next election campaign. In the summer of 2005, a slew of high-profile Democrats flocked to a meeting of the Democratic Leadership Council (DLC). This is the group that, according to *The American Prospect* magazine, has been funded by the likes of Enron, Texaco, and Philip Morris.[27] Not surprisingly, it is also the group that has most vociferously encouraged Democrats to embrace corporate-written trade deals[28]; the group whose leading policy spokesperson has pushed Social Security privatization[29]; and the group whose founder and CEO, Al From, actually brags that he gives Democrats "a game plan to try to contain the populism."[30] To really understand how incredible that is, consider that populism is defined in the dictionary as "supporting the rights and powers of the common people in their struggle with the privileged elite." Yet this top Democrat now haughtily talks about how he convinces politicians to reject that goal.

And, sadly, bought-off Democrats listen to this nonsense. For instance, just days after the DLC's meeting with the 2008 presidential contenders, a handful of Democrats provided the necessary votes to pass President Bush's latest corporate-written trade deal[31]—a trade deal aggressively pushed by the DLC.[32]

But it's not just the DLC—the willingness to sell out ordinary Americans' economic interests seems to pop up everywhere inside the elitist cadre of Washington, D.C.'s Democratic Party Establishment. For instance, when Robert Greenwald's movie exposing Wal-Mart's anti-worker agenda was released in 2005, evidence was uncovered showing that some high-profile Democratic operatives and pundits[33] were working not to promote the movie, but instead were on Wal-Mart's payroll. As just one example, the *New York Times* reported Wal-Mart recruited "Leslie Dach, one of Bill Clinton's media consultants, to set up a rapid-response public relations team in Arkansas" to defend the company's atrocious record.[34]

What's perhaps more nauseating about Democrats than Republicans is their willingness to sell out even if selling out means they will lose elections. The GOP at least has an electoral rationale for its corruption—they have ridden the trail of corporate money to winning elections. Democrats can't even say that. Yes, there are honest warriors within the party's ranks who win tough races on populist platforms. But they are largely ignored or undermined by Democrats' highest-profile leaders, who keep selling out because they simply don't know how to do anything else—even as polls show Americans want Democrats to start standing up for people's economic rights. The sustained fealty to the DLC is the perfect example of this. The DLC's marginalization of populist leaders within the Democratic Party has perfectly coincided with the party's electoral decline. Yet top Democrats still genuflect to the DLC's Big Business donors and its corporate agenda. With the wild-eyed lunacy of a crack addict, many Democrats are so singularly focused on raking in corporate campaign cash and reinforcing the status quo that they are unable to see that their genuflecting to corporate power—not their spin, not their language, not their television ads—is really the core of their problems.

And even now, as Democrats decry the Repbulicans "culture of corruption" and a group of lawmakers courageously propose a crackdown on the most egregious pay-to-play practices in Congress, some of the party's top leaders seem physically unable to resist the smell of corporate cash, despite the fact that it means undermining their own party's electoral prospects. According to the *Roll Call* newspaper in late 2005, "a House Democratic project designed to dip into deep K Street wallets" was entering a new phase, as the second ranking House Democrat, Rep. Steny Hoyer (D-MD) convened a meeting "with roughly 50 business-minded Democratic consultants, lobbyists, and corporate officers to get them to commit to writing checks" to the party. Hoyer even posted an earlier newspaper story on his taxpayer-funded website detailing his intricate plans to collect cash from lobbyists—a clear sign that in Washington, D.C., a corporate shakedown operation is a trophy to be publicly flaunted even during a corruption scandal. Topping it all off was a report that year by the *National Journal* noting that Hoyer actually has one of his senior legislative staffers in his congressional office serve simultaneously as his political fundraising operation's chief "liaison to K Street and the business community."

It is all proof positive that corruption has become such a mundane and ubiquitous part of the Washington, D.C., political culture, that many top Democrats view corporate money and public policy as totally inseparable.

BAD NEWS: The media largely ignore the hostile takeover.

The second piece of bad news is that most of the media today are no longer interested in telling Americans what's going on with their government. This is not about the minor inaccuracies, mischaracterizations, or misspellings—this is about media that have become wholly unwilling to even acknowledge the most basic realities. Specifically, almost everything you see on television, read in the newspaper, or hear on the radio from reporters makes political debates out to be ideological clashes between conservatism and liberalism, or partisan battles between Republicans and Democrats, when in fact those story lines are overly simplistic euphemisms for what's really going on. It is as if the media see the public as children, and thus tell us stories about birds and bees instead of telling us what we really need to know, which is the ugly, offensive, not-for-the-faint-of-heart truth about the X-rated ways public policy is conceived.

The truth is, almost every major political conflict and legislative battle is fueled by a clash between Big Money interests and the rest of us, regardless of political ideology or party. But you would never know it, because the media is either too lazy to explain this simple story line, too afraid to tell the truth, too dismissive of the public, too biased in favor of the corporate forces who run the show, or too dumb to realize they are making an inane sitcom out of a political debate that has very severe, real-life consequences for millions of Americans.

This says nothing of the media's increasing timidity in holding politicians' feet to the fire. In ages past, reporters actually challenged political power by asking tough questions. By contrast, today's reporters seem more interested in preserving their spot on politicians' Christmas card lists than actually confronting them. Just look at what the *New York Times*'s top White House correspondent Elisabeth Bumiller said when someone asked her why the media didn't challenge President Bush before the Iraq War about clearly questionable assertions. "We were very deferential because . . . it's live, it's very intense, it's frightening to stand up there," she said. "There was a very serious, somber tone . . . and no one wanted to get into an argument with the president at this very serious time."[35] Translation: Many reporters believe it is better to transcribe lies and be liked by politicians than call bullshit and risk being frowned upon by the powers that be.

And that leads us to the sad truth: If major reporters openly admit they were afraid to question government policy at the most critical time before a war, should we really expect these same pathetic chickens to have the guts to ask questions about things like corruption and corporate vote buying? Of course not.

GOOD NEWS: Americans are smart.

The good news is, first and foremost, that the American public is very smart. We not only know that corporations and the superwealthy have too much power. We know that this excess power is the product of Big Business's hostile takeover of our government—a hostile takeover that is being solidified by an insulated elite in Washington. As a 2005 poll showed, almost three-quarters of Americans believe both political parties in Washington fundamentally see the world differently than they do.[36] That suggests a broad understanding that the elitists who run our nation's capital are selling public policy to the highest corporate bidder, with no regard to the consequences for average citizens.

It is true—this awareness is often a vague feeling in people's minds, rather than a detailed, blow-by-blow understanding of exactly what's wrong with our government (that's what this book is supposed to be for). But that awareness unto itself is a major asset, because it is a prerequisite for any type of grassroots social movement that will ultimately clean up the mess.

GOOD NEWS: The good guys are getting more support.

Americans' heightened awareness about the corruption that plagues our political system hasn't happened in a vacuum. The rise of the Internet, weblogs, and alternative media is building a resurgence of political consciousness not seen since the pre-television days, when politics was an almost exclusively grassroots exercise. Innovative organizations like Moveon.org and New York's Working Families Party are now harnessing this grassroots resurgence and channeling it into campaigns that actually exert serious pressure on lawmakers to stop selling out and start representing their constituents.

Much of this is being backed up by a new fundraising apparatus whereby political candidates can actually raise campaign resources from small grassroots donors rather than huge corporations. Slowly but surely, there is a support system being built to amplify the work of those courageous (though outnumbered) lawmakers who have been fighting the good but all-too-lonely fight in the political trenches for years.

Thanks to all this, we are starting to see some results. A new generation of leaders is forging its political fortune on populism and principle, rather than cynicism and capitulation. A farmer who stands up to corporate special interests and corruption was elected governor of Montana, a state that the national media ignorantly and incorrectly write off as a right-wing backwater. A crusader against corporate crime has become one of the most popular politicians in the same state that houses Wall Street. And a candidate made a serious bid for his party's presidential nomination in 2004 by talking about how our country is increasingly divided into "two America's," split by economic class.

Better still, the battle to reclaim our country is going beyond just the election of individual politicians and into intense skirmishes over concrete policies. Some campaigns, like the fight to raise workers' paychecks, have been successful. While the bought-off politicians in Washington have let the minimum wage languish at poverty levels, seventeen states fought off Corporate America's dishonest propaganda and raised their own minimum wages.[37] That includes New York, where the Working Families Party did the seemingly impossible by successfully pressuring the Republican-controlled State Senate to override Republican governor George Pataki's veto and pass the wage increase.[38]

Other battles have been lost or are still pending, but the mere fact that there are battles at all is a major step forward. For instance, in Montana, a group of cities in 2005 made a bid to buy out an energy company after citizens got sick and tired of being gouged by high prices.[39] In Alabama, conservative Republican governor Bob Riley turned his religious convictions into political action and boldly proposed a landmark reform package that would have raised taxes on his state's wealthiest residents and corporations in order to lower the tax burden on the poor.[40] Though he lost, he showed that it is possible to start redefining the terms of America's tax debates and start challenging the immorality of our current system.

Even in Washington, there has been some progress, such as when Ohio representative Sherrod Brown (D) built a bipartisan coalition that came within one vote of blocking the corporate-written Central American Free Trade Agreement—a pact that will probably mean more job losses here at home and more worker exploitation abroad. And though, as mentioned before, a handful of Democrats provided the critical votes for passage,[41] Brown showed that with some guts and sustained tenacity, even Big Business's greed can be challenged in Congress.

STILL, THE truth nags: for every victory or near victory, there are many more defeats. That is because American politics still has all the qualities of a casino. Think about it. The casino industry is wildly profitable because the games are fundamentally fixed to make sure gamblers lose. You can win a pull of the slot machine every now and again, but if you play long enough, you will go broke. Likewise, Big Business has succeeded in its hostile takeover of government because money has tilted the political system in Corporate America's favor. Sure, the establishment occasionally throws regular folks a transparent win and makes a big deal of it, just the way the casino occasionally lets us get three 7s and then sounds a big alarm. But it's all a hustle to perpetuate the illusion that we have a chance to regularly win, and to make sure we don't think about the fundamental truth: that for all the rhetoric, the system is rigged against us.

It is this fundamental truth that we must ultimately confront if we are ever to see lasting change. And that is not easy. Not only is there Corporate America's matrix of lies, myths, and half-truths that this book details. There is a natural desire to pretend that for all the problems we know exist, the system is still sound. It is the same kind of denial a middle-aged man goes through when he loses his hair: it's more comforting for him to wear a toupee—no matter how bad—rather than just publicly admit he's bald.

In all different ways, we put on this toupee of denial no matter how ridiculously fake we all know it is. Some of us stomp our feet and insist that democracy is flourishing in America, even as we watch votes sold to the highest bidder. Others use terms like "unpatriotic," "traitor," or worse to attack those who criticize government corruption, even as more and more pay-to-play scandals are uncovered. And the media packages it all as some sick form of infotainment, marginalizing those who have the nerve to speak truth to economic power, even as ordinary Americans are bled dry.

So, you ask, how can we overcome all these obstacles and fight back? The power players have auctioned off their services to the highest bidders, the media dismiss real issues, and Corporate America continues to widen its conquest of our government. How can we ever hope to fundamentally alter a system that has aided and abetted all of this?

There are many answers to this question. Some of them are about changing our psychology to really focus on what's important. Others are concrete steps we can take. Here are just a few:

Reject the idea that you can't change anything.

In the movie *The Usual Suspects*, the main character says "the greatest trick the devil ever pulled was convincing the world he didn't exist." Likewise, the greatest trick Big Money elitists ever pulled was convincing ordinary Americans we can't change things, we can't make a difference, and we must become just another cog in a soulless machine that ignores anything other than the quest for private profit.

This destructive attitude manifests itself in all sorts of ways: some don't vote because they think their one vote doesn't matter, others don't pay attention to how their elected representatives behave, because they don't think it is important. But really, nothing could be further from the truth.

Not to sound like a cheesy public service announcement, but it is a fact: almost every story of progress venerated in American history books started out with an unfathomably small group of people. The truth is, you have far more ability than you think to change things, and the idea that you don't is just another myth that Corporate America wants you to believe. Why? Because when ordinary people disengage from the political process, we hand over a huge amount of power to the establishment— power the establishment would not have otherwise. Breaking out of this psychology is a prerequisite to changing anything, because it is this psychology more than anything that allows our political process to be needlessly corrupted in perpetuity.

Get your head in the game.

Once we get past the myth that we can't change anything, the next thing to do is figure out where we can get the best information about how the hostile takeover is advancing. If you've read this far, the hope is you've gotten a start on that, but if you are committed to engaging in this fight, you will need a constant source of reliable information about the day-to-day struggle.

It is true—most political reporting nowadays is downright awful. The profession of journalism once inspired hardscrabble reporters who dreamed of breaking hard-hitting stories. Now it has essentially become a venue dominated by glamour-desperate louses who were either too ugly or too untalented to make it in Hollywood. These people dream not of breaking real stories but of spewing the latest unimportant gossip on some inane television talk show hosted by one of a number of robotic dolts like Tucker Carlson and watched by all of twelve people, the majority of whom live in the well-guarded confines of gated communities in northern Virginia or northwest Washington, D.C.

That said, there are still places to get good information. First and foremost are financial-focused media like *BusinessWeek* and newspapers' business sections. These are publications written exclusively for people who rely on the information to make money—and that means there is no room for punditry, spin, or inaccuracy. What you read in these publications is as close to rock-solid information about the hostile takeover as you will get anywhere.

There are also a handful of good reporters still toiling in daily journalism who are serious about covering both economic issues and the critical intersection of money and politics. They include the *New York Times*'s David Cay Johnston and Robert Pear; the *Wall Street Journal*'s David Rogers and Ellen Schultz; the *Washington Post*'s Tom Edsall and Jeffrey Birnbaum; and the *Los Angeles Times*'s Peter Gosselin and Tom Hamburger. Mind you, these aren't "liberal" or "conservative" reporters—they go after both sides with equal vigor, which is exactly what they are supposed to do, and exactly why they are so valuable. These reporters are the ones who don't fall prey to the faux story lines that have destroyed modern journalism.

But don't take my word for it—find the reporters you trust in the publications you read. There are still some good ones out there. The trick is to remember who writes the stories about the economic issues you care about; to develop your own list of reporters you can rely on; and then to read those writers' articles religiously.

Finally, do your own research. There are terrific nonpartisan resources readily available on the Internet that can tell you everything from how members of Congress voted on a given issue to how much they are taking from different industries. To start, you can go to www.davidsirota. com to see the sites and research techniques that were used to write this book, and you can build your personal list from there.

Information has always been power in politics, but throughout most of American history, only those in the smoky backrooms have had the information. That's why perhaps the biggest threat the Internet poses to corporate control of our government is its sheer ability to deliver previously inaccessible information to citizens—information that helps us debunk the lies and fight the hostile takeover.

Be a big fish in small pond.

One of the reasons we feel so powerless is that we've forgotten how to actually influence, pressure, and change the political system. Part of that is because the media write citizens out of the political narrative from the get-go, presenting public policy as the exclusive property of moneyed interests who hand down laws as if they were royal edicts. Another factor is the incessant focus on the White House to the exclusion of every other locus of political power. Today, you are more likely to hear about the president's vacation plans than you are a report about the critical bill moving through your city council that affects your daily life. That naturally leads us to believe that the only office worth influencing is the presidency.

This one-two punch has been devastating: first citizens' power is downplayed, and for those who still muster political energy, everything tells us the focus should be on trying to pressure the White House, probably the single most difficult institution in the world for ordinary citizens to influence. The key to getting out of this downward spiral is for us to focus our energies on battles we can actually win. We need to be bigger fishes in smaller ponds.

A group of motivated citizens are far more likely to sway the position or vote of their city councilman by meeting with him/her and making demands than they are getting the president of the United States to do anything. As corrupt as politics is, you would be surprised at how malleable a local official can be when confronted by a group of motivated citizens making demands, and promising electoral consequences if those demands are not met. The same thing goes even for members of Congress—when trying to create change, citizens are far more likely to move their congressional representatives than they are a candidate for the White House. The reason is obvious: the smaller the election, the more a small group of people can overcome the influence of big money and sway the outcome through grassroots activity.

This is not to say that we should entirely divorce ourselves from national politics. But it is to say that we shouldn't continue to focus *exclusively* on presidential elections, as many of us do to the almost full exclusion of closer-to-home politics that we can more intensely impact. Sure, adopting this big-fish-small-pond attitude will at first seem less glamorous. It sounds so much more exciting to try to influence the president of the United States than it does to try to influence your local state legislator, right? Yes, until you actually see your local legislator change his/her position because of political pressure you brought to bear. And with enough persistence over enough time, that influence will steadily move up the food chain. Get better state legislators, and you get better governors. Get better House members, and you get better senators. Ultimately, this model will bring us a better president—but only if we start smaller.

Remember the real fight, and forget the cocktail party arguments.

As described in the beginning of this book, the debates that happen in our nation's capital often seem as though they are occurring on another planet, and the people who report on those debates self-importantly believe they and the insulated world they cover are the only things that matter. It is why, for instance, you see reporters breathlessly and incessantly speculating about which senators are thinking of running for president three years from now at the same time they largely ignore the fact that America is going through a health care, energy, and jobs crisis. For high-paid reporters hobnobbing in the world of Washington cocktail parties, the gossip is more important than the day-to-day economic challenges facing the average American.

Changing this attitude in Washington may be impossible, but preventing ourselves from buying into it is not. The simple fact is, the fight against the hostile takeover isn't contingent on changing the opinion of a small cadre of Washington columnists, editorial writers, and reporters. Their opinions can't be changed because so many of them make their living justifying the hostile takeover instead of challenging it. But what's even more important is that as powerful as the Washington media establishment thinks it is, its opinions do not matter. What matters is organizing regular citizens for political action.

Corporate America seems very attuned to this reality. It is why the advocacy organizations Big Business funds basically ignore what the pundits say, and focus on more and more sophisticated methods of indoctrinating voters through direct propaganda, and organizing these voters for action. The fact that this organizing often misleads people into helping undermine their own economic rights does not take away from the bottom line: Educating and organizing works.

On the other side, however, the old-line Democratic Party operatives in Washington haven't figured this out. Until a recent infusion of new blood, the party has seemed all too obsessed with winning the increasingly irrelevant battles for the media elite's approval, and all too dismissive of the on-the-ground battles that will actually change our country. This is probably one of the reasons Democrats have been relegated to seemingly permanent minority status.

For you, the concerned citizen who has no interest in being co-opted into Corporate America's organizing and sees very little from either political party, that means looking for alternative channels for political action. They are out there, but they require far harder work than just slapping a bumper sticker on your car, or calling in to the local radio show.

If your employer is paying you and your colleagues poorly, start a drive to unionize your workplace. If your congressman is consistently voting against your economic interests, organize groups of citizens to go out, knock on doors, and vote him/her out of office. If your local government is about to harm the community with a new law, organize a citizens' group to protest, or start a petition to get the issue on the ballot for a voter referendum. Don't just sit there and write a letter to the editor when the *Washington Post* or the *Wall Street Journal* writes an editorial supporting yet another awful policy. Engage in the real fight in your own backyard to change things where it matters.

Push to publicly finance elections, and until that happens, donate what you can.

Whatever economic concern motivates your personal political action, there is one debate that transcends them all: how elections are financed. Right now, we have legalized bribery, where candidates rely on contributions from wealthy corporate donors to get elected, and pay those contributors back once in government through legislative favors. To understand how out of control this system really is, just look at how Big Money interests now routinely and publicly threaten retribution when politicians consider defying Corporate America's wishes and actually serving the public.

For instance, in 2005, *New York* magazine reported that "Republican billionaire Ken Langone is waging a self-proclaimed 'holy war' against New York attorney General Eliot Spitzer." Why? Because Spitzer had the guts to go after crooked Wall Street firms that were ripping off ordinary stockholders. "One way or another, Spitzer's going to pay for what he's done to me," Langone said, promising to abuse the current campaign finance system by dumping a huge amount of cash into defeating Spitzer's campaign for governor.

Days later, there was a story in the *National Journal*, barely noticed because it was so mundane. The headline said it all: "Business to '06 Candidates: Wise Up or Prepare to Lose." The piece then described how Big

Business was threatening to spend millions to defeat congressional candidates who dared to defy Corporate America's wishes.

The only way to change this rule-by-Big-Money system is to use all the tactics described in the sections above to not only push for better economic policies, but also for publicly financed elections.

In various state and municipal elections, if candidates pass certain minimum thresholds, they become eligible for public money to run their campaign. These systems let candidates actually run on the merits of their positions, rather than their willingness to capitulate to corporate wishes, or their skills as a telemarketer shaking down special interests for cash. The criticism of public financing of elections is that it costs taxpayer money. But it costs far less than the amount of taxpayer money politicians currently waste paying back favors to their big donors, and it loosens the stranglehold Corporate America has on our political process. And in case you thought this was just a "liberal" idea, just head to Arizona, one of the most conservative states in America, where voters approved public financing of elections in a statewide referendum.

Still, getting to a full publicly financed election system is a very long-term project, which means in the interim more citizens need to contribute money to political campaigns. Big Business can buy elections not only because companies have a lot of money but also because, as the nonpartisan Center for Responsive Politics reports, "only a tiny fraction of Americans actually give campaign contributions to political candidates."[42] That has to change.

After getting through a book that details and decries the incredibly extreme financial pressures ordinary Americans are under, you may be wondering, "How am I now reading a call for ordinary Americans to shell out money to politicians?" The answer is pretty simple: Until we get publicly financed elections, money will play a big role in politics, and that means ordinary Americans have two choices: we can continue to not contribute anything to political candidates, essentially walking off the field and forfeiting. Or we can hold our nose and play in an albeit unfair game. The latter is clearly the better choice—at least then we have a chance to win a victory here and there, and make our presence felt, especially if we are smart about where we spend limited resources.

There is no rule that says politics, even in our corrupt system, has to be so thoroughly dominated by a few very large contributors (though those large contributors will always be somewhat powerful). Groups like Moveon.org are flipping the old smoky backroom model on its head, gathering a very large group of contributors who each give just a little bit. Such a model doesn't require regular folks to cough up hundreds of dollars. On the contrary, if millions of people kicked in $5 or $10, we might have a whole different country.

Getting more people to contribute small sums of money to political causes will require a change in mind-set. We need to look at political giving in the same way we look at the basket that comes around at our place of worship. We chip in what we can, no matter how modest, because we believe in the work that our money funds. That is the way we need to think about supporting good people running for office, because government can have an impact on society that is as big—if not bigger—than almost any other institution.

THERE IS not a shred of doubt in my mind that this book will be assaulted from all sides within the political establishment, with all sorts of hyperbole. The worst will be the red-baiters, who will call this book "antibusiness," "anticapitalist," or an affront to America's supposedly "free market" system. But after you read this book, it should be clear that America isn't a free market in the first place. We live in an economy that is highly regulated—but regulated to help an elite few reap all of society's economic gains. It has all the facets of socialism that red-baiting politicians supposedly hate, but they say nothing about it because it is a socialism that benefits their biggest campaign contributors.

Think about it: The same self-described "free market" proponents that want to cut government assistance to the poor in the name of eliminating the "welfare state" support billions in government welfare checks to already-wealthy corporations. The same self-described "capitalist" advocates of deregulation who eliminated bankruptcy protections for ordinary people in the name of "accountability" are the people who created special bankruptcy protections exclusively for the superwealthy and large corporations. The same proponents of "free" trade are the people who write restrictive clauses into trade deals that prevent Americans from buying cheaper medicines from other countries. And the list goes on. These hypocritical politicians, lobbyists, and spin artists are the real socialists—the corporate socialists who are running this country into the ground.

Both Republican and Democratic party operatives in Washington will undoubtedly claim this book proposes some sort of extreme, out-of-step shift to the left—even though polls show nearly every problem and policy prescription identified is neither to the "left" nor the "right" but well within the mainstream of American public opinion. One thing is true: what is written here may not be well within the mainstream of thinking among political elites, but then that is exactly the point of this book—to show how the elitists that run our country are so bought-off and out of touch, they actually argue that their extremist positions represent America.

None of this is a surprise. Throughout history, the establishment has always criticized threats to its power, and there is always the same thread running through the attacks. The truth teller is, in one way or another, criticized for "waging class warfare"—supposedly the quintessentially unpatriotic behavior in the country that mythologizes a rags-to-riches American dream. But just as someone once said patriotism can be used as the last refuge of scoundrels, the truth is decrying "class warfare" is being used as a last refuge of wealthy elitists—the very people who have waged a brutal class war since the dawn of American history. Whether busting mining unions at the turn of the century, or busting Wal-Mart unions today; whether decimating people's life savings during the Depression, or doing the same today; whether depriving citizens of basic health care fifty years ago or this year; whether paying workers slave wages back then or right now—Corporate America's goal has been the same: do whatever it takes to squeeze as much cash out of ordinary folks as possible.

The only difference between today and yesteryear is that in past eras we tried to divide the corporate raiders from the government regulators— a divide designed to blunt the sharpest edges of unbridled capitalism. That divide has been eliminated thanks to the hostile takeover. Corrupt politicians have worked to make the sharp edges of capitalism sharper than ever before, helping Big Business slash jobs, wages, health care benefits, and the overall well-being of millions of hardworking Americans.

For politicians, the task of publicly justifying the hostile takeover has gotten all the harder. Why? Because though the financial rewards for corrupt politicians to sell out have gotten bigger, the hypocrisy inherent in the hostile takeover has become more obscene than ever. In one breath politicians claim to sympathize with the economic squeeze we all know we are going through. In another breath they claim the policies they supported that created this squeeze are actually helping us. Now, though, more and more Americans are awakening to the scam, and the politicians have to come up with new, even more slick ways of glossing over the situation. The result is more lies and a new distraction game that attempts to steer the political debate away from economic issues entirely.

Is it really a coincidence that as Americans' economic situation gets worse, more and more of our political debate is focusing on the relatively small number of social issues that divide ordinary citizens, instead of focusing on the economic ones that unify us? Is it really just a coincidence that as our economic challenges get bigger, the amount of time political candidates spend discussing economic issues gets smaller? Of course not. Divide, distract, and conquer is a mantra both Big Business and its political cronies know a lot about. Perpetuate fights over racially and religiously divisive issues, sprinkle in more lies about critical pocketbook issues, and throw in some vicious attacks on people who tell the truth about this sham and you keep the broad population from unifying in a fight against the hostile takeover of our government.

Still, there is a silver lining. So used to getting its way for so long, Big Business has overreached. Today even the most politically disengaged citizens know that a hostile takeover has occurred. They might not know exactly what's happened, but they know something is very, very wrong. Therefore, those who are fighting the hostile takeover no longer have to worry about a lack of public awareness. We can focus on the real battle at hand: convincing our fellow citizens that this country can do better.

To be sure, that is no small task. Every message that comes from the establishment says in one way or another that the status quo, no matter how bad it gets, is just an immutable fact of life, as if handed down from a divine power, instead of what it really is: the artificial result of a long, well-funded, and well-orchestrated campaign to undermine our democracy and further empower the already powerful.

But if history is any guide, things are about to change. The story of America is not a story of pessimistic, passive people who sit back and get fooled. It is the story of a tenaciously optimistic people who stand up and fight back. From labor's fight to create the five-day workweek, to women's fight for the right to vote, to African-Americans' fight for civil rights, our country's heritage is citizens reacting to extraordinary circumstances with a pugnacious attitude and triumphing in the face of seemingly all-powerful forces.

The same attitude will mark the battle against the hostile takeover. In one way or another, every great American social movement has been about people taking back their government, finding their voice, and acting on their justifiable sense of outrage. It is a sense of outrage that comes with being abused by corrupt politicians, cheated by the establishment, insulted with lies, and denied honest answers. It is a sense of outrage that has fueled our country's past historic battles against injustice. And it is a sense of outrage that will always lead America to a better future.

—DAVID SIROTA

January 2006
Helena, Montana

Notes

INTRODUCTION

1. James Drew and Steve Eder, *Toledo Blade*, 10/30/05. "Ohio Bush donors richly rewarded," http://www.toledoblade.com/apps/pbcs.dll/article?Date=20051030&Category=NEWS24&ArtNo=510300346&SectionCat=NEWS&Template=printart.

2. Jeffrey H. Birnbaum and Renae Merle, *Washington Post*, 6/17/05. "MZM and Wade also donated money to Cunningham's reelection effort. The company and its affiliates, for instance, contributed $20,000 in 'soft money' to Cunningham's American Prosperity PAC State Fund between 2000 and 2002, according to PoliticalMoneyLine.com." http://www.washingtonpost.com/wpdyn/content/article/2005/06/16/AR2005061601414.html.

3. Toby Eckert, Copley News Service, 6/17/05. "Cunningham also lived aboard Wade's yacht in Washington and was a personal friend of the defense contractor." http://www.signonsandiego.com/news/metro/20050717-9999-1n17duke.html.

4. Toby Eckert, Copley News Service, 6/17/05. "Last month, an article in the *San Diego Union-Tribune* revealed that Wade bought Cunningham's Del Mar—area home in 2003 for $1.675 million and sold it at a $700,000 loss nearly a year later." http://www.signonsandiego.com/news/metro/20050717-9999-1n17duke.html.

5. Jerry Kammer and Marcus Stern, Copley News Service, 6/5/05. "Wade is the founder of MZM Inc., a Washington, D.C.—based company which has received $163 million in defense contracts since 2002." http://www.signonsandiego.com/news/metro/20050705-9999-1n5duke.html.

6. *BusinessWeek*, 9/11/00. "BUSINESSWEEK's poll shows that nearly three-quarters of Americans think business has gained too much power over too many aspects of their lives. In a response that surprised the pundits, the public seemed to rally around the sentiment expressed at the Democratic convention, when Al Gore declared that Americans must 'stand up and say no' to 'Big Tobacco, Big Oil, the big polluters, the pharmaceutical companies, the HMOs.' Gore sensed the frustration of many voters and their desire to blunt some of the power of business, crafting a new campaign strategy that so far is working. . . . Indeed, 74 percent of those polled by BUSINESSWEEK agreed with the Veep's remarks." http://www.businessweek.com/2000/00_37/b3698001.htm.

7. Tamara Straus, *San Francisco Examiner*, 12/13/00. "According to a September 2000 BusinessWeek/Harris Poll, between 72 percent and 82 percent of Americans believe that "business has gained too much power over too many aspects of American life" and 74 percent to 82 percent believe that big companies have too much influence over

"government policy, politicians, and policy-makers in Washington." http://www.
commondreams.org/views/121400-106.htm.

8. *Washington Post*/ABC News, 7/16/02. "Vast majorities of Americans express distrust
in the nation's business executives and their companies' financial accounting, and
most say President Bush has not moved strongly enough to fight corporate fraud.
Fifty-four percent in an ABCNews/*Washington Post* poll say Bush's proposals to curb
corporate wrongdoing are 'not tough enough.' " http://abcnews.go.com/sections/
business/DailyNews/corporatecrimes_poll020716.html.

9. CBS News, 1/17/04. "Perceptions that the administration caters to the wealthy also
persist—in this poll, 57 percent think the administration's policies favor the rich.
11 percent think they favor the middle class and 25 percent think they treat all
groups the same." http://www.cbsnews.com/stories/2004/01/17/opinion/polls/
main593849.shtml.

10. David Sirota, "Debunking 'Centrism,' " *The Nation*, 1/3/05. "A 2002 *Washington Post*
poll taken during the height of the corporate accounting scandals found that 88 percent of Americans distrust corporate executives, 90 percent want new corporate
regulations/tougher enforcement of existing laws. . . . September 2004 CBS News poll
found that 72 percent of Americans say they have either not been affected by the Bush
tax cuts or that their taxes have actually gone up . . . [a] national poll found that almost
two-thirds of Americans say they prefer a universal health care system 'that's run by the
government and financed by taxpayers' as opposed to the current private, for-profit
system. . . . A March 2004 Associated Press poll, for instance, showed that two-thirds of
Americans favor making it 'easier for people to buy prescription drugs from Canada or
other countries at lower cost.' . . . A 1999 poll done on the five-year anniversary of the
North American trade deal was even more telling: Only 24 percent of Americans said
they wanted to 'continue the NAFTA agreement.' "
http://www.thenation.com/doc/20050103/sirota.

11. PR Newswire, 6/6/05. "The Feldman Group released a survey Thursday showing that
voters share a set of national ideals. Sixty-two (62) percent believe America is the
greatest country on Earth and cite self-determination and equal rights as core ideals
on which American Exceptionalism rests. Voters are deeply critical of elected officials,
as 72 percent believe that elected officials in Washington do not see the nation's problems and opportunities in the same way they do." http://releases.usnewswire.com/
printing.asp?id=48410.

12. Klaus Marre, *The Hill*, 12/8/04. "Sen. Don Nickles is about to become The Nickles
Group. The Oklahoma Republican and Budget Committee chairman said yesterday that
he will start his own political consulting and business venture company after he ends his
24-year Senate career next month." And Tory Newmyer, *Roll Call*, 1/31/05: "Lobbyists
estimate that Breaux could be collecting $4 million a year these days." http://www.
hillnews.com/thehill/export/TheHill/News/Frontpage/120804/nickels.html.

13. E.J. Dionne, *Washington Post*, 9/16/03. "Warning against the idea of child
care as an entitlement, Sen. Rick Santorum, a Pennsylvania Republican,
reassured us: 'Making people struggle a little bit is not necessarily the worst thing.' "
http://www.washingtonpost.com/ac2/wp-dyn?pagename=article&contentId=
A15664-2003Sep15&notFound=true.

14. David Grann, *The New Yorker*, 10/25/04. " 'We try to channel what the chattering
class is chattering about, and to capture the sensibility, ethos, and rituals of the Gang of
500, which still largely sets the political agenda for the country,' Halperin explained
during one of several recent conversations."

CHAPTER 1: TAXES

1. CBS News, 3/17/03. http://www.cbsnews.com/stories/2003/03/17/eveningnews/main544367.shtml.
2. Joe Newman, *Orlando Sentinel*, 3/26/03.
3. Mark Murray, James Kitfield, et al., *National Journal*, 8/10/02.
4. Matthew Wald, *New York Times*, 4/23/02.
5. Jonathan Turley, professor of public interest law at George Washington University, *USA Today*, 12/17/03. http://www.usatoday.com/news/opinion/editorials/2003-12-17-turley_x.htm.
6. Tom DeLay, *CongressDaily*, 3/12/03. http://www.house.gov/georgemiller/lineoftheday31303.html.
7. Tim Fleck, *Houston Press*, 1/7/99. http://www.houston-press.com/issues/1999-01-07/columns2.html.
8. David Francis, *Christian Science Monitor*, 12/1/03. http://www.csmonitor.com/2003/1201/p13s01-wmgn.html.
9. Bill Gates Sr. and Chuck Collins, *The Nation*, 1/9/03. http://www.thenation.com/doc.mhtml?i=20030127&s=gates.
10. Kevin Phillips, *Politics of Rich and Poor*, 1990, Chapter 4, Table 3, page 83.
11. Citizens for Tax Justice report entitled "The Bush Tax Cuts So Far, 2001–2010," July 2005. http://www.ctj.org/pdf/gwbdata.pdf.
12. Ibid.
13. R.G. Ratcliffe, *Houston Chronicle*, 3/13/05. http://www.chron.com/cs/CDA/ssistory.mpl/metropolitan/3082519.
14. Ibid.
15. Citizens for Tax Justice report entitled "Surge in Corporate Tax Welfare Drives Corporate Tax Payments Down to Near Record Low," 4/17/02. http://www.ctj.org/html/corp0402.htm.
16. Taxpayers for Commonsense press release, 5/5/04. http://www.taxpayer.net/TCS/PressReleases/2004/5-5fsc.htm.
17. Jonathan Weisman, *Washington Post*, 4/19/04. http://www.washingtonpost.com/ac2/wp-dyn/A22581-2004Apr18?language=printer.
18. Citizen Works report, "How Corporations Are Using Offshore Tax Havens to Avoid Paying Taxes," 4/15/03. http://www.citizenworks.org/corp/tax/taxbreif.php. Statement of Senator Max Baucus at Senate Finance Committee Hearings, April 11, 2002. http://finance.senate.gov/hearings/statements/041102mb.pdf.
19. Public Campaign report, 4/15/04. http://www.campaignmoney.org/spotlight/sis04_15_04.htm.
20. Center for Responsive Politics spring newsletter, 2001. http://www.opensecrets.org/newsletter/ce75/repeal.asp.
21. Peter Dizikes, ABC News, 2/9/01. http://abcnews.go.com/Politics/story?id=121854&page=1.
22. Jonathan Weisman, *Washington Post*, 4/19/04. http://www.washingtonpost.com/ac2/wp-dyn?pagename=article&contentId=A22581-2004Apr188&notFound=true.
23. George W. Bush, Presidential Debate, 10/3/00.
24. Citizens for Tax Justice, report, "The Bush Tax Cuts So Far, 2001–2010," July 2005, page 2. http://www.ctj.org/pdf/gwbdata.pdf.
25. CBS News, 1/11/04. http://www.cbsnews.com/stories/2004/01/09/60minutes/main592330.shtml.

26. Center on Budget and Policy Priorities, 1/15/03. http://www.Center_on_Budget_and_Policy_Priorities.org/1-9-03tax.htm.

27. David Francis, *Christian Science Monitor,* 2/2/04. http://www.taxpolicycenter.org/newsevents/cite_surprise.cfm.

28. Jonathan Weisman, *Washington Post,* 8/13/04. http://www.washingtonpost.com/wp-dyn/articles/A61178-2004Aug12.html.

29. Christopher Lee, *Washington Post,* 2/19/03.

30. National Conference of State Legislatures, report entitled "State Budget & Tax Actions 2005: Preliminary Report," table entitled "Net State Tax Changes by Year of Enactment, 1995–2005." http://www.ncsl.org/programs/fiscal/presbta05.htm.

31. Kathleen Hunter, Stateline, 3/8/05. http://www.stateline.org/live/ViewPage.action?siteNodeId=136&languageId=1&contentId=16909.

32. National Council of State Legislatures, State Budget and Tax Actions Preliminary Report, 2004, Figure 7. http://www.ncsl.org/programs/fiscal/presbta04.htm.

33. Mike Smith, Associated Press, 2/24/05. http://www.ftimes.com/main.asp?SectionID=1&SubSectionID=1&ArticleID=25699&TM=61957.

34. Ray A. Smith, *Wall Street Journal,* 7/13/04. http://www.county.org/resources/news/dynContView.asp?cid=399.

35. Alan Fram, Associated Press, 2/8/05. http://www.detnews.com/2005/politics/0502/10/politics-82885.htm.

36. *New York Times*/CBS Poll, 1/12–1/15/04, cited in *New York Times,* 1/18/04.

37. Will Lester, Associated Press, 4/14/04. http://www.post-gazette.com/pg/04105/300467.stm.

38. David Milstead, *Rocky Mountain News,* 4/15/04.

39. David Cay Johnston, *San Francisco Chronicle,* 4/11/04. http://www.sfgate.com/cgi-bin/article.cgi?f=/c/a/2004/04/11/INGV560VO41.DTL.

40. Brian Riedl, Heritage Foundation, 6/16/04. http://www.heritage.org/Press/Commentary/ed061604b.cfm.

41. Stephen Moore, *National Review,* 8/9/93. http://www.findarticles.com/p/articles/mi_m1282/is_n15_v45/ai_13284505/print.

42. David Cay Johnston, *San Francisco Chronicle,* 4/11/04. http://www.commondreams.org/headlines04/0411-05.htm.

43. Representative Jim DeMint (R-SC), speech to the Heritage Foundation, 5/8/01. http://www.heritage.org/Research/PoliticalPhilosophy/loader.cfm?url=/commonspot/security/getfile.cfm&PageID=4327.

44. *Wall Street Journal* editorial, 11/20/02.

45. Tim Noah, *Slate,* 12/16/02 http://slate.msn.com/id/2077294/.

46. J.T. Young, *Washington Times,* 12/3/02.

47. Jonathan Weisman, *Washington Post,* 12/16/02. http://www.washingtonpost.com/ac2/wp-dyn?pagename=article&contentId=A59577-2002Dec15&notFound=true.

48. Brian DeBose, *Washington Times,* 8/4/04. http://washingtontimes.com/national/20040803-110115-1762r.htm.

49. Robert McIntyre, Citizens for Tax Justice, congressional testimony, 5/17/95. http://www.ctj.org/html/armchr.htm.

50. Ibid.

51. Representative Larry Combest (R-TX), chairman, House Agriculture Committee, 6/9/00. http://agriculture.house.gov/press/106/pr000609.html.

52. Senator Evan Bayh (D-IN), Official Senate press release, 6/12/02. http://bayh.senate.gov/www/Press/2002/12JUNE02pr.htm.

53. Scotty Johnson and Sam Husseini, FAIR, September/October 2000. http://www.fair.org/extra/best-of-extra/farm_bureau_3-00.html. Defenders of Wildlife report entitled "Amber Waves of Grain: How the Farm Bureau Is Reaping Profits at the Expense of America's Family Farmers," April 2000. http://www.defenders.org/fb/amberwaves.pdf.

54. American Farm Bureau press release, 4/4/01. http://www.fb.org/news/nr/nr2001/nr0404.html.

55. National Public Radio with Terry Gross, 10/2/03. http://www.commondreams.org/views03/1008-07.htm.

56. Center on Budget and Policy Priorities, 2/6/01. http://www.Center_on_Budget_and_Policy_Priorities.org/5-25-00tax.htm.

57. David Cay Johnston, *New York Times*, 4/8/01. http://www.commondreams.org/headlines01/0408-02.htm.

58. Ibid.

59. Bush signed the Economic Growth and Tax Relief Reconciliation Act on June 7, 2001. The *Atlanta Journal-Constitution* reported on 6/8/01 that the bill is "a high-profile down payment on a long-range plan that includes reduced income tax rates, phasing out the estate tax."

60. Center on Budget and Policy Priorities, 2/6/01. http://www.Center_on_Budget_and_Policy_Priorities.org/5-25-00tax.htm.

61. Center on Budget and Policy Priorities, 7/27/05. http://www.Center_on_Budget_and_Policy_Priorities.org/7-27-05tax.htm.

62. Ibid.

63. Jeffrey H. Birnbaum and Jonathan Weisman, *Washington Post*, 8/12/05. http://www.washingtonpost.com/wp-dyn/content/article/2005/08/11/AR2005081102013.html.

64. Grover Norquist, Americans for Tax Reform, 5/15/03. http://www.atr.org/press/editorials/0515030ped.html.

65. Chris Edwards, Cato Institute director of fiscal policy, 4/02. http://www.cato.org/pubs/tbb/tbb-0204.html.

66. Christian Weller, Center for American Progress Senior Economist, citing GAO 2004 data and GAO report "Comparison of the Reported Tax Liabilities of Foreign and U.S.-Controlled Corporations, 1996–2000", page 2. http://www.americanprogress.org/atf/cf/{E9245FE4-9A2B-43C7-A521-5D6FF2E06E03}/profitstaxes.pdf; http://www.gao.gov/new.items/d04358.pdf.

67. Citizens for Tax Justice, 5/15/02. http://www.ctj.org/html/corp0302.htm.

68. Robert McIntyre, Citizens for Tax Justice congressional testimony, 6/18/03. http://www.ctj.org/html/corp0603.htm.

69. Warren Vieth, *Los Angeles Times*, 4/15/04. http://taxpolicycenter.org/newsevents/cite_breaks_cost.cfm.

70. Curt Anderson, Associated Press, 12/17/99.

71. Curt Anderson, Associated Press, 3/13/02. http://bernie.house.gov/documents/articles/20020318173422.asp. Citizenworks, "List of Corporate Tax Dodgers." http://www.citizenworks.org/corp/tax/taxdodgerslist.php.

72. Institute for Taxation and Economic Policy report, 10/19/00. http://www.ctj.org/itep/corpoopr.htm.

73. Citizens for Tax Justice, 9/22/04. http://www.ctj.org/corpfed04pr.pdf.

74. Elliot Blair Smith, *USA Today*, 2/25/05. http://www.usatoday.com/money/perfi/taxes/2005-02-24-taxes-usat_x.htm.

75. *St. Petersburg Times* editorial, 4/15/04. http://www.sptimes.com/2004/04/15/Opinion/Another_corporate_tax.shtml.

76. David Cay Johnston, *New York Times*, 11/3/04. http://64.233.161.104/search?q= cache:oUsVL6sbZP8J:www.iht.com/articles/2004/11/02/business/irs.html+11,000+ audit+taxes+irs+international+herald+tribune&hl=en.

77. Jonathan Weisman, *Washington Post*, 4/12/04. http://www.detnews.com/2004/ politics/0404/13/a06-119903.htm.

78. GAO report, February 2004. http://www.gao.gov/new.items/d0495.pdf.

79. Griff Witte and Robert O'Harrow Jr., *Washington Post*, 6/16/05. http://www. washingtonpost.com/wp-dyn/content/article/2005/06/15/AR2005061502511. html?sub=AR.

80. Mary Dalrymple, Associated Press, 2/12/04. http://www.usatoday.com/news/ washington/2004-02-12-defense-taxes_x.htm.

81. Government Accountability Office, 2/04. http://www.gao.gov/new.items/d0495.pdf.

82. Lee Drutman, Citizen Works, 4/8/03. http://www.citizenworks.org/enron/ offshoretax-leg.php.

83. Jonathan Weisman, *Washington Post*, 12/19/03. http://www.washingtonpost.com/ ac2/wp-dyn?pagename=article&node=&contentId=A13403-2003Dec18&notFound= true.

84. David Cay Johnston, *San Francisco Chronicle*, 4/11/04. http://www.commondreams. org/headlines04/0411-05.htm.

85. President Bush, 8/9/04. http://www.whitehouse.gov/news/releases/2004/08/ 20040809-3.html.

86. David Cay Johnston, *San Francisco Chronicle*, 4/11/04. http://www.commondreams. org/headlines04/0411-05.htm.

87. Brian Tumulty, Gannett News Service, 2/11/03.

88. Max Sawicky, Economic Policy Institute report, "Do-it-yourself tax cuts," 4/12/05. http://www.epinet.org/content.cfm/bp160; statement of Leonard E. Burman before the United States House of Representatives Committee on Ways and Means; On Waste, Fraud, and Abuse, 7/17/03.

89. Joe Achenbach, *Washington Post*, 9/22/05. http://blogs.washingtonpost.com/ achenblog/2005/09/gop_to_audit_th.html. The specific proposal is on page 12 of the Republican Study Committee's 9/21/05 report "Operation Offset."

90. Max Sawicky, Economic Policy Institute report, "Do-it-yourself tax cuts," 4/12/05. http://www.epinet.org/content.cfm/bp160.

91. Juliet Eilperin and Jonathan Weisman, "Congress Targets Tax Havens; House Vote Shows Perception of Corporate Abuse," *Washington Post*, 6/30/02. House roll call vote #366, 7/26/02. http://clerk.house.gov/evs/2002/roll366.xml.

92. House roll call vote #351, June 30, 2005. http://clerk.house.gov/evs/2005/ roll351.xml. DeLauro press release, 6/30/05. http://www.house.gov/delauro/press/ 2005/June/corporate_expats_06_30_05.html.

93. Rahm Emanuel, "The Democrats Can Win on Taxes," *Wall Street Journal*, 10/15/03. http://online.wsj.com/article/0,,SB106617977825169900,00.html.

94. Linda Feldmann and David T. Cook, "The Man Who Democrats Hope Can Take That Hill," *Christian Science Monitor*, 3/11/05. http://csmonitor.com/2005/0311/ p01s01-uspo.htm.

95. President Bush, 7/20/02. http://www.whitehouse.gov/news/releases/2002/07/ 20020720.html.

96. Daniel J. Mitchell, Heritage Foundation Executive Memorandum #913, 2/12/04. http://www.heritage.org/Research/Taxes/em913.cfm.

97. Melvin Claxton and Ronald J. Hansen, *Detroit News*, 9/26/04. http://www.detnews. com/2004/specialreport/0409/26/a01-284666.htm.

98. Center on Budget and Policy Priorities, 8/26/03. http://www.Center_on_Budget_and_Policy_Priorities.org/8-26-03bud.htm.

99. Center on Budget and Policy Priorities, 1/23/04. http://www.Center_on_Budget_and_Policy_Priorities.org/1-23-04tax-fact.htm.

100. Grover Norquist quoted in *New York Times Magazine* piece by Paul Krugman, 9/14/03.

101. Senator Rick Santorum quoted in a *Los Angeles Times* piece by Elizabeth Shogren, 9/11/03.

102. Al Hunt, CNN, 9/13/03.

103. Daniel J. Mitchell, Heritage Scholar, 2/12/04. http://www.heritage.org/Research/Taxes/em913.cfm.

104. CNN, 12/23/04. http://www.cnn.com/2004/EDUCATION/12/23/pell.grants/. Dan Morgan, *Washington Post,* 12/24/04. http://www.commondreams.org/cgi-bin/print.cgi?file=/headlines04/1224-03.htm.

105. John Fountain, *New York Times,* 12/4/02. http://www.jessejacksonjr.org/issues/i1205026531.html.

106. Minneapolis *Star Tribune* editorial, 2/8/05. http://democraticwhip.house.gov/media/2006_presidential_budget/star_tribune.cfm.

107. David W. Chen, *New York Times,* 2/25/05. http://www.nytimes.com/2005/02/22/nyregion/22housing.html.

108. Mary Dalrymple, Associated Press, 2/13/05. http://www.truthout.org/cgi-bin/artman/exec/view.cgi/37/8956.

109. Paul Krugman, *New York Times,* 2/11/05. http://www.truthout.org/cgi-bin/artman/exec/view.cgi/38/8927.

110. Melissa B. Robinson, Associated Press, 8/1/02.

111. Leonard E. Burman and Jeff Rohaly, Brookings Tax Policy Center, 1/7/03. http://www.taxpolicycenter.org/publications/template.cfm?PubID=1000422.

112. Center on Budget and Policy Priorities, 1/15/03. http://www.Center_on_Budget_and_Policy_Priorities.org/1-9-03tax.htm.

113. Edward Walsh, *Washington Post,* 1/17/03. http://www.washingtonpost.com/ac2/wp-dyn/A4064-2003Jan16.

114. Mark Benjamin, United Press International, 10/17/03. http://www.upi.com/view.cfm?StoryID=20031017-024617-1418r.

115. Center on Budget and Policy Priorities, 1/30/04. http://www.Center_on_Budget_and_Policy_Priorities.org/1-22-04tax.htm.

116. Reuters, 1/10/04. http://www.cnn.com/2004/ALLPOLITICS/01/10/bush.radio.reut/.

117. Niels Sorrells, *Congressional Quarterly,* 2/4/04.

118. Bush's FY 2005 budget, released on 2/2/04. http://www.whitehouse.gov/infocus/budget/index.html.

119. Eric Umansky, *Slate,* 2/18/04. http://slate.msn.com/id/2095705/.

120. Melinda Liu, John Barry, and Michael Hirsh, *Newsweek,* 4/25/04. http://www.msnbc.msn.com/id/4825948/.

121. David Chu quoted in a story by Greg Jaffe of the *Wall Street Journal,* 1/25/05.

122. Mark Benjamin, Salon.com, 1/27/05.

123. Robert Pear and Carl Hulse, *New York Times,* 2/7/05. http://www.sfgate.com/cgi-bin/article.cgi?file=/c/a/2005/02/07/MNGM5B72E01.DTL.

124. Tony Blankley, *Pittsburgh Tribune-Review,* 2/20/2005. http://pittsburghlive.com/x/tribune-review/opinion/columnists/guests/s_305273.html.

125. Citizens for Tax Justice, "The Bush Tax Cuts So Far, 2001–2010," July 2005, page 4. http://www.ctj.org/pdf/gwbdata.pdf.

126. Ibid., page 2.
127. Ibid.
128. Ronald J. Hansen and Melvin Claxton, *Detroit News*, 9/26/04. http://www.detnews. com/2004/specialreport/0409/26/a01-284666.htm.
129. Genaro C. Armas, Associated Press, 10/12/04.
130. http://www.whitehouse.gov/news/releases/2004/03/20040313.html.
131. PBS *Newshour*, 6/7/01. http://www.pbs.org/newshour/updates/june01/tax_6-7.html.
132. *New Orleans City Business*, "Port of New Orleans Winces at President's Budget Hatchet," 4/16/01.
133. Ronald J. Hansen and Melvin Claxton, *Detroit News*, 9/28/04. http://www.detnews. com/2004/specialreport/0409/29/a09-286527.htm.
134. Bruce Alpert, New Orleans *Times-Picayune*, 7/16/03.
135. Bill Sammon, *Washington Times*, 1/20/04. http://washingtontimes.com/national/ 20040120-120924-6281r.htm.
136. New Orleans *Times-Picayune*, 6/8/04.
137. Mark Schleifstein, New Orleans *Times-Picayune*, 2/8/05.
138. ASCE report card 2005. http://www.asce.org/reportcard/2005/page.cfm?id=eq23. Study was released March of 2005, Associated Press, 3/9/05: http://www.usatoday. com/news/washington/2005-03-09-infrastructure_x.htm.
139. Jason Vest and Justin Rood, *National Journal*, 9/1/05: http://www.govexec.com/ dailyfed/0905/090105iv1.htm.
140. CNN, 3/6/02. http://archives.cnn.com/2002/ALLPOLITICS/03/06/army.secretary/.
141. John McQuaid and Mark Schleifstein, New Orleans *Times-Picayune*, 6/25/02.
142. Center for Tax Justice analysis July 2005 shows the richest 1 percent will receive $53.7 billion in tax cuts in 2006, $57.4 billion in 2007, $66.6 billion in 2008, $61.4 billion in 2009, and $97.2 billion in 2010 for a total of $336 billion. http://www.ctj.org/pdf/ gwbdata.pdf.
143. Associated Press, 9/14/05. http://www.foxnews.com/story/0.2933.169356.00.html.
144. ABC News poll, 1/22/02. http://www.abcnews.go.com/sections/business/DailyNews/ taxcut_poll_020122.html.
145. CNN/Money, 4/15/04. http://money.cnn.com/2004/04/15/news/economy/ election_moneypoll/.
146. Center for American Progress report, "State of the Union Rhetoric vs. Reality: Job Training Proposal." http://www.americanprogress.org/site/pp.asp?c=biJRJ8OVF&b= 22536.
147. Ronald Hansen and Melvin Claxton, *Detroit News*, 9/26/04. http://www.detnews. com/2004/specialreport/0410/03/a15-284398.htm.
148. Congressional Budget Office, report entitled "Cost Estimate of the Jobs and Growth Tax Relief Reconciliation Act of 2003," 5/23/03. Notes in the table on page 2 that the tax cut will cost $135.3 billion in 2004–$180 million is a little more than one-tenth of 1 percent of $135.3 billion. http://www.cbo.gov/ftpdocs/42xx/doc4249/hr2.pdf.
149. Center on Budget and Policy Priorities, 3/20/03. http://www.Center_on_Budget_and_ Policy_Priorities.org/3-5-03bud-fact.htm.
150. Edmund L. Andrews, *New York Times*, 1/29/05.
151. Ibid.
152. Bob Anez, Associated Press, 3/8/05. http://www.billingsgazette.com/index.php?tl= 1&display=rednews/2005/03/07/build/state/35-taxcheats.inc.
153. Amy Schatz, *Wall Street Journal*, 5/12/05.
154. U.S. House Report 109-203, "Safe, Accountable, Flexible, Efficient Transportation Equity Act: A Legacy for Users," 7/28/05, pages 1163 and 1164. http://frwebgate.

access.gpo.gov/cgi-bin/getdoc.cgi?dbname=109_cong_reports&docid=f:hr203. 109.pdf.

155. Judy Hasson, *Federal Computer Week*, 1/30/03. http://www.fcw.com/fcw/articles/ 2003/0127/web-irs-01-30-03.asp.

156. Mark Basch, *Florida Times-Union*, 3/30/05.

157. William Raspberry, *Washington Post*, 2/12/01.

158. CNN, 7/30/01. http://www.cnn.com/2001/ALLPOLITICS/07/30/bush.social.security/.

159. Maya MacGuineas, *Atlantic Monthly*, 1/20/04. http://www.newamerica.net/index. cfm?pg=article&DocID=1452.

160. Ibid.

161. Nicholas Confessore, *New York Times Magazine*, 1/16/05.

162. Citizens for Tax Justice, 5/8/04. http://www.ctj.org/pdf/earnpr.pdf.

163. Warren Buffett, *Washington Post*, 5/20/03. http://www.responsiblegov.net/ Dividendpercent20Voodoo.htm.

164. Center for American Progress tax plan. http://www.americanprogress.org/site/ pp.asp?c=biJRJ8OVF&b=310260.

165. David Wessell, "Politicians Must Decide How to Raise Taxes," *Wall Street Journal*, 10/13/05.

166. Greenberg, Quinlan & Rosner poll for Responsible Wealth, 5/6–9/02. http://www. responsiblewealth.org/press/2002/americans_support_pr.html.

167. Center for Tax Justice analysis, July 2005, shows the richest 1 percent will receive $53.7 billion in tax cuts in 2006, $57.4 billion in 2007, $66.6 billion in 2008, $61.4 billion in 2009, and $97.2 billion in 2010, for a total of $336 billion. http://www.ctj.org/pdf/ gwbdata.pdf.

168. Caroline Daniel, *Financial Times*, 9/20/05. Mary Dalrymple, Associated Press, 9/14/05.

169. Rick Maze, *Navy Times*, 9/21/05. http://www.navytimes.com/story.php?f= 1-292925-1117445.php.

170. CBS/Associated Press, 9/28/05. http://www.cbsnews.com/stories/2005/09/28/ national/main888226.shtml.

171. Mary Dalrymple, Associated Press, 9/21/05. http://news.yahoo.com/s/ap/ 20050921/ap_on_go_co/hurricanes_washington_hk4;_ylt=A12N0LtE8BE.tpcsJt4k9. g8KbIF;_ylu=X3oDMTBiMW04NW9mBHN1YwM1JVRPUCUl.

172. Jonathan Weisman, *Washington Post*, 9/22/05. http://www.washingtonpost.com/ wp-dyn/content/article/2005/09/21/AR2005092102394.html.

CHAPTER 2: WAGES

1. Fed chairman Alan Greenspan statement, 7/18/01.

2. Fed chairman Alan Greenspan's commencement address at the Wharton School, University of Pennsylvania, 5/15/05. http://www.federalreserve.gov/boarddocs/speeches/ 2005/20050515/default.htm.

3. AFL-CIO, Labor Day report, 2004. http://www.aflcio.org/mediacenter/resources/ upload/ld2004_report.pdf. Congressman George Miller Calls for Minimum Wage Increase, press release, 7/8/04. http://edworkforce.house.gov/democrats/releases/ rel7704c.html.

4. 2005 HHS Poverty Guidelines say the poverty line for a family of 3 is $16,090. http:// aspe.hhs.gov/poverty/05poverty.shtml.

5. Arandrajit Dube, "Are Jobs Getting Worse," 10/14/04. www.iir.berkeley.edu/research/ jobquality.pdf.

6. Stan Cox, Alternet, 6/10/03. http://www.corpwatch.org/article.php?id=7048.

7. Jonathan Krim and Griff Witte, *Washington Post,* 12/31/04. http://www.washingtonpost. com/ac2/wp-dyn/A37628-2004Dec30?language=printer.

8. Grant Gross, Industry Standard, 12/22/04. http://www.thestandard.com/ movabletype/datadigest/archives/003187.php#trackbacks.

9. Janco Associates press release, "Recovery Does Not Help IT—Demand and Pay Flat in Janco Associates Inc. 2005 Salary Survey," 1/11/05. http://www.e-janco.com/ PressRelease/press_releasepercent20Sal_percent20Survey_percent2020050111.htm.

10. Economic Policy Institute snapshot, 4/20/05. http://www.epinet.org/content.cfm?id= 2012.

11. Christopher Swann, *Financial Times,* 5/10/05. http://news.ft.com/cms/s/ f269a8f4-c173-11d9-943f-00000e2511c8.html.

12. Art Pine and Will Edwards, Bloomberg News, 1/4/05. http://quote.bloomberg.com/ apps/news?pid=nifea&&sid=aiYj4kedJz18.

13. Charles Stein, *Boston Globe,* 5/5/04. http://www.commondreams.org/headlines04/ 0505-03.htm.

14. Mark Trumbull, *Christian Science Monitor,* 8/22/05. http://www.csmonitor.com/ 2005/0822/p01s03-usec.html?s=hns.

15. *BusinessWeek* press release, 4/7/05. http://www.businessweek.com/magazine/content/ 05_16/b3929100_mz017.htm?campaign_id=nws_insdr_apr8&link_position=link4.

16. Ibid. $9.6 million divided by $33,176 = 289.

17. Rachel Koning, Marketwatch, 7/25/05.

18. Center for Responsive Politics. http://www.opensecrets.org/cmteprofiles/ indus.asp?cycle=2004&CmteID=S18&Cmte=SLAB&CongNo=108&Chamber=S; http://www.opensecrets.org/cmteprofiles/indus.asp?cycle=2004&CmteID= H08&Cmte=HEDU&CongNo=108&Chamber=H.

19. Carol Hymowitz, *Wall Street Journal,* 11/17/04. http://www.careerjournal.com/ columnists/inthelead/20041117-inthelead.html.

20. Center for Responsive Politics data found Domino's gave roughly $71,000 in soft money to GOP and $30,000 in PAC money to the GOP. http://www.opensecrets.org/ softmoney/softcomp2.asp?txtName=Dominopercent27s+Pizza&txtUltOrg=n&txtSort= name&txtCycle=1998; http://www.opensecrets.org/pacs/lookup2.asp?strID=C00366088.

21. George Weeks, *Detroit News,* 4/29/04.

22. 2003 November Occupational Employment and Wage Estimates for Michigan. Annual average wage: $38,619.

23. Ron French, *Detroit News,* 3/7/04. http://www.detnews.com/2004/specialreport/ 0403/11/a01-84173.htm.

24. President Bush, 10/30/04. http://www.whitehouse.gov/news/releases/2004/10/ 20041030-3.html.

25. Public Citizen's White House for Sale project shows 43 Bush Pioneers/Rangers in the construction industry, 17 in the agriculture industry, 19 in the manufacturing industry, and 6 in the nursing home/hospital industry.

26. Laura Meckler, Associated Press, 7/13/96.

27. Laura Kurtzman and Ann E. Marimow, *San Jose Mercury News,* 9/3/04.

28. Jordan Rau, *Los Angeles Times,* 9/19/04.

29. Lauren Mayk, *Sarasota Herald-Tribune,* 9/23/04.

30. Sonni Jacobs and Carlos Campos, *Atlanta Journal-Constitution,* 3/29/05. http://www.ajc.com/metro/content/custom/blogs/georgia/entries/2005/03/29/ legislature_voids_atlantas_living_wage_provision.html.

31. American Legislative Exchange Council, report entitled "Can America Survive on 'Living Wages?,' " 4/01. http://www.alec.org/meSWFiles/pdf/0103.pdf.

32. American Legislative Exchange Council's model bill. http://www.alec.org/viewpage.cfm?pgname=1.1f.

33. Ed Kilgore, *The New Democrat*, 9/1/99. http://www.ndol.org/ndol_ci.cfm?kaid=114&subid=144&contentid=1115.

34. CNN, 6/27/03. http://money.cnn.com/2003/06/26/news/economy/epi/.

35. Eric Pianin, *Washington Post*, 11/22/03.

36. Leigh Strope, Associated Press, 1/6/04.

37. Tom Edsall, *Washington Post*, 9/9/05. http://www.washingtonpost.com/wp-dyn/content/article/2005/09/08/AR2005090802037.html.

38. Yochi J. Dreazen, *Wall Street Journal*, 9/12/05. http://online.wsj.com/article/0,,SB112648366967837577,00.html?mod=yahoo_hs&ru=yahoo. Opensecrets.org issued a March 12, 2003, report showing Fluor and Bechtel are both major donors to the Republican Party. http://www.capitaleye.org/inside.asp?ID=69.

39. Yochi J. Dreazen, *Wall Street Journal*, 9/12/05. http://online.wsj.com/article/0,,SB112648366967837577,00.html?mod=yahoo_hs&ru=yahoo.

40. New Bridge Strategies front page. http://www.newbridgestrategies.com/index.asp.

41. Dan Balz, *Washington Post*, 9/1/05.

42. Reuters, 9/10/05. http://www.cnn.com/2005/POLITICS/09/10/katrina.contracts.reut/.

43. Charles Lewis, *Multinational Monitor*, 10/93. http://multinationalmonitor.org/hyper/mm1093.html.

44. Bill Clinton, 11/10/93.

45. *Rochester Business Journal*, 5/12/00.

46. Public Citizen, report entitled "Purchasing Power: The Corporate-White House Alliance to Pass the China Trade Bill Over the Will of the American People," 10/2/00. http://www.citizen.org/documents/purchasingpower.PDF.

47. Center for Responsive Politics data finds that General Electric gave roughly $756,000 in soft money to the GOP since 2000 and $1.66 million hard money to the GOP since 2000 (2004: $653,626 + 2002: $519,824 + 2000: $505,450). http://www.opensecrets.org/softmoney/softcomp1.asp?txtName=General+Electric.

48. National Public Radio, 1/3/01.

49. John Sununu, 5/23/89.

50. Robert Rubin, 6/9/99.

51. House Speaker Newt Gingrich, 7/18/95.

52. Nik I. Kovac, *Harvard Crimson*, 2/24/00. http://www.thecrimson.com/article.aspx?ref=99582.

53. Bruce Bartlett, former Reagan Treasury official, CNN, 2/13/04.

54. Kantor's biography at Mayer, Brown, Rowe and Maw law firm notes that he "specializes in Market access issues • expanding client activities in foreign markets through trade, direct investment, joint ventures and strategic business alliances." http://www.mayerbrownrowe.com/lawyers/profile.asp?hubbardid=K534008205&lawyer_name=Kantor_percent2C+Michael+.

55. Mickey Kantor, 1/5/99, quoted on page 278 of John R. MacArthur, *The Selling of "Free Trade,"* 2000.

56. Lou Dobbs, CNN, 3/1/05. http://www-cgi.cnn.com/2005/US/02/28/cafta.politics/.

57. Robert Rubin press conference, 5/3/96.

58. President Bush, 4/17/01.

59. Paul Blustein, *Washington Post*, 10/26/01. http://lists.essential.org/pipermail/ip-health/2001-October/002270.html.

60. Sheldon Alberts and Joe Paraskevas, Can West News Service, 3/4/05.

61. Sandra Boodman, *Washington Post*, 11/25/03.

62. David Wahlberg, Cox News Service, 11/29/03.

63. Associated Press, 2/26/05. http://www.sfgate.com/cgi-bin/article.cgi?f=/n/a/2005/02/26/national/w081015S32.DTL.

64. Center for Responsive Politics data shows agribusiness gave $7,618,679. http://www.opensecrets.org/presidential/sector.asp?id=N00008072&cycle=All.

65. Center for Responsive Politics data shows Bush received $1 million from the pharmaceutical industry in 2004, and $500,283 in 2000. http://www.opensecrets.org/industries/recips.asp?Ind=H04&Cycle=2004&recipdetail=A&Mem=N&sortorder=U; http://www.opensecrets.org/industries/recips.asp?Ind=H04&Cycle=2000&recipdetail=A&Mem=N&sortorder=U.

66. Harold Myerson, *Washington Post*, 3/30/05. http://www.washingtonpost.com/wp-dyn/articles/A11310-2005Mar29.html.

67. Ibid. And Evelyn Iritani, *Los Angeles Times*, 1/9/06.

68. John Lyons, *Wall Street Journal*, 5/3/05. http://www.bilaterals.org/article.php3?id_article=1813.

69. Mark Weisbrot, Knight-Ridder, 4/19/01. http://www.commondreams.org/views01/0419-05.htm.

70. Minority Leader Dick Gephardt (D-MO) quoted on page 105 in John R. MacArthur, *The Selling of "Free Trade,"* 2000.

71. Jim Siegel, *Cincinnati Enquirer*, 9/5/04.

72. John Snow, 10/12/04.

73. Center for Economic and Policy Research, 10/11/01. http://www.commondreams.org/news2001/1011-05.htm.

74. Public Citizen fact sheet. http://www.citizen.org/trade/ftaa/workers/index.cfm.

75. Richard Stevenson, *New York Times*, 4/30/99.

76. Delphi CEO Robert "Steve" Miller, *Fortune*, 10/31/05.

77. Mark Weisbrot, *Miami Herald*, 4/16/05.

78. Public Citizen fact sheet. http://www.citizen.org/trade/ftaa/workers/index.cfm.

79. Elizabeth Becker, Clifford Krauss, and Tim Weiner; *New York Times*, 12/27/03.

80. Ibid.

81. PIPA poll, 3/28/00. http://www.pipa.org/OnlineReports/Globalization/AmericansGlobalization_Maroo/AmericansGlobalization_Mar00_apdxb.pdf.

82. PIPA/University of Maryland poll, "Majority Disapproves of Government Approach to Trade," press release, 1/22/04.

83. John R. MacArthur, *The Selling of "Free Trade,"* 2000, page 299.

84. Lou Dobbs, CNN, 3/1/05. http://www-cgi.cnn.com/2005/US/02/28/cafta.politics/.

85. Timothy Noah, *Slate*, 7/24/02. http://slate.msn.com/id/2068449/.

86. Erin Billings, Roll Call, 9/20/05. http://www.rollcall.com/issues/51_25/news/10551-1.html.

87. Rahm Emanuel, "Free Trade Is a Winner for Democrats," *Wall Street Journal*, 5/23/00.

88. Bruce Alpert, New Orleans *Times-Picayune*, 2/10/01.

89. Ari Fleischer, 10/1/01.

90. Joe Stange, Associated Press, 9/20/00.

91. MSNBC, 9/22/04. http://www.msnbc.msn.com/id/4448630.

92. President Bush, 7/14/04. http://www.whitehouse.gov/news/releases/2004/07/20040714-11.html.

93. Presidential debate, 10/13/04. http://www.washingtonpost.com/wp-srv/politics/debatereferee/debate_1013.html.

94. Elizabeth Fulk, *The Hill*, 11/18/04. http://www.hillnews.com/news/111804/unions.aspx.

95. Associated Press, 3/7/05. http://www.cbsnews.com/stories/2005/03/07/politics/main678648.shtml.

96. Economic Policy Institute press release, 3/4/05. http://www.epinet.org/newsroom/releases/2005/03/050304-Minimum_Wage.pdf.

97. John Baer, *Philadelphia Daily News*, 4/11/05. http://www.philly.com/mld/dailynews/11364119.htm.

98. National Public Radio, 3/3/05. http://mediamatters.org/items/200503050001.

99. Harry Bernstein, *Los Angeles Times*, 9/15/92.

100. Fiscal Policy Institute, 4/20/04, pages 11–12. http://www.fiscalpolicy.org/minimumwageandsmallbusiness.pdf.

101. Card and Krueger, 1995. http://www.epinet.org/content.cfm/issuebriefs_ib149.

102. Sen. Arlen Specter (R-PA), 3/7/05. http://frwebgate.access.gpo.gov/cgi-bin/getpage.cgi?dbname=2005_record&page=S2134&position=all.

103. Economic Policy Institute report. http://www.epinet.org/issueguides/minwage/table3.gif.

104. Sen. Orrin Hatch (R-UT), 5/7/05. http://frwebgate.access.gpo.gov/cgi-bin/getpage.cgi?dbname=2005_record&page=S2128&position=all.

105. Fiscal Policy Institute, 4/21/04. http://www.fiscalpolicy.org/press_040421.stm.

106. Jerome Levy Economics Institute, 3/98. http://www.levy.org/default.asp?view=publications_view&pubID=f73a2071a3 (page 2). Cited by Bruce Alpert, New Orleans *Times-Picayune*, 3/22/99.

107. Center on Budget and Policy Priorities, 5/29/98. http://www.Center_on_Budget_and_Policy_Priorities.org/5290rmw-pr.htm.

108. Sen. Arlen Specter (R-PA), 3/7/05. http://frwebgate.access.gpo.gov/cgi-bin/getpage.cgi?dbname=2005_record&page=S2134&position=all.

109. On 10/7/02, the Manchester Union Leader reported John H. Sununu "has his own lobbying and consulting business, JHS Associates, sits on several boards."

110. Sen. John Sununu (R-NH), Senate floor statements, 3/7/05. http://frwebgate.access.gpo.gov/cgi-bin/getpage.cgi?dbname=2005_record&page=S2117&position=all.

111. Philip Mattera and Anna Purinton, "Shopping for Subsidies," Good Jobs First, 5/04. http://www.goodjobsfirst.org/pdf/wmtstudy.pdf.

112. House roll call vote #348, 9/21/01. http://clerk.house.gov/evs/2001/roll348.xml.

113. House roll call vote #210, 6/5/02. http://clerk.house.gov/evs/2002/roll210.xml.

114. Rep. Bernie Sanders (I-VT), testimony before the House Financial Services Committee, 5/6/04.

115. Paul Kersey, Heritage Foundation, testimony to House Small Business Committee, 5/3/04. http://www.heritage.org/Research/Labor/tst042904a.cfm.

116. 2005 HHS Poverty Guidelines say the poverty line for a family of 3 is $16,090. http://aspe.hhs.gov/poverty/05poverty.shtml.

117. E! Online, 7/17/01. http://www.eonline.com/News/Items/0,1,8552,00.html.

118. Rush Limbaugh, 1/7/04.

119. National Low Income Housing Coalition report, 2004. http://www.nlihc.org/00r2004/introduction.htm.

120. Dr. Robert Pollin, Dr. Mark Brenner, Ms. Jeannette Wicks-Lim, report for Center for American Progress, page 11. http://www.americanprogress.org/atf/cf/_percent 7BE9245FE4-9A2B-43C7-A521-5D6FF2E06E03percent7D/minimumwage-layout8.pdf. Derived from H. Boushey, C. Brocht, B. Gundersen, and J. Bernstein, *Hardships in America: The Real Story of Working Families*, 2001.

121. Economic Policy Institute, 7/24/01. http://www.epinet.org/content.cfm/press_releases_hardships.

122. U.S. Mayors 2004 report. http://www.usmayors.org/uscm/ hungersurvey/2004/onlinereport/HungerAndHomelessnessReport2004.pdf.

123. Jonathan Weisman, *Washington Post,* 10/11/04. http://www.washingtonpost.com/ ac2/wp-dyn/A22773-2004Oct10?language=printer.

124. Holly Sklar, Knight-Ridder News Service, 8/29/01. http://www.commondreams.org/ views01/0829-08.htm.

125. House Education and Workforce Minority Committee report, "FY 2006 Bush Budget: Breaks Promises, Underfunds K-12 Funding, and Forces Students to Pay More for College," 2/7/05, page 9. http://edworkforce.house.gov/democrats/photos/ FY06budgetsummary.pdf and http://www.Center_on_Budget_and_Policy_Priorities. org/2-5-03tanf.pdf.

126. Mark Wilson, Heritage Foundation, 6/28/01. http://www.heritage.org/Research/ Labor/WM19.cfm.

127. PR Watch press release. http://www.prwatch.org/prwissues/2002Q1/ddam.html.

128. Employment Policies Institute, June 2001. http://www.epionline.org/study_detail. cfm?sid=24.

129. Sen. Mike Enzi, 4/1/04. http://enzi.senate.gov/wagehike.htm.

130. Economic Policy Institute table and report. http://www.epinet.org/issueguides/minwage/ table3.gif.

131. USDA Agriculture Information Bulletin #747-03, 5/00, page 4. http://www.ers.usda. gov/publications/aib747/aib74703.pdf.

132. Sirota interview with Ross Eisenbrey, spring 2005.

133. Matthew B. Kibbe, Cato Institute, report entitled "The Minimum Wage: Washington's Perennial Myth," 5/23/88. http://www.cato.org/pubs/pas/pa106.html.

134. Vice President Dick Cheney, 5/21/04. http://www.whitehouse.gov/news/releases/ 2004/05/20040521-2.html.

135. John King, CNN, 9/16/03. http://www.cnn.com/2003/ALLPOLITICS/09/16/cheney. halliburton/.

136. James Toedtman, *Newsday,* April 14, 2004. http://www.spokesmanreview.com/local/ story_txt.asp?date=041404&ID=s1509377.

137. Economic Policy Institute snapshot, 5/27/04. http://www.epinet.org/content.cfm/ webfeatures_snapshots_05272004.

138. President Bush, 6/19/04.

139. Economic Policy Institute, "Economic Snapshot," 1/21/04. http://www.epinet.org/ content.cfm/webfeatures_snapshots_archive_01212004.

140. Stephen Roach, *New York Times,* 7/22/04.

141. Eric Torbenson, *Dallas Morning News,* 02/05/2003.

142. Randolph Heaster, *Kansas City Star,* 4/10/03. http://www.twincities.com/mld/ kansascity/business/companies/5597020.htm.

143. *Christian Science Monitor,* 4/28/03. Edward Wong and Micheline Maynard, *New York Times,* 4/27/03.

144. Brad Foss, Associated Press, 4/25/03.

145. Art Pine and Will Edwards, Bloomberg News/*Pittsburgh Post-Gazette,* 1/4/05.

146. PRNewswire release about *BusinessWeek's* Annual Executive Pay Scoreboard, 4/7/05. http://www.prnewswire.com/cgi-bin/stories.pl?ACCT=104&STORY=/ www/story/04-07-2005/0003339105&EDATE=.

147. Julie Moran Alterio and Jerry Gleeson, *Westchester Journal News,* 12/19/02. http://www.detnews.com/2002/careers/0212/19/b04-39624.htm.

148. Tony Gnoffo, *Philadelphia Inquirer,* 2/4/05.

149. Marcia Gelbart, *Philadelphia Inquirer,* 12/3/04.

150. Tony Gnoffo, *Philadelphia Inquirer,* 4/9/05. http://www.philly.com/mld/philly/business/11349970.htm.

151. Jane M. Von Bergen, *Philadelphia Inquirer,* 4/11/04. http://www.philly.com/mld/inquirer/8402784.htm?1c.

152. Charles Stein, *Boston Globe,* 5/5/04. http://www.commondreams.org/headlines04/0505-03.htm.

153. Tony Reid, Knight-Ridder, 4/14/05.

154. Copley News Service, 1/27/05.

155. AFL-CIO Paywatch database. http://www.aflcio.org/corporateamerica/paywatch/ceou/database.cfm?tkr=CAT&pg=1.

156. Julie Moran Alterio and Jerry Gleeson, *Westchester Journal News,* 12/14/02. http://www.detnews.com/2002/careers/0212/19/b04-39624.htm.

157. Tony Reid, Knight-Ridder, 4/14/05.

158. David Francis, *Christian Science Monitor,* 9/4/01. http://www.faireconomy.org/press/ufenews/2001/Exec_Excess_CSM.html.

159. Economic Policy Institute, 3/2005. http://www.epinet.org/content.cfm/issueguides_minwage_minwagefacts.

160. Stanley Holmes and Wendy Zellner, *BusinessWeek,* 4/12/04.

161. Lisa DiCarlo, *Forbes,* 12/7/04. http://www.forbes.com/personaltech/2004/12/07/cx_ld_1207overachiever.html.

162. *BusinessWeek,* 5/31/04. http://businessweek.com/magazine/content/04_22/b3885011_mz001.htm.

163. Scott Adams and David Neumark, Public Policy Institute of California, 8/04. http://www.ppic.org/content/pubs/WP_804SADNWP.htm.

164. *Christian Science Monitor,* 3/15/02. http://www.csmonitor.com/2002/0315/p01s02-usec.html.

165. Charles S. Johnson, *Billings Gazette,* 2/16/05. http://www.billingsgazette.com/index.php?id=1&display=rednews/2005/02/16/build/state/68-living-wage.inc.

166. Daniel B. Wood, *Christian Science Monitor,* 3/15/02. http://www.csmonitor.com/2002/0315/p01s02-usec.html.

167. David Smith, *Arkansas Democrat-Gazette,* 8/4/02.

168. Anthony Bianco and Wendy Zellner, *BusinessWeek,* 10/6/03.

169. PIPA Poll, survey analysis page 2, 1/22/04. http://www.pipa.org/OnlineReports/Globalization/GlobalTradeFarm_Jan04/GlobalTradeFarm_Jan04_rpt.pdf.

170. Leigh Strope, Associated Press, 1/5/04. http://www.msnbc.msn.com/id/3882629/.

171. *Nashville Business Journal,* 6/21/01.

CHAPTER 3: JOBS

1. White House economic adviser Greg Mankiw quoted by Peter Brownfeld, Fox News, 2/9/04. http://www.foxnews.com/story/0,2933,111287,00.html.

2. CBS News, 2/16/04.

3. David Streitfeld, *Los Angeles Times,* 12/29/03. http://www.commondreams.org/headlines03/1229-01.htm.

4. Dana Milbank, *Washington Post,* 3/9/04. http://www.washingtonpost.com/ac2/wp-dyn?pagename=article&contentId=A41479-2004Mar8.

5. Economic Policy Institute's Jobwatch, 4/21/05. http://www.jobwatch.org/email/jobwatch_20050401.html.

6. Edmund Andrews, *New York Times,* 7/8/04.

7. *Washington Post,* 9/15/04.

8. Ibid.

9. University of California at Berkeley study by Ute Frey and Kathleen Maclay, 10/29/03. http://www.haas.berkeley.edu/news/20031029_outsourcing.html.

10. Paul McDougall, *Information Week*, 4/4/05. http://www.crn.com/sections/breakingnews/dailyarchives.jhtml?articleId=160403369.

11. Bill Clinton, 6/12/92.

12. Ibid.

13. Clinton signed NAFTA on 12/8/03.

14. James Robinson, CEO of American Express, quoted on page 275 of John R. MacArthur, *The Selling of "Free Trade,"* 2000.

15. White House press release, "The Clinton-Gore Administration: Strengthening Manufacturing for the 21st Century," 2/4/00.

16. Cato Institute handbook for the 107th Congress, Section 32, page 347. http://www.cato.org/pubs/handbook/hb107/hb107-32.pdf.

17. Economic Policy Institute, "Unemployment Insurance: Facts at a Glance," 8/04. http://www.epinet.org/content.cfm/issueguides_unemployment_facts.

18. Center for American Progress, "State of the Union Rhetoric vs. Reality: Job Training Proposal," 1/20/04. http://www.americanprogress.org/site/pp.asp?c=biJRJ8OVF&b=22536.

19. Ronald J. Hansen and Melvin Claxton, *Detroit News*, 9/28/04. http://www.detnews.com/2004/specialreport/0409/29/a01-286728.htm.

20. Ibid.

21. Carlos Alberto Becerril, United Press International, 1/20/05. http://www.washtimes.com/upi-breaking/20050120-050209-7965r.htm.

22. William Daley, 10/21/93.

23. Karen M. Lundegaard, *Cincinnati Business Courier*, 11/22/93.

24. Liz Moyer, *American Banker*, 5/21/04.

25. Robert Scott, Economic Policy Institute report entitled "Fast Track to Lost Jobs: Trade Deficits and Manufacturing Decline Are the Legacies of NAFTA and the WTO," 2001. http://www.epinet.org/briefingpapers/117/bp117.pdf.

26. Robert E. Scott, EPI Briefing Paper entitled "NAFTA at 7," 4/01. http://www.ratical.org/co-globalize/NAFTA@7/us.html#fn1.

27. Robert Scott, Economic Policy Institute, 11/17/03. http://www.epinet.org/content.cfm/briefingpapers_bp147.

28. Gil Klein, *Tampa Tribune*, 12/21/97.

29. Bill Clinton, White House press release, 5/17/00. http://www.clintonfoundation.org/legacy/051700-presidential-statement-on-pntr.htm.

30. Robert E. Scott, Economic Policy Institute, Working Paper #270, 1/2005. http://www.epinet.org/workingpapers/epi_wp270.pdf.

31. Daniel Griswold, Cato Institute, 2/21/01. http://www.cato.org/dailys/02-21-01.html.

32. Martin Crutsinger, Associated Press, 12/14/05.

33. President Bush, 8/13/02. http://www.whitehouse.gov/news/releases/2002/08/20020813-5.html.

34. White House press secretary Ari Fleischer, 1/18/02.

35. Donald L. Barlett and James B. Steele, *Time*, 11/9/98. http://www.time/com/time/archive/preview/0,10987,140395,00.html.

36. http://www.commondreams.org/news2002/0501-14.htm.

37. Donald L. Barlett and James B. Steele, *Daily Press* (Newport News, VA), 10/6/96.

38. *Boston* magazine, 6/04.

39. Center for Responsive Politics data shows PAC money from corporations in 2002:

General Electric gave $1,774,414, AT&T gave $980,332, Boeing gave $938,123, and Bechtel gave $164,661. http://www.opensecrets.org/pacs/lookup2.asp?strid= C00024869&cycle=2002; http://www.opensecrets.org/pacs/lookup2.asp?strid= C00185124&cycle=2002; http://www.opensecrets.org/pacs/lookup2.asp? strid=C00142711&cycle=2002; http://www.opensecrets.org/pacs/lookup2.asp? strid=C00103697&cycle=2002.

40. *Inside U.S. Trade,* 8/10/01. http://bernie.house.gov/documents/articles/ 2001-08-10-ex-im_bank.asp

41. Donald L. Barlett and James B. Steele, *Time* magazine, 11/16/98; Bernie Sanders, *The Nation* magazine, 5/21/02.

42. Leslie Wayne, *New York Times,* 9/3/02. http://www.bernie.house.gov/documents/ articles/20020903115232.asp.

43. Patrick Thibodeau, *Computerworld* reports on Forrester Research Data, 5/17/04. http://www.computerworld.com/managementtopics/outsourcing/story/ 0,10801,93217,00.html.

44. Dana Milbank, *Washington Post,* 2/29/04. http://www.washingtonpost.com/ac2/ wp-dyn?pagename=article&contentId=A15634-2004Feb28&notFound=true.

45. Mark Leibovich, *Washington Post,* 8/1/03.

46. Associated Press, 6/22/05.

47. John Chambers, CEO of Cisco, quoted in *Manufacturing and Technology News,* 10/21/04.

48. Andrew Stein, CNN, 8/31/04: Cites an 8/31/04 study by the Institute for Policy Studies. http://money.cnn.com/2004/08/31/news/economy/outsourcing_pay/.

49. Andrew Leckey, *Chicago Tribune,* 1/9/05. http://www.latimes.com/business/ yourmoney/sns-yourmoney-0109leckeyfile,1,3959077.story?coll=la-utilities-business.

50. Center for Responsive Politics data shows Crowley has taken $292,404 from securities and investment firms. http://www.opensecrets.org/politicians/allindus.asp?CID= N00001127.

51. Rediff.com, 3/16/03. http://www.rediff.com/money/2003/apr/16bpo.htm.

52. Rachel Konrad, Associated Press, 4/27/04.

53. Aziz Haniffa, *India Abroad,* 6/11/04.

54. Clint Swett, *Sacramento Bee,* 7/3/04.

55. Steve Lawrence, Associated Press, 9/30/04. http://www.calchamber.com/Chamber_in_ the_news/09-30-04_outsourcing_contracosta.htm.

56. CBS, *60 Minutes,* 8/1/04. http://www.cbsnews.com/stories/2003/12/23/60minutes/ main590004.shtml?CMP=ILC-SearchStories.

57. Stella M. Hopkins, *Charlotte Observer,* 2/20/05.

58. President Bush's weekly radio address, 2/7/04. http://www.whitehouse.gov/news/ releases/2004/02/20040207.html.

59. David Streitfeld, *Los Angeles Times,* 12/29/03.

60. Bloomberg News, 3/16/04. http://quote.bloomberg.com/apps/news?pid= 10000103&refer=us&sid=aO5a6z1BsWOQ.

61. David Cay Johnston, *New York Times,* 2/20/04.

62. Cliff Haas, Associated Press, 9/24/81.

63. Dana Priest, *Washington Post,* 1/31/92.

64. Associated Press, 1/5/03. http://www.news-star.com/stories/010503/New_81.shtml.

65. David Lazarus, *San Francisco Chronicle,* 1/3/03.

66. Representative John Boehner (D-OH), 10/16/01.

67. Peter Gosselin, *Los Angeles Times,* 10/10/04. http://www.latimes.com/news/ printedition/la-fi-riskshift10oct10,1,3174836.story.

68. Center on Budget and Policy Priorities, 1/14/03. http://www.Center_on_Budget_and_Policy_Priorities.org/1-6-03ui.htm.

69. Center on Budget and Policy Priorities, 10/4/02. http://www.Center_on_Budget_and_Policy_Priorities.org/10-4-02ui-pr.htm.

70. Federal Reserve chairman Alan Greenspan, 5/21/03.

71. Center on Budget and Policy Priorities, 5/23/03. http://www.Center_on_Budget_and_Policy_Priorities.org/5-22-03ui.htm.

72. Center on Budget and Policy Priorities, 10/15/03. http://www.Center_on_Budget_and_Policy_Priorities.org/10-15-03ui-pr.htm.

73. Fawn H. Johnson, "DeLay Sees 'No Reason' to Extend Federal UI Program into Next Year." Bureau of National Affairs (BNA) Daily Labor Report, 11/20/03. http://www.Center_on_Budget_and_Policy_Priorities.org/11-25-03ui.htm#_ftn4.

74. Center on Budget and Policy Priorities, 12/3/03. http://www.Center_on_Budget_and_Policy_Priorities.org/11-25-03ui.htm.

75. Center on Budget and Policy Priorities, 10/13/04. http://www.Center_on_Budget_and_Policy_Priorities.org/10-13-04ui.htm.

76. Economic Policy Institute, 3/4/04. http://www.afscme.org/action/fy2006.htm.

77. Representative John Boehner (R-OH), 10/16/01.

78. AFL-CIO FY 2006 fact sheet. http://staging.aflcio.org/issuespolitics/bushwatch/2006budget_main.cfm. Economic Policy Institute, 3/4/04. http://www.epinet.org/content.cfm/webfeatures_viewpoints_FY2005_FedBudget_and_jobs; AFSCME 2006 budget fact sheet. http://www.afscme.org/action/fy2006.htm.

79. Malia Rulon, Associated Press, 2/7/05. http://www.ohio.com/mld/beaconjournal/news/state/10841074.htm.

80. Greg Wright, Gannett News, 3/17/05.

81. Center on Budget and Policy Priorities, Table 1 in Isaac Shapiro's report, 10/13/04. http://www.Center_on_Budget_and_Policy_Priorities.org/10-13-04ui.htm.

82. Center on Budget and Policy Priorities, 2/2/04. http://www.Center_on_Budget_and_Policy_Priorities.org/1-29-04ui.htm.

83. House Roll Call vote #18, 2/4/04. http://clerk.house.gov/evs/2004/roll018.xml. Alex Wayne, *Congressional Quarterly*, 6/3/04. http://www.cnn.com/2004/ALLPOLITICS/02/05/congress.unemployment/.

84. AFL-CIO FY2006 Budget fact sheet. http://www.aflcio.org/issues/bushwatch/2006budget.cfm.

85. CBS/Associated Press, 2/7/05. http://www.cbsnews.com/stories/2005/02/08/politics/main672275.shtml

86. Representative Ralph Regula (R-OH), 2/13/02.

87. William McCall, Associated Press, 2/4/02.

88. Jonathan Riskind and Catherine Candisky, *Columbus Dispatch*, 1/20/02.

89. Ibid.

90. President Bush, 7/1/02.

91. Mei-Ling Hopgood, *Dayton Daily News*, 4/4/02.

92. Melvin Claxton and Ronald J. Hansen, *Detroit News*, 9/28/04.

93. Cory Reiss, *Sarasota Herald-Tribune*, 1/19/04.

94. Vice President Dick Cheney, 11/1/04.

95. President Bush, 10/28/04.

96. Denise Smith Amos, *Cincinnati Enquirer*, 10/10/03. http://www.enquirer.com/editions/2003/10/10/loc_pellgrants10.html. Cleveland *Plain Dealer* editorial, 11/24/04.

97. Peter Gosselin, *Los Angeles Times*, 10/10/04. http://www.latimes.com/news/printedition/la-fi-riskshift10oct10,1,3174836.story.

98. Melvin Claxton and Ronald J. Hansen, *Detroit News,* 9/28/04. http://www.detnews. com/2004/specialreport/0409/29/a01-286728.htm.

99. Federal Reserve chairman Alan Greenspan, 1/24/02.

100. Susan Milligan, *Boston Globe,* 11/21/03. Josh Richman, *Alameda Times-Star,* 5/12/2004.

101. Jim Luther, Associated Press, 10/4/85.

102. Marcus Gleisser, Cleveland *Plain Dealer,* 1/18/93.

103. Sandra Sobieraj, Associated Press, 8/6/02. http://www.bernie.house.gov/documents/ articles/20020806181033.asp.

104. President Bush, 9/17/02.

105. Brad Foss, Associated Press, 12/1/03.

106. Louis Uchitelle, *New York Times,* 12/10/03.

107. President Bush, 12/11/03.

108. CNN, 2/12/04. http://www.cnn.com/2004/US/02/12/bush.outsourcing/.

109. Lou Dobbs, CNNfn, 3/23/04.

110. President's Export Council charter. http://www.ita.doc.gov/TD/PEC/charter.html.

111. CNN/Lou Dobbs's list of companies we've confirmed are "Exporting America." http://www.cnn.com/CNN/Programs/lou.dobbs.tonight/popups/exporting.america/ content.html.

112. Saritha Rai, *New York Times,* 2/25/05.

113. President Bush, 3/4/04.

114. Bureau of Labor Statistics, Monthly Metropolitan Area Unemployment Report, 3/04. ftp://ftp.bls.gov/pub/news.release/History/metro.04282004.news.

115. Alan Zibel, *Oakland Tribune,* 9/2/03.

116. Richard McCormack, *Manufacturing and Technology News,* 10/12/05. http://www. manufacturingnews.com/news/05/1012/art1.html. *BusinessWeek,* 10/17/05. http:// www.businessweek.com/magazine/content/05_42/c3955025.htm.

CHAPTER 4: DEBT

1. Paul Harris of the *London Observer* quoting *The Faith of George W. Bush* by Stephen Mansfield, 11/2/03. http://observer.guardian.co.uk/international/story/ 0,6903,1075950,00.html.

2. Linda Stern, *Newsweek,* 2/21/05.

3. Consumer Financial Services Law Report regarding Fleet Bank, 11/21/02: "A federal District Court granted a consumer's class certification motion against Fleet Bank R.I.).

4. *Concord Monitor,* 11/23/04. http://bernie.house.gov/documents/articles/ 20041124142440.asp.

5. *Consumer Reports,* 5/04. http://www.consumerreports.org/main/content/display_ report.jsp?FOLDER_percent3Cpercent3Efolder_id=422623&ASSORTMENT_ percent3C_percent3East_id=333147#. *Motley Fool,* 2/28/05. http://www.fool.com/ News/mft/2005/mft05022801.htm.

6. Peter Gosselin, *Los Angeles Times,* 3/4/05.

7. New York attorney general Eliot Spitzer, press release, 4/3/03. http://www.oag.state. ny.us/press/2003/apr/apr03a_03.html New York attorney general Eliot Spitzer, press release, 6/6/04. http://www.oag.state.ny.us/press/2004/jul/jul06a_04.html.

8. Demos, press kit on bankruptcy. http://www.demos-usa.org/pubs/bankruptcy_ press_kit.pdf.

9. Roughly 100 million households, Census 2000. http://www.census.gov/prod/2003pubs/ censr-5.pdf.

10. Center for Responsive Politics data shows that between 2000 and 2004 the finance/ credit industry gave politicians $25.3 million, and the commercial banking industry gave $77.9 million for a total of $103.2 million. http://www.opensecrets.org/ industries/indus.asp?cycle=2006&ind=F03; http://www.opensecrets.org/industries/ indus.asp?cycle=2006&ind=F06.

11. Barry Yeoman, *Rolling Stone*, 3/10/04.

12. Center for Responsive Politics data shows that in 2004, Sen. Richard Shelby (R-AL) was the sixth-largest recipient of financial industry cash in the U.S. Senate, raising $1.9 million. That same year, Representative Michael Oxley (R-OH) was the second-largest recipient of financial industry cash in the U.S. House, raising $975,750. http://www. opensecrets.org/industries/recips.asp?Ind=F&cycle=2004&recipdetail=S&Mem= Y&sortorder=U; http://www.opensecrets.org/industries/recips.asp?Ind=F&cycle= 2004&recipdetail=H&Mem=N&sortorder=U.

13. Center for Responsive Politics data shows that Sen. Mitch McConnell (R-KY) has raised $304,755 from commercial banks over his career. http://www.opensecrets.org/ politicians/allindus.asp?CID=N00003389.

14. John Solomon, Associated Press, 8/2/00.

15. Public Citizen, report entitled "White House for Sale." http://www.whitehouseforsale. org/ContributorsAndPaybacks/pioneer_profile.cfm?pioneer_ID=1041.

16. *Washington Post*, 3/13/86. John D. Hawke was U.S. comptroller of the currency when the announcement was made—he was appointed by Clinton, and before that was the chairman of Arnold & Porter, a major banking law firm. According to the 6/14/86 *National Journal*, "Hawke clients [are] primarily regional banks."

17. Tom Oliphant, *Boston Globe*, 8/29/04. http://www.boston.com/news/globe/ editorial_opinion/oped/articles/2004/08/29/a_gop_fleecing_of_card_users/.

18. Jeanne Sahidi, CNN, 4/20/05. http://money.cnn.com/2005/04/20/pf/bankruptcy_bill/.

19. Senate roll call #13, 3/1/05. http://www.senate.gov/legislative/LIS/roll_call_lists/ roll_call_vote_cfm.cfm?congress=109&session=1&vote=00013.

20. Diana Henriques, *New York Times*, 12/7/04.

21. Associated Press, 3/1/05. http://www.msnbc.msn.com/id/7032779/.

22. Senate roll call vote #21, 2005. http://www.senate.gov/legislative/LIS/roll_call_lists/ roll_call_vote_cfm.cfm?congress=109&session=1&vote=00021.

23. Public Campaign Action Fund. http://ga3.org/campaign/sensenbrenner/explanation.

24. http://www.opensecrets.org/industries/recips.asp?Ind=F03&Cycle=2000&recipdetail= S&Mem=Y&sortorder=U.

25. Center for Responsive Politics data shows Sen. Joseph Lieberman (D-CT) has taken more than $267,000 from the commercial banking industry in his career. http://www. opensecrets.org/politicians/allindus.asp?CID=N00000616.

26. Sen. Joseph Lieberman (D-CT), press release, 3/11/05. http://lieberman.senate.gov/ newsroom/release.cfm?id=233340.

27. Senate roll call vote #29 (on cloture), 3/8/05. http://www.senate.gov/legislative/LIS/ roll_call_lists/roll_call_vote_cfm.cfm?congress=109&session=1&vote=00029.

28. Hans Nichols, *The Hill*, 3/23/05. http://www.hillnews.com/thehill/export/TheHill/ News/Frontpage/032305/podesta.html.

29. Rich Cohen, *National Journal*, 3/17/05.

30. Hans Nichols, *The Hill*, 4/14/05. http://www.hillnews.com/thehill/export/TheHill/ News/Frontpage/041405/crowley.html.

31. Center for Responsive Politics data shows Rep. Joe Crowley (D-NY) has taken $237,550 from the banking and credit industries since his 1998 election (8 years times 12 weeks

divided by $237,550 equals roughly $2,000 per week). http://www.opensecrets.
org/politicians/allsector.asp?CID=N00001127.

32. CNN, 12/1/04. http://money.cnn.com/2004/12/01/pf/debt/internet_loans/.

33. Gary Strauss and Barbara Hansen, *USA Today,* 3/31/03. http://www.usatoday.com/
money/companies/management/2003-03-31-ceopay2_x.htm.

34. Patrick McGeehan, *New York Times,* 11/21/04.

35. Ray Martin, CBS News financial analyst, 3/18/05. http://www.cbsnews.com/stories/
2005/03/17/earlyshow/contributors/raymartin/printable681246.shtml.

36. Donald Ogilvie, *USA Today,* 3/10/05. http://www.usatoday.com/news/opinion/
2005-03-10-bankruptcy-oppose_x.htm.

37. Patrick McGeehan, *New York Times,* 11/21/04.

38. Ibid.

39. Consumer Federation of America, press release, 2/27/01. http://www.consumerfed.
org/pdfs/travpr.pdf. Demos, report entitled "Credit Card Industry Practices in Brief."
http://www.demos-usa.org/pubs/IndustryPractices_WEB.pdf.

40. *USA Today,* 3/11/05. http://www.usatoday.com/news/opinion/
2005-03-10-bankruptcy-our_x.htm.

41. *Concord* (New Hampshire) *Monitor,* 11/23/04. http://bernie.house.gov/documents/
articles/20041124142440.asp.

42. Patrick McGeehan, *New York Times,* 11/21/04.

43. Ibid.

44. Robert Pear, *New York Times,* 12/27/83.

45. Center for Responsive Politics' Capital Eye, Courtney Mabeus, 3/2/05. http://www.
capitaleye.org/inside.asp?ID=157.

46. Shirley Ragsdale, *Des Moines Register,* 3/4/05. http://desmoinesregister.com/apps/
pbcs.dll/article?AID=/20050304/BUSINESS04/503040376/1029/BUSINESS.

47. HealthDayNews, 2/2/05. http://www.talkingpointsmemo.com/bankruptcy/
archives/2005/03/index.php#005043.

48. *Health Affairs,* 2/2/05. http://content.healthaffairs.org/webexclusives/index.dtl?year=
2005 http://www.talkingpointsmemo.com/bankruptcy/archives/2005/03/index.
php#005043.

49. Shirley Ragsdale, *Des Moines Register,* 3/4/05. http://desmoinesregister.com/apps/
pbcs.dll/article?AID=/20050304/BUSINESS04/503040376/1029/BUSINESS.

50. Mary Deibel, *Albany Times Union* (Scripps Howard), 12/2/98.

51. David U. Himmelstein, Elizabeth Warren, Deborah Thorne, and Steffie Woolhandler,
Study published in *Health Affairs,* 2/05. http://www.getsickgobroke.org/study.php;
http://www.getsickgobroke.org/Illness_Contributions_to_Bankruptcy.pdf.

52. Louise Witt, *New York Times,* 6/7/05. http://www.nytimes.com/2005/07/07/business/
07sbiz.html.

53. Rush Limbaugh, *Rush Limbaugh Show,* 3/2/05. http://press.arrivenet.com/industry/
article.php/611844.html.

54. Will Dunham, States News Service, 10/20/92. Lawrence Malkin, *International Herald
Tribune,* 2/1/95. http://www.iht.com/bin/print_ipub.php?file=/articles/1995/02/01/
deal.php Kate Snow, Dana Bash, and Ted Barrett, CNN, 9/24/01: "Congress Approves
$15 Billion Airline Bailout." http://cnnstudentnews.cnn.com/2001/fyi/news/09/24/
airline.bailout/.

55. AFSCME analysis of Bush 2006 budget. http://www.afscme.org/action/fy2006.htm.

56. Robert Atkinson, *Blueprint,* 7/27/03. http://www.ppionline.org/ndol/print.cfm?
contentid=251915.

57. Libby Quaid, Associated Press, 3/13/05. http://www.suntimes.com/output/elect/cst-nws-food13.html.
58. Libby Quaid, Associated Press, "House Panel to Slash Funding for Food Stamps," 10/29/05.
59. Center on Budget and Policy Priorities, 6/3/03. http://www.Center_on_Budget_and_Policy_Priorities.org/6-3-03tanf.htm.
60. Medicare Rights Center, 9/3/04. http://www.medicarerights.org/pressrelease2004_22.html.
61. Margaret Talev, *Sacramento Bee*, 2/21/05.
62. *Christian Science Monitor*, 5/12/04. Center on Budget and Policy Priorities, 3/17/04. http://www.Center_on_Budget_and_Policy_Priorities.org/3-17-04hous-pr.htm.
63. U.S. Conference of Mayors, 2/14/05. http://www.usmayors.org/uscm/us_mayor_newspaper/documents/02_14_05/budget_story.asp.
64. U.S. House Appropriations Committee Minority staff, report 3/15/05. http://www.house.gov/appropriations_democrats/pdf/paypell.pdf.
65. Lev Grossman, *Time*, 1/24/05.
66. Sylvia Smith, "Bayh Weighs Bankruptcy Law Changes," *Fort Wayne Journal Gazette*, 3/2/05. http://www.bankrog.com/node/175.
67. 2005 HHS Poverty Guidelines say the poverty line for a family of 3 is $16,090; minimum wage is a yearly salary of about $10,700. http://aspe.hhs.gov/poverty/05poverty.shtml; http://www.epinet.org/content.cfm/issueguides_minwage_minwagefaq.
68. Economic Policy Institute, 3/05. http://www.epinet.org/content.cfm/issueguides_minwage_minwagefacts.
69. Genaro Armas, Associated Press, 12/20/04. http://www.commondreams.org/headlines04/1220-01.htm; http://www.nlihc.org/oor2004/.
70. Karen Pallarito, HealthDayNews, 2/2/05. http://www.hon.ch/News/HSN/523782.html.
71. Robert E. Rector and Kirk A. Johnson, Heritage Foundation, 1/5/04. http://www.heritage.org/Research/Welfare/bg1713.cfm.
72. Steve Salerno, *Allentown Morning Call*, 9/13/04.
73. Jill Smolowe and Lisa Gray, *People*, 2/14/05.
74. Cindy Hadish, *Cedar Rapids* (Iowa) *Gazette*, 2/19/05. http://www.getsickgobroke.org/pubstories.php.
75. Senator Bill Frist (R-TN), Senate floor speech, 3/1/05. http://www.govtrack.us/congress/record.xpd?id=109-s20050301-6&bill=s109-256.
76. Albert Crenshaw, *Washington Post*, 3/20/05.
77. Jonathan Alter, *Newsweek*, 4/25/05.
78. Gretchen Morgenson, *New York Times*, 3/2/05.
79. Michael R. Crittenden, *CQ Weekly*, 7/9/05.
80. Mark Reutter, *Washington Post*, 10/23/05.
81. Bernard Simon, *Financial Times*, 10/13/05.
82. Mark Reutter, *Washington Post*, 10/23/05; Ted Evanoff, *Indianapolis Star*, 11/6/05.
83. Gretchen Morgenson, *New York Times*, 3/2/05.
84. Senate roll call vote #23, 3/3/05. http://www.senate.gov/legislative/LIS/roll_call_lists/roll_call_vote_cfm.cfm?congress=109&session=1&vote=00023.
85. Feingold press release, 3/1/05. http://feingold.senate.gov/~feingold/releases/05/03/2005301B05.html.
86. Maura Reynolds, *Los Angeles Times*, 3/2/05.
87. Ed Yingling on PBS's *Frontline*, 11/23/04. http://www.pbs.org/wgbh/pages/frontline/shows/credit/interviews/yingling.html.

88. Delroy Alexander, *Chicago Tribune*, 1/7/04.

89. PBS, *Frontline*, 11/23/04. http://www.pbs.org/wgbh/pages/frontline/shows/credit/interviews/yingling.html.

90. *The New Republic*, "Morally Bankrupt," 2/25/05. http://ssl.tnr.com/p/docsub.mhtml?i=20050307&s=editorial030705.

91. Data obtained from *American Banker–Bond Buyer*, "Highest Paid Card-Industry Executives," 6/03 and 6/04.

92. Rob Hotakainen, *Fresno Bee*, 3/11/05.

93. Peter G. Gosselin, *Los Angeles Times*, 3/4/05.

94. Ibid.

95. Center for Responsive Politics data shows Sen. Orrin Hatch (R-UT) received $158,350 from commercial banks in his career.

96. Senator Orrin Hatch (R-UT), floor statement, 3/3/05. http://frwebgate.access.gpo.gov/cgi-bin/getpage.cgi?dbname=2005_record&page=S1982&position=all.

97. Scott Reckard, *Los Angeles Times*, 1/8/04.

98. Senator Richard Shelby (R-AL), Senate floor speech, 3/3/05. http://frwebgate.access.gpo.gov/cgi-bin/getpage.cgi?dbname=2005_record&page=S1979&position=all.

99. Patrick McGeehan, *New York Times*, 11/21/04.

100. Diana B. Henriques, *New York Times*, 12/7/04.

101. "Credit card woes," *Concord Monitor* editorial, 11/23/04. http://www.cmonitor.com/apps/pbcs.dll/article?AID=/20041123/REPOSITORY/411230321/1027/OPINION01; http://bernie.house.gov/documents/articles/20041124142440.asp.

102. Senate roll call vote #20, 3/3/05. http://www.senate.gov/legislative/LIS/roll_call_lists/roll_call_vote_cfm.cfm?congress=109&session=1&vote=00020.

103. Senate roll call vote #251, 11/13/91. http://www.senate.gov/legislative/LIS/roll_call_lists/roll_call_vote_cfm.cfm?congress=102&session=1&vote=00251.

104. Center for Responsive Politics data calculating total campaign contributions taken from the commercial banking and finance/credit industry between 1991 and 2005 by the eighteen senators who voted for the 1991 D'Amato amendment and against the 2005 Dayton amendment. Those senators are Baucus, Biden, Cochran, Domenici, Kerry, Lott, McCain, Sarbanes, Shelby, Specter, Warner, Stevens, Burns, Kohl, Leahy, Reid, and Craig.

105. Center for Responsive Politics data shows Senator John McCain (R-AZ) accepted $195,328 from commercial banking interests in his 2004 election campaign, and $74,493 from commercial banking interests in his 1998 election campaign, for a total of $269,821 between the time he voted for the D'Amato amendment and against the Dayton amendment. http://www.opensecrets.org/races/summary.asp?id=AZS1&cycle=2004; http://www.opensecrets.org/1996os/indus/S6AL00013.htm.

106. PBS, *Frontline*, interview with Walter Wriston, former chairman of Citicorp/Citibank, 11/23/04. http://www.pbs.org/wgbh/pages/frontline/shows/credit/interviews/wriston.html.

107. Lawrence Lindsey, 1996 Federal Open Market Committee Meeting, 12/17/96. http://www.federalreserve.gov/fomc/transcripts/1996/19961217Meeting.pdf; http://www.talkingpointsmemo.com/bankruptcy/archives/2005/03/lindsey_speaks.php.

108. Ibid.

109. Marianne Means, *New York Times* News Service, 3/12/05.

110. Michele Heller, *American Banker*, 12/5/03.

111. PBS, *Frontline*, interview with Edmund Mierzwinski, 11/23/04. http://www.pbs.org/wgbh/pages/frontline/shows/credit/interviews/mierzwinski.html.

112. Peter G. Gosselin, *Los Angeles Times*, 3/4/05.

CHAPTER 5: PENSIONS

1. Ellen Schultz, "End Run: Companies Sue Union Retirees to Cut Promised Health Benefits," *Wall Street Journal*, 11/10/04. http://online.wsj.com/public/resources/documents/SB110003711129469246.htm.
2. Ibid.
3. Ibid.
4. *Forbes*, Richest People 2003, #67. http://www.forbes.com/finance/lists/10/2003/LIR.jhtml?passListId=10&passYear=2003&passListType=Person&uniqueId=L1XF&datatype=Person.
5. Paul Wilson, *Charleston Gazette*, 3/30/05.
6. Ellen Schultz, *Wall Street Journal*, 11/10/04. http://online.wsj.com/public/resources/documents/SB110003711129469246.htm.
7. Latin American News Digest, 3/16/05. CNNFn, 10/15/99. Business News Americas, 6/21/05. http://money.cnn.com/1999/10/15/deals/asarco/.
8. Associated Press, 7/3/05. http://www.helenair.com/articles/2005/07/03/montana_top/a06070305_01.txt.
9. Kelly Greene, *Wall Street Journal*, 3/2/05.
10. Eric Dash, *New York Times*, 4/3/05. http://www.kentucky.com/mld/kentucky/business/11037475.htm.
11. Curt Anderson, Associated Press, 5/19/02. http://reddingpalm.com/newsarchive/20020519bus016.shtml.
12. Catherine Toth, *Honolulu Advertiser*, 5/2/05. http://the.honoluluadvertiser.com/article/2005/May/02/bz/bz02p.html.
13. Christine Dugas, "Treasury Says Cash-Balance Pensions Are OK," *USA Today*, 12/10/2002. http://www.usatoday.com/money/perfi/retirement/2002-12-10-pensions_x.htm.
14. Alan Ota, *Congressional Quarterly Daily Monitor*, 9/10/03. http://www.washingtonpost.com/wp-dyn/articles/A50604-2004Jun17.html.
15. David R. Baker, *San Francisco Chronicle*, 5/11/05. http://sfgate.com/cgi-bin/article.cgi?f=/c/a/2005/05/11/BUG9NCN5QO1.DTL.
16. Ellen Schultz, "End Run: Companies Sue Union Retirees to Cut Promised Health Benefits," *Wall Street Journal*, 11/10/04. http://online.wsj.com/public/resources/documents/SB110003711129469246.htm.
17. Austan Goolsbee, University of Chicago, Graduate School of Business, 9/04; Bill Walsh, Newhouse News Service, 2/24/05. http://gsb.uchicago.edu/pdf/ssec_goolsbee.pdf; http://www.newhousenews.com/archive/walsh022405.html.
18. Ellen Schultz and Charles Gasparino, "Privatizing a Portion of Social Security Could Shower Billions on Mutual Funds," *Wall Street Journal*, 2/20/96. http://www.ourfuture.org/issues_and_campaigns/socialsecurity/key_issues/money_trail_and_wall_street/readarticle54.cfm.
19. Center for Responsive Politics data show the securities and investment industry contributed $92,956,969 to politicians in 2000, $60,447,437 in 2002, and $91,375,230 in 2004, for a total of roughly $244.6 million. http://www.opensecrets.org/industries/indus.asp?cycle=2006&ind=F07.
20. Bill Walsh, Newhouse News Service, 2/24/05. http://www.newhousenews.com/archive/walsh022405.html.
21. People for the American Way, Right Wing Watch. http://www.pfaw.org/pfaw/general/default.aspx?oid=9261.
22. Robert Dreyfus, *Mother Jones*, 11–12/96. http://www.motherjones.com/news/feature/1996/11/dreyfuss.html.

23. Trudy Lieberman, *The Nation*, 1/27/97. http://www.nationarchive.com/Summaries/v264i0003_09.htm.

24. Glen Kessler, *Washington Post*, 6/26/01.

25. Heritage Foundation website, Corporate Associate Membership. http://www.heritage.org/support/corporateassociates.cfm.

26. Deirdre Shesgreen, *St. Louis Post Dispatch*, 3/6/05. Landon Thomas Jr., *New York Times*, 11/21/04.

27. Cato Institute, 3/6/01. http://www.socialsecurity.org/daily/03-06-01.html.

28. Michael Tanner, "Signs of Crisis Are Clear," Cato Institute, 2/1/05. http://www.socialsecurity.org/pubs/articles/tanner-050201.html.

29. Media Matters for America, 4/14/05. http://mediamatters.org/items/200504140007.

30. Andrew Biggs's Cato Institute biography states, "Andrew Biggs is a former Social Security analyst and Assistant Director of the Cato Institute's Project on Social Security Choice." http://www.cato.org/people/biggs.html

31. "Administration Reform Principles Mirror Cato's," Cato Institute, 3/6/01. http://www.socialsecurity.org/daily/03-06-01.html.

32. Social Security Administration website. http://www.ssa.gov/policy/about/organization.html#orp.

33. Christian Berthelson, *San Francisco Chronicle*, 1/6/05. http://www.sfgate.com/cgi-bin/article.cgi?file=/chronicle/archive/2005/01/06/MNGJ1ALTFH1.DTL.

34. Marc Lifsher, *Los Angeles Times*, 1/22/05.

35. Albert B. Crenshaw, *Washington Post*, 6/7/05. http://www.washingtonpost.com/wp-dyn/content/article/2005/06/06/AR2005060601712.html.

36. Ibid. According to the article, there were 1,108 pension plans "whose assets are at least $50 million below the value of the benefits they promise." The *Post* also reports that "in 1999, for example, only 166 plans were underfunded by $50 million or more" (1,108 is 660 percent more than 166).

37. Dear Colleague letter from Rep. Sanders, Miller, and Gutknecht, 3/13/03. http://edworkforce.house.gov/democrats/cashbalancedc.html.

38. Ellen Schultz, "Workers of All Ages Lose Benefits in Switch to Cash-Balance Plans," *Wall Street Journal*, 11/5/05.

39. Mary Williams Walsh, *New York Times*, 6/7/05. http://www.teamster.org/05news/hn_050607_6.htm.

40. Albert Crenshaw, *Washington Post*, 6/7/05.

41. Dean Foust, *BusinessWeek*, 11/3/03. http://www.businessweek.com/magazine/content/03_44/b3856045.htm; Albert Crenshaw, *Washington Post*, 6/7/05. http://www.washingtonpost.com/wp-dyn/content/article/2005/06/06/AR2005060601712.html.

42. Kelly Greene, *Wall Street Journal*, 3/2/05.

43. Eric Dash, "The New Executive Bonanza: Retirement," *New York Times;* 4/3/05. http://www.law.harvard.edu/programs/olin_center/corporate_governance/MediaMentions/NYTimes_Apr.3.2005.pdf.

44. Ibid.

45. Associated Press, 8/12/00. http://archives.cnn.com/2000/ALLPOLITICS/stories/08/12/cheney.parachute.ap/.

46. Associated Press, 8/1/04. http://www.billingsgazette.com/index.php?id=1&display=rednews/2004/08/01/build/nation/84-halliburton.inc.

47. Donald L. Bartlett; James B. Steele; Laura Karmatz; Lisa McLaughlin; Dody Tsiantar; Joan Levinstein, *Time*, 10/31/05.

48. David Cay Johnston, *New York Times*, 12/17/02.

49. Donald L. Bartlett; James B. Steele, Laura Karmatz; Lisa McLaughlin; Dody Tsiantar; Joan Levinstein, *Time*, 10/31/05.

50. Deene Goodlaw analysis for the Pension Rights Center entitled "Anaysis of the Portman-Cardin Bill—the Pension Preservation and Savings Enhancement Act (H.R. 1776)" 2004. http://www.pensionrights.org/docs/PORTMANCARDIN.pdf.

51. Vineeta Anand, *Pensions and Investments*, 4/28/2003.

52. Marc Sandalow and Carolyn Lochhead, *San Francisco Chronicle*, 7/19/03. http://www.sfgate.com/cgi-bin/article.cgi percent3Ffile=/c/a/2003/07/19/MN292730.DTL.

53. *Bulletin*'s Frontrunner quoting the *Wall Street Journal* from 7/24/03.

54. Mike Casey, "Breaking the Pension Bank," *Kansas City Star*, 5/15/05.

55. Labor secretary Elaine Chao, National Press Club speech, 1/10/05.

56. Albert Crenshaw, "Big Pension Plans Fall Further Behind," *Washington Post*, 6/7/05.

57. Mike Casey, "Breaking the Pension Bank," *Kansas City Star*, 5/15/05.

58. Mary Williams Walsh, "Pension Loopholes Helped United Hide Troubles," *New York Times*, 6/7/05. http://www.teamster.org/05news/hn_050607_6.htm.

59. Labor secretary Elaine Chao, National Press Club speech, 1/10/05. http://www.dol.gov/_sec/media/speeches/20050110_retirement.htm.

60. PBGC press release, "PBGC Releases Fiscal Year 2004 Financial Results," 11/15/04.

61. Representative Jim Nussle (R), 6/9/05.

62. Lisa Zagaroli, *Detroit News*, 4/12/05. http://www.detnews.com/2005/business/0504/12/A01-147922.htm.

63. Representative George Miller (D-CA), press release, 6/6/05. http://www.house.gov/apps/list/press/ed31_democrats/rel6605.html.

64. Mike Casey, *Kansas City Star*, 5/15/05.

65. Simon Romero, "On Texas Coast, a Laboratory for Private Accounts," *New York Times*, 3/18/05. http://select.nytimes.com/gst/abstract.html?res=F30C12F63B580C7B8DDDAA0894DD404482.

66. President Bush, 12/16/04.

67. William Welch, *USA Today*, 3/23/05. http://www.usatoday.com/news/washington/2005-03-23-social-security-repor_x.htm.

68. Center on Budget and Policy Priorities, 6/14/04. http://www.Center_on_Budget_and_Policy_Priorities.org/6-14-04bud.htm; http://www.cbo.gov/showdoc.cfm?index=5530&sequence=2.

69. Representative Bill Thomas (R-CA), Federal News Service, 4/29/05.

70. Representative Jim Nussle (R-IA), Budget Committee hearing, 2/9/05. President Bush, 5/13/05.

71. Center for Responsive Politics data shows Representative Jim Nussle (R-IA) received $182,425 from the securities and exchange (financial services) industry in his career. http://www.opensecrets.org/politicians/allindus.asp?CID=N00004255.

72. William Welch, *USA Today*, 3/23/05. http://www.usatoday.com/news/washington/2005-03-23-social-security-repor_x.htm.

73. Center on Budget and Policy Priorities, 5/4/05. http://www.Center_on_Budget_and_Policy_Priorities.org/5-2-05socsec3.htm.

74. Robert Pear, *New York Times*, 1/16/05. http://www.house.gov/schakowsky/SocialSecurity_NYTIMES_Pear_1_16_05.html.

75. President Bush, 3/21/05. http://www.whitehouse.gov/news/releases/2005/03/20050321-13.html.

76. David Stout, *New York Times*, 6/14/05. http://www.nytimes.com/2005/06/14/politics/14cnd-bush.html.

77. Karen Olsson, *Texas Observer,* 6/25/99. http://www.texasobserver.org/showArticle.asp?ArticleID=1175.

78. President Bush, 10/30/00.

79. White House press secretary Scott McClellan, 6/17/05. http://www.whitehouse.gov/news/releases/2005/06/20050617-5.html.

80. Senator Robert Bennett (R-UT), Federal News Service, 3/8/05.

81. Robert Pear, *New York Times,* 1/16/05. http://www.truthout.org/docs_05/011705E.shtml.

82. Center on Budget and Policy Priorities, 2/7/05, Table 1. http://www.Center_on_Budget_and_Policy_Priorities.org/2-3-05socsec.pdf.

83. Center on Budget and Policy Priorities, 5/10/05. http://www.Center_on_Budget_and_Policy_Priorities.org/5-10-05socsec.htm.

84. Michael Getler, *Washington Post,* 3/20/05. http://www.washingtonpost.com/wp-dyn/articles/A50364-2005Mar19.html.

85. Ibid.

86. GAO chief David Walker, testimony to House Ways and Means Committee, 3/9/05.

87. Mike Allen, *Washington Post,* 3/13/05.

88. White House budget director Josh Bolten, 2/9/05.

89. Center on Budget and Policy Priorities, 5/10/05. http://www.Center_on_Budget_and_Policy_Priorities.org/5-10-05socsec.htm.

90. President Bush, 2/16/05.

91. Sean Hannity, Fox News, *Hannity & Colmes,* 3/4/05.

92. President Bush, 4/16/01. http://www.whitehouse.gov/news/releases/2001/04/20010416-5.html.

93. Larry Rohter, *New York Times,* 1/27/05.

94. President Bush, 4/29/05. http://www.whitehouse.gov/news/releases/2005/04/20050429-1.html.

95. CBS News, 6/2/04. http://www.cbsnews.com/stories/2004/06/01/eveningnews/main620626.shtml.

96. Jamie McIntyre, CNN, 12/12/03. http://www.cnn.com/2003/WORLD/meast/12/11/sprj.irq.halliburton/.

97. Cato Daily Comments, 4/21/03. http://www.socialsecurity.org/daily/04-23-01.html.

98. Representative Kevin Brady (R-TX), House Ways and Means Committee, 5/12/05.

99. Howard Witt, Knight-Ridder, "Case Study: What Happened When Texas Town Took the Private Investment Route?" 2/20/05.

100. Ibid.

101. Ibid.

102. Ibid.

103. Simon Romero, "On Texas Coast, a Laboratory for Private Accounts," *New York Times,* 3/18/05.

104. Howard Witt, Knight-Ridder, 2/20/05.

105. Republican National Committee chairman Ken Mehlman, remarks to RNC State Chairmen's Meeting, 4/29/05.

106. President Bush, 4/26/05.

107. Jonathan Weisman, *Washington Post,* 2/24/05. http://www.washingtonpost.com/wp-dyn/articles/A48438-2005Feb23_2.html.

108. Tom Curry, MSNBC, 2/18/05. http://msnbc.msn.com/id/6989229/.

109. Charles Babington, *Washington Post,* 4/2/05. http://www.washingtonpost.com/wp-dyn/articles/A19705-2005Apr1.html.

110. Minneapolis *Star Tribune,* 2/22/05.

111. Representative Jerrold Nadler (D-NY), 6/9/99. http://waysandmeans.house.gov/legacy/fullcomm/106cong/6-9-99/6-9nadl.htm.

112. Representative Peter DeFazio (D-OR), Dear Colleague letter, 11/30/01. http://www.ourfuture.org/issues_and_campaigns/socialsecurity/key_issues/legislation/readarticle116.cfm.

113. *National Journal*, 5/21/99. http://www.ourfuture.org/issues_and_campaigns/socialsecurity/key_issues/legislation/readarticle116.cfm.

114. Judy Woodruff, CNN, 4/29/05. http://transcripts.cnn.com/TRANSCRIPTS/0504/29/ip.01.html.

115. Catherine Toth, *Honolulu Advertiser*, 5/2/05. http://the.honoluluadvertiser.com/article/2005/May/02/bz/bz02p.html.

116. Representative Bernie Sanders (I-VT), 9/21/04. http://bernie.house.gov/statements/20040921190610.asp.

117. Representatives Gil Gutknecht (R-MN), George Miller (D-CA), and Bernie Sanders (I-VT), Dear Colleague letter about their Pension Benefits Protection Act of 2003 (HR 1677), 3/13/03. http://edworkforce.house.gov/democrats/cashbalancedc.html.

118. Eric Dash, "The New Executive Bonanza: Retirement," *New York Times*, 4/3/05.

119. Representative George Miller (D-CA), press release about H.R. 5292, 10/8/04. http://edworkforce.house.gov/democrats/releases/rel10804b.html; http://frwebgate.access.gpo.gov/cgi-bin/getdoc.cgi?dbname=108_cong_bills&docid=f:h5292ih.txt.pdf.

120. Lisa Zagaroli, *Detroit News*, 4/12/05. http://www.detnews.com/2005/business/0504/12/A01-147922.htm.

121. Representative George Miller (D-CA), press release, 6/29/05. http://www.house.gov/apps/list/press/ed31_democrats/rel62905.html.

122. President Bush, 12/9/02. http://www.whitehouse.gov/news/releases/2002/12/20021209-1.html.

123. President Bush, remarks at nomination ceremony of Bill Donaldson as chairman of the SEC, 12/10/02. http://www.whitehouse.gov/news/releases/2002/12/20021210-5.html.

124. CBS News, 12/10/02. http://www.cbsnews.com/stories/2002/12/10/politics/main532435.shtml.

125. Leigh Strope, "Proposed Regulations Protect Employers from Age Discrimination Liability," Associated Press, 12/10/02.

126. Representative Bernie Sanders (I-VT), 3/10/03. http://bernie.house.gov/documents/releases/20030310182243.asp.

127. Mary Williams Walsh, *New York Times*, 3/9/03. http://www.teamster.org/05news/hn_050607_6.htm.

128. Ibid.

129. Ibid.

130. Representative Bernie Sanders, Congressional Record, page H4038, 5/14/03. http://frwebgate.access.gpo.gov/cgi-bin/getpage.cgi?dbname=2003_record&page=H4038&position=all.

CHAPTER 6: HEALTH CARE

1. Malcolm Gladwell, *The New Yorker*, 8/22/05. http://www.newyorker.com/fact/content/articles/050829fa_fact.

2. Associated Press, 1/14/04. http://www.cnn.com/2004/HEALTH/01/14/uninsured.solutions.ap/.

3. Evan Halper, *Los Angeles Times*, 12/18/04.

4. Robert Pear, *New York Times*, 12/20/04.

5. Nicole Volhontseff, *Columbia Missourian*, 1/28/05. http://www.columbia-mo.com/news/story.php?ID=11760.

6. Elly Wiese, Associated Press, 3/31/05. http://www.showmenews.com/2005/Mar/20050331Busi003.asp.

7. Elly Wiese, Associated Press, 3/7/05. http://semissourian.com/story/160032.html.

8. Jonathan Weisman and Ceci Connolly, *Washington Post*, 3/23/05. http://www.washingtonpost.com/wp-dyn/articles/A58069-2005Mar22.html.

9. Families USA, study entitled "Health Care: Are You Better Off Today Than You Were Four Years Ago?", 9/04. http://www.familiesusa.org/site/DocServer?docID=4601.

10. Businesswire, "HMOs Earn $10.2 Billion in 2003, Nearly Doubling Profits, According to Weiss Ratings; Blue Cross Blue Shield Plans Report 63 percent Jump in Earnings," 8/30/04. http://www.weissratings.com/News/Ins_HMO/20040830hmo.htm.

11. The Irving Levin Health Care Executive Compensation Report, 2004, section entitled "Who's Making What in Health Care," page 12: sum of "Total Cash Compensation" of HMO/insurers executive compensation. http://www.levinassociates.com/publications/mam/mamprem/04execcomp.pdf.

12. Weiss Ratings, 5/24/05. http://www.weissratings.com/News/Ins_HMO/20050524hmo.htm.

13. Fortune 500 list, 2004 earnings by the health care industry, *Fortune*, 4/18/05. http://www.fortune.com/fortune/subs/fortune500/industrysnapshot/0,23615,28,00.html.

14. Christopher Rowland, *Boston Globe*, 10/5/04. http://www.boston.com/news/nation/articles/2004/10/05/medicare_bill_a_study_in_dc_spoils_system?pg=full.

15. Center for Responsive Politics data. http://www.opensecrets.org/industries/indus.asp?Ind=H.

16. Public Citizen report entitled "Blind Faith: How Deregulation and Enron's Influence Over Government Looted Billions from Americans," 12/2001. http://www.citizen.org/cmep/energy_enviro_nuclear/electricity/Enron/articles.cfm?ID=7104.

17. R. G. Ratcliffe, *Houston Chronicle*, 1/19/02. http://www.chron.com/cs/CDA/story.hts/politics/1218175.

18. Associated Press, 6/13/05. http://www.billingsgazette.com/index.php?tl=1&display=rednews/2005/06/13/build/state/91-racicot.inc.

19. Nancy Gibbs and Karen Tumulty, *Time*, 12/25/95. Brian Blomquist, *New York Post*, 7/19/00. http://www.mult-sclerosis.org/news/Jul2000/PWMSNewtsEx.html.

20. Steve Lohr, *New York Times*, 1/16/05.

21. Families USA study entitled "Health Care: Are You Better Off Today Than You Were Four Years Ago?," 9/04.

22. Center for American Progress report entitled "The Corporate Tax Void: Record High Profits and Record Low Taxes," 4/9/04. http://www.americanprogress.org/atf/cf/_percent7BE9245FE4-9A2B-43C7-A521-5D6FF2E06E03percent7D/profitstaxes.pdf.

23. David Welch, *BusinessWeek*, 6/6/05. http://www.businessweekasia.com/magazine/content/05_23/b3936037_mz011.htm.

24. John Ritter, *USA Today*, 3/2/04. http://www.usatoday.com/money/industries/retail/2004-03-02-wal-mart_x.htm. Andy Serwer, *Fortune* press release, 11/1/04; http://www.fortune.com/fortune/information/Presscenter/0,,11152004_walton.html.

25. Steve Greenhouse and Michael Barbaro, *New York Times*, 10/26/05.

26. CBS Poll, 6/18/05. http://www.cbsnews.com/stories/2005/06/17/opinion/polls/main702815.shtml.

27. White House press secretary Scott McClellan, 9/13/04.

28. Public Citizen report entitled "Ed Gillespie: The Embedded Lobbyist," 6/03: see "Insurance" and "Hospitals and Health Care" on page 9 chart. http://www.citizen.org/documents/Gillespie_June.pdf.

29. Republican National Committee chairman Ed Gillespie, National Press Club speech, 11/4/04.

30. Gary Langer, ABC News, 10/20/03. http://abcnews.go.com/sections/living/US/healthcare031020_poll.html.

31. ABC/*Washington Post* poll, 10/13/03, Question #48. http://abcnews.go.com/images/pdf/935a3HealthCare.pdf.

32. Pew poll, 8/7/03. http://people-press.org/reports/display.php3?ReportID=190.

33. Paul Krugman, *New York Times*, 6/13/05. http://www.nytimes.com/2005/06/13/opinion/13krugman.html?hp.

34. Alexandra Marks, *Christian Science Monitor*, 8/13/03. http://www.csmonitor.com/2003/0813/p03s01-ussc.html.

35. Kirstin Downey, *Washington Post*, 3/6/04. http://www.washingtonpost.com/ac2/wp-dyn/A34899-2004Mar5?language=printer.

36. Katie Merx, *Crain's Detroit Business*, 6/7/04.

37. President Bush, 10/30/04. http://www.whitehouse.gov/news/releases/2004/10/20041030-3.html.

38. Robert J. Blendon, Minah Kim, and John M. Benson, *Health Affairs*, 6/01. http://content.healthaffairs.org/cgi/reprint/20/3/10.pdf.

39. Vice President Dick Cheney, 6/13/03.

40. Senator Phil Gramm (R-TX), 7/15/98.

41. Official congressional biography of Senator Phil Gramm (R-TX). http://bioguide.congress.gov/scripts/biodisplay.pl?index=G000365.

42. Chris Viehbacher of GlaxoSmithKline, Fox News, 8/20/03.

43. Ben Hirschler and Mark Potter, *National Post* (Canada), 2/13/04.

44. William Welch, *USA Today*, 6/15/04. http://www.usatoday.com/news/washington/2004-06-15-uninsured-report_x.htm.

45. Kaiser Commission on Medicaid and the Uninsured report entitled "Underinsured in America: Is Health Coverage Adequate?" 7/02, citing Kaiser survey data. http://www.kff.org/uninsured/loader.cfm?url=/commonspot/security/getfile.cfm&PageID=14136.

46. Robert Wood Johnson Foundation report entitled "Working but Uninsured," 3/27/05. http://www.rwjf.org/newsroom/newsreleasesdetail.jsp?id=10347.

47. January W. Payne, *Washington Post*, 12/21/04. http://www.washingtonpost.com/wp-dyn/articles/A13690-2004Dec20.html. According to CNN, the 9/11 death toll was 2,752. http://www.cnn.com/2003/US/Northeast/10/29/wtc.deaths/.

48. Census Bureau report entitled "Income, Poverty, and Health Insurance Coverage in the United States: 2004, 8/05. http://www.census.gov/prod/2005pubs/p60-229.pdf.

49. Malcolm Gladwell, *The New Yorker*, 8/29/05. http://www.newyorker.com/fact/content/articles/050829fa_fact.

50. World Health Organization, World Health Report, 2000, page 200. http://www.who.int/entity/whr/2000/en/whroo en.pdf.

51. The U.S. Peace Corps operates in Morocco and Costa Rica. http://www.peacecorps.gov/index.cfm?shell=learn.wherepc.northafr.morocco; http://www.peacecorps.gov/index.cfm?shell=learn.wherepc.LatinAmerica.costarica.

52. Robert Pear, *New York Times*, 2/7/04.

53. Larry Bivins, *Nashville Tennessean*, 4/20/03. http://www.tennessean.com/government/archives/03/04/31786117.shtml. Reuters, 9/29/05. http://today.reuters.

com/news/newsArticle.aspx?type=domesticNews&storyID=2005-09-29T194923Z_
01_MOR947431_RTRUKOC_0_US-HCA.xml&archived=False. Jeffrey Birnbaum,
Washington Post, 10/24/05. http://www.washingtonpost.com/wp-dyn/content/
article/2005/10/23/AR2005102301201.html?sub=AR.

54. President Bush, 2004 presidential debate, 10/13/04.

55. Stephen Heffler, Sheila Smith, Sean Keehan, Christine Borger, M. Kent Clemens, and
Christopher Truffer of the Centers for Medicare and Medicaid Services, report entitled
"U.S. Health Spending Projections for 2004–2014." Tony Pugh, Knight-Ridder, 2/24/05.
http://www.commondreams.org/headlines05/0224-03.htm; http://content.
healthaffairs.org/content/vol0/issue2005/images/data/hlthaff.w5.74/DC1/Heffler05_
Ex1.gif; http://content.healthaffairs.org/cgi/content/full/hlthaff.w5.74/DC1.

56. Douglas Holtz-Eakin, head of the Congressional Budget Office, 1/28/04. http://www.
cbo.gov/showdoc.cfm?index=4989&sequence=0#table3.

57. Morton Mintz, *The Nation,* 12/15/04. http://www.thenation.com/doc.mhtml?i=
20041115&c=2&s=mintz. Physicians for a National Health Program, 8/22/03.
http://www.pnhp.org/news/2003/august/_important_new_data_.php.

58. Paul Krugman, *New York Times,* 4/22/05. http://healthandenergy.com/health_
insurance.htm.

59. Ceci Connelly, *Washington Post,* 5/5/04.

60. Peronet Despeignes, *USA Today,* 8/6/04. http://www.usatoday.com/money/economy/
2004-08-26-census-poverty_x.htm.

61. Physicians for a National Health Program, 8/13/03. http://www.pnhp.org/news/2003/
august/doctors_call_for_nat.php.

62. Public Citizen, 8/20/03. http://www.pnhp.org/news/2003/august/_important_new_
data_.php.

63. Victoria Colliver, *San Francisco Chronicle,* 8/27/04. http://www.sfgate.com/
cgi-bin/article.cgi?file=/c/a/2004/08/27/MNGPF8FF2U1.DTL.

64. Physicians for a National Health Program, 6/4/03. http://www.pnhp.org/news/2003/
june/study_estimates_that.php.

65. Citizens for Tax Justice report entitled "The Bush Tax Cuts So Far, 2001–2010," 7/05.
http://www.ctj.org/pdf/gwbdata.pdf.

66. Pew Research Center, 8/7/03. http://people-press.org/reports/display.php3?
ReportID=190.

67. Steve Irwin, "Toyota to Build 100,000 Vehicles per Year in Woodstock, Ont., Starting
2008." Canada Press, 7/10/05. http://www.cbc.ca/cp/business/050630/b0630102.html.

68. Steve Arnold, *Hamilton Spectator* (Ontario), 9/13/02.

69. Alan Ortbals, *Illinois Business Journal,* 7/12/04. http://www.ibjonline.com/print_
madison_county_judicial_hellhole.html.

70. Peter Baker, *Washington Post,* 1/6/05. http://www.washingtonpost.com/wp-dyn/
articles/A50603-2005Jan5.html.

71. Kaiser Family Foundation report entitled "Medical Malpractice Law in the United
States," 5/05, page 42. http://www.kff.org/insurance/loader.cfm?url=/commonspot/
security/getfile.cfm&PageID=53241.

72. Nick Anderson and Edwin Chen, *Los Angeles Times,* 10/22/04.

73. Jenny Anderson, *New York Times,* 7/7/06.

74. Jay Angoff, former insurance commissioner of Missouri and now a lawyer at Roger
Brown & Associates, report entitled "An Analysis of the Conduct, Performance and
Financial Condition of NCRIC, Inc., 2000–2004," 6/1/05. http://www.dcinjuryfacts.
com/law-justice-1039441.html.

75. Jay Angoff, former insurance commissioner of Missouri, report for the Center for Justice

and Democracy entitled "Falling Claims and Rising Premiums in the Medical Malpractice Insurance Industry," 7/05. http://www.centerjd.org/ANGOFFReport.pdf.

76. ISO press release, 4/12/05. http://www.iso.com/press_releases/2005/04_12_05.html. Center for Justice and Democracy report entitled "2004 Was the Most Profitable Year Ever for the Insurance Industry," 7/8/05. http://www.centerjd.org/free/mythbusters-free/MB_InsProfits2004.htm.

77. ISO press release, 3/14/04. http://www.piaofpr.com/sharpincreaseinp.htm.

78. ISO press release, 4/12/05. http://www.iso.com/press_releases/2005/04_12_05.html.

79. National Association of Insurance Commissioners, analysis entitled "2003 Profitability Report."

80. Doug Heller of the Foundation for Taxpayer and Consumer Rights, testimony to the U.S. Senate Commerce Committee, 10/22/03. http://www.consumerwatchdog.org/insurance/rp/1799.pdf.

81. Weiss Ratings study, 6/3/03. http://www.weissratings.com/News/Ins_General/20030602pc.htm.

82. Foundation for Taxpayers and Consumer Rights report entitled "How Insurance Reform Lowered Doctors' Medical Malpractice Rates in California," 3/7/03. http://www.consumerwatchdog.org/healthcare/rp/rp003103.pdf.

83. Tim Bonfield, *Cincinnati Enquirer*, 10/11/04. http://www.enquirer.com/editions/2004/10/11/loc_doctor.day2.html.

84. Foundation for Taxpayer and Consumer Rights press release, 10/26/04. http://releases.usnewswire.com/GetRelease.asp?id=38849.

85. Mark Silva, *Chicago Tribune*, 1/3/05. http://www.consumerwatchdog.org/malpractice/nw/?postId=2002&pageTitle=Bush's+tort+reform+efforts+to+start+at+'judicial+hellhole'percent3B.

86. Congressional Budget Office, official cost estimate for H.R. 4600, 9/25/02. http://www.cbo.gov/showdoc.cfm?index=3815&sequence=0.

87. Congressional Budget Office report entitled "Limiting Tort Liability for Medical Malpractice," 1/8/04. http://www.cbo.gov/showdoc.cfm?index=4968&sequence=0.

88. Representative Mike Rogers (R-MI), House Energy and Commerce Committee, 5/20/04.

89. Rogers was elected in 2000. Data from the Center for Responsive Politics show that in the 2003–2004 election cycle, he pocketed $43,500 in PAC contributions from the insurance industry and $150,267 in PAC contributions from the health industry, and in the 2001–2002 election he pocketed $57,100 in PAC contributions from the insurance industry and $23,500 in PAC contributions from the health care industry. http://www.opensecrets.org/pacs/memberprofile.asp?cid=N00009668&cycle=2004&expand=F; http://www.opensecrets.org/pacs/memberprofile.asp?cid=N00009668&cycle=2002&expand=F.

90. Representative Rick Lazio, debate with Hillary Clinton, 9/13/00. http://www.australianpolitics.com/news/2000/00-09-13.shtml.

91. President Bush, 10/8/04.

92. Senator Conrad Burns (R-MT), 10/14/03.

93. Robert Pear, *New York Times*, 6/18/00. http://www.consumerwatchdog.org/healthcare/nw/?postId=376&pageTitle=The+'R'+Wordpercent3B+Justice+Souter+Takes+on+a+Health+Care+Taboo.

94. Frank J. Murray, *Washington Times*, 6/13/2000. http://www.consumerwatchdog.org/malpractice/nw/?postId=373&pageTitle=Supreme+Court+Finds+No+Federal+Case+in+HMO+Lawsuit.

95. *Sacramento Business Journal*, 12/14/2001. http://www.bizjournals.com/sacramento/ stories/2001/12/17/editorial1.html.

96. *National Journal*, 7/28/99.

97. Gallup Polling Organization, Gallup Poll Tuesday Briefing, 7/15/03.

98. VFW commander-in-chief Edward S. Banas Sr., statement to Congress, 3/10/04.

99. Robert Pear, *New York Times*, 12/20/04.

100. Nicole Volhonstseff, *Columbia Missourian*, 1/28/05. http://columbiamissourian.com/ news/story.php?ID=11760.

101. University of Montana report, 2/04. http://www.dphhs.mt.gov/hpsd/uninsured/ healthreport.pdf.

102. Bob Anez, Associated Press, 9/1/00.

103. Center for Responsive Politics data shows Senator Conrad Burns (R-MT) has taken $277,902 from the health care industry in his career. http://www.opensecrets.org/ politicians/allsector.asp?CID=N00004638.

104. University of Montana report, 2/04. http://www.dphhs.mt.gov/hpsd/uninsured/ healthreport.pdf.

105. Commonwealth Fund and Kaiser Family Foundation press release, 11/10/93.

106. Families USA report entitled "One in Three: Non-Elderly Americans Without Health Insurance, 2002–2003," 6/04.

107. Malcolm Gladwell, *The New Yorker*, 8/22/05. http://www.newyorker.com/fact/ content/articles/050829fa_fact.

108. Center for Responsive Politics data show Representative Tom Coburn (R-OK) took $146,106 from health industry PACs in 1995–1996 and $74,999 from health industry PACs in 1997–1998. http://www.opensecrets.org/1996os/sector/H4OK02048.htm.

109. Representative Tom Coburn (R-OK), remarks at a House Commerce Committee hearing, 6/16/99. Coburn was speaking after a woman said, "I believe from their Web site, they are looking for a dentist, currently, so that they can include a dentist in their system." She also said, "I think I got it on the e-mail through Families USA, I think, somewhere on the Internet."

110. Paul Krugman, *New York Times*, 6/13/05.

111. Andy Miller, *Atlanta Journal Constitution*, 2/27/04. http://www.ajc.com/business/ content/business/0204/27walmart.html. Sydney P. Freedberg and Connie Humburg, *St. Petersburg Times*, 3/25/05. http://www.sptimes.com/2005/03/25/State/Lured_ employers_now_t.shtml.

112. Associated Press, 7/24/05. http://www.magicvalley.com/articles/2005/07/25/news_ localstate/news_local_state.6.txt.

113. *Health Business Week*, 5/28/04.

114. Kristen Gerencher, CBS.MarketWatch.com, 5/4/04. http://www.marketwatch.com/ news/story.asp?guid=percent7B04A2FC4E-12BE-4E77-B497-72D80479CDB8_ percent7D&siteid=google&dist=google&cbsReferrer=www.google.com; Physicians for a National Health Plan, 3/18/03. http://www.pnhp.org/news/2003/april/blue_cross_ of_califo.php.

115. Victoria Colliver, *San Francisco Chronicle*, 4/28/05. http://sfgate.com/cgi-bin/article. cgi?f=/c/a/2005/04/28/BUGVJCGF631.DTL&type=business; http://www.pnhp.org/ news/2003/april/blue_cross_of_califo.php.

116. Foundation for Taxpayer and Consumer Rights, 12/12/03. (Kaiser Family Foundation, California Health Benefits Survey, 2002, February 2003). http://releases.usnewswire. com/GetRelease.asp?id=24381.

117. Foundation for Taxpayers and Consumer Rights report entitled "How Insurance Reform

Lowered Doctors' Medical Malpractice Rates in California," 3/7/03. http://www.consumerwatchdog.org/healthcare/rp/rp003103.pdf.

118. Elizabeth Wolfe, Associated Press, 5/13/04.

119. Institute of Medicine, 1/14/04. http://www.iom.edu/report.asp?id=17632.

120. U.S. Department of Health and Human Services website entitled "HHS—What We Do." http://www.hhs.gov/about/whatwedo.html/.

121. Money in State Politics analysis of Tommy Thompson's 1998 campaign contributions. http://www.followthemoney.org/database/StateGlance/candidate.phtml?si=199848&c=384921&p=16#geography.

122. Associated Press, 1/14/04. http://www.cnn.com/2004/HEALTH/01/14/uninsured.solutions.ap/.

CHAPTER 7: PRESCRIPTION DRUGS

1. Irving Levin Associates, 10/17/01. http://www.levinassociates.com/pressroom/pressreleases/pr2001/pr110exec.htm.

2. Associated Press, 3/8/05. http://dailynews.muzi.com/news/ll/english/1353130.shtml.

3. Families USA, 7/9/03. http://www.policyalmanac.org/health/pr/drugs.shtml.

4. KGO-TV (ABC affiliate), San Francisco, report entitled "Cost of Prescription Drugs Rising Rapidly," 6/30/04.

5. Ed Garsten, *Detroit News,* 3/11/04. http://www.detnews.com/2004/autosinsider/0403/11/a01-88813.htm.

6. Theresa Agovino, Associated Press, 1/15/04. http://www.freep.com/news/health/health15_20040115.htm.

7. Ed Silverman, *Newark Star-Ledger,* 10/15/04. http://www.healthyskepticism.org/library/ref.php?id=1134.

8. Public Citizen, 3/17/02. http://www.citizen.org/documents/fortune500_2002report.PDF.

9. NBC *Today* show, 9/2/04. http://msnbc.msn.com/id/5886411/.

10. Public Citizen, 6/23/03. http://www.publiccitizen.org/pressroom/release.cfm?ID=1469.

11. Ibid.

12. About.com, United States Army. http://usmilitary.about.com/od/army/l/blchancommand.htm.

13. Center for Responsive Politics data on pharmaceutical/health products industry contributions. http://www.opensecrets.org/industries/indus.asp?Ind=H04.

14. Public Citizen's White House for Sale lists 15 Bush Rangers/Pioneers from the health/pharmaceutical industry: Ronald F. Docksai (Bayer Corp.), Bruce S. Gelb (Bristol-Myers Squibb), Ben & Vicki Hinson (Mid Georgia Ambulance), Jerry H. Hodge (Maxor National Pharmacy), Jonathan Javitt (Health Directions LLC), Stephen Kass (Meris Laboratories Inc.), Munr Kazmir (Direct Meds Inc.), Craig Keeland (ViaViente Ltd), Hank McKinnell (Pfizer), Malachi Mixon (Invacare Corp.), Christine Davis O'Brien (AstraZeneca), Mr. & Mrs. Nicholas T. Serafy Jr. (Proficiency Testing Service), John R. Stafford (Wyeth), Jeff L. Swope (Champion Partners Ltd.), Elliott Vernon (Healthcare Financial Group).

15. Anne Mulkren, *Denver Post,* 5/23/04. http://www.commondreams.org/headlines04/0523-02.htm.

16. *National Journal,* 11/19/02.

17. Wayne Washington and Susan Milligan, *Boston Globe,* 12/12/03. http://www.boston.com/news/nation/articles/2003/12/12/bush_allys_firm_vies_for_medicare_cards/.

18. NewsMax, 12/22/00. http://www.newsmax.com/archives/articles/2000/12/22/194305.shtml.

19. Representative Dan Burton (R-IN), *Indianapolis Star,* 12/30/02. Waters & Kraus press release, 3/17/02. http://www.mercurypolicy.org/new/documents/ WatersKrausPressRelease031702.pdf.

20. CBS News, 12/12/02. http://www.cbsnews.com/stories/2002/12/12/eveningnews/ main532886.shtml.

21. Associated Press, 7/14/04. http://www.usatoday.com/news/washington/ 2004-07-14-aids-defense_x.htm.

22. PhRMA website. http://www.phrma.org/whoweare/.

23. Connecticut Coalition for Better Health Care press release, 6/20/00. http://cthealth. server101.com/citizens_for_better_medicare_a_sham_group.htm.

24. John Broder, *New York Times,* 6/28/00.

25. Jim Drinkard, *USA Today,* 7/6/03. http://www.usatoday.com/news/washington/ 2003-07-06-medicare-drug_x.htm.

26. Springfield, Missouri, *News-Leader* editorial, 12/26/04.

27. Alan Holmer, president of PhRMA, *AARP Bulletin,* 8/02. http://www.aarp.org/ bulletin/faceoff/Articles/a2003-06-25-lowerdrugprices-.html.

28. Center for Responsive Politics data show Senator Jon Kyl (R-AZ) has taken $143,385 from the pharmaceutical/health products industry during his career. http://www. opensecrets.org/politicians/allindus.asp?CID=N00006406.

29. Senator John Kyl (R-AZ) press release, 4/27/04. http://kyl.senate.gov/record.cfm?id= 220803.

30. Robert Dreyfuss, *American Prospect,* 4/23/01. http://www.prospect.org/ print-friendly/print/V12/7/dreyfuss-r.html.

31. David Kendall, DLC's Progressive Policy Institute, 6/21/03. http://www.ppionline.org/ ppi_ci.cfm?knlgAreaID=111&subsecID=141&contentID=251891.

32. Center for Responsive Politics data show Senator Daniel Patrick Moynihan (D-NY) accepted $77,500 from the pharmaceutical/health products industry during his career. http://www.opensecrets.org/1994os/osdata/moynihan.pdf.

33. David Broder, *Washington Post,* 9/25/00.

34. Public Citizen, "2002 Drug Industry Profits: Hefty Pharmaceutical Company Margins Dwarf Other Industries," 6/03. http://www.citizen.org/documents/Pharma_Report.pdf.

35. John Fauber and Joe Manning, Knight-Ridder/Tribune News Service, 4/2/01. http://abcnews.go.com/GMA/MellodyHobson/story?id=127643&page=1.

36. From text of H.R. 626, the Health Care Research and Development and Taxpayer Protection Act. http://bernie.house.gov/prescriptions/hr626.asp.

37. Public Citizen report, "New Investigative Study Reveals How Congress' Addiction to Drug Industry Money Threatens Medicare Drug Bill," 7/6/00. Public Citizen was citing "Federal Taxation of the Drug Industry from 1990 to 1996," Congressional Research Service Memorandum, 12/13/99. http://www.citizen.org/documents/addicting.pdf.

38. CBS News, 10/10/04. http://www.cbsnews.com/stories/2004/10/10/sunday/ main648431.shtml.

39. Benjamin Romano, *Seattle Times,* 10/21/05. http://seattletimes.nwsource.com/html/ businesstechnology/2002574075_icos21.html. Colleen Flanagan, State Department Info, 12/3/03. http://usinfo.state.gov/gi/Archive/2003/Dec/04-679621.html.

40. Center for Responsive Politics data show Sen. John Breaux (D-LA) took $66,999 from the pharmaceutical/health products industry in his 1998 campaign, and another $81,150 from the industry between 1999 and 2004. http://www.opensecrets.org/ 1998elect/dist_indus/98LAS8indus.htm; http://www.opensecrets.org/politicians/ indus.asp?CID=N00005385&cycle=2004.

41. Kate Schuler, *Congressional Quarterly,* 4/27/04.

42. Patricia Barry, AARP *Bulletin,* 6/02. http://www.aarp.org/bulletin/medicare/Articles/a2003-06-23-drugprofitsvsresearch.html/page=2.

43. Public Citizen, "2002 Drug Industry Profits," 6/03. http://www.citizen.org/documents/Pharma_Report.pdf.

44. Gail Russell Chaddock, *Christian Science Monitor,* 7/19/00. http://www.commondreams.org/views/071900-102.htm.

45. Ibid.

46. Ralph Nader, Common Dreams, 11/28/03. http://www.commondreams.org/views03/1128-07.htm.

47. Jonathan Kaplan, *The Hill,* 11/18/03. http://releases.usnewswire.com/printing.asp?id=23476.

48. Amy Goldstein, *Washington Post,* 3/19/04. http://www.washingtonpost.com/ac2/wp-dyn/A6339-2004Mar18.

49. Robert Pear, *New York Times,* 5/4/04.

50. Ben Pech, Washington director of the Medicare Rights Center, *In These Times,* 12/11/03. http://www.inthesetimes.com/comments.php?id=489_0_3_0_C.

51. Bob Cusak, *The Hill,* 4/7/04. http://www.hillnews.com/business/040704_thomas.aspx.

52. Senate lobbying disclosure forms show Scully got a job with the health care/pharmaceutical lobbying/law firm Alston & Byrd. http://sopr.senate.gov/cgi-win/opr_gifviewer.exe?/2004/01/000/861/000861821|3. Tom Dickinson, *Mother Jones,* 5/04. http://www.motherjones.com/news/feature/2004/05/medicare.html.

53. Public Citizen, 1/13/04. http://www.citizen.org/congress/govt_reform/ethics/scully/index.cfm.

54. *National Journal,* 12/04/03.

55. Louis Jacobson and Peter H. Stone, *National Journal,* 4/9/04. http://38.118.42.202/story_page.cfm?articleid=28209&printerfriendlyVers=1&. According to Roskey's biography at Leading Authorities speakers' bureau, he was an adviser to Senator Charles Grassley (R-IA), who chairs the finance committee. http://www.leadingauthorities.com/23744/Colin_Roskey.htm. *National Journal,* 12/4/03. According to Public Citizen, Alston & Bird lobbies for drug companies such as, among others, Johnson & Johnson, AstraZeneca, Bristol-Myers Squibb, Pfizer and Praecis Pharmaceuticals. http://www.citizen.org/documents/Scully_Fact_Sheet.pdf.

56. Senate lobbying disclosure forms show that Jeff Forbes, chief of staff to Senator Max Baucus, registered as a lobbyist for PhRMA on 3/1/04. The Medicare bill that Forbes and Baucus worked on was signed into law on December 8, 2003.

57. April Fulton, *National Journal,* 12/4/03. Senate lobbying records show Forbes is now a paid lobbyist for PhRMA at the firm Cauthen, Forbes and Williams.

58. Bob Cusack, *The Hill,* 4/7/04. http://www.hillnews.com/business/040704_thomas.aspx.

59. Lauran Neergaard, Associated Press, 4/12/95.

60. Gerard O'Neill with Mitchell Zuckoff, Alice Dembner, and Matt Carroll, *Boston Globe,* 4/5/98.

61. Michael Unger, *Newsday,* 5/2/93.

62. ABC, *Primetime Live,* 6/18/92.

63. Associated Press, 5/27/04.

64. Gerard O'Neil with Mitchell Zuckoff, Alice Dembner, and Matt Carroll, *Boston Globe,* 4/5/98.

65. Jeffrey Leiden, chief operating officer of Abbott Laboratories, PR Newswire, 5/25/04; Maureen Groppe, Gannett News Service, 8/5/04.

66. Gerard O'Neil with Mitchell Zuckoff, Alice Dembner, and Matt Carroll, *Boston Globe,* 4/5/98.

67. CNN Talkback Live, 5/3/00, transcript.

68. Senate Roll Call vote #168, 6/30/00; BNA Daily Report, 10/15/01. http://lists. essential.org/pipermail/ip-health/2001-October/002090.html.

69. Ceci Connelly, *Washington Post*, 4/23/04. http://www.washingtonpost.com/ac2/ wp-dyn?pagename=article&contentId=A34822-2004Apr22&notFound=true.

70. Jane Bryant Quinn, *Newsweek*, 9/27/04. http://www.msnbc.msn.com/id/6039139/ site/newsweek/.

71. William K. Hubbard, FDA associate commissioner for policy and planning, statement at the joint hearing of the U.S. Senate Subcommittee on Health Care and Subcommittee on International Trade, Committee on Finance, 4/27/04. http://www.fda.gov/ ola/2004/importeddrugs0427.html.

72. Alan Holmer, *The Hill*, 8/6/01. http://bernie.house.gov/documents/articles/ 2001-08-06-PhRMA_response.asp?print.

73. Associated Press, 11/25/03. http://www.cbsnews.com/stories/2003/11/25/health/ main585608.shtml.

74. Marc Kaufman, "USDA Allowed Canadian Beef In Despite Ban," *Washington Post*, 5/20/04. http://www.washingtonpost.com/wp-dyn/articles/A41076-2004May19.html.

75. Sen. Debbie Stabenow (D-MI), Roll Call, 7/11/05.

76. Theresa Agovino, Associated Press, 9/9/03. http://www.pittsburghlive.com/x/ tribune-review/business/s_154185.html.

77. FDA warning letter, 2/18/04. http://www.fda.gov/foi/warning_letters/g4535d.htm.

78. President Bush, 8/18/04.

79. Eric Madigan, Stateline, 11/20/03. http://www.stateline.org/live/ViewPage. action?siteNodeId=136&languageId=1&contentId=15481.

80. Tony Pugh, Knight-Ridder, 11/28/03. http://reclaimdemocracy.org/weekly_2003/ canada_drugs_not_dangerous.html.

81. Ibid.

82. Doug Struck, *Washington Post*, 10/20/04. http://www.washingtonpost.com/wp-dyn/ articles/A46215-2004Oct19.html.

83. Tim Craig, *Washington Post*, 9/14/04.

84. Theresa Agovino, Associated Press, 10/2/04.

85. Center for Responsive Politics data show Richard Burr was the single largest congressional recipient of cash from the pharmaceuticals/health products industry. He took $299,184 in his successful 2004 run for the U.S. Senate from North Carolina. http://www.opensecrets.org/industries/recips.asp?Ind=H04&Cycle=2004& recipdetail=A&Mem=N&sortorder=U.

86. David Rice, *Winston-Salem Journal*, 10/27/04.

87. Peter Rost, *New York Times*, 10/30/04.

88. Tony Pugh, Knight-Ridder, 11/19/03. http://reclaimdemocracy.org/weekly_2003/ canada_drugs_not_dangerous.html.

89. Jessica R. Dart, sworn affidavit, 3/1/04. http://www.house.gov/hinchey/issues/fda2.pdf.

90. Rep. Maurice Hinchey (D-NY), report entitled "FDA Is Placing Corporations Above Public." http://www.house.gov/hinchey/issues/fda.shtml.

91. Rita Rubin, *USA Today*, 11/28/04. http://www.usatoday.com/news/health/ 2004-11-28-fda-vioxx_x.htm.

92. David Graham, associate director for science and medicine in the FDA's Office of Drug Safety, congressional testimony, 11/18/04. http://www.consumersunion.org/pub/ campaignprescriptionforchange/001651.html.

93. Robert Pear, *New York Times*, 2/25/04. http://www.policyimpact.com/news/ index.php?article=923.

94. Center for Science in the Public Interest, 12/3/03. http://www.cspinet.org/new/200312031.html.

95. Roger Yu, *Dallas Morning News,* 6/21/04.

96. Canadian Content, 12/4/04. http://www.canadiancontent.net/commtr/article_727.html.

97. James Kanter, Dow Jones Newswire, 1/6/04. http://www.globalaging.org/health/world/2004/bayer.htm.

98. Carla Marinucci, *San Francisco Chronicle,* 8/26/04. http://www.sfgate.com/cgi-bin/article.cgi?f=/c/a/2004/08/26/GOVERNOR.TMP.

99. Lisa Rapaport and Clea Benson, *Sacramento Bee,* 10/1/04. http://www.sacbee.com/content/politics/story/10935504p-11852899c.html.

100. Ceci Connolly, *Washington Post,* 11/11/04. http://www.washingtonpost.com/wp-dyn/articles/A41321-2004Nov10.html.

101. Center for Responsive Politics data show Rudolph Giuliani (R) took in $99,389 in campaign contributions from the pharmaceutical/health products industry in 2000. http://www.opensecrets.org/industries/recips.asp?Ind=H04&Cycle=2000&recipdetail=A&Mem=N&sortorder=U.

102. Deborah Barfield Berry, *Newsday,* 8/19/04.

103. Dick Johnson, from Brooklyn Center, Minnesota, was on the bus. He was quoted by Bill Hogan in *AARP Bulletin* on 6/04. http://www.aarp.org/bulletin/prescription/Articles/a2004-06-10-busstop.html.

104. Judd Legum and David Sirota, *The Nation,* 9/27/04. Associated Press, 8/12/04. http://www.commondreams.org/views04/0910-04.htm.

105. Robert Pear, "Medicare Law Is Seen Leading to Cuts in Drug Benefits for Retirees," *New York Times,* 7/14/04.

106. Thomas Scully, National Public Radio, 11/21/03.

107. Ellen Schultz and Theo Francis, *Wall Street Journal,* 1/8/04. http://online.wsj.com/public/resources/documents/SB107350927860976500.htm.

108. Center for American Progress report entitled "The $47 Million Retiree Sellout," 5/14/04. http://www.americanprogress.org/site/pp.asp?c=biJRJ8OVF&b=70999.

109. Robert Pear, "Medicare Law Is Seen Leading to Cuts in Drug Benefits for Retirees," *New York Times,* 7/14/04. http://www.yuricareport.com/Medicare/MedicareBillCostsRetireesMore.html.

110. Thomas Scully got a job with the health care/pharmaceutical lobbying/law firm Alston & Bird. Senate lobbying disclosures. http://sopr.senate.gov/cgi-win/opr_gifviewer.exe?/2004/01/000/861/000861821|3. Public Citizen report entitled "Lobbying Clients Represented by Thomas Scully's Potential Employers" notes that Alston & Bird represent major health care and pharmaceutical companies. http://www.citizen.org/documents/Scully_Fact_Sheet.pdf.

111. Representative Bill Thomas, *Congressional Record,* 11/21/03, page H12248. http://frwebgate.access.gpo.gov/cgi-bin/getpage.cgi?position=all&page=H12248&dbname=2003_record.

112. Center for Responsive Politics data show that during his career, Representative Bill Thomas (R-CA) has taken $940,001 from health professionals, $674,419 from the insurance industry, $535,050 from the pharmaceutical/health products industry, $317,286 from the hospital/nursing home industry, and $247 from the health services/HMO industry. http://www.opensecrets.org/politicians/allindus.asp?CID=N00007256.

113. Amy Goldstein, *Washington Post,* 3/19/04. http://www.washingtonpost.com/ac2/wp-dyn/A6339-2004Mar18?language=printer.

114. Tony Pugh, Knight-Ridder, 3/12/04.

115. Amy Goldstein, *Washington Post,* 11/24/03.

116. Melissa Davis, TheStreet.com, 11/24/03.

117. President Bush, 12/8/03. http://www.whitehouse.gov/news/releases/2003/12/ 20031208-2.html.

118. Families USA, 10/20/04. http://www.familiesusa.org/assets/pdfs/ Approximately-Half-of-Americans-in-Medicare-Are-at-Risk-of-Losing-Coverage.pdf.

119. Ibid.

120. Patented Medicines Price Review Board website description. http://www. pmprb-cepmb.gc.ca/english/View.asp?x=175&mp=87.

121. Jeremy Laurance, *London Independent,* 12/4/03.

122. Mark Sherman, Associated Press, 11/22/04; Todd Zwillich, WebMD Medical News, 11/22/04. http://my.webmd.com/content/article/97/104193?printing=true.

123. Terry Savage, *Chicago Sun-Times,* 11/27/03. http://www.suntimes.com/output/savage/ cst-fin-terry274.html.

124. Mark Sherman, Associated Press, 11/26/03. http://www.detnews.com/2003/politics/ 0311/26/a05-335804.htm.

125. Max Richmond, vice president of the National Committee to Preserve Social Security and Medicare, as quoted by Jason Daily, Aurora (IN) *Journal Press,* 7/8/04.

126. Representative Tom Allen (D-ME), 5/15/01. http://tomallen.house.gov/showart.asp? contentID=281.

127. Ben Peck, Washington director of the Medicare Rights Center; *In These Times,* 12/11/03. http://www.inthesetimes.com/comments.php?id=489_0_3_0_C.

128. Bloomberg News, 7/26/04. http://quote.bloomberg.com/apps/news?pid= 10000103&sid=afbDpPGzrT9w&refer=us.

129. Ellen Schultz and Theo Francis, *Wall Street Journal,* 1/8/04. http://online.wsj.com/ public/resources/documents/SB107350927860976500.htm.

130. Robert Pear, *New York Times,* 1/31/05. http://www.nytimes.com/2005/01/31/politics/ 31drug.html?oref=login.

131. Theresa Agovino, Associated Press, 9/10/04.

132. Lester Crawford, congressional testimony, 3/11/04.

133. Alan Fram, Associated Press, 11/21/04. http://www.suntimes.com/output/elect/ cst-nws-cong21s1.html.

134. Center for American Progress, 3/16/04. http://www.americanprogress.org/site/ pp.asp?c=biJRJ8OVF&b=38005.

135. Christopher Rowland, *Boston Globe,* 4/15/04. http://www.boston.com/business/ globe/articles/2004/04/15/study_says_drug_imports_may_not_hurt_profits/.

136. Ibid.

137. Melody Petersen, "Lifting the Curtain on the Real Costs of Making AIDS Drugs," *New York Times,* 4/24/01.

138. Peter Rost, *Los Angeles Times,* 12/26/04. http://onegoodmove.org/1gm/1gmarchive/ 001819.html.

CHAPTER 8: ENERGY

1. Charles DiBona, *Buffalo News,* 9/11/94.

2. Tim Appenzeller, *National Geographic,* June 2004. http://magma.nationalgeographic. com/ngm/0406/feature5/index.html?fs=www7.nationalgeographic.com.

3. Michael Kanell, *Atlanta Journal-Constitution,* 11/3/01.

4. David Garman, assistant Secretary of Energy, congressional testimony, 11/1/01.

5. Brad Wong, *Seattle Post-Intelligencer,* 1/17/03. http://seattlepi.nwsource.com/local/ 104601_hummer17.shtml.

6. Consumers Union press release, 5/11/04. http://www.consumersunion.org/pub/core_other_issues/001086.html.

7. The WSJ/Mercer 2004 CEO Compensation Survey, 4/11/05. http://www.mercerhr.com/summary.jhtml;jsessionid=ZPZBI4HMSL0HWCTGOUGCHPQKMZ0QYI2C?idContent=1089750.

8. Center for Responsive Politics data show that the oil and gas industry gave Republicans $26,793,906 in 2000, $19,914,232 in 2002, and $20,218,375 in 2004, for a total of $66,926,513 over 4 years (4×365 days = 1,460 days; $1,460 \times 24$ hours = 35,040 hours; $67 million divided by 35,040 hours = $1,912 per hour). http://www.opensecrets.org/industries/indus.asp?Ind=E01.

9. PBS, *NOW*, interview of Alex Gibney, director of the movie *Enron: The Smartest Guys in the Room*, 8/12/05, transcript. Associated Press, 5/7/02. http://www.usatoday.com/money/energy/enron/2002-05-07-enron-calif-memo.htm.

10. CBS News, 6/16/04. http://www.cbsnews.com/stories/2004/06/16/eveningnews/main623569.shtml.

11. *Electricity Daily*, 9/1/04.

12. Nelson Schwartz, *Fortune*, 4/18/05. http://www.fortune.com/fortune/ceo/articles/0,15114,1044779,00.html.

13. R.G. Ratcliffe, *Houston Chronicle*, 2/6/02. http://www.chron.com/cs/CDA/story.hts/special/enron/1244510.

14. Ronald Brownstein, Richard Simon, and Edmund Sanders, *Los Angeles Times*, 12/15/01. http://bernie.house.gov/documents/articles/20011219100052.asp.

15. Representative George Miller (D-CA), report entitled "A Sweetheart Deal," 2/14/03. http://www.house.gov/georgemiller/bushinsiders.pdf.

16. Center for Public Integrity, 1/14/02. http://www.public-i.org/report.aspx?aid=190&sid=200.

17. Public Citizen's Whitehouseforsale.org found 48 Bush Rangers and Pioneers in the oil and gas industry. http://www.whitehouseforsale.org/ContributorsAndPaybacks/pioneer_search.cfm.

18. Dave Boyer, *Washington Times*, 1/16/02. http://www.papillonsartpalace.com/lieberma.htm.

19. Larry Margasak, Associated Press, 1/17/02.

20. Noam Scheiber, *Washington Monthly*, 1/13/03. http://www.findarticles.com/p/articles/mi_m1316/is_1_35/ai_97173631.

21. George Ochenski, "Montana's Deregulation Dilemma," *High Country News*, 4/27/98. http://www.hcn.org/servlets/hcn.Article?article_id=4119.

22. Jonathan D. Glater, *New York Times*, 9/21/03. http://www.commondreams.org/headlines03/0821-12.htm.

23. Public Citizen report entitled "Blind Faith: How Deregulation and Enron's Influence over Government Looted Billions from Americans," 12/01. http://www.citizen.org/cmep/energy_enviro_nuclear/electricity/Enron/articles.cfm?ID=7104.

24. Consumers Union press release, 9/14/04.

25. Sierra Club oil fact sheet: http://www.sierraclub.org/wildlands/arctic/oilfactsheet.asp.

26. Josh Meyer, "Saudi Government Provided Aid to 9/11 Hijackers, Sources Say," *Los Angeles Times*, 8/2/03. http://www.truthout.org/docs 03/080303A.shtml. David E. Kaplan, *U.S. News and World Report*, 12/15/03. http://www.usnews.com/usnews/news/articles/031215/15terror.htm.

27. Center for Public Integrity, "Big Oil Protects Its Interests," 7/15/04. http://www.publicintegrity.org/oil/report.aspx?aid=345&sid=100.

28. National Petroleum Council website: "The National Petroleum Council (NPC), a federally chartered and privately funded advisory committee, was established by the Secretary of the Interior in 1946 at the request of President Harry S. Truman. In 1977, the U.S. Department of Energy was established and the NPC's functions were transferred to the new Department. The purpose of the NPC is solely to represent the views of the oil and natural gas industries in advising, informing, and making recommendations to the Secretary of Energy with respect to any matter relating to oil and natural gas, or to the oil and gas industries submitted to it or approved by the Secretary." http://www.npc.org/background.html.

29. Capital Research Center report. http://www.capitalresearch.org/search/orgdisplay.asp?Org=CTO100.

30. Robert Bradley, Cato Institute, 4/22/99: "The Increasing Sustainability of Conventional Energy." http://www.cato.org/pubs/pas/pa-341es.html.

31. Capital Research Center report. http://www.capitalresearch.org/search/orgdisplay.asp?Org=HER100.

32. Ed Fuelner, president of the Heritage Foundation, United Press International, 4/23/04. http://washingtontimes.com/upi-breaking/20040423-114855-9870r.htm.

33. http://www.townhall.com/townhall/townhall-history.html.

34. John Stossel, 9/7/05. http://www.townhall.com/opinion/columns/johnstossel/2005/09/07/155361.html.

35. John King, CNN, 9/16/03. http://www.cnn.com/2003/ALLPOLITICS/09/16/cheney.halliburton/.

36. Center for Responsive Politics data show the oil and gas industry has given George W. Bush $4,529,926 in his two runs for president. http://www.opensecrets.org/presidential/indus.asp?ID=N00008072&Cycle=All.

37. Jim Snyder, *The Hill*, 7/7/05. http://www.hillnews.com/thehill/export/TheHill/News/Frontpage/060705/brief.html.

38. Mike Dennison, *Great Falls Tribune*, 7/27/05. http://www.greatfallstribune.com/apps/pbcs.dll/article?AID=/20050727/NEWS01/507270302/1002.

39. Jennifer Lee, Resources for the Future, 4/11/01. http://www.rff.org/rff/Publications/weathervane/Features/2001/Proposed-Bush-Budget-Cuts-Renewables-and-Energy-Efficiency-Programs.cfm.

40. Congressional Research Service report IB10020, entitled "Energy Efficiency: Budget, Oil Conservation, and Electricity Conservation Issues," 7/27/01. http://www.ncseonline.org/NLE/CRSreports/energy/eng-48.cfm?&CFID=14334684&CFTOKEN=37037097.

41. Taxpayers for Commonsense, 12/12/03. http://www.taxpayer.net/TCS/whitepapers/SUVtaxbreak.htm.

42. Timothy Egan, *New York Times,* 2/4/05.

43. On June 14, 2001, the Appropriations Committee rejected 27−34 an amendment by Rep. Nancy Pelosi (San Francisco) which would have imposed price caps in the Western electricity market for twenty months. Also rejected were an amendment to provide federal loans and guarantees to improve electricity transmission and another to upgrade and repair hydroelectric dams. A fourth defeated amendment would have increased the LIHEAP boost to $600 million in fiscal 2001 and $1.4 billion in 2002. http://www.calinst.org/bulletins/bull819w.htm#_1_7.

44. H. Josef Hebert, Associated Press, 7/30/03.

45. Matthai Chakko Kuruvila, *San Jose Mercury News*, 7/16/05. Associated Press, 6/14/04.

46. Senator Pete Domenici (R-NM), *Congressional Record*, 7/30/03. http://frwebgate.access.gpo.gov/cgi-bin/getpage.cgi?dbname=2003_record&page=S10184&position=all.

47. Center for Responsive politics data show the energy/natural resources industry has given Senator Pete Domenici (R-NM) $1,097,870 over his career. http://www.opensecrets. org/politicians/allsector.asp?CID=N00006515.

48. Federal Energy Regulatory Commission (FERC) staff report, 3/26/03. FERC report entitled "The Western Energy Crisis, the Enron Bankruptcy, and FERC's Response," 4/13/05. http://www.ferc.gov/industries/electric/indus-act/wec/chron/ chronology.pdf; http://www.ferc.gov/industries/electric/indus-act/wec/enron/ summary-findings.pdf.

49. Richard Oppel, *New York Times*, 3/27/03. http://www.globalpolicy.org/socecon/tncs/ 2003/0327enron.htm.

50. David Lazarus, *San Francisco Chronicle*, 9/7/00.

51. Josh Meyer, *Los Angeles Times*, 8/2/03. http://www.truthout.org/docs_ 03/080303A.shtml.

52. Consumers Union press release, 5/11/04. http://www.consumersunion.org/pub/core_ other_issues/001086.html.

53. David Sirota interview with Consumers Union's Dr. Marc Cooper, 8/26/05. Alex Berenson, *New York Times*, 6/12/04.

54. Consumers Union press release, 5/11/04. http://www.consumersunion.org/pub/ core_other_issues/001086.html.

55. Consumers Union, 10/29/04. http://www.consumersunion.org/pub/core_other_ issues/001541.html.

56. Consumers Union report entitled "Record Prices, Record Oil Company Profits—The Failure of Antitrust Enforcement to Protect American Energy Consumers," 9/04. http://www.consumersunion.org/pub/FTCBOOKf.pdf.

57. Detroit Free Press, 5/22/04. http://www.freep.com/money/autonews/gas22e_ 20040522.htm.

58. Lauren Shepherd, *The Hill*, 7/21/04. http://www.thehill.com/news/072104/ftc.aspx.

59. Public Citizen, 3/31/04. http://www.citizen.org/pressroom/print_release.cfm?ID=1678.

60. Public Citizen, 3/04. http://www.citizen.org/documents/oilmergers.pdf; http://energy. senate.gov/hearings/testimony.cfm?id=531&wit_id=1339.

61. Foundation for Taxpayer and Consumer Rights, report by petroleum industry analyst Tim Hamilton, 9/1/05. http://www.consumerwatchdog.org/energy/rp/5083.pdf; http://www.consumerwatchdog.org/energy/pr/?postId=5084.

62. *New York Times*, 2/4/05. http://www.truthout.org/docs_2005/020505A.shtml.

63. Public Citizen report entitled "Mergers, Manipulation and Mirages: How Oil Companies Keep Gasoline Prices High, and Why the Energy Bill Doesn't Help," 3/04. http://www.citizen.org/documents/oilmergers.pdf.

64. Stuart Auerbach, *Washington Post*, 7/7/91.

65. Robert Ebel, testimony before the Senate Resources Committee, 4/12/00. http://www. anwr.org/features/ebel.htm.

66. Public Citizen's Stealthpacs.org. http://www.stealthpacs.org/profile.cfm?org_id=162. The Center for Public Integrity, Silent Partners. http://www.public-i.org/527/search. aspx?act=com&orgid=164&comid=371c.

67. Freedom Works, 2/27/01. http://www.freedomworks.org/informed/issues_template. php?issue_id=381.

68. Charli E. Coon, Heritage Foundation, 8/1/01. http://www.heritage.org/Research/ EnergyandEnvironment/WM27.cfm.

69. Center for Responsive Politics data show the oil and gas industries gave Senator John Thune (R-SD) $260,327 between 1999 and 2004. http://www.opensecrets.org/ politicians/indus_newmems.asp?CID=N00004572&cycle=2004.

70. Senator John Thune (R-SD), *Congressional Record*, 3/16/05, page S2773. http://frwebgate.access.gpo.gov/cgi-bin/getpage.cgi?dbname=2005_record&page=S2773&position=all.

71. Tom Doggett, Reuters, 10/1/03. http://www.climateark.org/articles/reader.asp?linkid=26033.

72. Josef Hebert, Associated Press, 3/16/05.

73. Sierra Club fact sheet citing Annual Energy Review 1999, Table 5.1, Energy Information. http://72.14.203.104/search?q=cache:kjJLp45SD1AJ:www.sierraclub.org/wildlands/arctic/oil_development.asp.

74. *Inside Energy*, 8/6/01.

75. Jerry Taylor, Cato Institute, National Public Radio, 10/5/00.

76. American Council for an Energy Efficient Economy cites the 1997 President's Committee of Advisors on Science and Technology (PCAST), a panel of research experts and private sector executives. The committee conducted a detailed review of the Department of Energy's energy-efficiency R&D programs and concluded: "R&D investments in energy efficiency are the most cost-effective way to simultaneously reduce the risks of climate change, oil import interruption, and local air pollution, and to improve the productivity of the economy." PCAST said R&D budgets for energy efficiency should be doubled over 5 years, and that such an investment would produce a 40-to-1 return for the nation, including energy cost reductions of up to $45 billion annually by 2010." http://www.aceee.org/energy/rdd.pdf.

77. Senate roll call vote #309, 7/29/03. http://www.senate.gov/legislative/LIS/roll_call_lists/roll_call_vote_cfm.cfm?congress=108&session=1&vote=00309.

78. Senate roll call vote #52, 3/16/05. http://www.senate.gov/legislative/LIS/roll_call_lists/roll_call_vote_cfm.cfm?congress=109&session=1&vote=00052.

79. Jeff Gerth, *New York Times*, 2/21/05. http://www.finebergresearch.com/files/bigoil.htm.

80. Judith Kohler, Associated Press, 10/3/05.

81. Elizabeth Arnold, National Public Radio, 9/19/03.

82. Charlie Cain, *Detroit News*, 11/18/01.

83. Associated Press, 3/17/05, and *Irish Times*, 3/18/05.

84. Tim Martin, *Lansing State Journal*, 7/8/01.

85. Charlie Cain, *Detroit News*, 11/18/01.

86. Center for Responsive Politics data show Representative Ray LaHood (R-IL) has taken $176,687 from the energy/natural resource industry over his career. http://www.opensecrets.org/politicians/allsector.asp?CID=N00004933.

87. *Peoria Journal Star*, 5/22/04. http://www.raylahood.com/articles/article05-22-04.htm.

88. Robert Pore, *Grand Island Independent*, 3/9/05. http://www.theindependent.com/stories/030905/new_nelsongas09.shtml.

89. President Bush, 4/20/05.

90. Elisabeth Bumiller and Carl Hulse, *New York Times*, 4/21/05. http://www.ewg.org/news/story.php?id=3948.

91. William Neikirk, *Chicago Tribune*, 7/29/05.

92. William Roberts, Bloomberg News, 8/9/05. http://www.rep-am.com/story.php?id=25477.

93. Eric Peters, *Washington Times*, 12/19/95.

94. MSNBC's *Hardball*, 8/1/01.

95. Sen. Ted Stevens (R-AK), *Congressional Record*, 4/17/02, pages S2777, and S2778. http://frwebgate.access.gpo.gov/cgi-bin/getpage.cgi?dbname=2002_record&page=S2777&position=all.

96. Opinion Research Corporation, 3/2005. http://www.40mpg.org/pdfs/031705_40mpg_survey_report.pdf.

97. Vice President Dick Cheney, 4/30/01.

98. Mike Allen, *Washington Post*, 8/26/03. http://www.commondreams.org/headlines03/0826-03.htm.

99. Congressional Research Service report on Cheney's deferred compensation and holdings, 9/25/03. http://lautenberg.senate.gov/~lautenberg/press/2003/01/2003925A22.html.

100. DeWayne Wickham, *USA Today*, 5/7/01. http://www.usatoday.com/news/opinion/columnists/wickham/2001-05-07-wickham.htm.

101. President Bush, 4/24/01. http://www.whitehouse.gov/news/releases/2001/04/20010424-1.html.

102. Joseph Kahn, *New York Times*, 5/6/01.

103. President Bush, 6/17/04.

104. Democratic National Committee report on energy, "Bush's Budgets Consistently Slash Renewable Energy Programs," 2004. http://www.democrats.org/specialreports/energyrecord/.

105. Statement of David M. Nemtzow, of the Alliance to Save Energy, PR Newswire, 4/6/01.

106. Scott Burns, CNBC Money, 4/23/05. http://moneycentral.msn.com/content/invest/extra/P115791.asp. Brad Wong, *Seattle Post-Intelligencer*, 1/17/03. http://seattlepi.nwsource.com/local/104601_hummer17.shtml.

107. Union of Concerned Scientists, backgrounder. http://www.ucsusa.org/clean_vehicles/cars_and_suvs/page.cfm?pageID=1280.

108. Jeff Plungis, *Detroit News*, 10/7/04.

109. Ibid.

110. Tom Incantalupo, *Newsday*, 8/8/05. http://www.newsday.com/business/ny-bzhybo84375601aug08,0,175722.story?coll=ny-business-headlines.

111. Jeremy W. Peters, "Congress Caps Credits for Hybrid Cars," *New York Times*, 7/30/05. http://www.nytimes.com/2005/07/30/business/30hybrid.html.

112. Associated Press, 1/5/05. http://www.msnbc.msn.com/id/6786521/.

113. Bernard Simon, *Financial Times*, 8/23/05.

114. Charles DiBona, *Buffalo News*, 9/11/04.

115. Bhushan Bahree, *Wall Street Journal*, 5/18/04.

116. CNNfn, 5/20/04. http://money.cnn.com/2004/05/20/markets/oil_reserves/?cnn=yes.

117. Daniel Yergin, *New York Times*, 4/11/04: He quotes "the head of exploration for a major oil company."

118. Greg Gordon, *Sacramento Bee*, 3/21/05.

119. Ibid.

120. Alexandra Marks, *Christian Science Monitor*, 3/29/05. http://www.csmonitor.com/2005/0329/p01s01-usec.html.

121. House Speaker Dennis Hastert (R-IL), 3/26/04. http://speaker.house.gov/library/econ/040326jobsenergy.shtml.

122. Katharine Abend of U.S. PIRG, testimony before the House Energy Subcommittee, 6/12/01. http://www.house.gov/science/energy/jun12/abend.htm.

123. The American Council for an Energy Efficient Economy lists the U.S. Department of Energy as one of its sponsors on its website. http://www.aceee.org/about/govt.htm; http://www.aceee.org/about/funding.htm.

124. Natural Resources Defense Council report entitled "Fuelish Claims," 11/2/01, cites Howard Geller, et al., "U.S. Oil Import Dependence and How It Can Be Reduced," *Energy Policy* 22, 6 (1994): 471–85. http://www.nrdc.org/land/wilderness/artech/farcjobs.asp.

125. U.S. Department of Energy brochure entitled "Tomorrow's Energy Today for Cities and Counties," 11/96.

126. University of Michigan's Office for the Study of Automotive Transportation report entitled "Fuel-Saving Technologies and Facility Conversion: Costs, Benefits, and Incentives," 11/04. http://www.greenmachinestour.org/HAD-final-11-22-04.pdf.

127. Paul Harris, *UK Observer*, 9/21/03. http://observer.guardian.co.uk/international/story/0,6903,1046363,00.html.

128. Sam Kazman of the Competitive Enterprise Institute, *Atlanta Journal-Constitution*, 7/1/03. http://www.cei.org/gencon/019,03541.cfm.

129. Keith Bradsher, *New York Times*, 7/17/01.

130. Ibid.

131. Myron Levin, *Los Angeles Times*, 2/18/03.

132. Jeffrey Runge, administrator of the National Highway Traffic Safety Administration, testimony to the Senate Commerce Committee, 2/26/03.

133. John Crawley, Reuters, 8/19/05. PBS, *Frontline*. http://www.pbs.org/wgbh/pages/frontline/shows/rollover/etc/before.html.

134. Ralph Vartabedian, *Los Angeles Times*, 1/22/03.

135. Laura Bly, *USA Today*, 10/2/02. David Pittle of Consumers Union, testimony to the Senate Commerce Committee, 2/26/03.

136. PBS, *Frontline*, 2/21/02.

137. Keith Bradsher, *New York Times*, 7/17/01.

138. Public Citizen, report entitled "SUVs: The High Costs of Lax Fuel Economy Standards for American Families," 7/11/03. http://www.citizen.org/pressroom/release.cfm?ID=1454.

139. Center for Responsive Politics data show Senator Kit Bond (R-MO) took $164,751 from the oil and gas industry in his 1998 election, and $127,650 from the industry in his 2004 election. http://www.opensecrets.org/1998elect/dist_indus/98MOS8indus.htm; http://www.opensecrets.org/politicians/indus.asp?CID=N00005178&cycle=2004.

140. Public Citizen, 3/04. http://www.citizen.org/documents/oilmergers.pdf.

141. Fred Tasker, Knight-Ridder, 8/23/03.

142. Jeffrey Stansbury, "How Kilowatt Socialism Saved L.A. from the Energy Crisis," *San Francisco Bay Guardian*, 5/9/01. http://www.sfbg.com/News/pgande/kilowatt.html.

143. Sarah Cooke, Associated Press, 6/30/05. http://seattlepi.nwsource.com/printer/ap.asp?category=1310&slug=NorthWesternpercent20Cities.

144. Daniel M. Kammen, professor of energy and society, director of the Renewable and Appropriate Energy Laboratory (RAEL) Energy and Resources Group (ERG), Senate Finance Committee testimony, 7/11/01.

145. Ken Bossong, Renewable Energy Access, 2/28/05. http://renewableenergyaccess.com/rea/news/story?id=23074.

146. Greg Schneider, *Washington Post*, 3/31/05. http://www.washingtonpost.com/wp-dyn/articles/A14232-2005Mar30.html.

147. Linda Sharp, Cox News Service, 1/5/05.

148. Bill Lambrecht, *St. Louis Post-Dispatch*, 5/17/05.

149. Ron Cogan, autoMedia.com, 7/30/02. Phillip Lampert of the National Ethanol Vehicle Coalition, testimony to the House Small Business Committee, 5/6/04. http://www.e85fuel.com/news/073002fyi.htm.

150. Thomas Friedman, *New York Times*, 6/17/05. http://www.nytimes.com/2005/06/17/opinion/17friedman.html?oref=login.

151. Energy Report, 2/11/02. U.S. Rep. Maurice Hinchey, 2/27/03. http://www.house.gov/apps/list/press/ny22_hinchey/022703energy.html.

152. White House fact sheet, 3/10/04. http://www.whitehouse.gov/news/releases/2003/02/20030206-2.html.

153. Robert Litan of the Brookings Institution, *Washington Post*, 5/21/01. http://www. brookings.edu/views/op-ed/litan/20010521.htm.

154. Opinion Research Corporation poll commissioned by 40mpg.org released on 9/22/05. http://www.40mpg.org/getinf/092205release.cfm.

155. Public Citizen, 3/04. http://www.citizen.org/documents/oilmergers.pdf.

156. CBS, *Marketwatch*, 4/1/05. *Philadelphia Inquirer*, 4/1/05.

157. Brett Arends, *Boston Herald*, 9/7/05.

158. Todd Richmond, Associated Press, 9/21/05. http://news.yahoo.com/news?tmpl= story&u=/ap/20050921/ap_on_re_us/katrina_gas_gouging.

159. Tom Doggett, Reuters, 9/21/05. http://abcnews.go.com/Business/wireStory?id=1145805.

160. *The Hill*, 7/21/04. http://www.thehill.com/news/072104/ftc.aspx.

CHAPTER 9: UNIONS

1. States News Service, 10/1/03.

2. David Moberg, *Newsday*, 2/4/04. http://www.commondreams.org/views04/ 0204-06.htm. Pamela Rohland, *Central PA Magazine*, 11/02. http://www.centralpa. org/archives/02dec3hershey.html.

3. Eric Brazil, *San Francisco Chronicle*, 8/28/01. http://www.sfgate.com/cgi-bin/ article.cgi?file=/chronicle/archive/2001/08/28/BU17298.DTL&type=business.

4. Deirdre Davidson, American Lawyer Media, 2/7/01; Wisconsin Employment Law Letter, 5/01; and Department of Labor press release, 4/11/01. Bush actually eliminated reporting requirements for companies. In 2001, Bush rescinded a Clinton order that required companies to disclose materials they received to aid in stopping union organizing campaigns, such as pamphlets, videos, scripts, and strategy advice. Prior to the Clinton order, the Department of Labor routinely exempted "advice" given directly to companies from the disclosure requirement. http://www.dol.gov/opa/media/press/ opa/opa2001098.htm.

5. Larry Lipman, *Palm Beach Post*, 4/1/01; OMB Watch, 4/4/01. http://www.ombwatch. org/article/articleview/198/1/68/.

6. Tim Hoover, *Kansas City Star*, 1/12/05.

7. Knight-Ridder newspapers, "Indiana Gov. Daniels Cancels Union Contracts for 25,000 State Workers," 1/12/05. AFL-CIO, 1/13/05. http://www.aflcio.org/aboutunions/ voiceatwork/ns01132005.cfm.

8. Glenn Feldman, associate professor at the University of Alabama at Birmingham, *Birmingham News*, 9/5/04.

9. Ibid.

10. Eric Zorn, *Chicago Tribune*, 9/4/97.

11. American Rights at Work fact sheet. http://americanrightsatwork.org/resources/facts/ remedies.cfm.

12. Michael Barbaro, *Washington Post*, 4/9/05. http://www.truthout.org/docs_2005/ 040905E.shtml.

13. Steven Greenhouse, *New York Times*, 12/14/04. http://www.truthout.org/docs_04/ 121504L.shtml.

14. David Bonior, Center for American Progress article, 6/25/04. http://www. americanprogress.org/site/pp.asp?c=biJRJ8OVF&b=99065.

15. John King, CNN, 2/23/04.

16. Juliet Eilperin, *Washington Post*, 2/8/03.

17. Representative Charlie Norwood (R-GA), *Washington Times*, 2/24/05.

18. Center for Responsive Politics analysis of contributions to members of the Senate

Health, Education, Labor and Pensions Committee and members of the House Education and Workforce Committee; Analysis shows that Big Business interests gave $98.8 million to members of these committees in 2004, while labor interests gave just $7.2 million. http://www.opensecrets.org/cmteprofiles/overview.asp?cycle=2004&CmteID= S18&Cmte=SLAB&CongNo=108&Chamber=S; http://www.opensecrets.org/ cmteprofiles/overview.asp?cycle=2004&CmteID=H08&Cmte=HEDU&CongNo= 108&Chamber=H#.

19. Bill Press, Tribune Media Services, 3/21/01. http://archives.cnn.com/2001/ ALLPOLITICS/03/21/column.billpress/.

20. Bob Borosage, *American Prospect*, 3/1/03. http://www.ourfuture.org/onmessage/ borosage/3_1_03.cfm.

21. Nancy Cleeland, *Los Angeles Times*, 8/5/02.

22. Richard O. Boyer and Herbet M. Morais, *Labor's Untold Story*, 1955, page 27.

23. Robert Novak, *Chicago Sun-Times*, 5/16/96.

24. Albert Fishlow and Karen Parker, introduction to the book *Growing Apart*, 1999. http://www.cfr.org/publication.html?id=3276&excerpt=1&.

25. David Francis, *Christian Science Monitor*, 3/31/89.

26. Amy Joyce, *Washington Post*, 7/27/05.

27. Wal-Mart's "Manager's Toolbox to Remaining Union Free." http://reclaimdemocracy. org/walmart/antiunionman.pdf.

28. Gary M. Galles, professor of economics at Pepperdine University, *Ventura County Star*, 9/6/98.

29. CNN, *Crossfire*, 2/15/00.

30. Mike Nemeth, *Ft. Myers News-Press*, 4/24/02 and 5/1/02.

31. Repesentative Charlie Norwood (R-GA), press release, 3/2/05. http://www.house.gov/ apps/list/press/ga09_norwood/UnionScandals.html.

32. Representative Charlie Norwood (R-GA), *Washington Times*, 2/24/05.

33. Sarah Fritz, *St. Petersburg Times*, 1/8/01.

34. Laura Meckler, Associated Press, 1/5/01.

35. Linda Chavez, Capital Research Center's "Labor Watch," 9/04. http://www. capitalresearch.org/pubs/pdf/LW0904.pdf.

36. Lawrence Mishel and Matthew Walters, "How Unions Help All Workers," Economic Policy Institute, 8/03; Labor Research Association, 11/15/05. http://www.laborresearch. org/story.php?id=367. AFL-CIO report entitled "The Union Difference." http://www. aflcio.org/joinaunion/why/uniondifference/uniondiff6.cfm.

37. AFL-CIO report entitled "The Union Difference" cites the Bureau of Labor Statistics Employee Benefits in Private Industry report of 3/04. http://www.aflcio.org/ joinaunion/why/uniondifference/uniondiff6.cfm.

38. Lawrence Mishel and Matthew Walters, Economic Policy Institute, 8/03. http://www. epinet.org/content.cfm/briefingpapers_bp143.

39. Economic Policy Institute report entitled "How Unions Help All Workers," 8/03. http://www.epinet.org/content.cfm/briefingpapers_bp143.

40. Bureau of Labor Statistics, 4/21/05. ftp://ftp.bls.gov/pub/suppl/empsit.cpseed19.txt; ftp://ftp.bls.gov/pub/news.release/wkyeng.txt.

41. Lawrence Mishel and Matthew Walters, Economic Policy Institute, 8/03.

42. Karen Parker and Albert Fishlow, *Growing Apart*, 1999. http://www.cfr.org/publication. html?id=3276&excerpt=1&.

43. Stuart Silverstein, *Los Angeles Times*, 2/14/99.

44. PBS, *Frontline*, 11/16/04. http://www.pbs.org/wgbh/pages/frontline/shows/walmart/ transform/employment.html.

45. Steve Bailey, *Boston Globe,* 2/12/99.

46. Joel Rogers and Richard Freeman, *The Nation,* 6/24/02. http://www.thenation.com/doc.mhtml?i=20020624&s=rogers&c=1.

47. Jim McKay, *Pittsburgh Post-Gazette,* 1/12/05.

48. Kent Hoover, *Atlanta Business Chronicle,* 9/6/02. AFL-CIO press release, 8/29/02. http://www.aflcio.org/mediacenter/prsptm/pro829b2002.cfm.

49. AFL-CIO press release, 4/19/05. http://www.aflcio.org/mediacenter/prsptm/pr04192005.cfm. Richard Peterson, emeritus business professor at the University of Washington, *Seattle Post-Intelligencer,* 4/21/05. http://seattletimes.nwsource.com/html/opinion/2002247724_peterson21.htm.

50. National Right to Work press release, 8/30/02. http://www.nrtw.org/b/nr_139.php.

51. Bureau of National Affairs's Daily Labor Report reprints the fact finding report of the Department of Labor's Commission on the Future of Worker-Management Relations, 6/3/94. http://www.nathannewman.org/EDIN/.labor/.files/.archive/.dunlop/DunlopPreliminaryReport.html.

52. Human Rights Watch 2000 labor report cites Charles J. Morris, "A Tale of Two Statutes: Discrimination for Union Activity Under the NLRA and RLA," *Employment Rights and Policy Journal* 327, 2 (1998). http://www.hrw.org/reports/2000/uslabor/USLBR008-07.htm#P830_200865.

53. Human Rights Watch 2000 labor report cites Richard B. Freeman and Joel Rogers, pages 62 and 88 of their book *What Workers Want.* http://www.hrw.org/reports/2000/uslabor/USLBR008-07.htm#P833_201798.

54. North American Agreement on Labor Cooperation. http://www.naalc.org/english/nalmcp_3.shtml.

55. *National Journal*'s Technology Daily, 1/2/02.

56. General Accountability Office report entitled "Occupational Safety and Health: Violations of Safety and Health Regulations by Federal Contractors," 8/96. http://www.gao.gov/archive/1996/he96157.pdf.

57. The Employee Free Choice Act (HR 1696) was introduced on 4/19/05 and gained 210 cosponsors in the House and more than 30 in the Senate, but the Republican leadership refused to allow it to go to the floor for a vote. http://www.americanrightsatwork.org/takeaction/efca/; http://www.americanrightsatwork.org/takeaction/efca/efca_summary.cfm; http://thomas.loc.gov/cgi-bin/bdquery/z?d109:HR01696:@@@P; http://thomas.loc.gov/cgi-bin/bdquery/z?d109:SN00842:@@@P.

58. *Investors Business Daily,* 8/8/01.

59. Stefan Gleason of the National Right to Work Committee, *Washington Times,* 9/3/01.

60. Mediatransparency.org cites multiple contributions to the National Right to Work Committee from right-wing donors including the Waltons. http://www.mediatransparency.org/recipientgrants.php?recipientID=1128. The United Transportation Union filed an amicus brief with the NLRB (court Case 8-RD-1976) in the Dana and Metaldyne cases asserting, "More than 80 percent of [the National Right to Work Legal Foundation's] contributions come from business and corporate sources." http://www.nlrb.gov/nlrb/about/foia/DanaMetaldyne/UnitedTransportation.pdf.

61. Nathan Newman, TPMCafe, 10/14/05. http://houseoflabor.tpmcafe.com/story/2005/10/14/94113/125. Eighth Circuit decision.

62. Alison Grant, Newhouse News Service/Cleveland *Plain Dealer,* 1/26/05.

63. Steven Greenhouse, *New York Times,* 12/14/04.

64. David Moberg, *In These Times,* 3/8/05. http://www.inthesetimes.com/site/main/article/2008/.

65. *The Progressive,* 6/1/02.

66. Philip Dine, *St. Louis Post-Dispatch,* 7/30/01.

67. Labor Research Association, 6/24/03. http://www.laborresearch.org/story.php?id=306.

68. AFL-CIO press release, 6/4/03. Statement by AFL-CIO president John Sweeney, 6/4/03. http://laborday.aflcio.org/mediacenter/prsptm/pro6042003.cfm.

69. Steven Greenhouse, *New York Times,* 1/2/05.

70. Julius Getman and F. Ray Marshall, *Los Angeles Times,* 12/12/03. http://www.commondreams.org/scriptfiles/views03/1212-08.htm.

71. David Bonior, Center for American Progress article, 6/25/04. http://www.americanprogress.org/site/pp.asp?c=biJRJ8OVF&b=99065.

72. Human Rights Watch report entitled "Workers' Freedom of Association in the United States under International Human Rights Standards," 8/00.

73. Human Rights Watch report entitled "Unfair Advantage: Workers' Freedom of Association in the United States under International Human Rights Standards," 2000, page 10. http://hrw.org/reports/pdfs/u/us/uslbr008.pdf.

74. Carolyn Barta, *Dallas Morning News,* 10/16/96.

75. Center for Responsive Politics, Money in Politics Alert, vol. 5, no. 37, 2/14/00. http://www.opensecrets.org/alerts/v5/alertv5_37.asp.

76. Senator John McCain (R-AZ), New Hampshire presidential debates, 1/26/00.

77. Linda Chavez from her book *Betrayal.* http://128.121.183.34/lindachavez/betrayal/betrayal_text_1.htm.

78. Public Campaign, 3/01. http://www.publicampaign.org/publications/studies/hardfacts/hardfactsfull.htm.

79. Senator Trent Lott (R-MS), Federal News Service, 3/19/01.

80. Tom Hamburger, *Wall Street Journal,* 3/6/01. http://www.organicconsumers.org/corp/corporate.cfm.

81. Center for Responsive Politics report entitled "Business-Labor-Ideology Split in PAC & Individual Donations to Candidates and Parties" for the 2004 election. http://www.opensecrets.org/overview/blio.asp?cycle=2002.

82. Center for Responsive Politics data show that in 2004 labor contributed $105,116,167 to 527s while Single Issue/Ideological groups spent $431,338,793. http://www.opensecrets.org/527s/527cmtes.asp?level=S&cycle=2004.

83. Center for Responsive Politics data show that between 2000 and 2004, business spent a total of roughly $9.7 billion on lobbying, whereas labor spent roughly $96 million (business is defined categorically as agribusiness, communcations/electronics, construction, defense, energy and natural resources, finance/insurance/real estate, health, lawyers/lobbyists, misc. business, and transportation). http://www.opensecrets.org/lobbyists/index.asp.

84. Ibid. ($9.7 billion divided by 4 years, then divided by 535 members of Congress, equals $4.5 million).

85. Micheline Maynard and Jeremy Peters, *New York Times,* 8/20/05. http://www.nytimes.com/2005/08/20/business/20northwest.html.

86. David Welch, *BusinessWeek,* 6/5/05. http://www.businessweek.com/magazine/content/05_23/b3936037_mz011.htm.

87. Barbara De Lollis, *USA Today,* 8/23/02.

88. Steven Greenhouse, *New York Times,* 4/17/05.

89. Marcy Gordon, Associated Press, 4/22/05. http://accounting.smartpros.com/x47948.xml.

90. Steven Greenhouse, *New York Times,* 4/17/05.

91. Ann McFeatters, Associated Press, 3/30/05. http://toledoblade.com/apps/pbcs.dll/article?AID=/20050330/NEWS08/503300373/-1/NEWS.

92. Matthew Barakat, Associated Press, 8/9/04.

93. Steven Greenhouse, *New York Times*, 3/29/03.

94. James Lakely, *Washington Times*, 6/17/03. http://washtimes.com/national/20030616-104110-4701r.htm.

95. Derrick Z. Jackson, *Boston Globe*, 3/8/02.

96. Edward Iwata, *USA Today*, 2/18/04. http://www.usatoday.com/money/industries/energy/2004-02-18-enron-skilling_x.htm.

97. Jeff Shields, *South Florida Sun-Sentinel*, Knight-Ridder/Tribune Business News, 9/13/02. http://www.hotel-online.com/News/PR2002_3rd/Sept02_Diplomat.html.

98. Douglas Hanks III, *Miami Herald*, Knight-Ridder/Tribune Business News, 8/4/04. http://www.hotel-online.com/News/PR2004_3rd/Aug04_DiplomatSuit.html.

99. Christine Dugas, *USA Today*, 12/10/02. http://www.usatoday.com/money/perfi/retirement/2002-12-10-pensions_x.htm.

100. Nathan Newman, *Progressive Populist*, 1/1/03. http://www.nathannewman.org/archives/000609.shtml.

101. Dan Haar, *Hartford Courant*, 4/24/05.

102. Department of Labor press release, 4/11/01. DNC Report on Bush's labor record. http://www.dol.gov/opa/media/press/opa/opa2001098.htm.

103. Dan Haar, *Hartford Courant*, 4/24/05.

104. Nathan Newman, *Progressive Populist*, 1/1/03. http://www.nathannewman.org/archives/000609.shtml.

105. Senator Trent Lott (R-MS), 1/6/96.

106. Representative Bill Thomas (R-CA), 6/5/96.

107. *National Journal*, 1/5/98.

108. Senator Mitch McConnell (R-KY), *Fox News Sunday*, 10/5/98.

109. Timothy Noah, Slate, 12/22/99.

110. Martin Kasindorf, *USA Today*, 5/18/98. Americans for Tax Reform, 10/14/05. http://www.atr.org/content/html/2005/oct/101405pr-prop75.html.

111. Robert Greene, Associated Press, 10/1/98.

112. Grover Norquist, *Reason*, 2/97.

113. American Rights at Work fact sheet on Employee Free Choice Act. http://www.americanrightsatwork.org/takeaction/efca/cardsummary.cfm.

114. Ibid.

115. American Rights at Work, report entitled "Employee Free Choice Fact Sheet: Why Stronger Penalties are Needed."

116. Nathan Newman, Labor Blog, 4/18/05. http://www.nathannewman.org/laborblog/archive/002616.shtml.

117. Jonathan Glater, *New York Times*, 4/17/05; Andrew Parker, *Financial Times*, 12/15/05. http://www.nytimes.com/2005/04/17/business/yourmoney/17sox.html.

118. Department of Labor press release, 4/11/01; DNC report on Bush's labor record. http://www.dol.gov/opa/media/press/opa/opa2001098.htm.

119. House Education and Workforce Committee—Minority, press release, 4/18/05. http://www.house.gov/apps/list/press/ed31_democrats/rel41805.html.

120. Ibid.

121. Ibid.

CHAPTER 10: LEGAL RIGHTS

1. Bob Anez, Associated Press, 2/7/05.

2. Environmental Working Group report entitled "The Asbestos Epidemic in America." http://www.ewg.org/reports/asbestos/facts/fact1.php.

3. Vice President Dick Cheney, 2/7/04.

4. President Bush, 2/9/04.

5. Electronic Policy Network, "Asbestos Bill Saves Companies Billions by Denying Victims Justice," 06/14/05. http://www.movingideas.org/content/en/on_the_hill/asbestos.htm.

6. Associated Press, 9/26/05. http://www.billingsgazette.com/index.php?tl=1&display=rednews/2005/09/26/build/state/30-libby-asbestos.inc.

7. Lynn Turner, SEC chief accountant from 1998 to 2001, PBS, *Frontline*, 6/02. http://www.pbs.org/wgbh/pages/frontline/shows/regulation/congress/.

8. President Bush, 9/4/04.

9. Center for Responsive Politics data of the top twenty industries/groups giving to the House and Senate Judiciary Committees show pro-tort reform interests (business) gave $54.2 million in 2004, while anti-tort-reform interests (lawyers/unions) gave just $29.3 million. http://www.opensecrets.org./cmteprofiles/indus.asp?cycle=2004&CmteID=S17&Cmte=SJUD&CongNo=108&Chamber=S.

10. Josephine Hearn, *The Hill*, 2/15/05. http://www.thehill.com/thehill/export/TheHill/News/Frontpage/021505/chamber.html.

11. Lobbying expenditure records at Political Moneyline. http://www.politicalmoneyline.com/cgi-win/lb_client.exe?DoFn=&SenateID=51172-12; http://www.politicalmoneyline.com/cgi-win/lb_client.exe?DoFn=&SenateID=38756-12; http://www.politicalmoneyline.com/cgi-win/lb_client.exe?DoFn=&SenateID=4733-12.

12. Public Citizen report entitled, "Unfairness Incorporated: The Corporate Campaign Against Consumer Class Actions"; 6/03. http://www.citizen.org/congress/civjus/class_action/articles.cfm?ID=9846.

13. PBS, *Frontline*, 6/02. http://www.pbs.org/wgbh/pages/frontline/shows/regulation/congress/.

14. Bill Fleckenstein, president of Fleckenstein Capital, CNBC, 2/10/03. http://moneycentral.msn.com/content/P40765.asp.

15. Senate roll call vote #9, 2/10/05. http://www.senate.gov/legislative/LIS/roll_call_lists/roll_call_vote_cfm.cfm?congress=109&session=1&vote=00009. House roll call vote #38, 2/17/05. http://clerk.house.gov/evs/2005/roll038.xml.

16. National Association of Mutual Insurance Companies fact sheet on Punitive Damage Reform. http://www.namic.org/reports/tortReform/PunitiveDamage.asp.

17. National Association of Mutual Insurance Companies, Collateral Source Rule Reform. http://www.namic.org/reports/tortReform/CollateralSourceRule.asp.

18. Public Citizen report entitled "Legal Myths: The McDonald's 'Hot Coffee' Case," 11/30/99. http://www.citizen.org/congress/civjus/tort/articles.cfm?ID=785.

19. Mortimer B. Zuckerman, *U.S. News and World Report*, 6/16/03. http://www.usnews.com/usnews/opinion/articles/030616/16edit.htm.

20. Howard Kurtz, *Washington Post*, 6/23/03. http://www.washingtonpost.com/ac2/wp-dyn/A21440-2003Jun22?language=printer.

21. Tucker Carlson, CNN, *Crossfire*, 12/16/04.

22. Public Citizen press release, 11/15/04. http://www.commondreams.org/news2004/1215-08.htm.

23. *USA Today*, 5/24/04.

24. Lou Dobbs, CNN, 1/6/05. http://www.cnn.com/2005/US/01/06/tort.reform/.

25. Center for Justice and Democracy report entitled "First Annual Zany Immunity Laws 2004," 12/13/04. http://www.centerjd.org/ZANY.pdf; http://www.centerjd.org/press/release/ZanyAwardRel.pdf.

26. Stephanie Mencimer, *Washington Monthly,* 10/04. http://www.washingtonmonthly. com/features/2004/0410.mencimer.html.

27. *St. Louis Business Journal,* 11/6/03. http://stlouis.bizjournals.com/stlouis/stories/ 2003/11/03/daily59.html.

28. President Bush, 1/5/05. http://www.whitehouse.gov/news/releases/2005/01/ 20050105-4.html.

29. Peter Baker, *Washington Post,* 1/6/05. http://www.washingtonpost.com/wp-dyn/ articles/A50603-2005Jan5.html.

30. Thomas B. Edsall, *Washington Post,* 8/10/03. http://www.cmh.pitt.edu/tobacco/news/ Newsbattle_081003.htm.

31. http://brownvboard.org/summary/.

32. Ana Acle, *Miami Herald,* 5/26/96.

33. President Bush, 1/5/05. http://www.whitehouse.gov/news/releases/2005/01/ 20050105-4.html.

34. Michele Chandler, *San Jose Mercury News,* 1/20/05.

35. Public Citizen report entitled "Six Common Transactions That Cost Less Because of Class Actions," 8/20/03. http://www.citizen.org/congress/civjus/class_action/ articles.cfm?ID=10278.

36. Senate roll call vote #9, 2/10/05. http://www.senate.gov/legislative/LIS/roll_call_lists/ roll_call_vote_cfm.cfm?congress=109&session=1&vote=00009.

37. *Los Angeles Times,* 7/9/03. http://www.kingchuck.com/Law/class.actions2.html.

38. Jim Drinkard, *USA Today,* 2/17/05. http://www.usatoday.com/money/ 2005-02-17-lawsuits-usat_x.htm.

39. Jackson Lewis website, 5/4/05. http://www.jacksonlewis.com/legalupdates/article. cfm?aid=795. Nathan Newman, 5/18/05. http://www.nathannewman.org/laborblog/ archive/002838.shtml.

40. Bonnie Herzog of Citigroup/Smith Barney, PR Newswire press release from the Coalition to Preserve Access to Justice, 2/17/05.

41. Public Citizen report entitled "Unfairness Incorporated: The Corporate Campaign Against Consumer Class Actions," 6/03. http://www.citizen.org/congress/civjus/ class_action/articles.cfm?ID=9846.

42. *Congressional Quarterly Weekly,* 10/24/03.

43. Center for Responsive Politics data from the 2003–2004 election cycle show Sen. Mary Landrieu (D-LA) raised a total of $262,386 in PAC money. Subtract $8,500 (labor), $2,550 (single-issue), $2,300 (other), $21,537 (lawyers) for a total of more than $227,000 from corporate PACs. http://www.opensecrets.org/pacs/memberprofile. asp?cid=N00005395&cycle=2004&remove=M.

44. Senate roll call vote #9, 2/10/05. http://www.senate.gov/legislative/LIS/roll_call_lists/ roll_call_vote_cfm.cfm?congress=109&session=1&vote=00009.

45. Representative Rick Santorum (R-PA) introduced the "Comprehensive Family Health Access and Savings Act" on 2/28/1994. Section 1105 says, "LIMITATION ON NONECONOMIC DAMAGES The total amount of noneconomic damages that may be awarded to a claimant and the members of the claimant's family for losses resulting from the injury which is the subject of a medical malpractice liability action may not exceed $250,000, regardless of the number of parties against whom the action is brought or the number of actions brought with respect to such injury."

46. Claude Marx, Associated Press, 12/19/99.

47. *Roll Call,* 12/9/99.

48. Claude Marx, Associated Press, 12/19/99.

49. Charles B. Camp, *Dallas Morning News*, 1/31/95.

50. Ross Ramsey, *Houston Chronicle*, 2/2/95.

51. Michael Holmes, *Austin American-Statesman*, 4/16/95.

52. Tim Burger, New York *Daily News*, 8/26/00.

53. Ibid.

54. Stephanie Mencimer, *Mother Jones*, 10/04. http://www.motherjones.com/news/ outfront/2004/09/09_400.html.

55. *Austin American-Statesmen*, 4/13/95.

56. Ibid.

57. Felicity Barringer and Jim Rutenberg, "Apology Highlights ABC Reporter's Contrarian Image," *New York Times*, 8/14/00. http://www.nytimes.com/library/financial/ 081400stossel-abc.html.

58. Ted Rose, *Brill's Content*, 3/00. http://www.mediatransparency.org/reprints/brill_ stossel.htm. John Stossel, speech to the Cato Institute, 6/2/99. http://www.cato.org/ pubs/policy_report/v21n5/catoevents.html.

59. John Stossel, ABC News's *20/20*, 3/29/04, transcript.

60. John Martin, *Providence Journal-Bulletin*, 10/26/94.

61. President George Bush, 10/17/02. http://www.whitehouse.gov/news/releases/2002/ 10/20021017-3.html.

62. Public Citizen, 10/4/04. http://www.citizen.org/pressroom/release.cfm?ID=1799.

63. Public Citizen report entitled "The Facts About Product Liability Lawsuits." http://www.citizen.org/congress/civjus/tort/articles.cfm?ID=568.

64. Ibid.

65. Public Citizen report, 10/4/04. http://www.citizen.org/pressroom/release.cfm?ID=1799.

66. Vice President Dick Cheney, 5/3/04. http://www.whitehouse.gov/news/releases/2004/ 05/20040503-7.html.

67. Michael Liedtke, Associated Press, 9/25/03.

68. Kirstin Downey, *Washington Post*, 4/10/04.

69. Halliburton Watch, 9/15/04. http://www.halliburtonwatch.org/news/cheneylawsuits_ 099.html.

70. Public Citizen report entitled "NAFTA Chapter 11 Investor-to State Cases: Bankrupting Democracy," 9/01.

71. Vice President Dick Cheney, 9/30/03.

72. Stuart Taylor Jr. and Evan Thomas, *Newsweek*, 12/15/03.

73. Associated Press, 9/30/03.

74. Foundation for Taxpayer and Consumer Rights, 11/15/03.

75. Leonard Post, *National Law Journal*, 6/21/04.

76. Ibid.

77. Marie Cocco, *Newsday*, 7/13/04.

78. Peter Baker, *Washington Post*, 1/6/05. http://www.washingtonpost.com/wp-dyn/ articles/A50603-2005Jan5.html.

79. President Bush, 9/7/04. http://www.whitehouse.gov/news/releases/2004/09/ 20040907-11.html.

80. Public Citizen press release, 12/15/04. http://www.commondreams.org/news2004/ 1215-08.htm. Stephanie Mencimer, *Washington Monthly*, 10/1/04. http://www. washingtonmonthly.com/features/2004/0410.mencimer.html.

81. Leonard Post, *National Law Journal*, 6/21/04.

82. Public Citizen fact sheet. http://www.citizen.org/congress/civjus/class_action/ articles.cfm?ID=770.

83. Phil Hirschkorn, CNN, 8/22/03. http://www.cnn.com/2003/LAW/08/22/fox.franken/.

84. Kerry-Edwards press release, 8/26/04. http://releases.usnewswire.com/GetRelease. asp?id=35269.

85. CBS News, 7/17/01. http://www.cbsnews.com/stories/2001/07/17/eveningnews/ main301947.shtml.

86. *Billings Gazette,* 5/19/05. http://www.billingsgazette.com/index.php?id=1&display= rednews/2005/05/19/build/state/96-secrecy-bill.inc.

87. Ibid; 2005 Montana Legislature, Senate Bill No. 196. http://data.opi.state.mt.us/bills/ 2005/BillHtml/SB0196.htm.

88. Bingaman-Feinstein amendment as described by Public Citizen. http://www.citizen. org/documents/bingamanconsumeramendmentfact_percent20sheetpercent20 UPDATE.pdf.

89. Senate roll call vote #7, 2/9/05. http://www.senate.gov/legislative/LIS/roll_call_lists/ roll_call_vote_cfm.cfm?congress=109&session=1&vote=00007.

90. *New York Business Journal,* 3/10/04. http://www.bizjournals.com/buffalo/stories/ 2004/03/08/daily18.html?jst=s_cn_hl; http://www.bc.edu/schools/csom/cga/ executives/events/greenberg/.

91. American Trial Lawyers Association press release, 2/25/04. http://www.atla.org/ pressroom/AIG.aspx.

92. Eamon Javers and Diane Brady, *BusinessWeek,* 6/5/05. http://www.businessweek. com/@@BMBgLYUQ@E@OgQwA/magazine/content/05_23/b3936085.htm.

93. AFL-CIO executive paywatch. Executive compensation data. http://www.ecomponline. com/cobrand/cobrand.asp?cobrand_id=2; http://www.aflcio.org/corporateamerica/ paywatch/ceou/database.cfm?tkr=AIG&pg=1.

94. James Bernstein, *Newsweek,* 6/1/05. http://www.newsday.com/business/ ny-bzaig4285414jun01,0,2147632.story?coll=ny-business-leadheadlines.

95. Ibid.

96. Bureau of Labor Statistics, Census of Fatal Occupational Injuries (CFOI)—Current and Revised Data, 2003: total fatalities: 5,575. http://stats.bls.gov/iif/oshwc/cfoi/ cftb0187.pdf.

97. AFL-CIO report entitled "Death on the Job: The Toll of Neglect," 4/05.

98. Kirstin Downey, *Washington Post,* 4/10/04.

99. CBS News, 2/12/05. http://www.cbsnews.com/stories/2005/02/12/national/ main673677.shtml.

100. House roll call vote #318, 6/24/05. http://clerk.house.gov/evs/2005/roll318.xml. *H. Amdt. 367* to *H.R. 3010,* an amendment to prohibit use of funds in the bill to enforce or carry out item 6B of the settlement agreement between the Wage and Hour Division of the Department of Labor and Wal-Mart Stores, Inc.

101. Russell Gold and Ann Zimmerman, "Papers Suggest Wal-Mart Knew of Illegal Workers," *Wall Street Journal,* 11/5/05.

CONCLUSION

1. John Yewell, *Salt Lake Tribune,* 3/9/05.

2. R. Jeffrey Smith, *Washington Post,* 10/21/05 http://www.startribune.com/stories/587/ 5683296.html.

3. Allie Rasmus, *Austin News 8,* 10/21/05 http://www.news8austin.com/content/ your_news/default.asp?ArID=148083.

4. John Emshwiller and Kara Scannell, "Business World Tells Government: Back Off," *Wall Street Journal,* 3/21/05. http://www.wlf.org/upload/WSJ042505OL.pdf.

5. Judd Legum, Think Progess, 6/2/05. http://thinkprogress.org/index.php?p=1006. Public Citizen, 7/25/05. http://www.citizen.org/pressroom/release.cfm?ID=1997. William Lerach and Al Meyerhoff, Los Angeles Times, 1/20/02. http://www. enronfraud.com/insidervslittle.html.

6. Bruce Rubenstein, *Corporate Legal Times,* 11/97.

7. Chuck Neubauer, Judy Pasternak, and Richard Cooper, *Los Angeles Times,* 6/22/03.

8. Ibid.

9. Jeffrey Birnbaum, *Washington Post,* 7/27/05. http://www.washingtonpost.com/wp-dyn/ content/article/2005/07/26/AR2005072601562.html.

10. Jeffrey Birnbaum, "The Road to Riches Is Called K Street," *Washington Post,* 6/22/05. http://www.washingtonpost.com/wp-dyn/content/article/2005/06/21/ AR2005062101632.html.

11. Geoff Earle, *The Hill,* 10/20/04. http://www.hillnews.com/news/102004/breaux.aspx.

12. Ibid.

13. Chuck Neubauer, Judy Pasternak, and Richard Cooper, *Los Angeles Times,* 6/22/03.

14. Tory Newmyer, *Roll Call,* 1/31/05.

15. Jeffrey Birnbaum, *Washington Post,* 6/22/05. http://www.washingtonpost.com/ wp-dyn/content/article/2005/06/21/AR2005062101632.html.

16. Andrew Revkin, *New York Times,* 6/8/05. http://select.nytimes.com/gst/abstract.html? res=F10710F6385C0C7B8CDDAF0894DD404482.

17. Ibid. http://www.nytimes.com/2005/06/08/politics/08climate.html.

18. Andrew Revkin, *New York Times,* 6/15/05. Wall Street Journal, 6/14/05. http://select. nytimes.com/gst/abstract.html?res=F20713FE3D5F0C768DDDAF0894DD404482.

19. Jeanne Cummings, "For a High Court Nomination, Business Has Its Own Agenda," *Wall Street Journal,* 6/28/05. http://www.post-gazette.com/pg/05179/529698.stm.

20. Jeffrey Birnbaum and Thomas Edsall, *Washington Post,* 7/9/05. http://www. washingtonpost.com/wp-dyn/content/article/2005/07/08/AR2005070801790. html?sub=AR.

21. Henry Weinstein, *Los Angeles Times,* 7/22/05.

22. Carrie Johnson and Jeffrey Birnbaum, *Washington Post,* 7/21/05. http://www. washingtonpost.com/wp-dyn/content/article/2005/07/20/AR2005072002382.html.

23. Jeffrey H. Birnbaum and Thomas B. Edsall, *Washington Post,* 7/9/05. http://www. washingtonpost.com/wp-dyn/content/article/2005/07/08/AR2005070801790.html.

24. Charles Babington and Peter Baker, *Washington Post,* 9/30/05. http://www. washingtonpost.com/wp-dyn/content/article/2005/09/29/AR2005092900859.html. http://www.washingtonpost.com/wp-dyn/content/article/2005/07/20/ AR2005072002382.html.

25. Dana Milbank and Jim VandeHei, *Washington Post,* 12/5/04. http://www. washingtonpost.com/wp-dyn/articles/A36039-2004Dec4.html.

26. Kelley Beaucar Vlahos, Fox News, 2/2/05. http://www.foxnews.com/story/ 0,2933,146185,00.html.

27. Robert Dreyfuss, *American Prospect,* 4/23/01. http://www.prospect.org/print-friendly/ print/V12/7/dreyfuss-r.html.

28. DLC's Progressive Policy Institute, report entitled "The Progressive Case for CAFTA," 7/05. http://www.ppionline.org/documents/CAFTA_0715.pdf.

29. Will Marshall, president of the DLC's Progressive Policy Institute, report entitled "A Grand Bargain on Social Security," 1/1/99. http://www.ppionline.org/ ppi_ci.cfm?knlgAreaID=125&subsecID=165&contentID=1307.

30. DLC president Al From, quoted by Robert Dreyfuss, *American Prospect,* 4/23/01. http://www.prospect.org/print/V12/7/dreyfuss-r.html.

31. House roll call vote #443, 7/28/05—15 House Democrats vote for CAFTA. http://clerk.house.gov/evs/2005/roll443.xml. Senate roll call vote #209—10 Senate Democrats vote for CAFTA, 7/28/05. http://www.senate.gov/legislative/LIS/roll_call_lists/roll_call_vote_cfm.cfm?congress=109&session=1&vote=00209.

32. DLC's Progressive Policy Institute report entitled "The Progressive Case for CAFTA," 7/05. http://www.ppionline.org/documents/CAFTA_0715.pdf.

33. Jonathan Tasini reported on 11/2/05. http://workinglife.typepad.com/daily_blog/2005/11/why_are_democra.html.

34. Michael Barbaro, *New York Times,* 11/1/2005. http://www.nytimes.com/2005/11/01/business/01walmart.ready.html.

35. Elisabeth Bumiller quoted by Alec MacGillis, *Baltimore Sun,* 3/22/04.

36. U.S. Newswire, 6/6/05. http://releases.usnewswire.com/printing.asp?id=48410.

37. Dennis Cauchon, *USA Today,* 5/30/05. http://www.usatoday.com/news/washington/2005-05-30-minimum-wage_x.htm.

38. Josh Getlin, *Los Angeles Times,* 12/7/04.

39. Charles Johnson, *The Missoulian,* 5/13/04. http://www.missoulian.com/articles/2004/05/13/news/top/news01.txt.

40. Mitch Frank, "Alabama's Most Courageous Politician," *Time,* 8/15/03. http://www.time.com/time/columnist/frank/article/0,9565,476249,00.html. Bonna de la Cruz, *The Tennessean,* 8/1/03. http://www.tennessean.com/local/archives/03/08/36968111.shtml.

41. Senate roll call vote #209, 6/30/05. http://www.senate.gov/legislative/LIS/roll_call_lists/roll_call_vote_cfm.cfm?congress=109&session=1&vote=00170. House CAFTA vote, 7/28/05. http://clerk.house.gov/evs/2005/roll443.xml.

42. Center for Responsive Politics report entitled "2004 Election Overview: Donor Demographics." http://www.opensecrets.org/overview/DonorDemographics.asp?cycle=2004.

Acknowledgments

There are so many people to thank in making a book like this possible that I could fill an entire book with just thank-yous. The truth is, whenever you take on the powers that be and delve into a taboo topic like corruption, you get attacked viciously—and the people who follow are those who have helped me not only complete this book, but fight off the reflexive pangs of anxiety and defeatism that come with trying to fight the good fight in today's fierce political environment.

First and foremost, to my wife Emily—I'm not going to try to put into words how much you mean to me, or how much you have helped me with this project. To be quite honest, naming only my name and not also yours on the cover of this book is to commit a form of deception, because without you, this book never would have been proposed, much less written or published. This book is truly as much yours as it is mine.

To my parents, Karen and Rob, and my brothers Jeff and Steven: I'm sure it has not always been easy to watch a son/sibling enter the political arena—and I'm sure the criticism and attacks one naturally weathers in this realm have probably bothered you perhaps even more than they have me. But you have always offered unyielding support and encouragement, and that has always been the fuel that has kept me going.

To my new family, Mom, Dad, Zach, Nate, Zsofia, and Oscar Lipp—from the first day I met you, you embraced me like one of your own and made me feel as if I were always a part of your family, even when I was behaving like a true spaz trying to finish this book. Thank you.

To my grandparents, here and since passed—this book is a tribute to you, who started out here at the bottom of the economic ladder, and who worked to improve this country for your families and your families' families. This book is meant to honor your lives and carry on your legacies.

To my extended family—the Chicago Sirotas, the Hallermans, and the Steins—I couldn't have asked for better people to be surrounded by in my life and to share all of the special times together with. To have a family like the one we have is to be truly blessed.

To my two political brothers in arms—Joel Barkin and Mike Levy—because of you, my mind has expanded and my thinking has (hopefully) matured. I never feel lonely in the populist fight because I know you two are out there in your own way fighting by my side.

To those friends I incessantly badgered to read drafts of this book and bounce ideas off at all hours of the day—Matt Villano, Jason Taylor, Karen Cohen, Jeff Weaver, David Brock, Anna Dubrovsky, Aaron Kleiner, Jordan Marks, Harper Lawson, and Eric Stern—thank you for your help, and for not hating me for nagging you through this process. And thank you to all of my friends from high school, Northwestern, Capitol Hill, and the political campaigns who continue to deal with me, despite my neurotic tendencies—you all know exactly who you are, and you all mean so much to me.

To Jon Baskin—there was almost no one else on Earth I would have trusted to help me fact-check this book, and there is definitely no one else who would have agreed to do as many read-throughs as I asked you to do. Thank you for dealing with me and for being willing to help me. I could not have done this without you.

To the brillant people who happily dedicated their precious time to helping me flesh out pieces of this book— Elizabeth Warren, Ross Eisenbrey, Jared Bernstein, Warren Gunnels, Doug Heller, Mark Cooper—thank you. I hope this book does your work justice and that it helps you in your cause.

To the organizations whose research this book relied on—Public Citizen, the Economic Policy Institute, the Center on Budget and Policy Priorities, Citizens for Tax Justice, the Center for Responsive Politics, and Families USA, to name a few—you do not get the credit you deserve in today's media, but you are absolutely essential in the fight to take our government back.

To the people who, over the years, have given me the chances that got me to this point of being able to publish this book—Howard Carroll, Joe Hoeffel, Michael Bloomfield, Jeff Weaver, Scott Lilly, John Podesta, Al Franken, Joel Bleifuss, Katrina Vanden Huevel, Mike Tomasky, Wes Boyd, Eli Pariser, Art Torres, Kathy Bowler, and Becky Bond—you invested in me when you didn't have to, and this book is the product of that investment. I can't thank you enough.

To Bernie Sanders, David Obey, and Brian Schweitzer—you are all very different political leaders from very different parts of this great country, but you all have one thing in common: You each have a very personal committment to standing up and fighting for the millions of ordinary Americans who our political system has forgotten. You have each shown the courage of your convictions in this cause, and you have shown that fighting this fight can be winning politics. I am honored that you gave me the chance to work with you, and am thankful to call each of you my friend. You are unique inspirations that have profoundly affected my life and have kept me an optimist, even in the darkest political days.

To my editor Chris Jackson—through all the bumps and bruises of trying to get this book done, you have kept a level head and kept me focused. You were very careful to let this book reflect my voice, while also helping to shape this book for the better—that is a very delicate balance, but one you have clearly mastered. I feel very lucky to have had you as my editor.

Finally, to my agent, Will Lippincott—what can I really say? You have been my sherpa from the very beginning of this project. You are the embodiment of everything Jerry Maguire strove to be, clearly dedicated to your clients not just as business investments, but as people. You have been far more than an agent. You have been a career counselor, a stress absorber, a trusted adviser—and most important, a friend. I will always be indebted to you for everything you have done.

Index

About the Author

DAVID SIROTA is a veteran political operative, campaign strategist, and writer. As a political operative, Sirota worked on Capitol Hill first as the spokesman for Independent Congressman Bernie Sanders, and then as the spokesman for Democrats on the House Appropriations Committee—the committee at the center of many of the recent Republican corruption scandals. He also was a fellow at the Center for American Progress. As a campaign strategist, Sirota was a top aide to Montana's Brian Schweitzer in his unsuccessful 2000 run for U.S. Senate and successful run for governor, where he became the state's first Democratic chief executive in sixteen years. Most recently, Sirota became the co-chair of the Progressive Legislative Action Network (PLAN), a research and advocacy group supporting state lawmakers.

As a writer, Sirota has been published in, among others, the *Los Angeles Times,* the *San Francisco Chronicle,* the *Baltimore Sun,* and the *Charlotte Observer.* He is a senior editor at *In These Times* and a regular contributor to *The Nation* and *The American Prospect.* He also writes a blog for Working Assets and appears twice weekly on Air America radio's *Al Franken Show.*

He lives in Helena, Montana, with his wife, Emily, and his dog, Monty.